EUROPEAN UNION AND NEW REGIONALISM

This book is dedicated to our colleagues and friends in
Asia, Africa and Latin America

The International Political Economy
of New Regionalisms Series

The International Political Economy of New Regionalisms series presents innovative analyses of a range of novel regional relations and institutions. Going beyond established, formal, interstate economic organizations, this essential series provides informed interdisciplinary and international research and debate about myriad heterogeneous intermediate level interactions.

Reflective of its cosmopolitan and creative orientation, this series is developed by an international editorial team of established and emerging scholars in both South and North. It reinforces ongoing networks of analysts in both academia and think-tanks as well as international agencies concerned with micro-, meso- and macro-level regionalisms.

European Union and New Regionalism

Regional actors and global governance in a post-hegemonic era

Edited by
MARIO TELÒ

Ashgate

Aldershot • Burlington USA • Singapore • Sydney

Published by
Ashgate Publishing Limited
Gower House
Croft Road
Aldershot
Hants GU11 3HR
England

Ashgate Publishing Company
131 Main Street
Burlington, VT 05401–5600 USA

Ashgate website: http://www.ashgate.com

British Library Cataloguing in Publication Data
European Union and new regionalism : Regional actors and
    global governance in a post-hegemonic era. - (The
    international political economy of new regionalisms)
    1. European Union 2. Regionalism 3. Globalization
    I. Telò, Mario
    327.4

Library of Congress Control Number: 00–111398

ISBN 0 7546 1748 3 (Hbk)
ISBN 0 7546 1749 1 (Pbk)

Typeset by PCS Mapping & DTP, Newcastle upon Tyne.
Printed and bound in Great Britain by TJ International Ltd, Padstow, Cornwall.

Contents

Part III: European Union as a New Civilian Power in the Making

Part IV: Reconsiderations

List of Figures and Tables

Figures

Tables

Planispheres

Notes on Contributors

Catherine Børve Monsen is researcher at the Norwegian School of Management, Centre for European and Asian Studies, BI Oslo. Her research areas are globalization, regional integration, and more particularly, European and Asian integration. She has published several articles on this subject. She is Assistant Director of the Master of Management programme in Asia.

Kjell A. Eliassen is Professor of Public Management and Director of the Centre for European and Asian Studies at the BI Norwegian School of Management, Oslo, Professor of European Studies at the Free University in Brussels and honorary professor at the Shangai Fudan University. He has published many books and several articles on European and Asian affairs. He has been visiting professor at several European, American and Asian universities. During the last three years he has built up a part-time Masters programme in Asia in cooperation with leading Asian universities and the Norwegian School of Management. Among his recent books is (1998) *The European Common Foreign and Security Policy*, Sage, London.

Andrew Gamble is Professor of Politics and Director of the Political Economy Research Centre at the University of Sheffield. He is co-editor of two journals, *New Political Economy* and *The Political Quarterly*, and his books include *Regionalism and World Order* (co-edited with Tony Payne), *Hayek: the Iron Cage of Liberty*, and *Britain in Decline*.

Carolyn Jenkins is research officer at the Centre for the Study of African Economies, University of Oxford, and research associate at the Centre for Research into Economics and Finance in Southern Africa at the London School of Economics. She has been a consultant to governments and international institutions on macroeconomic issues, trade policy and regional integration in southern Africa.

George Howard Joffé was, until March 2000, Deputy-Director and Director of Studies at the Royal Institute of International Affairs in London. He is now affiliated to the Centre of International Studies at the London School of Economics and to the Centre of International Studies at Cambridge University. He also teaches at the School of Oriental and African Studies in London University. His recent publications include "The Middle East and the West" in Roberson, B-A. ed. (1998), *The Middle East and Europe: the power deficit*, Routledge and "The European Union and the Maghreb in the 1990s" in Zoubir, Y. ed. (1999), *North Africa in Transition: state, society and economic transformation in the 1990s*, University Press of Florida.

Pablo Medina Lockhart is researcher at the IGEAT-ULB, Institute of Geography and co-author (with Vandermotten) of Electoral Geography of Europe in *Le Vote des Quinze. Les élections européennes de juin 1999*, Presses de Sciences Politiques, Paris.

Thomas Meyer is Professor at the University of Dortmund and Director of the Friedrich-Ebert Stiftung, Bonn-Berlin. His main research areas include: social democratic theory and practice, comparative research on fundamentalism, theory of politics. Among his recent books is *Fundamentalismus in der modernen Welt*, Suhrkamp, Frankfurt.

Pier Carlo Padoan is Professor of Economics at the University of Rome, La Sapienza, and Director of Economic Studies at the College of Europe, Bruges. His main research areas include international economics, international political economy, European integration. Among his recent articles on regionalism and globalization is Regional Agreements as Clubs: The European Case, in E. D. Mansfield and H. V. Milner, eds (1997), *The Political Economy of Regionalism*, Columbia University Press, New York. He is co-editor of the Bruges Report *Europe 2020*, Nomos, 2000. He represents Italy at the IMF.

Sebastian Santander, Lecturer at the Université Libre de Bruxelles, works on globalization and regionalism and particularly on European Union and MERCO-SUR. Among his publications *Aux origines de la globalisation*, in F. Nahavandy, ed (2000), *Globalisation et néolibéralilsme dans le Tiers-Monde*, Paris.

Alberta M. Sbragia is the Director of the Center for West European Studies as well as the UCIS Research Professor of Political Science at the University of Pittsburgh. She was Visiting Associate Professor at the Harvard Business School, served as the Chair of the European Community Studies Association (1993–95) and as the co-chair of the American Political Science Association (APSA) in 1999. She has published extensively on the institutional evolution of the EU, edited *Euro-Politics: Politics and Policymaking in the "New" European Community* (The Brookings Institution) and served on the editorial board of numerous journals in the United States, Canada, and Europe. Her current work examines the role of the European Union in global environmental politics.

Reimund Seidelmann is Professor for International Relations/Foreign Policy at Giessen University/FRG, honorary professor at Renmin University in Beijing/PRC and has an international chair at the Institut d'Etudes Européennes at the Université Libre de Bruxelles. His main areas of research are European security and integration, peace and conflict theory, EU-China relations and, more particularly, Eastern Europe, where he has directed a number of research projects and published books and articles.

Mario Telò is Professor of Political Science at the ULB, Brussels, and Research Director at the Institute of Sociology and Institute for European Studies. He is editor of three international journals, *Europa/Europe* (Rome), *Transitions* (Brussels) and *Journal of European Integration* (Essex), is honorary Chair Jean Monnet and served as expert for the Presidency of the EU and the EU Commission. Among his recent books, he co-edited *De Maastricht à Amsterdam, L'Europe et son nouveau traité*, Complexe, Brussels, 1998 and edited *Bobbio, L'Etat et la démocratie internationale*, Brussels, 1999.

Göran Therborn is Professor of Sociology at the University of Göteborg and Director of the SCASS (Swedish Academy of Advanced Social Studies), Uppsala. As political sociologist, he is particularly focusing his comparative research on the Welfare State and unemployment in Western Europe. Among his recent books is *European Modernity and Beyond. The Trajectory of European Societies, 1945–2000*, Sage, 1995.

Lynne Thomas is a researcher at the Centre for Research into Economics and Finance in Southern Africa at the London School of Economics. Her research focuses on macroeconomic convergence in Southern Africa; the role of regional integration in promoting growth; and the characteristics of capital flows in Southern Africa.

Álvaro Vasconcelos is Director of the IEEI, Lisbon, and the main driver of the "Euro-Latino-American Forum". He also works on new regionalism in the international system after the Cold War. He leads the Euro-Latino-American Forum which celebrates its tenth anniversary in 2000. He recently co-edited (1998) *La politique étrangère et de sécurité commune. Ouvrir l'Europe au monde*, Presses de Sciences Politiques, Paris.

Preface:
Regionalism – A New Paradigm?

George Howard Joffé

There is little doubt that the end of the Cold War has forced analysts of the state as the vehicle through which international relations is expressed to reconsider their assumptions of the basic paradigms involved. Although globalization has been highlighted as the obvious alternative, particularly from the point of view of the global economy and, latterly, in terms of the new knowledge economy, the reality of the contemporary world seems to be better expressed in terms of regionalism. In other words, the political, social and economic characteristics originally attributed to states seem increasingly to be expressed through regional constructs in which the traditional Westphalian state is now embedded.

Of course, this classic concept of the state – autonomous, sovereign and freed of all constraint – never reflected the reality of the international scene, despite the role it has played in realist and neo-realist theory for many decades. Indeed, some of the contributors to this volume highlight the ways in which, over the past forty years or so, new paradigms have emerged to account for the increasing restraints on the freedom of action of states. In addition, since the Second World War, there has been a growing momentum towards the creation of supra-state institutions that have a normative role in contributing towards such developments. The balance-of-power between the superpowers, however, prevented the emergence of genuinely new political constructs designed to respond to the conditions created by the evolution of international law and commerce.

Only in Europe – for quite specific reasons connected with a long and bloody history of conflict between Germany and France – did such a structure emerge. Yet, even here, the European Community emerged within the context of the Cold War, in part as a pragmatic response to the superpower confrontation. It was only in the 1990s that the profound theoretical implications of what European statesmen had achieved over the previous thirty-to-forty years began to become apparent. Furthermore, it has only been since 1990 that the implications of hegemonic stability and the role of the United States could have become a central concern of students of international relations, as a consequence of the end of the Cold War, balanced by a new interest in the alternative concept of regionalism.

It is therefore, perhaps, no accident that the second major initiative in modern regionalism took place in March 1991 when Mercosul-Mercosur was founded as an experiment in common political and economic development involving Brazil, Argentina, Uruguay and Paraguay. Drawing on the experience of the European Union, it sought to encourage parallel initiatives in political evolution and economic development and integration without engaging in a close federal structure to achieve its objectives. Yet other experiences in regionalist approaches since then have emphasized the variety of different models that exist, alongside the European experience. This study examines five of them – the European Union itself, Mercosul-Mercosur, the North American Free Trade Area (NAFTA), the Association of South East Asian Nations (ASEAN) and the Southern African Development Community (SADC) – some of which predate the end of the Cold War, although all of them were only able to develop their full potential after its end.

The novelty in the current concept of "New Regionalism", unlike earlier concepts during the Cold War period, resides in its potential as an alternative to hegemonic stability, within a globalized context, in which the region becomes the nexus of activity both at the state and the supra-state level. Without denying the state and the cultural specificities associated with it, regionalism binds states – that are usually contiguous – together through their voluntary derogation of sovereign rights into a collective economic endeavour. Such an endeavour may also, should the partners wish it, become a political project as well so that the collectivity retains a significant autonomy of political and economic action within the structures created by economic globalism.

The success of the regional model is attested to by the vitality of the initiatives that have been undertaken to date. The five models discussed here are only the most prominent of a far wider range of initiatives that have either been started or revived during the past decade. Their continued vitality demonstrates that regionalism is becoming a permanent and prominent feature of the contemporary international system, providing a degree of theoretical order to a world that appeared to be increasingly confused and confusing in the aftermath of the Cold War. Regionalism, in short, may become the preferred response in a post-modern world through which the threats and benefits of globalization are mediated.

In this context, the role of the European Union is primordial. Not only is it the vehicle in which many of the ideas that inform modern economic regionalism were first tested, it is also becoming an experiment in new forms of political cooperation. Its formal structure as a network of sovereign states is being gradually transmuted into a new political construction as states gradually cede sovereign power over economic policy, monetary control and external foreign policy in a series of bold constitutional initiatives. Quite where this experiment will lead is unclear. Will the Union become a global competitor with the United States, as some fear? Or will it become the "civil society of civil societies" that many anticipate – a political and social model for others to follow?

Whatever the outcome, there can be little doubt of the future role of regionalism inside the future international system as a theoretical and practical construct. Nor can there be any doubt that Europe will retain its particularity as the innovator in finding solutions to the future relationship between state, nation and the individual in a world in which the certainties of the past find no echo.

This distinctive collection of original contributions by leading specialists stems from an international and multidisciplinary network coordinated by Mario Telò with the aim to combine European studies and international relations. On the one hand, it situates the EC/EU and its external relations in the framework of the development of different forms of regional arrangements. This combination offers an original development of European integration studies and a vigorous response to the conventional wisdom on European international identity, by considering various scenarios for the evolving international identity of the EU: a continental trading state, a new mercantilist fortress or a new civilian power. On the other hand, it supplements the current literature in international relations by dealing with regionalism as a possible new paradigm for international relations in the contemporary world.

This innovative textbook provides a clear insight for graduate and undergraduate students and researchers, ideal for courses that include issues of regionalism, world governance, EU's evolving continental and global role.

August 2000

Acknowledgements

This book results from an international research project on "Europe, Globalization and New Regionalism" launched by the Université Libre de Bruxelles, in cooperation with several academic institutions including the Royal Institute of International Affairs, the Oslo Centre of European and Asian Studies (Business Institute), and the Institute for International and Strategic Studies, Lisbon. The papers published were presented, in their very first draft, at an international workshop, led by Mario Telò, that was part of an international conference on the economic and political implications of the globalization process, held in Brussels with the title "From capitalism to capitalism in the world and in Europe". We thank those colleagues and professionals of the Institut de Sociologie, ULB, who organized the conference and sponsored the publication of this volume.

The authors wish to extend their gratitude to all the scholars and students who contributed to the Brussels workshop and to the ongoing research project, first of all, F. Cerutti, J. Nagel, F. Nahavandi, E. Remacle, R. Higgott, G. Ross, P. Winand, F. Attinà, G. Edwards, J. Vogel, R. Kaweh, A. Viñas, T. That Nguyen, P. Pierson-Mathy and all of the other participants. Furthermore, the editor would like to thank the Institutions which gave him the opportunity to present drafts of his work in progress as well as the organizers of workshops and discussants, and particularly: the IEE, Centre of Excellence J. Monnet of Brussels; F. Laursen and the IPSA/Mexican Political Science Association (Manzanillo Conference, 1998); the ECPR, European–Japanese Network and the University of Kyoto (I. Otake); the Chuo University (T. Furuki) and the International Christian University (Prof. T. Ueta) of Tokyo; the Institute of Social Science of New Delhi (Dr. A. Giri and A. Mathew), the Euro-Latino American Forum, the IEEI of Lisbon (A. Vasconcelos); the Institute Sorensen of São Paulo and the INTAL, Buenos Aires (F. Peña); the Institute of European Studies of Macau (M. Ceu Esteves); the UNESCO, Caracas (F.L. Segrera); the SDIC, University of Bologna (G. Antonelli and P.G. Ardeni); the Forum on the Problems of Peace and War, Florence (R. Ragionieri); the University of Florence, Political Science (A. Varsori) and the Institute Sant'Anna of Pisa (B. Henry, A. Loretoni); the Centre d'Etudes Européennes, Institut d'Etudes Politiques, Paris (J.L. Quermonne); the Pantheion University of Athens; J.H.H. Weiler; the Center for European Studies, Harvard and particularly the 'Boston Group'; the Geneva University/ECPR summer school 2000 (G. Nivat, N. Levrat, R. Schwok, J. Caporaso, A. Moravcsik, R. Ginzberg and the students); the European Commission (Action J. Monnet); the IPSA/RCEU network led by P. Leslie and H. Wallace; and, finally, the Portuguese Presidency of the European Union (and particularly M.J. Rodrigues, special adviser to the Prime Minister and responsible for the "progressive governance experts network" as well).

Of course the editor and the individual authors are entirely responsible for what is asserted in the chapters of the book.

We are particularly indebted to those who had a special role in the compiling and amending of this book including G. Joffé, former Director of the Royal Institute of International Affairs, M. May and her staff, J. Fitzmaurice, E. Burke and M. Burke, and last but not least, J. Lowy whose precious help in the editing of the manuscript resulted in this volume.

List of Abbreviations

ACC	Arab Cooperation Council
ACM	Arab Common Market
ACP	African, Caribbean and Pacific countries
AFTA/FTAA	American Free Trade Area (or Free Trade Area of the Americas)
ALALC	Latin American Association of Free Trade
ALADI	Latin American Association for Development and Integration
AMU/UMA	Arab Maghreb Union
APEC	Asia-Pacific Economic Cooperation
ARF	ASEAN Regional Forum
ASEAN	Association of South-East Asian Nations
ASEM	Asia–Europe Meeting
BENELUX	Belgium, Netherlands, Luxemburg
CACM	Central American Common Market
CAEU	Council for Arab Economic Unity
CAO	Eastern African Community
CAP	Common Agricultural Policy
CARIFA	Caribbean International Free Trade Association
CARICOM	Caribbean Community
CCASG	Council of Cooperation between Arab States of the Gulf
CEPAL	Economic Commission for Latin America
CEEAC	Economic Community of Central African States
CEPGL	Economic Community of the Great Lakes Countries
CER	Closer Economic Relationship
CFSP	Common Foreign and Security Policy
CIS	Commonwealth of Independent States
COMESA	Common Market for Eastern and Southern Africa
CSCE	Conference on Security and Cooperation in Europe
CUSA	Customs Union of Southern Africa
CUSFTA	Canada–USA Free Trade Agreement
DG(s)	Directorate(s) General
EAEC	East Asian Economic Caucus
EBRD	European Bank for Reconstruction and Development
EC	European Community (subsequently EU)
ECB	European Central Bank
ECFA	Economic Commission for Africa
ECHO	European Community Humanitarian Aid Office
ECLA	Economic Commission for Latin America

ECOWAS	Economic Community of West African States
ECSC	European Coal and Steel Community
EDF	European Development Fund
EEA	European Economic Area
EEC	European Economic Community
EFTA	European Free Trade Association
EIB	European Investment Bank
EMU	Economic and Monetary Union
EMP	Euro-Mediterranean Partnership
EP	European Parliament
EPC	European Political Cooperation
ESCAP	Economic and Social Commission for Asia and the Pacific
ESCWA	Economic and Social Commission for West Asia
EU	European Union
FTA	Free Trade Area
FTAA	Free Trade Area of the Americas
FTCE	Free Trade Agreement of Central Europe
G7	Group of Seven most wealthy countries (United States, United Kingdom, France, Germany, Italy, Japan and Canada)
G8	G7 and Russia
GATT	General Agreement on Tariffs and Trade
GCC	Gulf Cooperation Council
GSP	Generalized System of Preferences
ICT	Information and Communication Technologies
IGC	Intergovernmental Conference
IMF	International Monetary Fund
LAS	League of Arab States
MAI	Multilateral Agreement on Investment
MERCOSUR	Mercado Comùn del Sur (MERCOSUL in Portuguese; Common Market of the South)
MFN	Most Favoured Nation
NAFTA	North American Free Trade Agreement
NATO	North Atlantic Treaty Organization
NGO	Non-governmental organization
NTBs	Non-tariff Barriers
OAS	Organization of American States
OAU	Organization of African Unity
OECD	Organization for Economic Cooperation and Development
OPEC	Organization of Petroleum Exporting Countries
OSCE	Organization for Security and Cooperation in Europe
PTAs	Preferential Trading Arrangements
SAARC	South Asian Association for Regional Cooperation
SADCC	Southern African Development Coordination Conference (subsequently SADC)

SEATO	South-East Asia Treaty Organization
SELA	Latin American Economic System
SPC	South Pacific Commission
TEC	Treaty of European Community
TEU	Treaty of European Union
UDEAC	Customs and Economic Union of Central Africa
UN	United Nations
WAEMU	West African Economic and Monetary Union
WEU	Western European Union
WTO	World Trade Organization

Introduction: Globalization, New Regionalism and the Role of the European Union

Mario Telò

This volume stems from the work of an international and multidisciplinary research group. The group includes political scientists, internationalists, and social scientists who do not neglect to recognize the international economic and financial structures shaping the new power hierarchies. It also includes economists who take into account the weight of the political dimension in the changing globalized economy.

This book begins by observing that globalization and new regionalism are not only economic but also political processes. Of course, it neither deals with the pros and cons of free trade nor with the theory of international trade; its subject matter is also not international politics itself. Its particular focus is the *comparative analysis of regional organizations and their interrelations with the globalized economy and world politics of the post-Cold War era*. To focus on the political dimension of regionalism involves going beyond controversies among economists on the regionalism versus globalization relationship. It involves instead explaining the flourishing of regional organizations and studying their current and potential impact on governance. Regionalism and globalization are two components of the same historical process of strengthening interdependence and weakening the state's barriers to free trade, even if there can also be conflicting parallel tendencies. This is shown by trade blocs, strategic traders and by current asymmetries and uncertainties.

The group of scholars included here is peculiar in many respects. Almost all of the authors are prominent specialists in European studies, in particular European integration studies, and they approach regionalism and globalization from a particular point of view. They focus on the comparison of regional arrangements with the EC-EU and the evolution of the EU as an international entity before and after the end of the Cold War. Consequently the book offers, on the one hand, a theoretical framework for new regionalism and a comparative analysis of other regional organizations, bearing in mind the European experience. On the other hand, it shows the characteristics of the European Union as a growing global player and also its proactive relationship with other regional organizations. The question is to what extent this can be considered as a significant part of its current and potential role as a new kind of "civilian power" in the uncertain world politics of the early 21st century.

1. Three types of regionalism in the history of the 20th century

The resurgence of regionalism must be placed in a broader historical perspective, including *three waves of regionalism during the 20th century*. The world experienced the tragedy of both an aggressive nationalism and an imperial regionalism during the inter-war period. The international economy was characterized by the crucial fact that the British-centred hegemonic multilateral stability came to an end, which was already perceptible with the Great Depression of 1873. The crisis started with World War I and publicly crashed in August 1931, with the end of the Gold Standard's basis for the pound being one of the direct consequences of the Great Depression. After the failure of the International Economic Conference in 1933, it was finally realized that the UK could no longer play the role of hegemonic power and that the US could not, as yet. The end of the long era of the self-regulated market and of free trade was an international event.[1] The American economic crash of 1929 had a huge global impact. It undermined the apparent economic boom of the twenties, which J. M. Keynes had warned of ten years earlier, in *The Economic Consequences of Peace*. International economics shifted from open trade order, and the first seeds of international liberalization (including the Most Favoured Nation Clause, MFN) to state protectionism, discriminatory and regionalist imperialisms.[2]

The crisis in the fragile League of Nations peace system, the breakdown of the first steps towards a farseeing European design, namely the Briand-Stresemann dialogue, and the parallel Japanese occupation of Manchuria, heralded the end of the first attempt to construct a modern multilateral collective security system able to cope with the challenges of the 20th century. During the thirties and the early forties, the world experienced the difficult times of both economic and political "malevolent regionalism", as a result of German and Japanese attempts to become regional hegemonic powers. The military and fascist regimes of Japan and Germany replaced the former "pax Britannica" with a new conflict for regional domination, in Asia/Pacific and Europe respectively, provoking the outbreak of World War II.

Until then, in spite of its financial and economic strength, the US was not able to take the place of the declining UK as the hegemonic power in the industrialized world. Post-war American hegemony took the form of an accelerated move towards a more institutionalized multilateralism, whose domestic roots are to be found in the New Deal pattern of regulated capitalism. Despite the evolving global system having its centre in European colonialism for four centuries, the main globalization tendencies no longer come from Europe since World War II. The 1944/47 multilateral political and economic institutions provided an effective framework to overcome the catastrophic instability of the inter-war period. These institutions attempted to include both former and potential enemies; for example the new monetary system based on the convertibility of the US dollar, the International Monetary Fund and the World Bank, GATT, the United Nations and so on.

The beginning of the Cold War (1947) was a fundamental historical change, breaking universalistic perspectives and even NATO was founded in 1949, according to the will to adapt multilateralism to the new bipolar strategic challenge. However, this new type of US-centred multilateralism has for three decades, been the basic architectural principle for such international cooperation and growing interdependence. The golden age of international economic growth only became possible due to harmony between the American design and practice of a "trading state" and national Keynesianism (Clarck, 1997). The double aim of containing the Soviet threat and of creating a transatlantic community made it possible to harmonize the interests and ideals of the US New Deal, associating realism and idealism, namely peace, prosperity and democracy. This was typical of the new stable hegemonic international system (Ruggie, 1993).

A second type of regionalism, an economic regionalism, was set up during the 1960s and 1970s, which was compatible with such American-centred hegemonic stability and its vision of multilateralism. Particularly important was the regional integration of the European Community, which was inconceivable without taking into account the huge impact of American hegemony. Even if less successful elsewhere in the "free world" and in the third world, regionalist experiments took place, for example in Asia, Africa and Latin America. During these decades the US, in spite of free trade ideology, tolerated many forms of national and regional protectionism abroad, which is clearly proven by the EC examples (for instance, Customs Union, Common Agricultural Policy, Lomé Convention etc), the Latin American (supported by CEPAL, etc.) and Japanese. With the exception of the EC, the results have been very poor.[3] Too many inward-looking economic policies, too weak institutional settlements, the legacy of colonialism and the weight of underdevelopment do explain the failure or the marginal impact of such a second type of regionalism.

As far as the EC is concerned, the harmony between transatlantic stability, which was centred on the trading state, the open market and national Keynesianism, started to decline with the end of the Bretton Wood Gold Standard system (1971) and the oil crisis of the 1970s. The first plans for a European regional monetary union (the "Werner Plan") began in the early 1970s, even though the single European currency was not established before 1999. There is no doubt that the end of the dollar as an international factor of stability undermined the American hegemony and also the idea of a 'Trilateral' Directorate of the capitalist world. This Directorate, the famous triad, including Japan, Europe and the USA, was supposed to rescue the former stability path but only announced the coming epoch of transition.[4]

However, the question of the relationship between American leadership and new regionalism seems to be crucial in the new era of transition in the international system. On the one hand, the scientific and public debate of the 1980s on the declining role of the US, though overemphasized, allowed one to speak of a "post-hegemonic" international system from then on.[5] On the other hand, the collapse of the USSR in 1991 confirmed the strength of the tendency towards a sole super-power. The successful New Economy of the nineties and the Bosnian and Kosovo wars confirm the leadership of the US as far as culture, military, politics, economy and technology are concerned. Nevertheless, no new international order has yet been established. The parallel and opposing tendencies towards the decentralization and globalization of the world economic and political system are continuing within this uncertain framework. Regionalism is about to evolve in many areas of the world, according to new patterns, trends and agendas. In continuity and discontinuity with the past, it is a matter of *a third, post-hegemonic, regionalism* as a component in a new turbulent world system.

This volume focuses on this complex phenomenon and its theoretical implications. The current globalization process entails a broader and deeper (even if highly differentiated) new type of regionalism. During the last twenty years the world has witnessed, in parallel with the boom in international trade and foreign investments, the simultaneous development, or revival, of numerous and varied regional arrangements and regional organizations: the most well-known are the EU, NAFTA, ASEAN, Andean Community, MERCOSUR, SADC, SAARC and so on.[6]

Is this new regional dimension of international society a transient feature or is it able to constitute a long-term third trend between the anarchy of nation-states and the international markets and globalism as developers of world governance? What is the balance between the economic and political dimensions of new regionalism and what are its systemic and domestic causes? To what extent is current asymmetric multilateralism conflicting with unipolarism and, at the same time, is it unable to hinder moves towards fragmentation? Can it lead to an upward trend towards a new kind of multilateralism, including not only continental states (such as India and China) but also five or six regional trading blocs and regional entities and thus contribute to a new post-hegemonic stability? Will it contribute to economic stability and world governance, by hindering globalization or increasing it? To what extent do external relations and responsibilities have an impact on regional arrangements towards enhanced coherence and institutional consistency? Which particular role does and could the European Union play in the foreseeable future, as an international entity supporting regionalism worldwide? And finally, what is the difference between its approach to regionalism and that of the US?

2. Domestic and Systemic Causes of New Regionalism

This book offers, first of all, *a general overview of the common causes and features of new regionalism*. Important schools of thought conflict on two salient scientific issues. Firstly, what is the balance between domestic and systemic factors of regional integration? Secondly, how does regionalism interact with globalization? Let's start by deepening the first cleavage. On the one hand, domestic factors play an important role in developing new regionalism: the will of nation-states, and mainly of regional leaders, to rescue their sovereignty and recover their international bargaining power, or the wish of minor states to balance the regional leader within a common framework. The second cause is the private interest of export industries lobbying and networking on a regional basis. Thirdly, there is the internal functional spillover as a consequence of successful – even if limited to relatively marginal sectors and branches – cooperation agreements. Finally, there is the desire of developing countries to gradually cope with global competition.[7]

The so-called "domino theory" stresses the importance of mutual emulations and reactions as far as the development of regional organizations is concerned, particularly emphasizing the "multiplicating effect" induced by the recent evolution of the EU and NAFTA, in Latin America and worldwide.[8]

On the other hand, many scholars focus on the impact of systemic economic and political causes, which make it easier to underline what is common among regional organizations and to analyze variations provoked by the influence of national or subnational causes. As R.O. Keohane points out, without an overview of common problems, constraints and challenges set by the international system, we would miss the analytical basis to better understand the weight of domestic factors and distinguish them from external causes.[9] The particular approach of this volume combines both these classical schools of thought. It focuses, however, not only on the controversial economic effects of regionalism on globalization, but mainly on the political dimension of regional agreements and their impact on world governance.

The main systemic even if ambiguous explaining factor is globalization. The influence of the global system on national societies and on the regions of the world increased during the 20th century and was accelerated after 1945, and even more particularly in the two last decades.[10] International forces, political actors and multinational companies are working on and shaping the relations and hierarchies between states, economic interests and regions of the world. From an economic point of view, regional arrangements provide clear advantages in terms of location (trade and investment, saving in transport and economy of scale). Furthermore, regional adjustments ease the recovery of the developing regions of the world and also help them to cope gradually with the constraints of international competitiveness. Finally, larger regional markets make it possible for large companies to expand and to train for world competition. Whatever their institutional features are, preferential trade arrangements, regional arrangements and regional organizations have proliferated. Regionalism stands more and more in the centre of international economics and world politics.

There are two dominant explanations for this boom. The first explanation is based on the *GATT-WTO vision of regionalization* as part and antecedent of systemic globalization. In other words, regional trade liberalization and coopera-tion arrangements are seen as necessary intermediate steps, enabling nations and companies to cope with the risks and opportunities of the global market and to accept new multilateral rules. Of course, this assessment is partially correct. In many cases, regional cooperation is certainly a good preparation for an open inter-national economy, as proven, for example by the conclusion of the Uruguay Round (where integration into the EU induced some member states to accept the GATT deal[11]) or by the high impact of NAFTA on investments liberalization. As authori-tative illustration of such a harmonic school of thought, Larry Summers argues that regional liberalization is the best way towards liberalization and globalization and that regionalism did not only damage the multilateral world trading system, but will increasingly be the decisive drive towards liberalization (and also the reverse).[12] By contrast to such an optimistic vision, a second classical and varied school of thought emphasizes *regional and subregional discriminatory agreements as reactions to globalization and potential regional blocs*. For instance, according to Bhagwati,[13] regionalism slows down worldwide liberalization and threatens the multilateral trade system. Bergsten[14] is of the opinion that it sets unilateral priori-ties in conflict with global ones, as illustrated by the example of the European Monetary Union. According to Luttwack,[15] regionalism will be the new form of various geo-economic conflicts, with potential for political consequences.

The chapters in this book highlight many facts which cast some doubts on this controversy. Our goal is firstly to explain the resurgence of regionalism at the end of the 20th century and its common features and variations, independent of any qualitative appreciation of its potential to damage trade liberalization. The aim is secondly to go beyond this controversy, namely concerning the systemic causes of regionalism and its political dimension and consequences.

Many contributors stress the impact of the *contradictory evolution of multilat-eral trade bargaining on the strengthening political dimension of new regionalism*. On the one hand, the aforementioned GATT agreement in Marrakesh (1994) welcomed regional free trade agreements (article XXIV) as a step in the right direction. On the other hand however, the problems raised by the hard bargaining of the Uruguay Round and the failure of the WTO to commence a "Millennium Round" in Seattle (1999) provoked uncertainty for many actors and a changing balance between regionalism and multilateralism. Fear of over-asymmetric global-ization strengthens discriminatory agreements and competition on a regional basis. Region building is seen by many actors as a willingness to react to uncertainties and to compete better with other regions and economic powers (EU, USA and Japan). The question remains open whether new regionalism can better provide the rare public goods of governance and stability or instead damage global economic liberalization.

In this framework the meaning of the changing attitude of the USA towards regionalism needs also to be correctly interpreted. Firstly, the decision to create NAFTA is a new chapter in the economic foreign policy of the only remaining superpower. This can be seen as a new leverage within a general strategy, including also multilateralism and bilateralism. Secondly, the participation of the US in many interregional groupings (APEC, Free Trade Area of the Americas and so on) makes the asymmetries of the globalized or regionalized world's economy clearer and several conflicts between such "globalism" and new regionalism more possible.[16]

Another issue mentioned in many chapters is the complex impact of financial, technological and market globalization on the traditional *territorial state power*.[17] New regionalism can be seen as an attempt by states to react by strengthening regional control when traditional centralized national sovereignty no longer functions and to bargain collectively with extra-regional partners. The re-emerging geographical – or territorial – dimension of political regulation and external relations is regional, instead of national. In other words, territorial logic interacts critically with functional logic. Domestic social factors, political pressures and democratic participation are strengthening a new demand for the rescue of a territorial authority, as granting a better balance between *global* economy and *regional* values. States are attempting to revive political regulation by pooling authority at regional level, both as a voluntary and original decision and as an imitation of neighbour states or of models imported from abroad. According to a part of the literature, regionalism makes a partial rescue of national authority easier. In many areas of the world, new regionalism also limits the fragmenting and disintegrating impact of subnational regionalism, ethnic fundamentalism and the proliferation of movements for national self-determination by creating a new supranational framework. Often the success story of the manner in which the European Union copes with both traditional internal conflicts and the globalized economy, by transforming states' functions and structures, plays an important role as a reference for new regionalism.

Ultimately, a salient political systemic cause of the growing political dimension of regionalism (summarizing the two former explanations) is the impact of the double transformation of the *hegemonic stability*, which existed after 1944/45. This combined American interests, the economic expansion of the western world and the political goal of containment. Let us emphasize again the above-mentioned troubles of the American leadership during the seventies (end of the Bretton Woods system and oil crises) and 1980s, which allowed some international relations scholars to raise the huge question of "post hegemonic" stability. The second political transformation to be mentioned, because it is particularly useful in understanding the political dimension of regionalism, is the end of the Cold War and of the West–East confrontation. The unification of the world economy, with the end of its political division, the erosion of the previous blocs of alliances and the changing strategies of the world's main powers, the combination of fragmentation and the creation of new economic and political centers were all features of this time. Most of the security challenges of the post-Cold War era are regional, and thus the answer must be, at least partially, regional. It is true that in some places new regionalism is a matter of the resurgence of old regionalist organizations born in the 1950s and 1960s, but which were for years in lethargy until the mid 1980s–early 1990s. The end of the bipolar world certainly played an important role in giving them a broader scope. Indeed, for many decades, communism figured as a potential alternative model for many developing countries. Its collapse turned out to be a huge unifying factor, not only for the world economy and financial market (linking the former second world to the west and shaping the former third world), but also for political democratization and for world culture, changing worldwide, for example, attitudes towards economic liberalization. Many chapters inevitably ask two questions. Is a strengthened regionalism a type of substitute, somehow replacing East–West cleavage with regional trading bloc competition? To what extent does it interfere with the transforming political dimension of international order?

In fact, new regionalism matters, namely inside by conditioning states' and companies' strategies, and outside by affording a dynamic contribution to the changing international system. It is not a transient but instead a structural phenomenon of international relations. Its problems and challenges are analyzed in the following chapters. Unipolarism and unilateralism, nationalist and local fragmentation, growing world economic players and new mercantilist policies provoked by fears of marginalization, unstable transnational functional dynamics – all of these can play, directly or indirectly, either a supporting or a conflicting role in the development of regional cooperation and new regionalism.

Many chapters consider a final question: how did the worldwide economic and financial crisis of 1997/98 affect regional integration? The biggest post-WWII depression could be seen either as pressure towards greater integration or as a factor of the weakening regional cooperation of states, which were tempted to return to inward-looking policies or aggressive regionalism. Even worse: ethnic conflict, social chaos and political fragmentation can provoke not only renationalization but true disintegration as far as many parts of the globe are concerned.[18] However, many authors of the present book observe that the financial and economic crisis of 1997/98 did not halt new regionalism and that regional organizations proved to have an edge to go on. Furthermore, the fact that many countries belonging to the same region share the same problems and receive the same policy recommendations from world organizations (i.e. liberalization, transparency, new regulatory frameworks, increased infra-regional trade, fiscal and monetary cooperation) is encouraging them to strengthen their cooperation at regional level. This is for the very simple reason that it seems easier to achieve domestic reforms and face external constraints if part of the national power is shared at regional intergovernmental level. Finally, domestic democratization has been accelerated.

This volume is divided into three parts: a theoretical part, a second which includes a comparative analysis of new regional organizations and of the EU and a final part, focusing on the EU as international actor, strengthening new regionalism worldwide. The question is whether and how EU external relations provide a conscious and effective contribution towards extending and deepening regional cooperation. This applies, first of all, in the so-called "near abroad" (Mediterranean and Eastern Europe). It applies, secondly, in other continents where international relations could evolve from structural anarchy to regional or subregional regime building.

3. The Political Dimension of New Regionalism as an Alternative to the Theory of Hyper-Globalization and to New Medievalism

The new-regionalist paradigm and research on regionalization are theoretically challenged by many views sharing the thesis that the political dimension of regional integration is unlikely.[19] Among these are the approaches of the "globalizers" and the "new medievalists". Let us start with the first one. What is called in France *la pensée unique* and by business utopians "hyper globalization" entails a new- liberal vision of the cosmopolitan global economy, that of fast convergence of national economies, gradually rendering states and politics superfluous.[20] Some new-Marxist and former dependence theorists paradoxically agree with new liberals in emphasizing such an interpretation of globalized capitalism,[21] even if that is sometimes complemented by the radical utopia of periphery uprising[22] or by catastrophic forecasts.[23] Whatever the abuse of the concept may be, a huge economic change entailing important political implications comes into focus. Transnational companies, global financial markets, private and public cosmopolitan networks are increasingly taking fundamental decisions and creating new authorities. As a consequence, many national governments only have to choose whether to adjust, or not, to the constraints of the globalized economy.

In this theoretical framework, the crisis in the classic principle of territorial sovereignty (established for five centuries in the main European states and theoretically founded by J. Bodin, N. Machiavelli, T. Hobbes) is accelerating since the nation state is seen as simply obstructing economic development. Consequently, regionalization is considered only as a gateway to a global economy. As a consequence of the feeling of loss for a territorial political authority, competitiveness is taken into consideration only at the level of sectors and companies.

Such an approach has for many years now been a subject of harsh scientific criticism. The main issue raised by critical literature is that "globalizers" do not answer that very simple question: what remains for political power and political bodies? Political bodies does not necessarily mean nation state, but instead actors and institutions embedding capitalism in governance; i.e. state and non-state, formal and informal, institutionalized and non-institutionalized authorities.[24] Secondly, as said before, globalization is not only a technocratic bias. On the contrary, it includes globalism, one or more political projects, supporting various national interests, world policies, consistent rules and political alternatives.[25] Consequently, why should political projects not provoke political reactions? Regional arrangements are driven to a stronger political dimension. A third criticism is also that such discourse about globalization often becomes a kind of "rhetoric ideology", instrumental to domestic goals of national elites whose menu of policies is certainly changing, but not however their ability to choose it.

The mentioned critics converge in underlining that timing and forms of globalization are the subjects of policies and political decisions: that politics matters. Many of the contributors show that global, national and *regional* politics matter. When national authorities are overcommitted, new regional ones intervene as managers of the globalization process. Everywhere in the world, regional agreements are about to be founded and reinforced by state decisions. The emerging economic and political geography is regional rather than global.

We come again with new arguments to the very controversial question addressed by economists: how and in which form consolidated and deeper regionalist projects are compatible with globalization. Pessimistic assessments of new realists (whatever new Marxist or liberal) stress that the deepening of regional arrangements will inevitably provoke regional blocs, which will mean a zero sum game within inter-regional trade. In the worst scenario, hegemonic state-centred trade blocs will conduct tough economic conflicts, likely to shift towards demands for military security and, according to S. Huntington, to "holy wars".

The third approach and particularly the chapters by Gamble, Padoan and Meyer forward various arguments against such suggested catastrophic scenarios, and against various arguments and points of view from Bhagwati, Huntington, and Luttwack as well. Gamble is particularly clear about the different ways in which regionalism intersects with globalization and especially globalism. Some years ago R. Keohane emphasized the fact that, within complex interdependence, and beyond hegemonic stability, new transnational institutions and regimes are mediating conflicts, making a positive sum game possible and making economic welfare more likely for a larger number of countries.

Such an approach must not be confused with "Panglossian optimism". During these last two decades and particularly after 1989, from behind the embryonic cores which are apparently committed to "open regionalism", new *strategic traders emerged*, including EU, MERCOSUR, ASEAN....[26] These established themselves within the globalized economy, like USA and Japan. Regional cooperation often becomes a means of enabling regional companies and national economies to be internationally competitive, to weaken competitors and to strengthen the bargaining power of nations and groupings of nations within the WTO and multilateral negotiations. The US and EU are particularly proactive regarding programmes of training, research, investment, public procurement, infrastructure, projects to maintain legal and managerial control over firms, setting international negotiation agendas. They are the two main global players and it is obvious that other regional organizations are about to emulate them.

A part of the answer to the question of the remaining room for strategic traders is whether economic differences and variations tend to adapt or to survive within such a global economy. In fact, a huge convergence process occurred in world capitalism during the past decades. The US economy was able to impose its model everywhere and was able to marginalize different forms of capitalism, even if deeply rooted in very divergent historic national traditions. However, the existing capitalist diversity has not much to do with regionalism before 1945 (Germany, Japan ...) and this book shares the view that there could be substance behind trade disputes: "one of the forces driving the current regionalism is an attempt to protect models of economic and cultural organization".[27] The same economic pattern of global development is still giving birth to various regional balances with socio-cultural environments, institutional and legal frameworks and policies, beyond national limits. By way of conclusion, we do not need to share catastrophic scenarios if we question the scientific credibility of the globalizers' vision.

This book pays attention to the so-called new medievalist paradigm as well. Current globalization is characterized by transnational networking, by overlapping decision levels, declining distinction between the sources of authority and growing uncertainty about where sovereignty is located.[28] In this sense, the EU could be seen as the first post-modern state, because the European "regulation of deregulation"[29] helps to weaken traditional kinds of political authority and became in fifty years the first factor in the transformation of the nation-state. The second factor was the internal process of fragmentation and the empowering of subnational regions and entities – also supported by the EU. Nation-state crisis includes political apathy, the growth of subnational regionalist movements, the privatization and mediatization of power and so on. Moreover, in Europe, but particularly in other continents, private domestic and international violence and criminal networks mean the decline of state monopoly of force. The weight of transnational links and growing functional loyalties are giving birth to a geocentric technology, mainly a communication technology, unifying the world and opposing national politics. Nation-states are no longer able to form a protective shell and ought to be forced to share their authority. The result is a kind of confused multilevel global system of authority where states are involved with other entities (cities, particularly "global cities", companies, subnational and transnational interregional bodies, private and public networks, international organizations and so on), but no longer as dominant actors. Summing up, according to this approach, supranational regions are nothing but a factor in the decline of states.

This new transnationalism would exacerbate the conflict between the principle of territorial sovereignty (political power) and the functional but non-territorial principle of interdependence. The continual tension between the two principles would constitute (in the new medievalist vision) the very nature of the modern world system. After seventy years of a "kind of political disgression" (1917–89), such a reconfiguration of space-time would unify the contemporary world system.

The criticism of such an approach by this volume (A. Gamble and others) brings the reader back to the importance of political regionalism. Some of the current changes are permanent, some are transient. The state's authority is certainly declining, but is far from over in crucial sectors such as defence, security, and welfare. The nation-state changes rather than loses its role in one of several overlapping areas of governance. More generally, the unbundling of territoriality is only partial. New systems of law and forms of governance, which globalization itself does not provide, are demanded. Regional governance is often politically strengthened and legitimated, as a complementary or subsidiary level of national and local governance. External challenges may push regional authorities to a better political coordination orienting the multilevel fragmented governance.

Finally, many authors agree with the salience of both mentioned intellectual challenges, represented by hyperglobalization theories and new middle age concepts. However, they emphasize the impact of the current gap between demand and supply of good world governance. They suggest a third scenario: a kind of new political economy of world capitalism demanding "reregulation" at global level, by reinforcing regionalized democratic governance as a part of a renewed UN system. Many authors in this book find both the analytical and normative sides of such an approach very interesting. Yes, the evolution of some regional arrangements, and particularly of the European Union, shows that regional and supranational "reregulation" is likely to strengthen rather than replace the multilevel system of authority", rebalancing it, however, in favor of public centrally coordinated governance.[30] Whether new regionalism can support a new post-hegemonic multilateralism (at both political and economic levels) and balance unilateral and global strategies of world governance demands to be better explored from the point of view of international political economy.

4. The Political Economy of New Regionalism: Are strategic regional traders providers of good world governance?

Many authors welcome the concept of a "post-hegemonic world" as a general international framework in developing new regionalism. According to Padoan, the current global redistribution of power causes an institutional imbalance, since a single superpower can no longer provide an equilibrium between increasing demand and diminishing supply of international public goods. To what extent could the proliferation of regional arrangements provide the partial supply of a new multilateral equilibrium? Even when taking into account international literature on political economy, many authors come to the controversial question of the *ambiguity of new regionalism*, either conflict-oriented regional blocs or cooperative regional agreements as a precondition for cooperation on a global level. However, while pure economic rationale would support worldwide trade agreements in the current globalizing world, regional agreements exist and increase. Do their optimal size and internal cohesion have an impact on their contribution to world governance?

The number of countries demanding regional integration is important. It is a matter of fact that if associated with adjustments and reallocations, trade increases within regional agreements. Padoan proposes a "gravity model", emphasizing the advantages of *geographic proximity*: limited transfer costs, common policies, common social and environmental standards, giving comparative advantage to regions within world competition. Other writers in this book, such as Vasconcelos, Eliassen/Børve, Jenkins/Thomas, also agree in their chapters, that regional trade liberalization enables members – especially the poorer – to reap some of the benefits of trade, via larger markets and improved efficiency, without exposure to non-regional competition.

The trade-off between increasing size and internal cohesion could become problematic. Simple trade agreements and monetary clubs can both provoke an asymmetrical internal redistribution of benefits and affect the expected improvement in the welfare of members. However, domestic consensus and political support for regional agreements (and also for their changing size) are possible only through the notion of "cohesion". Cohesion involves balancing the inequalities and asymmetrical effects of liberalization and implying "a relatively equal social and territorial distribution of employment opportunities, wealth and income, corresponding to increasing expectations" (Padoan). The *optimal size* is achieved if the cohesion's costs do not outweigh benefits and if marginal costs (management, decision making, dramatically increasing with the number of member states[31] and demand for majority voting rules) equal marginal benefits, decreasing with the club's size.

The increasing demand for integration in regional clubs ("domino effect") due to globalization implies explicit and implicit admission fees, both in the case of trade and in monetary agreements. However, the marginal benefits, namely the security effects, are particularly relevant in case of an external threat (e.g. trade war and monetary instability). The number of members is viewed as crucial to the success and deepening of regional organizations. The "optimal size" varies in commercial or monetary clubs. According to this model, the international political economy is combined with a new institutionalist approach (importance of institutions as actors of internal cohesion, of majority voting rules, of issues linkage etc.).

Under these conditions regionalism can contribute to global governance. While globalization produces market instability, new regionalism can provide an answer to the demand for public goods and better conditions for new multilateralism at global level:

a) National actors are better prepared to adapt and to adjust. An agreement between national and regional levels is a good precondition for an international regime, since international organizations interact better with the regional level.
b) Regional agreements imply issue linkages (economy and security, monetary and trade), providing exchange of information and stability. This could be very useful for stabilizing international regimes.
c) The spectrum of national actors becomes necessarily wider, since integration means a relatively long-term commitment to regional rules. Their propensity to adjust increases, if the advantages of integration are relevant and consistent with domestic political equilibrium.

However, some final caveats. The main challenges are the contradictory implications of *the reduction in the number of actors* within the international arena. On the one hand, it can help international cooperation without hegemony, because bargaining between states is more difficult and less efficient than between regional blocs. On the other hand, regionalism is leading to a less cooperative regime: preferential agreements and selective market access increase the costs of exclusion. Furthermore, many member states demand regional clubs to provide them with better protection against global instability, which can consequently weaken the multilateral system. If it is true that multinational enterprises increase global interdependence, the convergence of policies and the diffusion of knowledge and innovation, asymmetrical capital mobility can, on the other hand, provoke protectionism in some countries or regional organizations. Furthermore, competition for location sites for multinational activities demands territorial regulation at either national or regional level. Competition among varying regulations can cause "a deterioration of rules or of rule enforcement, decreasing the costs of investment to the detriment of social costs".

Summing up, the economic perspective of new regionalism is remaining so ambiguous and open – cooperative and/or conflict oriented – that no clear theoretical conclusion could be drawn through a mere political economy approach. The relationship between the political dimension of new regionalism and the cultural implications of globalization has to be further explored.

5. Economic Rationale and Identities: Impact of the Cultural Factors on New Regionalism

Even though the influence of cultural differences is increasing in both international and infra-national conflicts after the end of the Cold War, we can neither observe nor foresee a growing consistency between civilizations and regional blocs. T. Meyer's chapter provides an analysis of the current theoretical debate on the relationship between cultural, political and economic factors, which shape the globalized world. Its main conclusion is that regional arrangements present a high degree of internal differentiation in styles of civilization (traditionalism, fundamentalism and modernism), the combination and balance of which change with the evolution of history. Furthermore, cultural global interdependence and transregional similarities are more important than tendencies towards regional cultural cohesion. This means that the catastrophic concept of a genetic mutual exclusion of main cultures is not in tune with the facts, and that the concept of culture, underpinned by Huntington's idea of "civilization's clash", is obsolete.[32] Of course political instrumentalizations of cultural values are also possible at subnational, national and regional levels, particularly in the hard times of economic and social crisis. However fundamentalism is not in itself a consequence of culture and there is no evidence that regionalism can better channel cultural fundamentalism.

The fact that regional blocs do not correspond to civilization but instead to infra-cultural state groupings is particularly clear if one observes the three partners of the transatlantic triangle: the European Union, NAFTA and MERCOSUR. All three belong to the same Christian and western culture, but are differentiated along West–West and North–South cleavages.

The current attempts to strengthen cultural factors as a background for a politics of identity at regional level are openly rhetoric: for example the call for "Asian values" by Mr. Mahatir, Malaysian Prime Minister, or for a "Christian Europe" by some Catholic democratic leaders. The so-called "fault lines" are not set between cultures but within cultures. Regionalism can be an opportunity for cross-cultural convergence, for practical examples of "trans-culturality", to allow internal differentiation, for cross-cultural overlapping and for cluster building of a new kind. This can be seen in the fact that for instance, ASEAN incorporates peoples belonging to six different religions. Also NAFTA still includes a historically very difficult border – a state border but also economic and ethnic borders, between perhaps two of the most distant neighbours in the history of the world, Mexico and the US. After its planned eastern (and southern) enlargement, the EU will include very varied subnational cultures, linguistic groupings and also various social and economic standards. New regionalism is likely to hinder the politics of exclusive national identity, impeaching political leaders from using ethnic or religious fundamentalism for their own aims, in times of economic crisis and growing social deprivation and exclusion. Moreover, new regionalism helps to diminish the conflict between states and changing stateless subnational identities. It often allows management of the negative implications of the "principle of self-determination", offering cultural or ethnic demands a broader and more encompassing alternative to sovereignty.[33]

However, identity matters and new regionalism is not always the result of a mere rational choice of convergent rational actors, multinational companies, and domestic interest groups. Both liberals and Marxists underestimate the importance of identities and of the cultural dimension. New regionalism goes beyond free trade arrangements. Some regional arrangements, such as SAARC, fail because of political tensions provoked by the instrumentalization of religious differences. Australia is excluded from ASEAN in spite of high trade and economic interdependence. Although it improved in 1999, the status of the relationship between the EU and Turkey is still a special and problematic one.

The question of the impact of regionalism on democratization has directly to do with this issue. Political and deeper regionalism can possibly exist between, on the one hand, a community building process based on a mere free trade area and, on the other hand, a kind of regional civilization, a "regional nationalism" (religiously or ethnically homogeneous), as a mutually exclusive background for new regionalist blocs. Many regional organizations already show, behind business networking and intergovernmental fora, a variety of legacies of a regional public sphere in the making: capitalist and social life diversities, cross-border political culture even if keeping national and local peculiarities. In normative terms, new regionalist organizations can set strict criteria for admission and enforce a commitment by member states to democracy, rule of law and human rights. Democratic regionalism and culture are the best reciprocal link and mutual support between international democracy and national democracy. When based on democratic core values, and shared institutions, they support the feeling of common belonging in spite of national and local different identities. Constructivist approaches in international relations[34] and new institutionalist views provide arguments for that scenario. Under such conditions, transnational cultural networks and transcultural dialogue can strengthen cross-cultural multilateralism and transregional coalitions. These help regional blocs to communicate with each other and to build a consensus, contributing to multilateral global governance.

In conclusion, even if cultural and political identity matters, new regionalism, in itself, does not have very much to do with scenarios of civilization clash. Of course, a populist leadership can instrumentalize it in order to support policies of regional fundamentalism and regional nationalism. However the cultural dimension of new regionalism can also ease both internal deepening and dialogue/cooperation between distinct entities outside macro-regions. The institutional features and particularly national and supranational democratization seem to be crucial variables in linking regional policies, public spheres and cultural and international identities of regional organizations. In many areas, like in the case of EU-Mediterranean relations, cultural interdependence can be strengthened by new telecommunication technologies and also provide an input into the development of civil societies and pluralism within the southern countries. This would have the consequence of enhancing the possibility of security partnerships within the area.

The cultural dimension of regionalism is not only a salient topic for comparative research. It supports our theoretical approach by overcoming the limits of the views of the globalizers and new medievalists.

Notes

1   K. Polanyi (1944); C. P. Kindleberger (1973); R. Gilpin (1981).
2   J. G. Ruggie (1993).
3   E. Haas (1975).
4   L. Thurow (1992).
5   R. O. Keohane (1984), R. Gilpin (1981). In the framework of a discussion focused on the so-called American decline, see also P. Kennedy (1985). R. Keohane, R. Cox, S. Gill and others transferred A. Gramsci's concept of hegemony to the international relations theory. Contrary to imperialism and dependence theories and according to Gramsci (1975), a hegemonic power dominates not only thanks to its economic strength and military, but also to its cultural and political supremacy, creating active consensus of both allies and subordinate states.
6   For a detailed description of existing regional organizations, see the Appendix.
7   European Commission and World Bank (1998), *Regionalism and Development. Report,*

Brussels, 2. 6. 1997, Studies series, n. 1.

8   R. Baldwin (1993).

9   R. O. Keohane, The World Political Economy and the Crisis of Embedded Liberalism, in J. H. Goldthorpe ed. (1984), *Order and Conflict in Contemporary Capitalism*, Clarendon Press, Oxford.

10 I. Clarck (1997), and L. Fawcett and A. Hurrell, eds. (1995).

11 D. Piazolo (1998), pp. 251–71.

12 Larry Summers, ed. (1991) and particularly the article, Regionalism and the World Trading System.

13 J. Bhagwati and P. Arvind, Preferential Trading Areas and Multilateralism: Stranger, Friends or Foes?, in Bhagwati and A. Panagariya, eds (1996).

14 F. Bergsten (1996), pp. 105–20 and F. Bergsten (1997).

15 G. Luttwack (1990).

16 See S. Haggard, Regionalism in Asia and in the Americas, in E. D. Mansfield and H. V. Milner eds, (1997).

17 See B. Badie (1999).

18 Among others, I. Wallerstein (1991).

19 For an introduction to this scientific discussion, E. D. Mansfield and H. V Milner (1997); Louise Fawcett and Andrew Hurrell (1995); W. Coleman and G. Underhill (1998), D. A. Lake and P. M. Morgan (1997).

20 K. Ohmae (1993), The Rise of the Region State, in *Foreign Affairs*, n. 78, Spring.

21 S. Latouche (1998).

22 S. Amin (1997).

23 J. Gray (1998).

24 P. Hirst and G. Thompson (1996).

25 According to Gamble's chapter, regionalism is also a state-project, a system of policies, just like *globalism* is a policy of a certain political authority, whereas "regionalization and globalization are complex processes of social change". On the political origins of globalization, see D. A. Lake, Global Governance, in A. Prakash and J. A. Hart (1999) pp: 32–51. *Planispheres* 2 and 3 show different global strategies towards regionalism (see *Appendix*).

26 L. C. Thurow (1992).

27 C. Crouch and W. Streeck (1997), Introduction. The Future of Capitalist Diversity, pp. 1–18.

28 H. Bull (1977) and S. Strange (1996)

29 G. Majone (1996), and G. Majone (1997), From the Positive to Regulatory State, in *Journal of Public Policy*, 17/2, pp. 139–67.

30 R. Cox ed. (1997), Prakash and Hart (1999), Ruggie (1998).

31 M. Olson (1965).

32 S. Huntington (1996) pp. 122–49 and the theoretical debate, which follows in *Foreign Affairs*. See also B. R. Barber (1995).

33 L. Fawcett and A. Hurrell, eds (1995), Conclusion, pp. 309–27.

34 The concept of a "shared sense of communal identity" has been proposed by C. A. Kupchan, Regionalizing Europe's Security, in E. Mansfield and H. Milner (1997).

Part I
Theoretical Perspectives

1. Regional Blocs, World Order and the New Medievalism

Andrew Gamble

The end of the Cold War and the reunification of the world economy have fuelled debate on the future of world order. Many of the changes that are taking place in the world system appear contradictory. There is a trend towards globalization which is creating a more interconnected world economy and world society, and is widely held to be associated with the erosion of the power of nation states to govern their economies. At the same time there appears to be a substantial regionalization of economic activity and the strengthening of regionalist projects launched by core states or groups of states.

This chapter will examine three alternative futures for the world system which have been identified in theoretical approaches to the issues of globalization and regionalization:

- a cosmopolitan global economy;
- regional blocs;
- a new medievalism.

1. A cosmopolitan global economy

There is a widespread view, encouraged by the approach of the millennium, that a fundamental change is taking place in the world system but that we lack an adequate language to describe what is going on or to identify the new principles by which the world system is ordered (Gamble, 1997). The old images and concepts remain powerful and seductive, none more so than the conventional international relations view of international politics as relations between states. However imperfectly the basic principle of the modern state system may have been realized in practice since it was first enunciated in the Treaty of Westphalia in 1648, it has provided the dominant perspective on international politics for 350 years. This basic principle is the claim of supreme authority over a given territory. All local, particular and personal sources of authority are consolidated into a single public power within a defined territorial space. This public power has two key spatial dimensions: the boundary between the public and the private, and the boundary between the internal and the external (Ruggie, 1993). This principle of territorial sovereignty depended on the repudiation of existing universal forms of religious and political authority using the new doctrines of *cuius regio eius religio* and *rex in regno suo est imperator regni suo*. These doctrines did not go uncontested, but they were increasingly in the ascendancy from the sixteenth century onwards and permitted the dividing up of the world into states which claimed absolute sovereignty over the territory they controlled, and recognized no superior jurisdiction.

1.1 Globalization

This way of conceiving the international state system is currently having to be rethought because of an increasing awareness that the idea of territorial sovereignty no longer captures very well the contemporary nature of political rule (Ruggie, 1993). This rethinking has been gathering pace since the 1970s as more and more changes appear which do not fit easily within the assumptions of the Westphalian perspective. It has produced an extensive literature around the new trends of globalization and regionalization, raising the question of whether the era of the nation-state is finally over. A popular wisdom has emerged in recent years that the nation-state has become an anachronism and is facing forces which it can no longer control. A global economy is emerging, dominated by new actors, such as transnational companies and banks, in which states are subordinate and reactive.

Globalization, as many have recognized, is not a new theory. Global economic forces and global markets have existed since the emergence of capitalism. In *The Communist Manifesto* 150 years ago Marx put forward one of the earliest and boldest theories of globalization, and he has been followed by many later writers, most recently world system theorists (Wallerstein, 1974). World systems theory emphasizes the contradictory character of the world system as a (relatively) unified economy and a (relatively) fragmented polity.

What all globalization theorists argue is that the world economy is best characterized as a global rather than as an international economy. An international economy is made up of separate national economies, controlled to a greater or lesser extent by states. Nation-states are at the centre of this world. They derive their legitimacy and their power from their control over discrete national territories, populations and resources. Flows of goods, people and capital have to be sanctioned by political authority.

A global economy, by contrast, is one in which the fundamental units are not nation-states and national economies but patterns of production and consumption organized by transnational companies, operating across national borders, and not reliant on any particular national territory or government. Economic decisions are shaped not at the level of national governments but through the workings of the global financial markets and the patterns of international trade and production.

Governments have to adjust their societies and economies to the changing requirements of the global economy, or risk impoverishment and isolation.

1.2 Hyper-globalization

The tendencies towards the creation of a global economy have existed since the
beginning of capitalism as a world system, but they have been stronger in some
periods than others. The period since the collapse of the Bretton Woods system in
1971 has seen the balance between transnational economic forces and national
governments appear to move in favour of the former. The international state system
and the principle of order which it embodies has come under severe strain.
Supporters and critics of the new global economy have argued that governments
lose their autonomy and become ciphers for global economic forces. A new
cosmopolitan society is said to have emerged, unified around a single set of political, social, economic and ideological principles, in which there is no room for
fundamental alternatives. History has ended (Fukuyama, 1992).

This strong version of globalization (or hyper-globalization, as it is sometimes
called) is put forward by, among others, Kenichi Ohmae, who argues that the nation-
state is no longer an appropriate unit of analysis because economic activity in the
global economy no longer coincides with political or cultural boundary lines (Ohmae,
1995). The nation-state, although increasingly irrelevant, is also seen as obstructing
the development of the global economy. It uses its centralized powers to raise taxes
and redistribute resources according to the pressures of special interests. The result is
a cumbersome, inefficient bureaucracy which makes national government the enemy
of the public interest. Ohmae argues that the powers of the nation-state should be
dismantled and the growth of region-states encouraged. These region-states, which
he sees as the ports of entry to the global economy, are typically urban conglomerates
and their hinterlands, with populations of between 5 million and 20 million people;
their borders are defined economically, not politically. They depend on the existence
of factor endowments which are located close together, not necessarily within
national borders. Competitiveness is determined at the level of sectors and firms, not
at the level of the national economy. The key issue for Ohmae is whether national
governments have the will and ability to embrace the global economy and resist
pressure for national policies of protection and subsidy. The only role for governments is to facilitate the globalization of their national economies. By doing so, they
bring nearer the nineteenth-century dream of a global cosmopolitan society which is
coordinated and managed without the need for politics and governments and in which
national attachments have become insignificant.

1.3 Critics of globalization

The globalization thesis does point to some important and real changes which have
been taking place in the world economy and have led to a weakening of nation-

states and an erosion of their sovereignty. But in its extreme form the argument is overblown. The evidence for the emergence of a global economy which overrides the modes of governance organized through nation-states and exists independently of them is remarkably thin (Hirst and Thompson, 1996). Global economic forces and global markets are always embedded in governance, both state and non-state. These forms of governance have been changing, but the global markets themselves lack the capacity to supply their own internal mechanisms of governance.

In discussing globalization it is important to distinguish between, first, the trends which are extending and deepening connections of many different kinds (Perraton et al., 1997), and second, the normative political project, globalism, which supports particular policies and rules out alternatives. Globalization rhetoric has been increasingly adopted by state elites to justify substantial changes in domestic policies, particularly on public spending, welfare and industrial intervention. But how constrained are national policies? Even if some of the changes which global-ization highlights have altered the limits within which national governments may act, some argue that at most it has changed the menu of policies from which govern-ments have to choose, rather than the ability to choose itself (Hirst and Thompson, 1996). From this perspective states still operate in an international rather than a global economy.

2. Regional blocs

This position – the assertion that the global economy has regional and national foundations – is the starting point for the second theoretical perspective on world order (Zysman, 1996). Politics and the state remain of vital importance to the way in which the global economy develops and to the institutional and cultural variety within it. Far from globalization sweeping away all political structures, it is creat-ing new ones. The political response to globalization has been the setting up of new structures and new projects. The emerging economic geography is regional rather than global, and a distinctive aspect of the emerging world order is the creation or consolidation of regionalist projects (NAFTA in the Americas, the EU in Europe and ASEAN in Southeast Asia).

The existence of these regionalist projects is clear enough, although they are very different from one another (Gamble and Payne, 1996). A key theoretical and practical question is what they signify. Are they compatible with globalization, even steps towards it, or do they foreshadow a turn away from the cosmopolitan world economy and a return to closed, antagonistic regional blocs? The latter view has its roots in realist perspectives in international relations, both liberal and Marxist. At its heart is a pessimistic assessment of the workings of the international state system. Left to themselves, states will be single-minded and ruthless in the pursuit of their security; the normal state of international relations is conflict.

2.1 The interwar crisis

This is not a new view. Writing in the 1940s, E. H. Carr analysed how the world order sustained by British hegemony in the nineteenth century had fallen apart in the twentieth. Carr described this world order as 'the golden age of continuously expanding territories and markets, of a world policed by the self-assured and not too onerous British hegemony, of a coherent "Western civilization" whose conflicts could be harmonized by a progressive extension of the area of common development and exploitation' (Carr, 1946: 224). The First World War had shattered this world beyond repair. During the 1920s there was a tendency towards disintegration and fragmentation of larger political units, particularly in Europe, but this was quickly followed by the reorganization of the world into a system of regional blocs:

> *The more autarky is regarded as the goal, the larger the units must become. The United States strengthened their hold over the American continents. Great Britain created a sterling bloc and laid the foundations of a closed economic system. Germany reconstituted Mittel-Europa and pressed forward into the Balkans. Soviet Russia developed its vast territories into a compact unit of industrial and agricultural production. Japan attempted the creation of a new unit of 'Eastern Asia' under Japanese domination. Such was the trend towards the concentration of political and economic power in the hands of six or seven highly organized units, round which lesser satellite units revolved without any appreciable independent motion of their own.* (Carr, 1946: 230)

Carr analysed the trend towards regional blocs in terms of power politics, distinguishing between military, economic and ideological forms of power, and interpreted world politics as a struggle for power between rival states. Classical Marxism reached similar conclusions in its analysis of the formation of regional blocs in the 1930s. Marxists ascribed the breakdown of the world order of the nineteenth century to the emergence of a new phase of capitalist development, one of whose main characteristics was competition between the leading capitalist powers for territory and resources. Lenin predicted that the world would be divided among the great international monopolies. The law of uneven development suggested that in any historical period capitalism would be advancing more swiftly in some regions, while in other older and more mature states it would become parasitic and start to decay. The increasing dominance of finance capital and monopoly forms of organization was the reason for the export of capital and the increasing competition between capitalist powers, which rapidly assumed a military as well as an economic aspect as different states attempted to divide up the whole world and establish exclusive spheres of influence (Sweezy, 1942; Brewer, 1990).

2.2 Hegemonic stability

One of the implications of Carr's analysis was that the breakdown of the world order in the 1930s and the formation of regional blocs followed inevitably from the collapse of British hegemony. This argument became the main theme of the hegemonic stability school which developed in the 1970s. Charles Kindleberger argued that it was the absence of a state capable of providing world leadership that accounted for the Great Depression in the 1930s:

> *The explanation of this book is that the 1929 depression was so wide, so deep, and so long because the international economic system was rendered unstable by British inability and United States unwillingness to assume responsibility for stabilising it in three particulars: (a) maintaining a relatively open market for distress goods; (b) providing counter-cyclical long-term lending; and (c) discounting in crisis.* (Kindleberger, 1973: 292)

For Kindleberger, the institutions of the liberal world order collapsed because of the inability of Britain to continue to play the role of hegemon and supply the public goods necessary to stabilize the global economy, and because of the absence of any other power able or willing to fill that role. The Second World War created the conditions for the emergence of a new hegemon, the United States, which produced the successful reconstruction of the world economy and the long period of prosperity in the 1950s and 1960s. But the erosion of the economic supremacy of the United States meant that its hegemonic power began to decline in the 1970s, and it was no longer able to guarantee the conditions for a stable liberal world order. The results were the recessions and economic instability of the 1970s and 1980s. If no power is able to supply the public goods which a liberal world order requires then states will respond with mercantilist and protectionist policies, as they did in the 1930s. Many contemporary observers in the 1930s had similarly concluded that the breakdown in the world order meant that the future belonged to national economies and regional blocs. Hubert Henderson, for example, claimed:

> *The old international order has broken down for good. Nothing but futility and frustration can come from the attempt to set it up again. Individual countries must be free to regulate their external economies effectively, using control of capital movements, quantitative regulation, preferences, autonomous credit policies, etc.* (Henderson, cited in Kindleberger 1973: 305)

One of the characteristics of regional bloc scenarios in the first half of the twentieth century and again today is that the nature of the conflict between the blocs is assumed to be a zero-sum game in which each bloc competes to increase its relative share of territory, resources and wealth within a global total which is fixed. In this neo-realist perspective regionalism simplifies and intensifies this conflict, by combining the most important states into more or less cohesive groups under the leadership of the dominant state in each region. The pressure on a region to become cohesive increases in relation to the success of other regions in unifying themselves. As each regional power seeks to maximize its wealth and extend its territory, the risk of economic wars rises, because in a zero-sum world each regional power calculates that conflict will yield more benefit than cooperation.

Gloomy forebodings of economic wars and holy wars (Huntington, 1993) have reappeared in the last ten years; but they are challenged by other scenarios which predict a future of increasing prosperity and peace, the settling of the ideological conflicts which have dominated world politics for 200 years and the universal acceptance of a common set of ideas about economic and social organization associated with the idea of a cosmopolitan global economy. On this view the clash of civilizations predicted by Huntington will not materialize because there is only one civilization – Western civilization – which is adapted for survival. The ethics of ultimate ends contained in Confucianism, Islam and Christianity all belong to the pre-modern stage of social development, and are destined to be left behind.

Liberal institutionalists further argue that as the world economy becomes more interdependent, it becomes rational for states to prefer cooperation to conflict (Keohane, 1984). States increasingly face common problems which can only be handled through agreement on new institutions and rules. As interdependence deepens, so the risk of major economic or military conflict should decline. Democracies do not fight one another, so as democratization spreads, the less likely it becomes that conflicts between states will be settled in the future by resort to arms. New transnational institutions develop to mediate conflicts. These theories reject the assumption that states face a zero-sum game. Instead, they assume that there is a positive-sum game in which states can cooperate either through competition or through intergovernmental negotiation to increase the total output of goods and services available for distribution. Economic welfare can be improved for everyone so long as positional goods such as territory and resources do not become the focus of competition. An earlier Marxist version of this argument can be found in the theories of ultra-imperialism, the peaceful joint exploitation of the world by the united finance capital of the great powers (Brewer, 1990).

2.3 Regionalism and globalization

If, however, the world is not facing a return to regional blocs, what explains the recent growth of regionalism and how far is it compatible with globalization? One of the problems is the different levels of analysis at which these concepts operate. Regionalism is a type of state project which can be distinguished from other types of state project such as globalism. Globalization and regionalization are not state projects but complex processes of social change which involve distinctive new patterns of social interaction between non-state actors. State projects like regionalism typically seek to accelerate, to modify, or occasionally to reverse the direction of social change which processes like globalization and regionalization represent.

In practice, regionalism as a set of state projects intersects with globalization. The relationship between the two has come into particularly sharp focus with the end of the Cold War. The world order now has not two but three cores: North America, the European Union and East Asia. The former core around the Soviet Union has disintegrated, allowing the three embryonic cores within the former capitalist world economy to emerge as the constituent elements of the new order, each with its own regionalist project. The relationships between these three cores and between the cores and their peripheries is both complex and diverse. No single pattern has become established. What they all share, however, is a commitment to open regionalism; policy is directed towards the elimination of obstacles to trade within a region, while at the same time minimizing trade barriers to the rest of the world. Policy debate has been conducted not between advocates of free trade and of protection, but between advocates of free trade and of strategic trade. The strategic traders have argued that maintaining and improving international competitiveness needs to be the central goal of economic policy. Instead of insulating the economy from foreign competition, the aim is to expose it to competition while at the same time ensuring that it is able to meet it. Strategic trade arguments deny free trade arguments that an optimum specialization of labour dictated by comparative advantage will arise spontaneously. Rather, states must act strategically to protect key sectors and ensure that they become international leaders in those areas (Reich, 1991, Thurow, 1992).

All the current regionalist projects have been driven to some extent by a strategic trade view. One of the benefits of greater regional cooperation has been the possibility of enabling regional companies and sectors to be successful in global markets. The emphasis is placed on training, research, investment, public procurement and infrastructure, and the need to maintain legal and managerial control over firms. Strategic trade assumptions have always been important in some states, but they have become more prominent recently. Free traders regard them as a diversion from the task of building a non-discriminatory open world trading system, and dispute claims that states are equipped to plan strategically in the way that companies attempt to do (Krugman, 1994).

The strategic trade argument has been carried further by those like Michel Albert who argue that there are distinctive models of capitalism which are regionally specific (Albert, 1991). The dominant Anglo-American model, with its emphasis on free trade, arm's-length banking and a *laissez-faire* policy regime, contrasts with the Japanese and Rhenish models, which emphasize strategic trade, long-term investment, and corporatist and partnership modes of corporate governance and policy formation. Such models, however, are ideal types. Although there are some significant differences between national institutional patterns which give rise to competing strategies for coping with competitive pressures in the global economy, they are easily exaggerated. Strategic trade considerations, for example, have always been important in some sectors of the United States, particularly defence, while some sectors in Europe and Japan have been governed entirely by the rules of free trade.

The new regionalism is contained within quite narrow ideological parameters, reflecting the continuing ideological and cultural leadership of the United States. The competition between models of capitalism of the last twenty years is much less fundamental than the earlier conflict between national capitalisms. Charles Maier, for example, argues: 'Viewed over the whole half century the American international economic effort of the era of stabilization centred on overcoming British, Japanese, and especially German alternatives to a pluralist, market-economy liberalism' (Maier, 1987: 1183). That battle was won, but important differences remain. One of the forces driving the current regionalism is an attempt to protect different models of economic and cultural organization. A limited regionalism emphasizing the diversity of the capitalist world has been the result.

3. New medievalism

Hyper-globalization, with its image of a politics-free cosmopolitan global economy, and hyper-regionalism, with its image of imminent return to an Orwellian world of unceasing struggle between three rival blocs, Oceania, Eurasia, and Eastasia, both seem inadequate to grasp the changing shape of world order. An alternative approach is *new medievalism*, a term first employed by Hedley Bull (1977).

New medievalism is best thought of as a metaphor which draws attention to some similarities between contemporary developments and certain features of the medieval political system in Europe. No one suggests that there could be a return to the medieval era. The issue which the use of the term is intended to raise is whether the principle of exclusive territorial sovereignty so typical of the modern era will turn out to be a unique and aberrant phase in political development (Kobrin, 1996). New medievalism involves contrasting the modern with the medieval state system and arguing that some of the features of the latter are becoming salient again (Tanaka, 1996).

The fundamental aspect of old medievalism in Europe was that there was no ruler with supreme authority over a particular territory or a particular population. Authority was always shared: downwards with vassals, upwards with the Pope – and, in Germany and Italy, with the Holy Roman Emperor. The source of authority was religious, not secular; it was derived from God. The medieval system was theocratic, and this gave it its unity. In 1400 European Christendom still thought of itself as one society (Mattingley, 1964). Authority was multiple and boundaries were overlapping. No centre of universal competence was recognized. There were three separate systems of law – canon law, customary law and civil law – based on three different traditions – Christian, German and Roman – making the administration of justice complex.

Political authority was organized through elaborate hierarchies, a chain of dependent tenures and fiefs. Some of the apparent anomalies which this threw up have been frequently noted. Charles the Bold was the feoffee of the Emperor for part of his lands and of the King of France for another part; but the King of France was also feoffee of Charles the Bold for some of his territories. Such interlocking relationships promoted stability because sovereignty was distributed not concentrated, with the functions of the state split up and assigned to different levels and locations, such as manors and cities.

All this made the centre extremely weak. Monarchs were not supreme authorities above their subjects as they subsequently strove to become. They had to rely for financial resources on their own personal domains. Their vassals owed them military service but not taxes, while the existence of the vassals and their local authority meant that monarchs had no way of communicating directly with the whole population. The absence of a mechanism to integrate and consolidate authority at the centre of the feudal system posed a permanent threat to its stability and survival, and made conflict endemic (Anderson, 1974).

Critics of the idea of a new medievalism can rightly point to major differences between the medieval and the contemporary world order. First, European medievalism was only one, local, political and cultural order in the world at that time. In place of the separate and largely self-sufficient civilizations of this period there now exists an increasingly interdependent global system, and Europe and East Asia, for example, are interdependent parts of this system rather than separate worlds. Second, there is no theocratic basis to the modern state system, except for a few Islamic states, and no universal doctrine in the way that Christianity was a universal doctrine for Europe. Third, the Westphalian system of discrete territorial sovereignties is still strong; indeed, in some respects, with the creation of many new nation states following the breakup of the Soviet Union, it has grown stronger. The modern conception of the public power as the capacity to create new laws and impose obedience to them has been challenged and weakened in some areas, but remains intact in others, and is even being strengthened (Anderson and Goodman, 1995).

But there is still some value in the idea of a new medievalism. The reason for using the term is to aid thinking about the implications of the evident weakening of the state system in the last twenty-five years, which have seen boundaries become blurred and the source of authority less distinct. States have been obliged to share authority with other actors, and their ability to command the exclusive loyalty of their citizens in some areas has diminished. Hedley Bull identified five major trends which gave support to the idea of a new medievalism in this sense. The first was the trend towards regional integration, of which the European Community (EC) was the most prominent example. Bull speculated as to whether the EC was developing into a new superstate, in which case it would not disturb the old Westphalian system, or whether it was a new hybrid, in which sovereignty would be shared between the Community and the member states indefinitely, producing perpetual uncertainty about where sovereignty was located. Bull here anticipated the more recent discussion of the European Union as a new type of political system, the first postmodern state (Ruggie, 1993; Anderson and Goodman, 1995).

A second trend was the disintegration of existing states as a result of new secessionist movements (Nairn, 1981). Again, Bull noted that this trend would be of significance for new medievalism only if the disintegration stopped short of the creation of new states. In that case, the basic principles of the Westphalian system would be upheld, not denied. Of interest to the thesis of new medievalism would be the intermediate stage, in which existing sovereignty is questioned but new sovereignty is not fully asserted, creating uncertainty as to where sovereignty was actually located.

A third trend was the revival of private international violence. Bull was thinking primarily of the growth of international terrorism, but others have also talked about the spread of disorder, corruption, business mafias and private violence more generally. One of the crucial aspects of territorial sovereignty was the claim to monopoly of the means of coercion, both internally within the private/public divide and externally. Only states were recognized as having legitimacy to wage war or to coerce their citizens. States have not lost this legitimacy, but in some areas their ability to enforce their claims to a monopoly of the means of violence has declined.

A fourth trend was the growth of transnational organizations. Bull detected an explosion in such organizations, ranging from companies, political movements and religious associations to international and intergovernmental agencies. He argued that every organization should be classified as national, multinational or transnational in terms of three dimensions: who controlled it, its personnel, and the geographical scope of its operations. The increasing number of organizations defined as transnational in terms of all three criteria suggested a growing divide between a geocentric technology and an ethnocentric politics. The nation-state could still be considered strong in certain areas, such as the deployment of military forces and the ability to command the loyalty of citizens. New medievalists do not think the nation-state will disappear or become unimportant, but argue that it is forced to share authority in some areas, and that it has lost much of its claim to exclusive sovereignty.

A fifth trend identified by Bull was the technological unification of the world, particularly in communications, transport and cultural networks, captured in ideas such as the global village. As Bull pointed out, a better term is global city, since this way of life – nervous, tense, agitated and fragmented – is more characteristic of urban than of village life. The emergence of new economic and cultural spaces which are global rather than national is another potential challenge to the state system and its authority, because it allows citizens to escape its control. But even here many spaces remain obstinately national and local.

3.1 Multi-level systems of authority

Although he set out the case for new medievalism as a possible alternative future for the international political system, Hedley Bull remained sceptical as to how far any of these trends would actually lead to permanent changes in the international state system rather than induce a number of adjustments to it. But the metaphor has proved powerful.

One of the most important contributions has come from Robert Cox. Starting from Susan Strange's observation that the world is beginning to look more like the European middle ages with multi-level systems of authority than the Westphalian system of territorial sovereignty, Cox (1996) cites a number of key developments.

Cities are once again meaningful centres of global interaction and exchange. Provinces and sub-national regions are achieving autonomy as states lose efficiency. Macro-regions are taking on some of the roles performed by states. The loyalty of companies is now multiple rather than unique. Finally, a new global consumerism is being established which promulgates universal norms of economic and political conduct and assists the convergence of tastes and hierarchies of values.

These trends lead to the emergence of a new world order which is characterized by a multi-level structure and the breakup of the old state system. The new order is a complex structure of political–economic entities: micro-regions, traditional states and macro-regions with institutions of greater or lesser functional scope and formal authority, and world cities. The development of this new order poses a fundamental challenge to the old system because it sets up rival transnational processes of ideological formation as well as institutions for concertation and coordination, and multilateral processes for conflict management, peacekeeping and regulation. States are involved in these processes, but not always as the dominant agents (Cerny, 1990).

This new world order exacerbates the conflict which has always existed in the world system between the principles of interdependence and territorial sovereignty. Interdependence is non-territorial, and is characterized by competition in the world market, global finance unconstrained by territorial boundaries, and global production. The territorial principle is state-based and grounded in military and political power. The strength of Cox's analysis is that, like Wallerstein (1974) he sees clearly that one has not risen at the expense of the other. The two principles define the nature of the modern world system and there is a continual tension between them.

3.2 Unbundled territoriality

Ruggie has taken the idea of new medievalism one stage further by arguing that the term is useful if it helps us to understand that we are living through a major transition as significant as the one between the medieval and the modern eras. The inability of many theorists, journalists and politicians to understand the EU is attributable to its being the first postmodern international political form. It is neither national nor supranational; instead, there are overlapping layers of economic and political space. Ruggie strongly attacks the neo-realists who argue that unless the EU becomes a unified state it has no real significance in the international state system, and that since it was primarily a by-product of the superpower conflict, the disappearance of that conflict has removed its rationale. What this ignores is the growth of new institutions, new jurisdictions and new spaces which signal a new form of political rule which cannot be fitted into the old categories.

Ruggie accepts the arguments of Jameson and Harvey that it is not just the international state system which is in crisis but modernity itself. Capitalism is moving into its third great phase of expansion. The first was the national market; the second was the imperial system; and the current phase is the production and manipulation of signs, images and information (Jameson, 1984, 1989). Central to this new phase of capitalism is the reconfiguration of space–time experiences, the first major upheaval since the Renaissance (Harvey, 1989). The experiences, Ruggie argues, have changed; but the perceptual equipment is lacking to make sense of them. Crucial to the concept of space in the modern era was single-point perspective, developed by Filippo Brunelleschi in 1425. Its original application was in painting, but it came to influence the form of all intellectual enquiry. In international relations it helped shape the concept of sovereignty, the viewing of all political relations from a single fixed point.

The specific spatial and temporal coordinates of modernity have been overturned by what Ruggie, following Halford Mackinder, terms the spatial and temporal implosion of the globe. Mackinder, writing at the beginning of the twentieth century, declared that the age of Columbus (the age of European expansion) was over and predicted the emergence of a unified post-Columbian world system (Mackinder, 1904). The Bolshevik revolution delayed that outcome for seventy-five years, but with the collapse of the USSR there is now no major barrier to the integration of all territories and states into a single world system. The ideology of globalization is a reflection of that.

This new stage in the development of the world system will be characterized, Ruggie argues, by a new system of rule of which the EU is the first harbinger. The basis on which the international political system is segmented into units and spaces is changing. The old mode of differentiation – territorial sovereignty – is being 'unbundled' by the globalization of the economy and culture. Instead of one perspective there are now multiple perspectives, and instead of one identity there are multiple identities. It is impossible to grasp the contours of this world with the categories of modernity. In this sense the intellectual perspective which is required is one closer to that of medieval times in Europe than of the modern period.

3.3 The future of the nation-state

As noted above, the idea of a new medievalism has been criticized, mainly on the grounds that the concept encourages looking back rather than looking forward. The contrasts with old medievalism may be much greater than the similarities. At the time of the European middle ages the world system was not unified and interdependent in the way that it is now; the extent of the division of labour and of interdependence was low. It was a period before the monopolization of government functions by sovereign nation-states (Hirst and Thompson, 1996). The extent of the integration of modern economies and societies means that no return to that earlier era is possible.

Nor is there anything comparable in the contemporary world system to the universal doctrine of Christianity. A new secular universal doctrine embracing human rights and environmentalism has begun to be elaborated, but it is a long way from enjoying the authority that Christianity enjoyed in medieval Europe.

Other features of medieval universalism, such as a common elite language, are also less developed. Further criticisms focus on the extent to which nation-states have actually been weakened. In some areas state powers have increased (Anderson and Goodman, 1995). The unbundling of territoriality is therefore only partial. Distinctions have to be made between the different roles which states perform. In security, defence and welfare, nation-states' loss of sovereignty is much less marked than in economic policy.

The advantage of new medievalism is that it does focus attention on systems of rule, which globalization does not. But the conditions for rule in the contemporary world system are clearly vastly different from those prevailing in the European middle ages. Different modes of governance – markets, hierarchies, networks and communities – are required to sustain and coordinate such a complex global division of labour and organize the distribution of work and income among sectors, regions, classes and households. Ohmae's dream of a politics-free cosmopolitan society is wide of the mark. The actual need is for new forms of governance to be established to handle the increasingly serious problems of the world system – population pressure, environmental sustainability, poverty and ethnic conflict (Held, 1995; Gamble, 1993).

What cannot be denied is that both the authority and the competence of the nation-state have been weakened in certain areas in the last twenty-five years. Eric Hobsbawm speaks of the nation-state being on the defensive against a world economy it cannot control, and against institutions such as the EU which it originally constructed to remedy its own weaknesses. It has suffered a loss of will and capacity. It can no longer financially maintain the public services which were so confidently established only a few decades ago; nor can it maintain public law and order (Hobsbawm, 1994). This judgement needs qualifying. Not all states in all parts of the world suffer the same incapacity and incompetence. But the general position is broadly accurate. The nation-state appears weak in relation to many of the problems it faces. But although it is weak it is still indispensable within the governance structure of the world system.

The key test of the thesis of new medievalism is whether this weakness of the nation-state is transient or permanent. If the factors which cause it are transient then the nation-state may re-emerge with enhanced powers and legitimacy. If they are permanent – as most analysts suspect – then the nation-state might just wither away as Ohmae desires; or, more probably, it might, as the new medievalism thesis suggests, be gradually changed into one of several overlapping areas of governance (Cerny, 1990).

One of the causes of the weakness of the state is that the era of national protectionism has ended, an era which enhanced the powers of national government and gave meaning to the concept of a national economy as an object of public policy. The 1980s and 1990s have witnessed a reconfiguration of the relationships between states and the global economy, with the emergence of new regions and speculation about regional blocs. As yet, the trend towards the formation of regional blocs remains weak, certainly compared with the 1920s and 1930s, and the new forms of regional political structures that have been established are more in tune with the governance mechanisms of the new medievalism than with those of the old international state system (Gamble and Payne, 1996).

3.4 Reregulating the economy

New medievalism is consistent with different scenarios for the future of the world system. Robert Cox has recently speculated that we may be witnessing a new phase in the alternation between deregulation and reregulation (Cox, 1996). Karl Polanyi argued that the conscious deregulation of the nineteenth century meant overreliance upon the market as the mode of governance (Polanyi, 1944). The state was steadily withdrawn from direct involvement in economic activity and was confined to the role of enforcing the rules of the market. Once established, markets were regarded as self-regulating. The consequences of self-regulating markets, however, were so socially destructive that resistance multiplied and the state found a new legitimacy as the regulator of the economy and the guarantor of minimum levels of welfare. Control was exercised at the level of the nation-state, through forms of governance reliant upon hierarchies, such as government bureaucracies, and associations such as trade unions.

Polanyi expected that this would be irreversible, but it has not proved so. The regulated system lost legitimacy in the 1970s because it was unable to cope with the problems of accelerating inflation, decelerating growth and the consequent tendency for public spending to outpace revenues. At the same time, it had to deal with the emergence of an increasingly global economy, manifested particularly in the financial markets. As a result, in the last thirty years there has been a pronounced swing away from regulation, and new experiments with deregulation, privatization and the dismantling of public sectors and public programmes have proliferated, particularly in Britain and the United States. The doctrine of globalization has codified many of these policy ideas into dogmas which are routinely expressed in the conditions for financial assistance imposed on national governments by international agencies like the IMF and the World Bank.

Cox asks whether the same pressures that led to the imposition of social control in the nineteenth century will develop again, as a result of the increasingly destructive nature of neo-liberal policies and the self-regulating market throughout the world system. This time, however, control would need to be reimposed not at the national level but at the global level. The practical difficulties in the way of such a development are immense, since the conditions for world government are nowhere fulfilled, and the systems of rule within the world system remain so fragmented. Nevertheless, pressure for some form of reregulation is growing as the financial turmoil in world financial markets has increased. But such reregulation, if it occurs, is likely to strengthen rather than replace the multi-level system of authority that now defines the international state system, rebalancing the various modes of governing the global economy, and thus privileging certain national strategies and institutional patterns over others.

4. Conclusion

'New medievalism' is at best a metaphor but, used properly, it can provide insights into the changing forms of governance of the world system. One of the key tests for this perspective is whether the EU is a peculiar and unique phenomenon, as peculiar and unique as the Holy Roman Empire – which, as Ruggie reminds us, was neither holy nor Roman nor an empire; whether it is the first embodiment of a new form of political rule which will spread to other regions; or whether it is embryonically a new unified regional bloc, a United States of Europe. Nationalist opponents of European integration believe that it is the last of these. The UK Referendum Party campaigned in the 1997 British general election for the principle of an independent nation, which it defined as possessing:

- the right to make laws which are supreme in our own country;
- the right to run our own economy for the benefit of our own people;
- the right to decide our foreign policy;
- the right to determine our national security;
- the right to control our own frontiers.

The debate increasingly turns on the extent to which these rights are any longer deliverable through territorially sovereign nation-states, and whether they can only be achieved by recognizing the fundamental changes in the way in which political and economic and social space is now structured.

One of the paradoxes of the current debate is that there is a double movement. On the one hand there are pronounced trends towards globalization in finance, production and commerce. On the other, the legitimacy of the nation-state as the preferred locus of political rule has never been stronger, and many nations, as in eastern Europe, still seek self-determination and the creation of their own independent state. The fears about regionalist projects and the revival of fears about the formation of blocs is in part the anxiety that the pluralism and overlapping authorities so characteristic of the present time will not last, and that there will be a swing back to unified centralized political authority.

One problem in thinking about the problems of world order is that the contrasts that are often proposed between different periods oversimplify. Since the world system began there have always been three types of order present: cosmopolitan, organized around markets; imperial, organized around security and global hegemonic functions; and territorial, organized around legitimacy and frontiers. The relative weightings of these three have changed in different periods, but they have always coexisted. What we are witnessing today is a rebalancing of these types of order. Realist conceptions of international relations for too long have obscured the fact that there have always been rival and overlapping sources of authority and order. There never was a pure Westphalian world. If new medievalism can help us appreciate that fact, it will have served a useful purpose.

2. Political Economy of New Regionalism and World Governance

Pier Carlo Padoan

The international system is much more complex today than it was twenty-five years ago when the regime which had been set up at the end of the Second World War – the Bretton Woods system – collapsed. Understanding this complexity is one of the major challenges facing international relations scholars, and any attempt to do so carries a high risk of adding confusion rather than clarity.

Let me first state, therefore, what this chapter does not intend to do. It does not try to provide a 'grand theory' of the international system today. It does not even pretend to offer indications of the direction in which such a theory might be found. More simply, it starts by noting that the evolution of the international system stems from the interaction of three levels of behaviour: the systemic level, the national level and the new intermediate level, the regional one. The distinction, and often the contrast, between the first two levels of analysis has long been one of the dividing lines among international relation scholars, and only recently we have been witnessing a resurgence of the debate, basically pointing at the possibility of combining the systemic and nation-state levels of analysis.[1] The discussion on regionalism has, on the other hand, largely followed a path of its own,[2] with few attempts to link it to the other two levels of analysis.

Starting from this point, the chapter seeks to offer suggestions on how to link the three levels of analysis. This will be done largely by drawing on the existing literature, and the discussion will take a dual approach. The 'top-down' approach considers the influence which the higher level exerts on the lower one: how the globalization of the international system affects the evolution of regional agreements, and how the latter influences the domestic policies of nation-states.[3] The 'bottom-up' approach looks at the opposite direction of influence: how changes at the national level impinge upon the dimensions and characteristics of regional agreements, and how the development of regional agreements and their interaction shape the characteristics of the new international system.

1. The global system in institutional disequilibrium

The global system is now in what has been called a post-hegemonic condition (Gilpin, 1987): that is, a situation in which no single country can provide unilaterally the public goods required for the operation of the system itself. This can also be expressed by saying that the international system is in 'institutional disequilibrium' in the sense that there is an excess demand for international public goods which in turn is the result of a decrease in supply, because of the redistribution of power away from a hegemonic structure,[4] and an increase in demand because of increased globalization.

The current configuration of the global system, however, is also often described as one of 'regionalism', which should be understood not so much as the result of concentration of trade and investment activities around major integrated regions (Europe, North America, Asia) but rather as a policy option pursued as a response to the failure of the post-hegemonic world in providing international public goods. As has been argued,[5] regionalism may be 'conflict oriented' or 'cooperative'. In the first case regional agreements provide collective goods for countries included in each region and exclude non-members from their consumption (an example of this would be a discriminatory trade agreement). Cooperative regionalism, on the contrary, could be understood as the formation of regional agreements as a precondition for cooperation at a global level, i.e. with a view towards multilateralism. To proceed from this point one needs to consider two factors: first, the conditions for cooperation without hegemony, i.e. within a multipolar world; and second, the interactions among domestic, regional and international policy.

The theory of international cooperation without hegemony offers a list of conditions that must be met if agreements to supply international public goods are to be reached:[6] 1) the number of actors involved must be small; 2) the time horizon of actors must be long; 3) actors must be prepared to change their policy preferences; 4) international institutions must be available. Condition 1 allows for the possibility of dealing with free riding. Condition 2 allows for repeated interaction among players, which is both necessary and unavoidable in an increasingly interdependent world. Condition 3 requires nation-states to be prepared to adjust to the international environment to reach agreements. Condition 4 relates to the fact that institutions support cooperation as they facilitate exchange and information among different actors.

Conditions 1 to 4 imply, among other things, that cooperation is achieved if nation-states adjust both their economic and their political equilibria. This leads us to the interaction between international and domestic politics. Robert Putnam (1988) has suggested that international regime formation requires that an agreement be reached at two levels of political activity: both level I, i.e. between national governments, and level II, i.e. between each national government, the legislator, and domestic interest groups. So, while commitments made at political level II must be consistent with the agreement struck at level I, the opposite relation must hold as well: level I agreements must be designed so as to be consistent with the specific level II agreements in each of the participating countries. The interaction between level I and level II politics in determining the success of international cooperation is a complex one and its implications are still being developed in the literature.[7]

Regionalism adds a third level of politics, regional politics, to be understood as the definition of a common regional policy which operates between domestic and international politics. The answer to the question whether regionalism will assume benign or malign characteristics, then, requires looking at the role regional (level III) politics can play as a bridge between level I and level II politics. This, in turn, requires a closer look at the conditions that must be met in order for regional agreements to be consolidated, i.e. the conditions in which level II politics can be 'melted' into level III (regional) politics. Once this is accomplished, international (level I) politics interacts with regional (level III) rather than with domestic (level II) politics.

De Melo, Pangaya and Rodrik (1993) develop this point analytically. Their framework considers regional integration as both an economic and a political process which is the outcome of a relationship between national governments and domestic pressure groups (level II politics in Putnam's terminology).[8] They show that the formation of supranational institutions – regional agreements – has a positive effect on the economic efficiency of national economies when these integrate because of the lower impact of domestic pressure groups on the policy stance of the supranational institution, compared to the corresponding impact on national governments. Without integration, national governments would provide excessive intervention – excessive, that is, with respect to the economically optimal – because of the strong influence of domestic pressure groups (the so-called 'preference dilution effect'). However, if there are large differences among national preferences concerning the degree of government intervention, the incentive to integrate may be insufficient (the 'preference asymmetry effect'). To operate efficiently, supranational institutions must be designed so as to minimize the weight of countries whose domestic pressure groups demand a high degree of government intervention (the 'institutional design effect'). The first effect relates to the increased role of national systems when international regimes are weak. The second effect relates to the role of differences in national systems in favouring or hindering international regime formation. The third effect underlines the point that regional politics requires the formation of some kind of supranational institution, to avoid the risk of being captured by special interest action.

The 'two-level' approach is a first useful step in trying to establish relations between national systemic and regional mechanisms of cooperation. The next step requires looking more closely at level III. More specifically, the following questions arise: first, why are regional agreements formed and why do they expand (or contract)? Second, how do countries respond to the formation of regional agreements?

2. Economic aspects of regional agreements

The establishment of a regional agreement requires the selection of those who are to join and also those who are to be excluded; regionalism is as much a question of cooperation as it is of exclusion. The extent of membership, therefore, must be determined. When is the optimal number of members reached? Why does it change over time?

Standard trade theory gives a precise answer to the question of number: the optimal size of a trade agreement is the world. Short of full liberalization, however, partial elimination of barriers following integration will improve the allocation of resources and welfare. Although the welfare gain might be partially curtailed by trade diversion, which could offset gains from trade creation, reallocation of resources generated by the integration process allows the exploitation of national comparative advantages. Differences in national resource endowments will lead to a deepening of specialization patterns which will benefit all countries involved in the integration process. Factors of production will be allocated in sectors where the country enjoys a comparative advantage, while production in other sectors will stop or be reduced. The process will, of course, involve adjustment costs and temporary unemployment, the severity and duration of which could be alleviated by appropriate financial support. Once reallocation is completed, inter-industry trade, i.e. trade in goods belonging to different sectors (e.g. textiles and food products), within the region will increase. Note that the benefits of integration, in such a framework, could be equally obtained by the reallocation of factors among countries, i.e. by migration and/or capital movements.

Within traditional trade theory the reason why the organization of international trade falls short of global liberalization, and therefore why regional rather than global integration develops, is usually found in the presence of special interests that, given imperfect political markets, have the resources and the ability to obtain protection from national or regional governments.

'New trade theory' has pointed at another possible source of gains from integration, deriving from the exploitation of (static and dynamic) gains from trade.[9] The larger market generated by integration allows (oligopolistic) firms to exploit increasing returns. This leads to further specialization within the same sectors as competition rests both on lower costs deriving from expanded production and on product (quality) differentiation. Intra-industry trade, i.e. trade of similar goods between countries, will be generated. Welfare gains from integration will ensue from lower costs and broader quality range as well as the exploitation of dynamic returns to scale generated by the learning process following the introduction of new technologies.

In this case, too, costs could arise from integration; however, they would be permanent, rather than temporary. In addition to the standard adjustment costs, economies of scale could generate agglomeration effects as both capital and labour would concentrate in specific areas, leading to permanent core–periphery effects within the region. Employment opportunities would concentrate in some areas, exacerbating the asymmetrical distribution of net benefits (Krugman, 1993).

The 'gravity model' of trade flows, which has recently become popular again, suggests that countries are more likely to trade with one another the closer their per capita and absolute income levels. This intuition can be given theoretical foundations according to the 'new trade theory' stressing economies of scale and diversity as source of (intra-industry) trade (see Baldwin and Venables, 1994). The gravity model assigns an important role to distance, predicting that geographical proximity will enhance the probability of trade between countries, other things being equal. While the economic justification of this element is related to transport costs, it is also possible (Alesina and Grilli, 1993) that geographically close countries also share similar preferences about the provision of common policies, thus increasing the incentives to integrate. Their analysis also points to a more general topic which is increasingly being addressed in the literature: namely, the role of social standards, in particular labour and environmental standards, in setting the 'comparative advantages' of countries and regions and the consequent trade-offs that emerge from the pressures of globalization.[10]

In general, trade integration would increase both inter- and intra-industry trade and, in both cases, increased competition would activate pressures to resist adjustment and/or demand for compensatory measures on the part of countries and regions most severely hit by the asymmetric distribution of net benefits.

The emergence of inequalities generated by the process of integration raises the notion of 'cohesion', which may be defined as '[a principle that] implies ... a relatively equal social and territorial distribution of employment opportunities, of wealth and of income, and of improvements in the quality of life that correspond to increasing expectations' (Smith and Tsoukalis, 1996: 1). An important implication is that, without cohesion, political support for a regional agreement is likely to fail.

Consensus to the regional agreement, and ultimately its size, will then depend on the degree of cohesion among its members. Cohesion problems will be greater the larger the asymmetric distribution effects, and therefore the larger the impact of scale effects generated by integration. These effects, in turn, will be greater the larger the diversity among members of the integrating region. Once the costs for cohesion management (i.e. the costs that must be borne to offset the asymmetry effects) exceed the benefits from integration, the widening process will come to an end. A number will have been determined.

Monetary integration, too, both when it implies fixing exchange rates and when it takes the form of full monetary union, can produce an asymmetric distribution of net benefits. (Economic) benefits from monetary integration stem from three sources (see de Grauwe, 1992): the elimination of transaction costs, the elimination of currency risk and the acquisition of policy credibility for inflation-prone countries. The first two benefits can be fully obtained only with monetary union. The third benefit has to be weighed against the costs of real currency appreciation which hits high-inflation countries once they credibly enter an exchange rate agreement (Krugman, 1993). If the latter are also the peripheral countries from a trade point of view, the adverse effects of real and monetary integration will cumulate, leading to further demand for compensation. Low-inflation countries, on the other hand, would be adversely affected by entering a monetary agreement with excessively expansionary partners, so that ultimately they would refuse the latter permission to join (Alesina and Grilli, 1993). In both cases the extension of the monetary agreement will stop short of global integration. Again, a number will be determined.

To conclude, economics can provide several contributory elements to the understanding of the number problem; however, a satisfactory theory of regional integration should explain the optimal number of members through the interaction of economic, institutional and political variables. One way of approaching the issue is to consider regional agreements as clubs.

3. Regional agreements as clubs

The economic analysis of club formation started to develop in the 1960s with the contributions of James Buchanan (1965) and Mancur Olson (1965), and since then has been applied to several economic and political issues such as community size, production of local public goods, two-part tariffs, congestion problems, political coalitions and, more recently, international organizations (Casella and Feinstein, 1990). The literature has been surveyed by Sandler and Tschirhart (1980), Frey (1984), Cornes and Sandler (1985) and Bolton et al. (1996).

Club theory deals with problems related to the establishment of voluntary associations for the production of excludable public goods. Optimal membership is determined by marginality conditions, when the spread between an individual member's cost and benefit is maximized. Marginal costs and benefits are functions of the size of the club.[11]

Costs are related to management and decision-making activities; hence management costs should not be confused with congestion costs arising for example from cumulative effects such as those discussed in the previous section, which will be considered as factors affecting the level of net benefits from club provision.

Marginal costs increase with the extension of club membership because management problems rise with the number of members. As Fratianni and Pattison (1982) stress, decision theory suggests that the addition of new members will raise the costs of reaching agreements in a more than proportional manner. Costs will also rise more than proportionally for organizational reasons and because, for political balance, each new member will have to be given equal opportunity, irrespective of its economic size, to express its viewpoint (Ward, 1991). Institutional arrangements alter the behaviour of costs. For example, a shift from a unanimity rule to a majority rule in decision making within the club lowers marginal costs. On the other hand, individual members' marginal benefits decrease with this change, assuming that the equal-sized share of total benefits from integration increases more slowly as the number of members rises, because congestion lowers the quality of the club good.

Optimal club membership is obtained when marginal benefits (B) equal marginal costs (C). We can consider the following simple rule. The incentive for a change in the extent of a regional agreement emerges whenever there is a discrepancy between marginal benefits and marginal costs of the club. Note that this allows us to consider possible (and not at all unrealistic) contractions in the size of the club (here determined by the number of members Q).

A trade agreement responds to some of the crucial requisites for the definition of a club: it produces freer trade, virtually a public good; it guarantees partial exclusion of non-members from free trade benefits; and, in the case of a customs union, it guarantees the benefits of a common external trade policy. To the extent that standards contribute to the determination of comparative advantage, groups of countries sharing common standards are forms of trade clubs.

Marginal benefits of a trade club may be thought of as depending on both exogenous and endogenous components, i.e. on the size of the club itself. The first include the 'security' effect of trade agreements. This implies that membership in a trade club is more valuable in the presence of a possible outside threat. This may be a genuine military threat, as Gowa and Mansfield (1993) have argued. The present global environment, however, may present other forms of threat, such as those deriving from the formation of regional and aggressive trade blocs. In such a case the incentive for joining a trade club lies not only in the trade creation and/or scale effects benefits but also in the 'insurance' that club membership provides against the harm that a trade bloc war could produce to small, isolated countries (Perroni and Whalley, 1994; Baldwin, 1993). A larger club membership will benefit existing members as well as new entrants. If the size of the alliance increases it reinforces resistance to the outside threat. This implies that the value of a club rises with the degree of conflict in the global system.

Exogenous factors also include purely political benefits from trade agreements, i.e. the fact that members will be admitted to the club in so far as they share the same political beliefs as the existing members, for example the full acceptance of democratic rules. This element has played a crucial role in the enlargement of the European Community to the southern countries, Greece, Portugal and Spain (Winters, 1993), and will play a similar role in the future enlargement of the EU.

A monetary agreement, whether in the form of a currency union or of an exchange rate agreement, also responds to the requisites of a public good. The public good nature of a single currency is well established in the literature. In the case of an exchange rate agreement such as the European Monetary System – or rather, its Exchange Rate Mechanism (ERM) – the public good involved is monetary stability extended to the participants of the ERM. Common intervention rules extended to members – not to unilateral peggers – allow for at least partial excludability of the good.

Globalization and outside threats increase the benefits of a monetary club as capital mobility and deeper financial integration increase the desirability of monetary unions as a protection against destabilizing capital movements (Eichengreen, 1994). Outside threats may come from 'aggressive' behaviour (or behaviour perceived as such) as part of foreign monetary policies. For example, Henning (1996) argues that one of the driving forces behind European monetary integration over recent decades has been the espousal of an aggressive macroeconomic policy attitude by the United States. Finally, one should include the 'non-economic' benefits of monetary membership which play a relevant role in the success, or failure, of monetary agreements (Cohen, 1993).

Marginal benefits increase, other things being equal, with the level of economic activity. The pressure of rising inequality due to integration will be lower the more sustained is the level of economic activity, as more sustained growth will benefit all club members. Another way of looking at this component is to recall that protectionist pressures increase in times of economic depression.[12] It is widely recognized that the pressure to enlarge the EU eastward has been slowed down by the recession that hit Europe during the first part of the 1990s. Also, more favourable macroeconomic conditions make it easier to implement the necessary policies for members of a monetary club (e.g. higher growth makes fiscal adjustment less costly).

Let us now consider the endogenous determinants of club size, i.e. the number of club members. Marginal benefits are related to club membership and decrease with club size because of rising congestion problems in club formation, as discussed in the previous section. Marginal benefits, other things being equal, decrease with the diversity of countries wishing to join the club: increasing diversity implies larger congestion costs in the case of a trade club or increasing divergences in the preference for a stable macroeconomic policy in the case of a monetary club.[13] This explains why members of a monetary club must fulfil appropriate requirements (e.g., in terms of financial stability in the EU, the 'Maastricht conditions' for membership of the single currency), and why new members may lower the quality of the public good if their monetary and fiscal policies follow non-convergent courses.[14]

Marginal costs also include exogenous and endogenous components (depending on club size). Marginal costs are determined by management problems. In the case of the EU, as Baldwin (1994) describes (see also Widgren, 1994), voting rules are complicated by the increase in the number of members, and hence by the increasing diversity of preferences, as each member country will use its voting power to increase the welfare of its citizens. Thus, for example, it is unlikely that the EU can successfully enlarge without a change in the voting procedure. As Fratianni (1995) stresses, the entrance of the central and east European countries into the Union will make the formation of a blocking minority much easier, given the current voting system.

Exogenous components can be thought of as associated with the amount and quality of international cooperation already existing among club members in other areas; that is, if institutions linking countries involved in negotiating the agree-

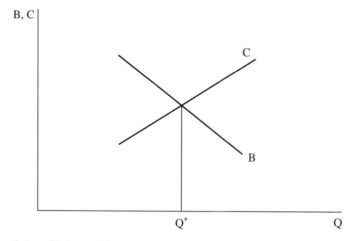

Figure 2.1   Club equilibrium

ments already exist, this will facilitate the formation and management of the new institutions. While several reasons can be advanced to support such a claim, it is a well-established fact in international relations theory that institutions provide information about other actors' behaviour, thus facilitating communication and information exchange.[15] In the case of monetary unions, the exogenous component may be thought of as representing the costs associated with the loss of monetary sovereignty as perceived by club members.

A simple representation of club equilibrium is offered in Figure 2.1. The equilibrium club size is Q^* where the marginal cost and benefits curves intersect.

Starting from Q^*, optimal club membership will vary according to a number of factors. There will be an enlargement process if macroeconomic conditions improve; if the degree of outside conflicts increases, thus raising the insurance value of membership; if the strength and efficiency of institutional arrangements among members other than trade relations increase; if diversity among countries – both members and candidates – decreases; and/or if the voting system becomes more flexible. The first three factors can be represented by a shift of the B curve to the right; the fourth factor may be represented by a shift of the C curve to the right.[16]

Finally, as suggested by Mansfield and Branson (1994), the presence of a leader (or k-group in Schelling's terminology) may increase the degree of cohesion of a regional agreement. This could also be represented by a shift of both curves to the right, as a regional leader would increase the value of the club good (e.g. by providing monetary discipline or unilateral access to domestic markets) and lower management costs.

In conclusion, equilibrium club size will vary because exogenous conditions and/or endogenous conditions change. This last point needs to be further clarified. Changing endogenous conditions here means that, as a result of changes in the international environment, countries outside the agreement become willing to undertake the alterations in their domestic political economy necessary in order to be 'admitted to the club', i.e. to become 'more similar' to the current club members, thus decreasing the degree of diversity. This is the basic insight in Baldwin's (1993) 'domino theory of regionalism', where the demand for integration increases in countries previously not interested in joining a regional agreement. However, as the final regional equilibrium will depend on both demand for and supply of membership. Linking the regional to the national level requires examination of this point.

4. Narrowing diversity: the demand for integration

As noted above, we may think of an integration 'equilibrium' as the outcome of the interaction between 'demand for integration', i.e. the decision of individual countries to apply for membership of integration agreements and to undergo the necessary adjustments for that request to be fulfilled, and the 'supply of integration', i.e. the willingness of regional agreements to accept new members. Let us take a closer look at the determination of the demand for integration.

Economic integration delivers benefits and costs, both economic and political, to the integrating countries. We have already briefly reviewed costs and benefits as discussed in the economics literature; here we consider them from the point of view of individual countries, in other words, as country-specific, as they reflect the economic and political structure of each country. If we consider this aspect we see that a given level of integration, exogenously determined,[17] will deliver different costs and benefits according to the initial level of market liberalization. From integration theory we know that costs of integration (Ic) are decreasing, and benefits of integration (Ib) are increasing with the degree of integration, i.e. with the degree of liberalization of the economy. Costs derive from the adjustment an economy has to undergo in the reallocation process that integration requires. They are initially high as one can assume that the production structure of a closed or isolated economy is quite distant from the one that is optimal in an integration equilibrium. Hence resource allocation may be quite distant from, and distorted in comparison to, an allocation consistent with trade liberalization. Costs can be measured both in terms of sectors that must be closed down and in terms of the political resistance to change; i.e. the Ic curve reflects both economic and political costs. Similarly, integration costs will be larger the higher the degree of protection and the larger the share of the economy that is not exposed to international competition, i.e. the non-tradeable sector. Benefits increase with the degree of integration as beneficial effects of international competition spread over a larger part of the economy through a better

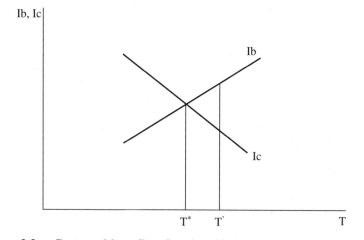

Figure 2.2   Costs and benefits of regional integration

resource allocation. The *Ib* curve also reflects political benefits in terms of the support of the interest groups that are likely to be favoured by liberalization.[18] We can also consider the non-economic aspects of integration, as benefits will be larger if members of the integrating region are also part of an alliance – not necessarily a purely military one (Gowa and Mansfield, 1993).

Figure 2.2 describes these elements. The respective positions of the *Ic* and *Ib* curves depend on the share of the non-tradeable sectors (a larger non-tradeable sector shifts the *Ic* curve to the right), and on the presence of an alliance, an outside threat, elements that would shift *Ib* to the right. The *Ib* curve would also shift to the right if a larger number of sectors of the economy would benefit from increased liberalization. As shown, there is a critical level of integration – *T** – beyond which benefits are larger than costs, making it expedient to pursue the integration option. The level of liberalization is exogenously determined by the characteristics of the agreement (e.g. the level of the tariff for a trade club or the degree of financial liberalization for a monetary club), say at level *T'*. Joining the agreement implies accepting this level of liberalization. At *T'* net integration benefits (*Ib – Ic*) may be positive or negative. In the first case it would obviously be beneficial for the country to join the agreement (or to ask for membership). In the second case positive net benefits would materialize only following a shift in the position of the two curves (the *Ib* to the right and/or the *Ic* to the left), which could be seen as the consequence of a shift in domestic preferences with respect to the integration option. The role of globalization is relevant in this process to the extent that increased market globalization shifts the preferences towards more open economies and away from sheltered sectors.

5. Interaction between supply of and demand for integration

Net integration benefits for a particular country are only a necessary condition for membership. Entering a club requires the payment of an admission fee. The justification for a club admission fee is obvious. New club members must guarantee that they will behave according to club rules and will not lower the quality of the club good. Hence the admission fee requires a policy change in any country wishing to join the agreement We may think of two simple examples of policy change as admission fee. In the case of a monetary club the admission fee may be explicit (as in the case of the fulfilment of the Maastricht conditions for joining the European single currency). In the case of a trade club a policy change is needed to rule out support to the domestic industry through instruments such as subsidies, transfers, etc. We may also think of 'implicit fees'. For instance, we may consider the case that the adjustment entailed in the process of integration has a macroeconomic dimension. This aspect is enhanced by globalization. Globalization is beneficial if, among other things, it enhances the possibility of attracting foreign capital. This requires a 'sound macroeconomic environment'. Macroeconomic stabilization must be implemented to obtain the dual objective of making the potential benefits of integration effective and of obtaining the international credibility that is necessary to attract funds from abroad, both from official institutions and from private investors. In short, the admission fee to the club must be paid to obtain the reputation for creditworthiness necessary to gain access to international capital markets and/or to be accepted in a club.

We can assume that the cost of reputation (R) increases with the degree of liberalization (integration) as deeper integration requires deeper transformation in policy, and/or a larger amount of funds from abroad is needed the larger the dimension of the adjustment process. In short, membership in a club implies an exogenous degree of liberalization T' and a corresponding amount of reputation R^* that must be obtained (the club admission fee). These two elements determine the conditions of the supply of membership.

Matching up the two elements, the level of liberalization and the reputation level, produces a new threshold in the choice process, illustrated in Figure 2.3. The value of T' determines a critical value of reputation (R^*) which must be reached in order to gain access to international finance and/or to be admitted to a club. Reputation can be obtained by implementing an adjustment programme, which in our framework can be, very simply, represented by an inverse relationship between R and X, the policy variable controlled by the government (public expenditure). This implies that a minimum level of R requires a maximum level of X.

To complete the picture, we must take into account the consequences of the admission fee for domestic political equilibrium. A government faces a domestic problem, which may be represented by assuming that the policy-maker maximizes the probability of staying in power. In order to obtain this goal the government will use X to maximize P, the government's popularity, to which the probability of

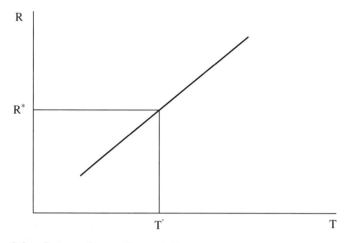

Figure 2.3   Integration and reputation

staying in power is positively related. We can assume that there is a minimum level of popularity (P^*) which is required to stay in power for a given institutional and political setting. The way in which X influences (directly) P reflects the social and institutional characteristics of the country. The amount of X necessary to obtain a given amount of P will increase with the degree of social sclerosis in Olson's (1965) sense (which is larger the larger the number and strength of interest groups, and the greater the degree of fragmentation of the society), the size and power of the nation-state bureaucracy and the degree to which government is divided (Helen Milner, 1997). A minimum level of popularity implies a minimum level of X, X^*. The position of the P curve is influenced by the nature of the state. A strong state, where the degree of social sclerosis is low, will obtain a higher amount of P out of a given amount of X than a weak state where the degree of social sclerosis is high.[19]

The framework is now set for its purpose, i.e. to answer the question: under what circumstances will a country find it desirable to ask for membership of an integration agreement? A positive answer requires that a positive net benefit from integration is obtained. This is larger the more market-oriented is the economy, the stronger the integration process in place (a higher value of T'), the stronger the outside threat (e.g. regional blocs worldwide) and the stronger are the non-economic ties with the integration partners. As the net integration benefits must be set against the amount of the admission fee, the pattern described boils down to one choice. The government may set the amount of X, its policy variable, at a value that is consistent with the integration option.

We may now recapitulate the steps in the domestic policy process. The intersection between benefits and costs from integration determines a minimum level of

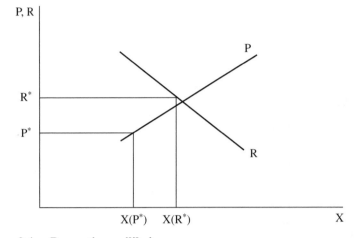

Figure 2.4   Domestic equilibrium

integration, T^*. This leads to a minimum level of reputation, R^*, to be obtained (the admission fee). Figure 2.4 brings together the reputation function and the popularity function, both determined, although in an opposite relationship, by the level of the domestic policy variable X. To use Putnam's (1988) terminology (see also Guerrieri and Padoan, 1989) the upper and lower bounds to X, established respectively by the reputation – $X(R^*)$ – and the popularity – $X(P^*)$ – constraints, determine a 'win set', i.e. a set of feasible policies that are consistent with both domestic and international policy goals.

If the reputation constraint is more binding than the popularity constraint – $X(R^*)<X(P^*)$ – a win set does not exist. The emergence of an integration option, however, may be exploited by the government to force an adjustment on the domestic economy by lowering the popularity constraint below the reputation constraint. This is the familiar case where international politics is used as a leverage to impose change in the domestic political and economic arena. This option will be more attractive the larger are the benefits promised by integration. This option will also be more easily pursued the more powerful are the domestic interest groups that will benefit from integration (whose relative position and size determines the relative position of the *Ib* and *Ic* curves). As the country adjusts towards the liberalization level T' and the reputation level R^* requested by club membership, the diversity between existing and candidate members decreases and this allows for an expansion of club size (the endogenous component of club size determination increases).

6. From top-down to bottom-up

In the sections above we have followed a 'top-down' approach, suggesting some linkages between the collapse of the post-war international (hegemonic) system – which has produced a state of institutional disequilibrium – and the emergence of regionalism, which can be thought of in part as a response to the excess demand for international public goods. We have then suggested that the formation of regional clubs has increased both the supply of and the demand for integration. The latter is signalled by the willingness of an increasing number of countries to adjust their domestic political economies in order to pay the entry fee to regional clubs (the 'domino effect').

It is now appropriate to follow a 'bottom-up' approach to examine a question raised earlier: namely, is the spreading of regionalism leading to a more cooperative global system – i.e. to the formation of a 'global multilateral regime'?

This issue can be addressed by reconsidering the conditions for cooperation without hegemony.[20] The discussion earlier in this chapter suggested that the willingness to adjust, hence the willingness to change national preferences (condition 2), is fulfilled to the extent that the supply of integration generates positive net benefits from integration to the domestic economy and that the club admission fee is not inconsistent with domestic political equilibrium. The same discussion suggested that condition 3 – a long time horizon – is also fulfilled, by definition, to the extent that club membership is seen as a long-term commitment. This is the case for participation in trade agreements and monetary unions,[21] as they both imply the payment of large sunk costs in order to make the national economies consistent with club requirements. Condition 4 – the role of institutions – is fulfilled if we consider that regional agreements are usually based on strong issue linkages, e.g. between economy and security, between monetary and trade relations, etc. Issue linkages may be explicit, as when members of an economic agreement (like the EU) are also part of a security agreement (like NATO), or implicit, as when security goals are pursued through economic integration. In general, issue linkages provide information about partners' behaviour in an area different from the one in which the agreement is being sought, thus fulfilling the role of institutions in international cooperation.

Condition 1 – a small number of actors – is also, by definition, fulfilled by the spreading of regionalism. What is less clear is whether such a condition does indeed lead to deeper global integration. Krugman (1993) has argued that the formation of regional blocs will lead to conflict rather than cooperation, and he has also shown that, under specific conditions, the number of regional actors less conducive to cooperation is three. Condition 1 then becomes the crucial one. To see whether a small number of actors leads to more or less global cooperation one must introduce a hypothesis about the behaviour of regional clubs facing each other in the international system.

One approach has been suggested by Oye (1992). He posits that, in a post-hegemonic, multipolar world, regional (and national) actors tend to pursue 'unrestricted', i.e. selective, bargaining vis-à-vis each other in order to obtain selective market access and, to this purpose, are ready to reciprocate with their partners to obtain liberalization of their domestic markets. He also notes that a strong incentive to pursue unrestricted (selective) bargaining comes from globalization as selective market access is a form of competition in global markets (which are not uniform markets). In addition, selective market access reinforces the incentives of third parties to barter over market access, as the formation of preferential agreements increases the costs of exclusion.

This line of argument (which is very similar to the 'domino approach' to regionalism) may be reinforced by the exploration of issues in the recent literature on the political economy of protection and liberalization. Grossman and Helpman (1996) suggest that domestic lobbying for *domestic* liberalization will come from pro-free trade groups that see domestic opening as a condition of obtaining market access abroad as the result of reciprocal bargaining. They also suggest that the predominance of protectionist interest groups arises from the fact that industries seeking protection are usually declining industries where the prospective market size is simply not big enough to compensate for entry costs, hence the potential for free-riding is much lower and the possibility of organizing collective action larger. On the contrary, industries that benefit from liberalization usually face expanding markets where free-riding firms would be able to enter without contributing to the lobbying effort. However, if 'sunrise' markets expand fast enough, the incentive to pursue reciprocal domestic liberalization may overcome the free-riding costs. In addition, the value of sunk costs investment in lobbying for protection declines over time in 'sunset' industries. This point can be extended to bargaining between regional agreements by noting that if reciprocal liberalization is carried out on a regional basis it will benefit firms belonging to the regional agreement which, in principle, have already paid an admission fee.[22] Therefore, participation in a regional agreement that engages in selective bargaining partially offsets the free-riding problem. In other words, reciprocal bargaining between regions may be more efficient than reciprocal bargaining between countries. On the other hand, Winters (1999) has argued that regionalism may make the multilateral system more fragile because, among other things, countries joining a regional agreement are doing so because they want more and not less protection; hence they would oppose regional policies leading to a more open and multilateral system.

Globalization can speed up the process in the direction of more openness. The most powerful forces of global integration are represented by the activities of multinational enterprises (MNEs). One relevant aspect is that these activities not only increase the degree of economic interdependence, but may also lead to convergence in governments' polices (through reciprocity).

The relevance for economic convergence derives from the fact that MNEs are powerful vehicles of innovation diffusion. In a world in which technological progress is the key determinant of growth and competitiveness, the degree of diffusion of knowledge is the crucial factor for the dissemination of the benefits of growth.[23] MNEs, however, may also become a powerful factor in 'political' convergence. As Froot and Yoffie (1991) have shown, MNE activities decrease the incentives for national governments to supply protection to their economies. In a world of highly mobile capital, MNE activities are one typical response to protectionist barriers – whether erected to protect nations or regions. As the amount of foreign investment in protected areas increases, the rents from protection increasingly accrue to foreigners, i.e. to the owners of foreign capital in the region, rather than to domestic residents. Hence protectionist governments receive a decreasing share of political support in exchange for their intervention, and their benefit from this form of political exchange decreases. On the other hand, the benefits from both reciprocal market access and international diffusion of knowledge increase. In short, in a world of countries or regions, each pursuing a policy of protection, international mobility of capital tends to weaken the strength of protectionistic policies and, indirectly, to decrease the differences in national or regional political economies.

This is true as long as this process is symmetrical, i.e. if capital mobility is a two-way activity. If capital flows only in one direction, the government of a region or country where foreign capital does not penetrate will be able to preserve the political benefits of protection. Only as long as investment flows in both directions do global market forces represent a powerful vehicle of economic integration. Further, if capital integration is not symmetrical, the region where foreign investment does not penetrate will also lose part of the (potential) benefits of innovation diffusion and of growth associated with it. It follows that in a world of high mobility of capital new incentives emerge to attract foreign MNE activities. This reinforces the incentives of industrial sectors to obtain liberal policies on a reciprocal basis.

Support may not come only from business groups. As several scholars show, lobbying activity by trade unions interested in creating new employment opportunities does not necessarily take the form of requests for more protection. Rather, unions will be interested in policies that attract capital, and so may lobby governments for more rather than less openness. This is one of the consequences of the fact that globalization has produced a new form of competition – competition for location sites – which requires (and is also dependent on) regulation: in the first place, because location advantages may be created by the investment of regional development funds, the overall amount of which may be afterwards judged excessive, and secondly, because of 'competition among rules', i.e. regulations affecting locational incentives such as environmental and labour market regulations. The attempt to attract foreign investment might create an incentive to relax rules, or rule enforcement, so as to decrease the private costs of investment at the expense of social costs, a problem facing both NAFTA and Europe.

To summarize, increasing capital mobility may indeed represent a powerful element of convergence in the sense that it creates incentives in domestic politics to pursue more open and less protection-oriented (more 'market'-oriented) policies, which tend to favour more cooperative international policies. This last and crucial point stems from the fact that, by definition, MNE operations are global and MNEs themselves can be less and less considered as tied to a specific country or region. This reinforces the need to establish regimes that will facilitate the operation of market forces at a global level: that is, globalization increases the demand for international public goods.

7. Summary and conclusion

The points developed in this chapter may be summarized in the following steps.

Step 1 The international system is in a state of 'institutional disequilibrium' in the sense that there is an excess demand for international public goods. This is the result of a decrease in supply, because of the redistribution of power away from a hegemonic structure, and of an increase in demand, because of increased globalization.

Step 2 The excess demand for international public goods spurs the formation of regional agreements. Regional agreements are a source of supply of (partially excludable) international public goods (club goods). At the same time, globalization provides incentives for the formation of regional agreements based on norms and standards that contribute to the build-up of regional comparative advantage. To the extent that globalization is conducive to market instability it is itself a source of spreading regionalism.

Step 3 Regionalism and globalization increase the demand for integration and encourage structural adjustment at country level. The demand of integration increases because access to the global market (globalization) requires new standards for the domestic economy and regional standards are a source of comparative advantage, but also because clubs offer protection against global instability. Domestic adjustment and demand for integration will respond positively to the supply of integration (as provided by existing regional agreements) to the extent that they are not inconsistent with domestic political equilibrium.

Step 4 As a growing number of countries joins regional agreements, regionalism provides a new equilibrium in the production of international public goods. It also leads towards the fulfilment of conditions of cooperation under anarchy since (a) the time horizon increases as regional agreements are by definition long-term commitments, (b) the propensity to adjust increases, and (c) issue linkages increase the exchange of information.

Step 5 The fulfilment of the fourth condition – a small number of actors – does not necessarily imply that regionalism leads to the construction of a new global system (to be understood as a global equilibrium between the supply and demand of international public goods) However, this might be obtained under unrestricted bargaining (Oye, 1992). The incentive to pursue unrestricted (selective) bargaining comes (also) from globalization as selective market access is a form of competition in global markets.

As presented, the sequence above can easily deliver the impression that almost inevitably a new global order will emerge from the collapse of the old one. We should be careful not to accept this view. What has been suggested in this chapter is only one possible reading of the existing literature in the attempt to establish linkages between the different levels of analysis. Several other approaches, and sequences, are possible, leading to different conclusions about the evolution of the international system.

Notes

1 See e.g. Milner, 1997.
2 On regionalism see, among others, de Melo and Panagariya, 1993: Winters, 1999; Baldwin, 1998.
3 In this chapter globalization is defined as the increasing elimination of barriers that separate local and national markets of factors and products from one another, accompanied by an increasing mobility of capital.
4 On hegemonic stability theory the standard reference is Kehoane, 1984.
5 For an analysis of the characteristics of regionalism see Winters, 1996.
6 See the articles in Oye, 1986, in particular the paper by Axelrod and Keohane; also Guerrieri and Padoan, 1989.
7 See e.g. Guerrieri and Padoan, 1988; Mayer, 1992; Milner, 1997; Grossman and Helpman, 1994.
8 Both the volumes offer empirical evidence that successful integration processes require the fulfilment of both economic and political conditions.
9 For a survey see Baldwin and Venables, 1994.
10 For a recent assessment of the debate see Rodrik, 1997.
11 A more extended analysis is presented in Padoan, 1997.
12 It can be argued that the operation of an international trade regime is influenced by the operation of an international macroeconomic regime. See Guerrieri and Padoan, 1988.
13 Collignon (1997) shows that the benefits of a currency union, a clear example of a monetary club, decrease with the increasing divergence in preferences among the union members for active stabilization policies.
14 This is also consistent with the view (see Bayoumi, 1994) that the incentives for non-members to join a monetary union are larger than the incentives for union members to accept new countries.
15 See Powell, 1994, for a survey of the role of institutions in international cooperation.
16 A more formal treatment is contained in Padoan, 1997.
17 For instance membership in a trade agreement implies that all member countries adopt the same level of tariff.

18 The role of interest groups in determining international agreements is analysed in Grossman and Helpman, 1996; Milner, 1997.
19 See Alesina and Perotti, 1995, for an empirical survey of the role of government institutions in determining fiscal policy behaviour.
20 A review of the debate on this issue is offered in Winters, 1999.
21 The same is not true for currency arrangements such as pegged exchange rates which, on the contrary, tend to be increasingly short-lived in a world of deep financial integration. See Eichengreen, 1994.
22 The admission fee is 'paid' by governments but this obviously reverberates on the country's firms.
23 On this point see Padoan, 1997. A formal assessment is provided by Grossman and Helpman, 1991.

3. The Cultural Factor in the Process of Globalization/ Regionalization

Thomas Meyer

There is a widespread consensus in political science today that issues of culture will play an increasingly significant role in both national and transnational politics in the new era of globalization that has succeeded the ideological Cold War. The politics of identity will be high on the political agenda, in all parts of the world and in relations among them.

1. Theories on the increasing global role of the cultural factor

A variety of causes for the unprecedented prominence of the cultural factor has been advanced in recent years. Three analyses in particular, espoused respectively by Huntington, Barber and Cox, will be considered in more detail below.[1] Irrespective of their different approaches, all three of these authors share the view that the foreseeable future of the globalized world will be marked by the interaction of economic, political and cultural factors, with cultural differences playing a particular role in generating and aggravating conflict. What are the causes of this new constellation, and do they vary from one situation to another? The answer to this question will contribute in no small measure to our understanding of the processes, the risks and the positive prospects of globalization.

2. The analytical concept of culture

To understand how the cultural factor actually works, we must turn to empirical and historical research. Normative methods, or over-reliance on hermeneutic approaches, will generate only speculative analysis or textual exegesis – though hermeneutic approaches, which deal with the nature of religions and cultures, can contribute significantly to a fuller picture of the potential for mutual cooperation and coexistence.

Cultures, broadly defined, are valued-based systems of collective orientation. They generate motives for action and ideas of legitimate conduct in all realms of social life: personal, economic and political. They also form the basis for the justification of public policy. Though cultural systems are flexible and subject to change induced by other social subsystems, for example economic activity, science, public discourse and political experience, at any given moment they can work as very rigidly limiting factors at the levels of both empirical motivation and normative justification for action. This is what Parsons' concept of culture as a 'latent pattern' of social structure and restructuring means.[2]

It is therefore a profound misunderstanding of the nature of culture to discuss the relation of the cultural factor to the economy and politics merely or mainly in terms of normative factors, rather than as one of the key forces of social reality. In political science, 'cultures' and their consequences for political action are analysed as empirical entities but also as resources for the legitimization of political action. The difference between the two functions may be substantial even in one and the same social unity.[3] To a certain extent, values, norms and attitudes direct social and political action spontaneously, because they are part of the collective mindset. But culture also provides norms and ideals as legitimate with a strong appeal that they should be followed, leaving however some scope for individual and collective deviation in terms of practical behaviour.

In the context of recent discussions on globalization the cultural factor, broadly defined, plays a key role at both levels. At the normative level, some form of global consensus is required for global political action, whether this is seen in terms of 'global culture' or 'global ethics'. At the empirical level, some of the theories on the increasing influence of the cultural factor on world economy and world politics, particularly that propounded by Huntington in his 'clash of civilizations' thesis, rule out the very possibility of any kind of global culture or global ethics on the grounds that the differences between cultures and civilizations are not only great but insurmountable.

It is widely acknowledged that the 1980s and 1990s saw a substantial increase in the number of intranational and international conflicts in which cultural differences, whether ethnic or religious, played a discernible role – in the Balkans, in Central Asia (Caucasus), South Asia (India, Sri Lanka) and Africa, for example – and that tendencies towards xenophobia and aggressive cultural self-assertion by minority groups became stronger and more visible in almost all multicultural Western societies. The politics of identity have started to loom large on the political agenda almost everywhere in the world.[4]

The three hypotheses which have tried to explain this recent development are to a great extent mutually exclusive. Huntington argues that, the deadening hand of the great, dominant ideologies of the twentieth century having been removed as a result of the influence of globalization, it is now clear that the basic social and political values which structure the world's major religion-based cultures and civilizations are inevitably hostile to each other. The value gaps between them are too vast to be bridged and sustained coexistence is therefore impossible.

Barber maintains that the popular cultural power inevitably linked to the consumer goods generated by the hegemonic American economy reshapes behaviour and is therefore considered as a deadly threat to indigenous cultural identity in many parts of the world. Fundamentalist hatred and aggression towards the West is an increasingly frequent response to that challenge, but will persist only as long as the worldwide hegemony of the present type of American economy is maintained.

Cox suggests that economic globalization in its present capitalist form creates socially and economically depressed sectors in all societies which tend to express their protest in radical forms of cultural identity because of the lack of adequate alternative ideologies. On this interpretation, conflicts disguised as cultural are but a side-effect of economic deprivation within the context of a traditional class conflict.

All three hypotheses claim to accord with the realities of recent developments in global politics and to deliver valid causal explanations for them. Each, if true, would imply consequences for the future of multilateralism in a globalizing world very different from, and even contrary to, the others; and each would generate very different potential strategies on how to tackle them.

3. Huntington – the leading paradigm

How can these competing hypotheses be evaluated in the light of empirical research, and what social theories would accurately reflect their assumptions?

The crucial point in Huntington's hypothesis is not that there are cultural conflicts – whatever that might really mean for a truly empirical analysis – but that all the great cultures and civilizations are based on mutually exclusive innate value programmes. According to Huntington, the 'fault lines of civilization' run particularly deep in the field of basic social and political values, over for example equality/inequality, individualism/collectivism, gender relations, the linkage between religion and politics, freedom and tradition, pluralism and regulation. As these values are precisely the crucial pillars supporting social relations and the structure of a polity – and its associated legitimate political process – there cannot be any sustainable coexistence between cultures, either within a society or between states.

Huntington argues that there are only three possible modes of interrelation between these mutually exclusive value sets, conceived by him as cultural metastructures: separation/apartheid; hierarchies of dominance; or conflict/war. Huntington himself favours a mixture of the second and third options, proposing that the West try to contain and dominate the Islamic and Confucian parts of the world, or otherwise prepare for a global cultural war in which decisions on permanent hierarchies of dominance and subordination will have to be taken by force.

The discourse on 'Asian values', including 'guided democracy', 'culturally interpreted' human rights and 'Confucian Dynamism' as the 'Protestant ethic' of the twenty-first-century global economy are heavily influenced by this theory, which is quoted by proponents of these values as Western corroboration of their claims. The picture of Islam as 'essential fundamentalism' (Barber), unfit for cooperation with, or understanding by, the rest of the world, and requiring eventually to be contained by force, is another offspring of this line of thinking. A cultural Cold War thus looms into view, with a triangular constellation of conflicts as its core: Confucianism against Westernism against Islam. This pattern of conflict is then expected to impact severely on both the economic and the political processes of globalization, impeding the smooth development of the global economy and of an equitable political multilateralism.

4. Cross-cultural empirical data

Fortunately for the prospects of globalism, however, Huntington's model is not in tune with the facts.[5] It is built on a gross methodological assumption: that overt political instrumentalization of real and ascribed cultural differences for the purpose of controlling power is the inevitable political consequence of cultural determinants. Furthermore, the very concept of culture or civilization which he uses is obsolete even as a rough description of contemporary cultural differentiation.

The results of contemporary empirical and historical research on cultural differentiation can be summarized as follows.[6] All cultural units are marked by an extremely high degree of internal differentiation. The first level of this might be called mutually contradicting *styles of civilization*, that is to say patterns of response within a particular cultural tradition to the challenges of the present. One of the most striking results of the worldwide research in fundamentalism conducted by Marty and Appleby is that even a single culture in today's world presents itself as a dialectical discourse-system in which three principal styles or modes of civilization struggle for hegemony: *traditionalism*, which aims at a very defensive adaptation of only those elements of modern culture which cannot be avoided; *modernism*, which interprets tradition strictly in the light of the predominance of the values of individualism, pluralism, activism and rationalism, and allows for major differences in the interpretation of the reference culture; and *fundamentalism*, which is a self-contradictory modern reaction against modernity, making use of some of the most effective products of modernity such as weaponry, organization and mass communication – but only to fight against the basic values of modernism itself, particularly against innate social and cultural differences, openness, relativism, pluralism, democracy, gender equality and individual rights. By a process of retrieval of historic stages in its mother culture, fundamentalism dogmatizes one particular historical pattern of interpretation as the essence of cultural identity; and acceptance of this standard is incumbent on everybody who wishes to be recognized as a true member of the given cultural community. Differences of understanding or interpretation are considered to be destructive, alien to the true nature of the given culture and poisonous taints of modernism within it. Various models of closed society and closed polity are erected on the basis of these presumed certainties of cultural identity.

No religion or culture is by its very nature inherently fundamentalist. Fundamentalism can never rightfully claim to be the unchallenged expression of cultural identity. Yet today this style of civilization is manifest in every religion-based culture – Buddhism, Hinduism, Judaism, Islam, Christianity, Confucianism – and indeed in the West itself. The relative political and social power of each of the three competing styles of civilization within each culture fluctuates at a rate that depends acutely upon the historical situation, the socio-economic constellation, the performance of the political class and the patterns and rate of change induced by the globalized economy and communications in any given society. At present it is the fundamentalist mode which seems set to be dominant.

Islam seems to be the main scapegoat in the contemporary cultural Cold War. The relative dominance of Islamic fundamentalism in many parts of the Muslim world, however, is itself only a product of the specific historical developments of the last few decades. Since the middle of the nineteenth century, attempts to modernize Islamic tradition have been prominent in Egypt, British India and other countries. Between the 1920s and 1960s, Islamic secularism – often within a socialist framework – was one of the most dynamic forces in Islamic culture. It is only since the 1970s that fundamentalist Islam has become the most visible force in the Muslim world; and even now, as Tibi has pointed out, the three principal tendencies are still apparent,[7] represented by the mainstream style of civilization in three countries: traditionalism in Saudi Arabia, secularism in Turkey and fundamentalism in Iran.

This analysis leads to three clear conclusions. First, what determines the social and political role of different cultures is not cultural identity itself, but the social and political forces which control the dominant interpretation; and which interpretation is dominant depends on the particular historical, social and economic experiences of the social groups which support the various interpretations. Second, all cultures in the modern world allow for significant internal differentiation and even for overt contradiction between the various attempts designed to render them relevant to contemporary practice. Third, contradictory tendencies in civilization patterns have more in common with their counterparts in other cultures than with their rivals within the same culture. Culture-based coalitions for the sake of political action may, therefore, be transnational rather than transcultural, as is illustrated by multilateral networks of civil society institutions. Indeed, the very concept of cultural identity has to be redefined in the light of this pattern of internal differentiation within classical cultural units.

Cross-cultural comparison of relevant socio-political values in sixty-five societies, all members of the major cultures, has generated informative results. On a national basis their significance is negative rather than positive: for they refute hypotheses about the unifying power of shared cultural access, while making clear that the crucial units of cultural identity and difference are sub-national socio-cultural environments.

The results of Hofstede's and Inglehart's cross-cultural study of the distribution of basic socio-political values can be summed up as follows. In the first place, in respect of their positions on various value scales (acceptance of equality/inequality, individualism/collectivism, soft [feminine]/hard [masculine] social values and uncertainty avoidance/tolerance), the maximal score difference between countries sharing the same culture and the average difference between countries of different cultures as a whole are almost the same. Some of the countries with the largest overall score difference belong to the same culture – Portugal and Denmark, Greece and Sweden, Portugal and Great Britain; whereas some of the countries with the closest similarities in their basic value profiles belong to different cultures – East Africa and Thailand, the Arab countries and Mexico, Brazil and Turkey, Portugal and South Korea. This demonstrates clearly that there is no such thing as 'fault-lines' between cultures in the distribution of *socio-political values* in today's world.

In this context, it must be stressed that there is a precise set of socio-political values that underlies the pattern of social relations in each society and in the related polity. Obviously, these patterns of socio-political values are not statically determined by religion-based cultural traditions. Yet there are characteristic relative differences in values such as individualism and equality, as well as cross-cultural similarities in other value dimensions and a considerable degree of overlapping across most societies from all cultural strands in all value dimensions.

Inglehart has recently demonstrated that the salience of the key value set for postmodernism – whose characteristic values include participation in political and employment structures, a more personalized society, civil liberties – varies among societies with the level of GNP, whatever the prevailing culture. This value set is of particular relevance for the cultural identity of any society, as it has a major impact on political culture, the political process, preferred political structures and the acceptance of economic, ecological and civil rights, and security policies.

This result indicates an increasing tendency towards cross-cultural convergence in a crucial value dimension, as postmodernism is most widespread among the younger generations and, once acquired, is sustained throughout their lifetimes. Since Pierre Bourdieu's studies in the formation of habitus and socio-cultural milieux, cross-national and cross-cultural studies have been carried out (notably by the Sigma Institute, Mannheim) with the aim of analysing the structure and dynamics of socio-cultural milieu building in European, North American and Asian societies. The main conclusion of these studies has been that in all these societies there is a strong internal cultural differentiation into relatively homogeneous subgroups (eight to ten milieus), whose members share a universe of values with respect to work, consumption, partnership, meaning of life, politics, family, leisure, lifestyle, attitude towards religion, and aesthetics of everyday life, and at the same time consciously and unconsciously distinguish themselves strictly from other milieux – the more so the further they are removed from them on the dynamic axis of value modernization.

In all the societies studied to date, social stratification along the lines of income, profession and formal education works only as a loose framework within which a variety of socio-cultural options is open to the individual, who may join one of three or four milieux. The main difference between the milieu cultures lies in the degree to which their generative value set is traditional, traditionless hedonistic, semi-modernized, modernized or affected by postmodernism.

The members of all these different milieux may still share some very basic values which makes it meaningful for them to coexist in the same polity, but the more advanced the milieux are on the value-change scale from 'traditional' to 'affected by postmodernism' the more values and attitudes they tend to share with members of corresponding socio-cultural milieux cross-nationally and even cross-culturally. With respect to social and political values, they may be more removed culturally from some of the milieu groups of their own society than from those of societies with different cultural traditions. Though they may still share with the former some of the same religious cults and soteriologies, they no longer share the socio-cultural orientations which are of relevance for economic, social and political action.

This is why the relevant socio-cultural units in an empirical sense will increasingly be sub-national milieux, many of which overlap cross-culturally in terms of their value structures. This holds true not only for what Huntington calls the 'Davos milieu' but also, increasingly, for the numerous younger and better-educated groups which play a key role in social and political life. This confirms that fundamentalism – as the most effective and most widespread form of the politics of identity – is today neither the purest nor the least challenged expression of cultural identity, but is rather a conscious instrumentalization of a particular retrieval of cultural social history for the purpose of accumulating political power.

If the politics of identity is to operate effectively as a form of instrumentalization, co-players are required. Some set out to instrumentalize for their own purposes; others lend themselves to instrumentalization for the sake of their own perceived motives and needs. Since the outset of modernity there has always been fundamentalist criticism of society's various crises, combined with an offer to retrieve a better past, but social and political fortunes have changed from one situation to another. In some circumstances fundamentalism survives, but only as a persistent small social splinter group with no political influence. But in certain combinations of social, economic and political crisis large segments of traditionalist milieux may suddenly be transformed into an aggressive and determined group of fundamentalist supporters.

This is most likely to happen in historical situations where traditionalist milieux find their socio-cultural identity abruptly challenged – often by the political class itself – and experience socio-economic deprivation. In turn, they express distrust of the ruling class, considering it to be corrupt and unable to deliver protection. Such a constellation of factors may have various causes. Typically, there is often a combination of the effects of globalization and the failure of the political class, aggravated by mechanisms of mass communication and extreme and aggressive social pressures for change.

5. Consequences for globalism and regionalism

On the basis of this analysis, the role of culture within globalization can be summed up in five theses.

In the first place, for the purposes of both political analysis and political action we have to relinquish the traditional concept of culture (Herder) and replace it by the more adequate concept of trans-culturality (Welsch).[8] Most contemporary theory about cultural factors is still based on Herder's concept, which is obsolete. Its four premises are the equation between ethnic and cultural identity, the homogeneity of the cultural unit, the total inclusion of all individuals into the homogeneous culture of their society, and the mutual failure of these cultures to understand one another. None of these applies in the contemporary world. The concept of trans-culturality accommodates regular internal differentiation, cross-cultural overlapping and new kinds of cluster-building by drawing on influences from different traditions and innovations.

Second, ascribed cultural identity is a relatively easily available resource for political instrumentalization within particular constellations of social, political and economic crises, but is not the inevitable cause of social and political conflict. If political interests do not intervene and acquire strong support through expressions of cultural identity for other reasons, sufficient consensus across cultural divisions can be mobilized to ensure political cooperation both intranationally and internationally. The relative strength of fundamentalist and liberal streams within a socio-cultural unit depends to a large extent upon economic, social and political conditions.

Third, the cultural factor may be expected to play three substantially divergent roles in such multilateral contexts of political action.

1   Political and religious leaders in power will constantly tend to use it as a multi-purpose mechanism to justify, for example, authoritarianism and the denial of human rights in the name of the true identity of the culture they represent. It will be used by opposition leaders to mobilize ruling elites, as a means of restoring a more 'genuine' national identity in the face of perceived threats from foreign influence or domestic cultural minorities.

2   Trans-cultural patterns of cultural differentiation will counter such developments by facilitating 'cross-cultural' multilateralism at the level of civil society along the lines of shared civilizational styles. As the increasing interaction

between transgovernmental organizations and international institutions on the one hand and trans-societal networks at the level of civil society on the other hand will be one of the factors shaping multilateral politics in the era of globalization, this trend will play an increasingly relevant role. A representative example was the Parliament of World Religions held in Chicago in 1994, which issued a declaration entitled *Towards a Global Ethics*.

3   Much depends on the social and economic consequences of the process of economic globalization. Both intranational and international exclusion, social degradation and economic deprivation will encourage those who aim to exploit cultural differences for political ends.

Fourth, it is often not realized that the common values which are needed for political regional cooperation are not the transcendent doctrines of salvation or shared practices in everyday life but certain basic socio-economic values such as liberty, equality and tolerance. Even in Europe, with its highly developed cultural identity, it has been shown that such an identity exists only to a very limited degree and as the result of constant and conscious political activity.[9] The comprehensive religious identity which European societies once shared often served as a source of division and civil war, lending itself at differing stages of history to substantially contradictory sets of socio-political values and polities. Only when European societies began to share socio-political values such as human rights, pluralism, democracy and tolerance could regional cooperation at the political level succeed.

Fifth, and conversely, in South Asia an emerging system of regional cooperation (SAARC) includes most of the world religions, either as majority communities (Buddhism in Sri Lanka and Nepal; Hinduism in India; Islam in Pakistan) or as large minorities (Islam and Christianity in India and Sri Lanka). In all these countries there are groups which encourage political cooperation and regional integration, and others who pay lip service to the ideal while fuelling national conflict.

The consensus that is required for successful regional cooperation is based not on common religious belief or common lifestyle/culture, but on two other shared convictions. These are that some common socio-political core values are shared, and that cooperation will benefit all participants in a mutual and fair manner. The interaction of these two ideas can create a sufficient basis of shared identity and a feeling of distinction from the rest of the world, particularly when – as in the case of South Asia – a history of close interaction has already been experienced.

To conclude, the influence of cultural factors in a globalizing world will continue to be contradictory and unpredictable. In pursuit of better frameworks for transnational cooperation and global governance it would be wise not to trust trans-cultural dialogues alone but to make use of the trans-cultural consensus that already exists in order to work towards a more equitable economic world order and to minimize exclusion. The cultural divergence of today's world allows for global effort to bring the economic forces of the neo-liberal global market back under the control of shared socio-cultural values (such as justice and mutual recognition) and an appropriate measure of political regulation and governance.[10] The politics of identity does pose a danger for regional cooperation and global governance, but feasible alternatives can and do exist.

Notes

1 S. P. Huntington, (1996) *The Clash of Civilizations and the Remaking of World Order,* Simon and Schuster, New York. B. R. Barber, *Jihad vs. McWorld* (New York: Times Books, 1995); R. W. Cox, ed., *The New Realism: Perspectives on Multilateralism and World Order* (London: Macmillan, 1997).

2 T. Parsons, *The Social System* (New York: Routledge & Kegan Paul, 1951).

3 G. Hofstede, *Culture's Consequences: International Differences in Work-Related Values* (Beverly Hills, CA: Sage, 1980).

4 Cf. F. Cerutti, 'Identität und Politik', *International Zeitschrift für Philosophie*, 1997, no. 2.

5 For details see T. Meyer, *Identitäts-Wahn: Die Politisierung des kulturellen Unterschieds* (Berlin: Aufbau, 1997).

6 See M. E. Marty and R. S. Appleby, *Fundamentalisms Observed* (Chicago: University of Chicago Press, 1991); G. Hofstede, *Cultures and Organizations: Intercultural Cooperation and its Importance for Survival* (New York: HarperCollins, 1994); R. Inglehart and P. A. Abramson, *Value Change in a Global Perspective* (Michigan: University of Michigan Press, 1995); Sigma Institut, Mannheim, Germany, unpublished research papers on socio-cultural milieu stratification in Japan, Thailand, Canada, USA, Germany, Great Britain, France and Italy.

7 B. Tibi, *The Challenge of Fundamentalism* (Berkeley, CA: University of California Press, 1998).

8 W. Welsch, 'Transkulturalität: die veränderte Verfassung heutiger Kulturen', in *Sichtweisen, Die Vielheit in der Einheit* (Frankfurt am Main: Stiftung Weimarer Klassik, 1994).

9 G. Delanty, *Inventing Europe: Idea, Identity, Reality* (Basingstoke: Macmillan, 1995).

10 The Commission on Global Governance, *Our Global Neighbourhood* (New York: Oxford University Press, 1995).

Part II
Comparative Analysis of Regional Groupings

4. Between Trade Regionalization and Deep Integration

Mario Telò

The complexity and ambiguity of new regionalism and its economic and political implications warrant an empirical analysis. The second main topic of this book is the comparison between the existing regional organizations, constantly keeping the EU experience in mind. Five main case studies are particularly taken into account: two in the Americas (NAFTA and MERCOSUR), one in Asia (ASEAN), one in Africa (SADC), while comparative references are made to other regional groupings (Communidad Andina, SAARC, ECOWAS).

New regionalism is in many respects a multiple reality first because of the great variety of institutional and informal features it covers. We are witnessing the revival of old regional organizations and the birth of new ones. Such differences suggest a basic methodological question: is the observer confronted with a variety of institutional forms of regionalism or with different forms of the same pattern? All the chapters embrace the general idea of European exceptionalism; namely that historical, cultural, and societal features underpin European identity and the unique institutions of the EU.[1] However, the comparison with the successive steps of the European integration process has proven to be very useful to the international literature. Even if out of any teleological vision, thus far we can distinguish between the following forms of regional groupings:

a) By *regionalization* we understand the different, private and public, forms of societal and economic association and cooperation within a region. Their number and influence have increased considerably since the early 1980s, according to the *Yearbook of International Organization*.[2]

b) A *regional forum* is the first step towards intergovernmental dialogue and cooperation, formal and informal, by institutionalized bodies or looser structures, mainly open to civil society representatives (business community, NGO's and so on).

c) *State-promoted regional cooperation* involves policy decisions by governments to remove barriers to trade and investments towards a free trade area and set intergovernmental cooperation, mainly limited to some sectors and branches[3] which could also include dispute settlement mechanisms.

d) *A customs union and a common trade policy*: these include common external tariff and foreign economic policy (for example, MERCOSUR, the EU and SACU, including five members of SADC).

e) By *economic integration* we understand a common market and an economic union, including not only cooperation but also coordination of national policies, through intergovernmental and, rarely, supranational institutions.

f) *Regional cohesion and complete economic integration*: examples include the five above and a socio-political construction: *political unity* (pooling national sovereignties) and high institutional capacity to minimize internal asymmetries and maximize external influence.[4]

Since new regionalism as a concrete phenomenon is often still unclear and overlapping within the current transition of the post-bipolar world system, this book's contributing researchers do not aim to create a general theory of new regionalism. On the contrary, the chapters begin by describing, classifying and raising questions and problems. What we can say is that there is no evidence at all that different regional models correspond to an evolutionary process where the limit and the end are established from the very beginning. Steps backward or stagnation are possible. There is no continuum either between the different degrees of formalization of regional cooperation. Finally, different models cannot be explained through the integration theory that was created and developed with Western Europe and on the basis of the political background of the European Nation-State, a so peculiar historical construction. However, comparison is useful and its main goal is not only to stress similarities but also to underline variations. It would be a methodological mistake to isolate a single regional organization and underestimate the general trends and the common features. Europe is a laboratory and a reference – even if the kind of high institutionalization found in European regionalism is not to be found elsewhere in the world.[5] Some of the current forms of regionalization do emulate the European pattern, namely the Common Market and Single European Act, while some others react against them or consciously avoid the European way.

Regarding the *international factors of new regionalism*, in reality regional organizations do have the same global environment in common. They not only experienced the common challenges of the globalizing economy, but also of the turning points of the evolving world system: 1931, 1945, 1971, 1989/91. However, they have quite a different experience with regional leaders, with the American leadership and the past Soviet policy in the different parts of the world. For example, multilateralism became a common rule in the USA–Western Europe relationship whereas bilateralism characterized the USA–Asia relationship, in the framework of the huge heterogeneity of the Asian continent. They have been differently affected by the evolution in American economic and security foreign policy. Variations can be classified depending upon the impact of the international system or upon the degree of internal cohesion and domestic pressures.

As far as *internal factors* are concerned, regional organizations all have experience of networks and institutions, policy making and communities. They all give rise to multi-tier, multi-level, multi-channel, multi-actor regional systems, partly informal and partly formal. Continental and subcontinental (as far as Europe, Africa, the Americas or Asia are concerned) variations are explained through several historical, political and economic factors including the difference of the States' preferences, the degree of divergence among them, and the distribution of capabilities among members of regional organizations and so on.[6]

Finally, club size is important: very often regionalism regards subregional organizations, including only a part of the States, belonging to that region of the world. An important question raised by the literature is whether a regional leader is necessary and sufficient to build up a regional organization[7] and to shape membership and borders. The separate chapters provide both analytical and critical assessments to answer this question.

1. ASEAN, SAARC and the Asian way to new regionalism

The international literature on the Association of South-East Asian Nations (ASEAN) is characterized by a crucial question: how could ASEAN possibly survive the dramatic changes incurred as the security framework of this particularly turbulent region and the domestic post-colonial regime transition for over thirty years? On the one hand, ASEAN had to be flexible enough to cope with the challenges of internal diversity and the political fragility of regimes within Pacific Asia.[8] On the other hand, it had to be sufficiently innovative to be able to face huge strategic uncertainties and the negative regional legacy of bilateral experiences – including arms control.[9] A comparison with the very poor achievements of the South Asian Association for Regional Cooperation (SAARC) is particularly interesting in this respect.[10] In fact, this regional grouping with the largest population worldwide seems to have not only a very low degree of integration among national economies and societies and no incrementalism, but it is currently experiencing the worst period of its fifteen-year history. The four main reasons for the stagnation include the legacy of the colonial past, the problems of underdevelopment, the lack of harmonization between national economies and the political tensions within the region. Bilateral issues, and particularly the conflict between the two nuclear powers India and Pakistan, rigorously out from the SAARC agenda, do brake any further progress in regional cooperation. All in all, the results over fifteen years, often high level summits, many attempts to improve information exchange, coordination, networking etc. are so modest that, given the present circumstances, the survival of SAARC as a forum in one of the most dangerous regions of the world is a precious achievement.

Internal asymmetry is only a partial explanation of failures and stagnation. Certainly with 72 per cent of land and 77 per cent of population, India represents the giant of the region. However, even other regional organizations (including MERCOSUR, ASEAN and SADC) are characterized by huge internal asymmetries that do not stop regional agreements from progressing. Clearly a second internal negative factor (common to many regional groupings, including developing countries) must not be forgotten: the lack of functional dynamics of regional economic integration and of complementarity among national economies, which makes the bilateral political conflict so unsolved.

According to a more convincing political explanation, the absence of mutual confidence-building measures condemns regional cooperation to the margins. Bilateral understanding between the two major powers of the region – as in Western Europe (France and Germany) and in Latin America (Argentina and Brazil) – largely explains the success of regional agreements elsewhere. In Asia, the common feeling of an external threat, whether political (Soviet and Chinese expansionism) or economic (the growing fear of marginalization within the globalizing economy), has been an important integrative factor for ASEAN countries. However, the end of the Cold War is significantly reducing the impact of systemic political factors within the Asian continent with the consequence of increasing the influence of local factors.[11] By building no security in the post-Cold War era, the South Asian crisis shows that regionalism does not easily substitute bilateralism or multilateralism either. In Southern Asia, when bilateralism or globalism are unable to provide solutions for regional conflicts, regionalism does not yet offer a solution either.

Finally, even the limits of another possible positive external factor are clearly showing the case of the ambivalent and poor influence of the EU policy supporting regional cooperation in Southern Asia.[12] The EU supporting policies are more successful where internal factors of integration are well balanced with external factors, as in the case of ASEAN. The increasing political dialogue between the EU and India (Lisbon Meeting, spring 2000 between the EU Presidency and the Indian Prime Minister) is consistent with the Commission Communication of 1996; however, it has to be set in the framework of the new situation created by the military *coup d'état* in Pakistan and the anti-Pakistan evolution of SAARC, on the one hand, and of the triangular competitive relationship the US–EU–India,on the other hand.

In its presentation of Asia's most important regional organization, Eliassen/Børve's chapter raises a methodological issue by proposing the comparison of ASEAN with the EC of the 1970s rather than with the highly institutionalized EU of today. The question is to what extent can we consider the synchronic dimension of their controversial relation to a globalized world by comparing regional organizations to each other. Furthermore, to what extent must a diachronic approach be chosen in order to have a better understanding of the gradual evolution of regional organizations? This book aims to combine both of these approaches, which is particularly useful as far as this case study is concerned.

ASEAN states were able to develop their intergovernmental cooperation, in spite of unusual obstacles and extraordinary difficulties. For more than three decades, ASEAN has been looking for an Asian way to regional cooperation. At first glance, it is similar to the EU insofar as the scope and range of its activities are concerned. The willingness to emulate the Western European model and, more recently, to react to the danger of diluting ASEAN within the broader interregional liberalization carried out by APEC,[13] played a certain role. In its Jakarta meeting of 1994, APEC adopted an ambitious programme to set up an interregional free trade area by 2020. With the setting up of APEC, we are faced, in Asia as in Europe and elsewhere, with competitive concepts of regionalism. Two opposite barriers are paradoxically braking the US preference for a comprehensive and more institutionalized APEC as a model of so-called open regionalism,[14] that is, ASEAN's fear of being absorbed into an intercontinental US-centred organization and a preference of many Asian states for a very soft, multiple geometry, Most Favoured Nation based, kind of APEC.

Another apparent similarity with the EC is their common origin in the Cold War era. Nevertheless, such an external potential unifying factor was not as useful in the Asian-Pacific region as in Western Europe, which can be explained largely by underlining that the USA's preference in Asia was for bilateralism rather than multilateralism.

Considering the internal factors, one has to take into account the great economic disparities among ASEAN countries in terms of industrial and technological development, labour costs, and export capacity. Furthermore, many observers stress the cultural and political heterogeneity of the region and the particular state traditions (populism, religious parties, role of the army, corruption, etc.) as well as the difficulty of coping with the challenges of both global liberalization and regional cooperation.

As a consequence, ASEAN followed its own way and, in spite of the aforesaid weaknesses, it is about to undergo an important change. Despite its very political origins, ASEAN can currently be defined as a mainly network-based regional integration. After the end of the bipolar world, the main driving force became the business community. Business networks are demanding further integration and institution building. The project for an ASEAN Free Trade Area has a main instrument: a Common Effective Preferential Tariff. The most likely issue could be similar to the European Free Trade Association,[15] according to Eliassen/Børve's chapter. Indeed, the ASEAN way means that transnational private networks, ethnic business, technological clusters, subregional policy communities, and free trade areas are pushing the governments forward. Personal contacts and business networks created along ethnic and cultural lines certainly build a complex multi-tier system using geographical proximity and both formal and informal meetings as a means to strengthen regional interests in global competition. Of course, as a consequence of such an approach, the institutional structure still is, relatively speaking, rather weak. The Council of Foreign Affairs Ministers (taking decisions on the basis of a consensual procedure and in a collegial way), the permanent and *ad hoc* committees, and the small General Secretariat in Jakarta are still very limited in scope and authority and lack a credible dispute settlement procedure.

Might ASEAN progress as a political entity as well? As far as the political dimension is concerned, a curious process characterizes ASEAN. It was born as an anticommunist security community, even when the bipolar construct was less constraining and more flexible in Asia than in Europe (because of the impact of the USSR–China conflict). Furthermore, the internal divisions on security issues between neutral Indonesia, pro-UK Malaysia and Singapore, the influence of the US and bilateral conflicts between Member-States were some of the main factors restraining economic cooperation and regional integration. Ten years after its foundation, the Bali Summit of 1976 did essentially reconfirm the primacy of political cooperation as an attempt to defend a non-communist international identity within that turbulent area. Why has there been a change towards economic priorities since 1992?

This book focuses both on internal factors (business networks) and on a changed perception of common external threats acting as a catalyst on regional cooperation, particularly the new need to react to growing international competition and liberalization. This includes the consequences of the Uruguay Round, the implementation of the Single European Act, the creation of NAFTA, and so on. To increase the competitiveness of ASEAN companies became a new *raison d'être* of the regional organization. As a matter of fact, things changed very quickly in the nineties, as shown both by consolidation and by the simultaneous ability to expand and to include former enemies, such as Vietnam, which joined in 1995, Laos and Burma in 1997, and finally Cambodia.

What has to be underlined is that the economic dynamics towards a free trade area are establishing a new political framework and a new security agenda firstly with ASEAN states' decision to discuss regional security issues at the Annual Conference. Secondly, we are witnessing the development of a 'concentric circles' system with the creation of the wider ASEAN Regional Forum (ARF), including China, Japan, South Korea, the EU, the USA, India and the main Asian-Pacific countries, which is asserting an ASEAN pivotal role, at least as a driving force. The ARF was created in 1993–4 in order to pursue and adapt, in the new international context characterized by a form of security vacuum, the original aim of stability and peace in the area. The major challenge for South-east Asian states is to place ASEAN within the framework of the evolving Asia-Pacific security triangle between the three giants, the USA, Japan and China. This attempt is proceeding quite successfully, even though ARF is still far from becoming an East Asian OSCE. The ASEAN Regional Forum still is a weak structure based on consultation. However, in spite of the principle of non-intervention, and the method of intergovernmental political cooperation, something new is currently happening. Dialogue with the growing (and often feared) neighbour, China, seems to be improving. The management of this relationship to the potentially political hegemon, The People's Republic of China, within a multilateral framework, despite its current economic transition, its nationalistic tendencies and its internal uncertainty, is a crucial issue for the regional security agenda. That is why the achievements of the Bangkok Summit of 1994 and the consequent meeting of heads of states were so important in terms of establishing confidence-building measures, preventive diplomacy, and peaceful conflict settlement. Furthermore, the normalization process with Vietnam and the renouncement by the ASEAN countries and China of the use of force as a means of addressing conflicts over territory and natural resources with regard to territorial problems and the natural resources of the Southern Chinese Sea, were important steps forward. The relationship with China and the ability to settle quarrels – a very sensitive issue in South-East Asia – are crucial for ASEAN as a regional peacekeeping organization. ASEAN member states decided, as a consequence of the harsh financial crisis, to drastically reduce their military budgets and defence programmes. The success of the ARF is particularly commendable because, for the first time in Asian-Pacific history, the economic and political influence of both China and Japan is increasing simultaneously. The influence of the USA in the region is still crucial in order to push free trade, establish military cooperation, and campaign for democratization and the rule of law. However, the role of the post-hegemonic USA in the region is likely to decline, if not as an economic power, at least as the 'first range' military power.

The Hanoi Summit of 1998 was an attempt of change regarding the internal obstacles to deeper integration (heterogeneity, non-intervention principle). With reference to Cambodia (traditionally a difficult issue for ASEAN in spite of its participation to the Paris Agreement of 1991), the enlargement had been postponed to 1999, because of the *coup d'etat* by Hun Sen and the divergent points of view between ASEAN countries. The return of Vietnam to regional cooperation after many years of low-profile foreign policy was a success. Not only was there increasing interference during the two main political crises of 1998/99 in Indonesia and Malaysia, but also Thailand openly proposed a 'strengthened interaction' going beyond the principle of non-interference, which was typical of the Suharto era. Deeper integration and stronger institutional cooperation have been conditioned by the very heterogeneity and pre-democratic nature of almost all of the national regimes during the previous decades. This explains why, despite exceptions (supporting Corazon Aquino's campaign in 1987, recently criticizing Burma's junta and Hun Sen's *coup d'état* in Cambodia) and the paradoxical post-crisis democratization wave (Indonesia, Philippines), *new regionalism does not yet entail generalized domestic democratization.* The weight of a very diverse colonial and neocolonial past, the legacy of the Cold War, the cultural, religious, and linguistic diversity, the unique relation between state and society, are together making regional cooperation more difficult than elsewhere, even regarding common problems such as the fight against air pollution, AIDS, pirates and criminality.

In spite of such problems, economic and political regionalism is increasing. The normally sacred principle of non-intervention is starting to be questioned although no consensus yet exists on new regional post-sovereign rules. The current prudent interference in the domestic affairs of other Member-States is justified in the name of the huge external implications of national crises like those of Indonesia (difficult post-Suharto transition era; East-Timor-crisis, etc.) or Malaysia (limited democracy, human rights, and media freedom as shown by the arrest and trial of former President Mahatir's Minister, Mr. Anwar). The democratization of Myanmar, though openly requested by ASEAN Member-States along with the EU, is still an open issue. The European style troika created by the ASEAN Bangkok Summit of 2000 in order to face regional security problems is confronted the mainly domestic and internal nature of challenges. Summing up, the process of building an internal problem-solving authority will be very gradual.

The consequences of the economic and financial crisis of 1997/98 on the evolution of ASEAN are highly contradictory. At the beginning, it increased inward-looking policies and, later on, there was a growing expectation of a more institutionalized intergovernmental regional framework for settling disputes and strengthening regional cooperation. As for the ability of ASEAN to survive the financial crisis of the late1990s, the Hanoi Summit in December 1998 succeeded in launching a common anti-crisis programme and in relaunching financial cooperation with Japan. Step by step, a form of intergovernmental watchdog has appeared on the agenda of ASEAN: the Manila network of mutual surveillance will be substituted by something less vague. According to Eliassen/Børve, a kind of 'cognitive regionalism' could work better than the IMF monitoring and constraining system, which failed in the past and provoked a reaction in the name of an increased sense of Asian identity. A regional approach to internal adjustment could indeed be more effective than a global one. As far as the current expectations are concerned, in the best case scenario, facing common challenges could develop a new ASEAN awareness, help social cohesion and democratization (Indonesia, Philippines, East Timor) to increase and allow regional cooperation to grow. The worst case scenario is that economic and social crisis could increase infra-regional conflicts as elsewhere in the past decades. Refugee problems between Indonesia and Malaysia, protectionist conjunctural policies, the external consequences of Indonesian forest destruction, and new domestic political instability in Philipines and Indonesia (as shown by the Atjeh and Moluchs secession movements) could put into question the delicate balance between external and internal politics in the region. At present, economy and politics have closer links than in the past. The Action Plan 1999–2004 of December 1998 demonstrates the will to consolidate integration and to provide common answers to common problems: calling for foreign investments, planning infrastructures, and coordinating currency policies. Can Thailand's Foreign Minister's concepts of 'flexible engagement' and of 'strengthened interaction' among Member-States in a reinforced ASEAN cope with the current difficult two level game and further implement the ASEAN way of regional cooperation? The main variable is the complex interaction with the unstable economic and political environment.

A more active role within the international arena was part of the huge dynamism of ASEAN during the 1980s and 1990s. On the one hand, it participated in the APEC process and, on the other hand, in the Asia Europe Meeting (ASEM). The process leading to the ASEM was started in 1994 (Singapore project and Karlsruhe Summit) under the convergent pressure of strategic interests and private lobbying. The question remains about similarities and dissimilarities in the expectations of both partners. ASEAN has three main goals: to achieve an improved international status, to get better access to the EU market, and to attract European investment. Why is the EU interested in taking a step forward beyond old post-colonial patterns of cooperation with developing countries to reach a cooperation on equal basis? There are two main answers: to accede economically and politically to a strategic area of the planet and to strengthen regional organizations worldwide.

Both ASEAN and the EU want to complete a kind of world trade triangle (Europe, Asia, North America), diversify markets, enhance their respective bargaining power with the North Americans and, eventually, push the USA towards a multilateral approach. The first ASEM Summit, at Head of State level, which took place in Bangkok in 1996, succeeded, as is shown by the chairman's statement and the common final document setting a regular – though informal – biregional agenda. Further summits took place in 1998 and in 2000. Both organizations are definitely about to take the opportunity to strengthen their international role after the end of a bipolar era, through interregional cooperation, including political dialogue.

The common goals of economic and political cooperation and socio-cultural dialogue have been partly implemented through ministerial meetings, business forums, managerial and youth leader meetings and the new Europe–Asia Foundation project.

Of course, there are still problems to be faced: first of all, the EU's protectionism; secondly, the EU concept of political dialogue, sometimes seen as an intervention by Asian authoritarian or post-authoritarian regimes; and thirdly, the EU's relative passivity during the financial and political crisis in the region. One should add that the EU wishes to widen the ASEM process to include more Asian countries. India is particularly interested, as due to its size and the paralysis of SAARC, it cannot be encapsulated solely within the South Asian framework. However, to include India is not an easy issue for ASEAN.

In conclusion, two parallel and linked trends characterize ASEAN's evolution within the current post-hegemonic world. The Member-States of ASEAN have been able to overcome their worst financial crisis, to enlarge the regional association to up to ten Member-States and to take further steps (even if they are somewhat delayed) toward a Free Trade Area. One of the main challenges for ASEAN is how to combine its deeper cooperation with the broader liberalization programme established by the American APEC initiative. Politically, ASEAN is now focusing on stabilizing territorial integrity and order against domestic fragmentation (particularly within multi-ethnic Member-States), even though the East-Timor crisis of 1999 confirms that ASEAN States still are reluctant to get involved in the domestic politics of a Member State. Moreover, they are establishing a broader, less rigid, regional security dialogue involving the US, the EU, Australia and the two potential regional leaders, China and Japan.

Secondly, the defensive approach of ASEAN States to economic globalization is evolving toward a more strategic view on the one hand, strengthening the ASEM process and, on the other hand, 'ASEAN plus three', namely South Korea, China and particularly its relationship to Japan. The new role of the economic giant and technological leader of East Asia is beyond its previous inattention to regional policy[16] (and beyond a mere bilateral relationship with the USA) and is likely to become a very dynamic factor. Japan looks increasingly likely to become both the centre of an enlarged regional cooperation process (ASEAN countries plus South Korea – including projects for a common market) and also the treasurer (source of public financing and private investments, fund against poverty, etc.) for the whole area. Along with historical links and economic interests, trade tensions with the US and the failure of the WTO in Seattle help to explain the Japanese will to become a strong partner of Asian Pacific countries.

Coping with the relationship with China is traditionally the main issue at stake for ASEAN. Bringing both Japan and China within multilateral global and regional frameworks is crucial for the security of the region. Improving its relationship with the nuclear power and the coming economic giant really is salient for ASEAN, particularly because of the historical problems and the countervailing tendencies as far as the transformation of Pacific Asia in a Japan-centred region is concerned.

In spite of the weight of bilateralism and of the tripolar political structure of the region (China, Japan, US), Asian Pacific new regionalism is evolving in new ways in the wake of the economic crisis and the problems that arose within the globalized economy. Against inward-looking strategies, it is also aiming to complement trade and interregional openness with stronger, more specialized regional agreements. Even more than in the past decades, the institutional settlement of ASEAN will be crucial, as it adapts to internal differentiation but also becomes strong enough to cope with domestic concerns, and, particularly, to help to bring the whole region beyond current uncertainties. Economic dynamics was the way for the old ASEAN to revive. However, to settle a 'regional security architecture'[17] is the challenge not only to avoid competition for resources and exacerbating disputes but also to stabilize both current economic dynamics and peace.

2. MERCOSUR and the Transatlantic Triangle

Regional groupings in Latin America and particularly the Organization of American States were for decades weak and stagnant. Nevertheless, there currently are examples of vital subregional integration, namely MERCOSUR and the Andean Community.[18] MERCOSUR shows salient similarities with the EU: the customs union, the political aim and its political function of stabilizing domestic democracies of Member States. These are part of a post-sovereign political culture which explains, according to many observers, its outstanding success story in such a short time.[19]

The Italian philosopher of the eighteenth century, Giambattista Vico said that the true nature of things is to be found in their birth. As MERCOSUR is concerned, its origin as a 'security community' in Karl Deutsch's words[20] is crucial in order to understand its future developments. Indeed, the first step of the current integration process between the countries of the southern cone of Latin America was a confidence-building treaty between Argentina and Brazil. The countries agreed to abandon their nuclear programmes and their previous mutually suspicious and aggressive political culture like France and Germany did at the beginning of the European construction.

This kind of democratic conditionality and intergovernmental political cooperation worked quite efficiently, as far as the internal adjustments of the Member States were concerned. This was true for Paraguay, when General Oviedo unsuccessfully tried to return to dictatorship (1996 and during the 1999 political crisis) and in the framework of the negotiations with other Latin American States, such as Chile and Bolivia as well.[21]

If we compare this with the paralysis of the South Asian Association for Regional Cooperation (SAARC) and with the dramatic bilateral tension between the two nuclear powers India and Pakistan, we can see the highly positive effects of this political variable. These include deepening economic and trade integration, common trade policy, and steps towards a political community. Reciprocally, the political dimension has been strengthened and stabilized by the tremendous success of growth in infra-regional trade, and the functional dynamics of integration, thanks to the better harmonization of the national economies of the region.

The main difference between the EU and MERCOSUR is still the institutional deficit of the latter, which is on the whole an intergovernmental body, conditioned by the hesitations of one Member State, namely Brazil, regarding institutional progress in terms of supranationality and with a very limited General Secretariat in Montevideo. The 1998–1999 crisis between Brazil and Argentina was partly overcome, in spite of Brazilian devaluation and the consequent risk of a return to protectionist measures; however, it has confirmed the previous institutional weaknesses. The current debates on deepening integration, namely on a future single currency, macroeconomic coordination and on the creation of a Court regulating juridical and economical disputes, may have relevant institutional implications.

Listing the obstacles to this, one should not forget the negative weight of the internal structural imbalances between Member States – the reason why many observers still consider MERCOSUR as a great Brazil. Within every Member State, between *élites* and civil society, social imbalances are also important, which explains the limited support MERCOSUR currently gets from low-income social strata.[22]

As far as the international dimension of MERCOSUR is concerned the chapter by Vasconcelos focuses on the transatlantic triangle, NAFTA–EU–MERCOSUR.

This emphasizes, firstly, the weakness of one of the three sides, namely the one linking the EU and MERCOSUR and, secondly, the problems existing in the Pan-American project called the Free Trade Association of the Americas, which foresees a continental free trade area from the year 2005 onwards. The FTAA (ALCA), a common design of the Bush and Clinton administrations, took important steps forward at the Santiago Summit of the Americas in April 1998, but the question is still whether or not the US vision of open regionalism is compatible with the existence and further deepening of MERCOSUR. The current balance between the pro-FTAA and the pro-deepening-MERCOSUR tendencies in the southern cone's countries is due to participation in an FTAA process, as a relatively coherent and united group of States, helping to further deepen MERCOSUR. A new process is open with the Andean Community in order to establish a common South American FTA. Does the refusal of the American Congress of the fast-track procedure requested by the Clinton administration to implement the hemispheric free trade area and the failure of the WTO in Seattle in 1999 make such a deep regionalist scenario more realistic? The main Latin American variable is the future strategy of the regional power, Brazil, that hesitates between its tradition as a diplomatic dwarf, deeper MERCOSUR regionalism or revival of traditional Latin American discourse (as shown at the Brasilia Conference of August 2000). The Brasilia Declaration, signed by twelve Latin American states shows Brazil's natural leadership by launching a South American Free Trade Area including MERCOSUR and the Andean Community, by criticizing the Colombia Plan financed by the US, and by wishing a reform of world financial architecture (Cardoso's opening speech). Will such a new Brazilian ambition weaken MERCOSUR.

A second open problem is to what extent can the Euro–Latin American relationship be strengthened beyond the framework agreement of 1995, both as trade and as political ties are concerned. The relationship of the EU to MERCOSUR is often mentioned as an example of the Midas approach of the EU, namely of the replication of this model worldwide.[23] Since the very beginning (1991, one month after the Asunción Treaty) the EU forged deep links with the Common Market of the South and in general supported regional integration in the southern part of the continent.

The bilateral agreement of 1992 has been particularly important in helping MERCOSUR to benefit from the EU's experience, as far as regional integration is concerned, by providing technical assistance to the Secretary of Montevideo (missions of the EU public servants), and by setting norms and standards. The EU Council Declarations of Lisbon (1992), Corfu and Essen (1994) explicitly supported the interregional cooperation between the EU and MERCOSUR. In 1995, the European Parliament explicitly mentioned the competition between the policies of the EU and the US towards MERCOSUR. The framework agreement of 1995, a third-generation agreement, includes a democratic clause, a *clause évolutive* and a political dialogue. Its precondition is for MERCOSUR to have a legal personality. Its goal is to underline and strengthen the convergences between regional organizations within multilateral organizations. Even education and training are included as matters of regional cooperation. Foreign direct investments by European companies in MERCOSUR countries and interregional trade have dramatically increased during this decade. The EU is the first trade partner and the first foreign investor. The Rio de Janeiro biregional summit of June 1999, the Rio Declaration and the starting of negotiations for a free trade area between the EU and MERCOSUR (plus, separately, with Chile) can be seen as confirmation of both difficulties and progress.[24]

Indeed, important obstacles remain for the biregional Rio process. These include non-tariff barriers (NTB), agricultural interests, and the implications of ECSC and the MFA (the Multi Fibre Agreement) as shown by the huge bargaining difficulties both in June (before the Rio Summit) and during the biregional trade liberalization bargaining. Furthermore, the EU is increasingly forced to place its priorities elsewhere (Eastern Europe, Balkan and Mediterranean crises). The Helsinki Council of December 1999 strengthened the decision to proceed to a great Eastern European enlargement of the EU within the next decades, which could limit global policies. On the other hand, many European countries and the European Commission underline the importance of MERCOSUR, not only as an economic partner but as a potential strategic political ally in view of a more symmetric multilateral world. The Rio process is a salient innovation: a comprehensive framework for articulated biregional relations; regular meetings to supervise the implementation of priorities; proactive cooperation in development policies; emphasis on cultural, social and educational issues; supporting regional deep integration. In this respect, this example is crucial for the EU's future external relations.

The EU Member States are still to some extent divided with regard to the progress of relations with MERCOSUR. On the one hand, France, while strongly supporting political alliance with MERCOSUR as part of a worldwide political multipolarism, brakes the implementation of a free trade agreement and provoked the pre-Rio Summit mini-crisis of June 1999. Spain, Portugal, Italy and more particularly Germany (number one as for exports to and imports from this region) are on the European Commission's side in supporting an anti-protectionist and encompassing approach to biregional negotiations.

The need to adjust to the US initiative of 1994 of creating a FTAA is not seen as urgent by every European State. However the FTAA, in spite of domestic troubles, is moving faster than expected. With the Santiago Declaration (1998) and Toronto summit (1999) and in view of the Buenos Aires summit of 2001, it includes a wide range of issues beyond pure free trade (inclusive of participation by civil society and by NGOs) and discussions on accelerating liberalization.

To conclude, MERCOSUR and other Latin American subregional groupings, such as the Andean Community, will be at a crossroads. Either they go on deepening (macroeconomic coordination) and strengthening their political dimension (institutional settlement, democracy and protection of human rights, security, and international political dialogue), or they risk being absorbed into a dynamic FTAA. The compromise linking the advancement of biregional negotiations of sensitive subjects between the EU and MERCOSUR with the progress of the Millennium Round is becoming more problematic because of the uncertainties of the WTO and the dynamics of FTAA. All in all, after the failure in Seattle, multilateralism, new regionalism, and biregionalism have been challenged as far as this area is concerned. Both regional organizations, the EU and MERCOSUR, are adjusting their strategies: Brazil and other Latin American countries advocated deepening regional cooperation and the EU is requesting a reform of the WTO's bargaining procedure, paying more attention to requests of developing countries and regional organizations. However, that is not enough, given the current uncertainty. Of course, if the future confirms that the US commitment to liberalization meets growing domestic obstacles, most probably, the interregional dialogue between the EU and MERCOSUR will be directly affected. But if the US strengthen the hemispheric dynamics of FTAA, as a support to its global strategy, both MERCOSUR and EU will be obliged to make crucial decisions within the next few years.

According to Vasconcelos, it is possible to foresee an evolution of transatlantic relations at the beginning of the 21st century. A third strategic scenario is likely to emerge between that based on the hard political multipolarism concept proposed by French President Chirac, and the other one, coming from the American vision of globalization as emerging markets and hemispheric liberalization: a less asymmetric transatlantic triangle as a substantive component of a new multilateral world governance. The strengthening of biregional EU–MERCOSUR cooperation is one of the main pillars of such an alternative, a way to combine deeper regionalism, biregional negotiations, and multilateralism thanks to common interests and cultural affinities.

Strategic choices are urgent. The EU and MERCOSUR have shown their political interest in biregional cooperation, as proven by the process relaunched in 1999. Both regional organizations are challenged to react to Seattle by deepening regional integration and interregional dialogue.[25] The current uncertainty depends on the US but also on the EU options and on MERCOSUR States options. MERCOSUR is still openly following a multiple-tie tactics, bargaining with the US and with the EU, within the Latin American subcontinent and within the multilateral organizations.

3. Developing NAFTA. The US between unilateralism, regionalism and multilateralism

It is still a controversial issue amongst international scholars whether the US had a long-term interest or not in regionalism and NAFTA.[26] Many domestic political streams, lobbying and economic interest coalitions have been fighting for years for a free trade agreement with Canada and later on with Mexico. However, this does not explain the very crucial fact that this agreement was only finalized in the nineties, after the Uruguay Round and the revival of European integration.

The US decision to sign and implement a Free Trade Agreement with Canada (1989) and to extend it to Mexico (1994) opens, according to A. Sbragia, 'a new chapter in American foreign economic policy'. It raises the question: why such a new referential trade area along regional lines, in spite of a symbiotic relationship between European and American companies and the Atlantic Alliance?

Firstly, after the end of the Cold War, the US could decouple security and economy. Two economic regionalisms on both sides of the Atlantic would not undermine the transatlantic security community strengthened by the 'New Transatlantic Agenda'[27] and the revival of NATO. Moreover, NAFTA has no political underpinning as the EU, ASEAN or MERCOSUR have.

Secondly, the weight of the negative US perception of the Single European Act, the doubts provoked by the image of 'the European Fortress, and the willingness to react through a Northern American regionalist policy must be taken into account.

As far as the consequences are concerned, the Miami Conference of 1994 and the Santiago summit of the Americas of 1998 did set up a detailed schedule for a Free Trade Area of the Americas, namely a greater NAFTA, that is a continental liberalization process.

The problem is that the current free trade agreement with the poor Mexico and the rich Canada already emphasizes the problem of huge asymmetries in regional arrangements as far as the US is included. NAFTA is particularly asymmetric and the institutional capacity is so weak that asymmetries are not counterbalanced enough. Last but not least, the bipartisan US consensus in rejecting the Mexican President V. Fox's proposals for a deeper NAFTA clearly shows the very political limits of US regionalism.

As for the institutional features, the comparison with the EU shows a very long list of differences. However, some similarities do exist and they go beyond simple free trade. Sbragia's chapter underlines three of them: the Commission for Environmental Cooperation; the Commission for Labor Issues and the institutionalization of dispute settlements. International literature does agree that 'the selection of an effective mechanism for resolving commercial disputes is fundamental to generate compliance with these mechanisms by parties to preferential trade agreements'.[28] The question is whether or not functional arguments explain that increasing institutionalization (compared for instance with ASEAN). However, the establishment of such a dispute-settlement mechanism is not deepening the integration process amongst the three countries.

In conclusion, though it can be classified as a modest and soft regional agreement, NAFTA goes further than GATT-WTO, it also includes some important foundational norms, which constitute a *de facto* protection, as in the EU. The regionalist choice of the US is very important at international level, given the amount of Northern American trade, which represents, just like the EU, some 40 per cent of world trade.

As far as the future is concerned, NAFTA is far from being over. The Seattle WTO failure and the accidents of Clinton's free-trade agenda are pushing the US either to more inward-looking policies or to a strengthening of its own regional alliances, using them to influence trade globalization worldwide. In the first case scenario, Mexico and Canada will no longer be able to resist the temptation of achieving deeper trade deals with the EU and with Latin American countries, independently from the US.

4. African regionalism and the Southern African Development Community (SADC)

Like several Latin American and other regional or subregional arrangements, African regionalism is very poor with regard to its achievements, as proven by the rhetoric of the Organization of African Unity and by the other subregional organizations' inability to regulate the numerous current (around fifteen) military conflicts within the continent. *Longue durée* explanations are specially adapted to cope with the failures of African regionalism, including economic underdevelopment, weakness of states, various consequences of the colonial and neocolonial legacies, division between different metropolitan references, and problems of border conflicts.

However, the controversial regionalist experience of the 1980s is also to be taken into account. According to the Lagos Action Plan approved by the OAU summit of 1980, an African strategy has been implemented with the aim of diminishing dependence on the outside. It also aimed to increase African autonomous development through five projects of enhanced rather than protectionist-oriented regional cooperation. These are: the Economic Community of Central African States (CEEAC, founded in 1983), the Preferential Trade Area (1981), changed in 1994 to the Common Market of Eastern and Southern Africa (COMESA), the Arabian Maghreb Union in Northern Africa (AMU, in 1989) and the pre-existing ECOWAS in Western Africa. The SADCC was created in 1980 by the 'Front Line States' in order to increase the isolation of the apartheid regimes of South Africa and Namibia. In 1981, the Berg Report for the Organization of African Unity criticized the last illusion of African self-sufficiency and pointed out that priority should be given to a break with a state-led economy and the illusion of alternative development strategies. It also inaugurated the new era of gradual economic (and, later on, even political) liberalization, which really matured with the end of Soviet communism and its influence in Africa.[29] Global imperatives and structural adjustment programmes inspired by the IMF and World Bank prevailed during the 1980s and 1990s and regional cooperation became marginal. However, globalization and the disintegration of states and societies are inextricably linked in many African countries, leading to a deterioration of traditional problems, including huge external debt, increasing poverty, and ethnic and border conflicts.

Beyond such negative experience and historical obstacles to successful region-alist cooperation, there appears a basic weakness: the structure of demand and production is too similar to generate substantial trade creation (see the chapter by Jenkins and Thomas).[30] The huge problem for African regional agreements is to be able to cope with both a very low level of economic development (as for industry, technology, productivity, infrastructures, services, and skilled labour) and with a dramatic and broadly diffused fragmentation of political systems.

Nevertheless, regionalism has increased in Southern (SADC[31]) as well as in Western Africa (ECOWAS[32]), as a result of two main factors: the growing fear of African marginalization in the new international environment, characterized by the two parallel trends towards globalization and regional blocs, and the growing exter-nal pressure by the international community and particularly by the European Union's development policy.

The awareness of the first factor is increasing. The long-term plan approved at the Summit of the Organization for African Union at Abuja (Nigeria) of 1991, can be seen as the background to the current new wave of regional integration, at least at the level of rhetoric from heads of states. These include decreasing tariff barri-ers, building free exchange areas and customs unions, and strengthening sectorial integration, before 2025, towards an explicit emulation of the EU, the EMU and the political union.

Regional arrangements within the southern part of the continent appear to be an interesting case study, particularly after the end of the apartheid regime. Indeed the Southern African Development Coordination Conference (SADCC) became the current SADC (Southern African Development Community) with the signing of the Windhoek Treaty of 1992. The dynamics of the industrial economy of South Africa allows the neighbouring countries to increase infra-regional trade, beyond the mere political priority of the previous anti-apartheid organization. SADC is currently trying to maintain the difficult balance between national adjustment and global competition, regional cooperation, and decreasing international aid. This is characterized by many surrounding regional organizations, with partly overlapping memberships. Namibia is the only member of them all: the Community of Eastern and Southern Africa (nine members); the Southern African Customs Union (five Member States, started in 1910); the Common Monetary Area (four members); and the Cross-Border Initiative (seven members).

SADC shares huge internal asymmetries with other regional organizations. Since the 1994 enlargement, South Africa represents around 70 per cent of SADC's GDP (and 20 per cent of the population), but is not yet able – because of urgent domes-tic problems – to play the role of regional aid provider and big economic engine. The Democratic Republic of Congo, one of the poorest Member States with the largest population, joined in 1998. The GNP per capita of the richest Member State (Mauritius) is 18 times higher than in the poorest one, Mozambique. The diver-gences on macroeconomic policy are very important. Jenkins and Thomas provide very useful tables showing the disparities between the more open and the more closed economies.

From Africa's point of view, the last decade of globalization made asymmetries worse within the world economy. The share of sub-Saharan Africa's total net long-term resource flows decreased dramatically (from 17 per cent in 1990 down to 6 per cent in 1996) particularly if compared with the increasing share to East/Asia Pacific and Latin American/Caribbean regions. With three per cent of the world's population, SADC represents one per cent of the world's GDP and one per cent of the world global exports. For some years, either according to the rules of the WTO, or through aid-supported structural adjustment programmes, trade liberalization has been progressing. In spite of huge implementation problems, in 1996 SADC approved a protocol calling for the gradual establishment of a SADC Free Trade Area as a means of achieving a significant increase in infra-regional trade, foreign investment, and rate of economic growth. Jenkins and Thomas point out how important complementary policies are (education, health, political stability, institutions, infrastructures and so on) to give a country a chance to increase growth and to reduce the destabilizing effects the more closed economies inevitably face.

By comparing SADC and the EU in terms of convergence measures among Member States, the authors come to the conclusion that in 30 years (1960–90) SADC countries did not reach any convergence at all (per capita incomes). While within the smaller hard core formed by the SACU (Customs Union, South Africa plus four Members States) the dispersion of per capita incomes dropped more than half, exceeding the convergence rate realized by the EU countries in the same period. Free trade, currency union, transfers from South Africa, and similar macro-economic policies did achieve convergence. Deep regional integration looks as a working way. The question is whether an extension of such convergence factors to all of the members of SADC could allow dispersion to drop and catch-up convergence including the less developed countries. Such an extension might occur with mutual benefits for both South Africa and other Member States. A regional development fund, the development of sectorial coordinated regional activities and more consistent macroeconomic policies is vital to the FTA's establishment.

However, this optimistic vision is tempered by some caveats. The consequences of the huge internal asymmetry are the dominance of South Africa and its interest in fighting the temptation to create a regional trade bloc (on the contrary, regional integration is seen as an alternative to global liberalization by other Member States), searching for larger trade partners beyond the SADC, and setting a free trade agreement with the EU negotiated since 1994 and applicable from 2000. Such varied and controversial agendas regarding the correspondence between regionalism, bilateralism and globalization are aggravated by political tensions, as demonstrated during the Zaire–Democratic Republic of Congo crisis in 1998/2000. In fact, as a consequence of the divergent appreciation of the Kabila regime, we are currently witnessing the growing hegemonic power – both economic and political – of South Africa, as shown by the Blue Crane SADC joint military manoeuvre of April 1999. On the other hand, a new internal cleavage opposing Congo, Namibia and Zimbabwe to the others can be seen. Such political problems do undermine the fragile regionalist integration process in Southern Africa and can stop infra-regional trade liberalization issues.

The multiple uncertainties and internal weaknesses of African regional arrangements do enhance the weight of the external factors, namely the impulse coming from the EU.[33] In spite of traditional Pan-Africanism, Africa is a part of the world where the balance between the domestic factors of regionalism and external pressures is in favour of the latter. That is one reason why the success and failures of the EU's policies are also interesting from a comparative point of view. The EU African policy is about to take a further step in the framework of the Kotonou Convention of 2000,[34] the fifth stage of the Lomé process (convention between the EU and the African, Caribbean and Pacific countries, ACP) which started more than forty years ago.[35] In spite of its growing importance as far as its scope and complexity are concerned, the Lomé process is generally not considered a success story and needs renewal. Some causes of the failures in increasing ACP countries' exports are linked to the global economy, price trends, and liberalization, resulting in diminishing the relative advantages of ACP. However, the new stage (Lomé 5) provides some innovative even if controversial guidelines: the special trade relationship between European countries and the seventy-one ACP partners will get, even if gradually, more in tune with the WTO rules and restrict the preferential regime. On the other hand, the conditionality criteria have been gradually strengthened. They now take into account the short-comings of the past conventions and stress the peculiarities of the EU external policy. Firstly, in keeping with the IMF and the World Bank, European aid will be linked to progress in macroeconomic performance, in adjustment policies and in improvements to the productive capacities of ACP countries. Secondly, progress in fighting against poverty, good governance, and in respect of human rights has been set as fundamental criteria.[36] Thirdly, it is particularly interesting to see how an existing long-term trend was strengthened to make a model out of interregional cooperation with Africa and ACP countries for the integrationist approach of EU external relations. An essential part of the convention is focused on complementing trade and aid by including explicit support for regional cooperation.[37] Free trade partnership with the EU will only be further developed within the next decade under the precondition that regional groupings are already set up among ACP countries. The open question is whether such a new condi-tionality will improve the implementation of cooperation policies and correct the current decreasing competitiveness, broad corruption, and increasing poverty in Africa or rather disappoint if it raises a feeling of an unacceptable and useless external pressure. Ultimately, there are some doubts about the consistency between a Euro-centred African regionalism, even if formally allowed by WTO, and, on the other hand, the global economy, namely the economic adjustments requested by international markets and the IMF.

5. Regionalization and deep integration

By comparative analysis of regionalism, this book tries to go beyond the vague and quite ideological concept of open regionalism, opposed to the notion of new mercantilism and protectionism.[38] We classify the first aforesaid three forms of regional agreements (economic association, societal intergovernmental Fora, free trade areas and cooperation) as soft regionalism, while the latter three illustrate various forms of deeper regionalism (customs union, common market and policies coordination, full integration and political union). Practical experiences often overlap and borders between soft and deep regionalism are not always clear, never definite or final, for example, as the conflict settlement mechanisms are concerned. However, one could classify the EU, MERCOSUR and the Oceanian experience of ANZCERTA as 'deep integration', including regional awareness and stress on common identity as well. ASEAN, SADC and Andean Community, not only by their political origin and development, also show many dynamics beyond mere soft regional grouping. The latter two also include other important features, respectively, monetary union as a hard core, and a relatively complex institutional settlement.

In conclusion, deeper regionalism gradually gives birth to *negotiated and rule-based political space* (not yet necessarily democratic but under the influence of the external and internal democratization waves) going beyond the mere functional model, and including confidence-building measures, common rules and procedures, mutual expectations, and political dialogue or cooperation. It often includes security regimes regarding Member States and applicants as well, for example, Germany and neighbours; Spain and Portugal; Italy and Austria; Hungary and Rumania; Hungary and Slovakia; Greece and Turkey; Brazil and neighbours; South Africa and neighbours; Ecuador and Peru; and Indonesia and Malaysia. Economic cooperation and political dialogue help by overcoming border conflicts and minority problems only if no major bilateral political tension exists (as in the case of SAARC). Deepening regional cooperation does not necessarily entail a multipolar balance of power and an exclusive civilization identity either. The question is whether it can increase multilateralism instead of bilateralism within and outside the region; create common interests and a new understanding of national interest; enhance economic convergence instead of divergence, and encourage peaceful settlement of existing border conflicts. These questions and answers are salient for the development of the political theory, beyond the state-centric Westphalian paradigm.

This book stresses how salient the comparison with the European experience is when studying new regionalism. Even if unique and not exportable elsewhere, the European case study is particularly interesting. First of all, many regional arrangements have been created in order to emulate the EC–EU or to react to the success story of the EU. Secondly, the EU as a global actor in the making, establishes partnerships at world level and supports new regionalism in Latin America, Africa and Asia, both by institutional policies and private networking. The future of new regionalism is in various ways intrinsically linked to the evolving EU.

Notes

1   W. Wallace (1994).
2   Edited by Union of International Associations, published by K. G. Saur, München, New York, London and Paris. See the analysis of empirical data provided by Paul Taylor (1993), pp. 24–46.
3   B. Balassa, 'The Theory of Economic Integration: an Introduction', in B. Balassa (1961).
4   Leon N. Lindberg (1963) 'Political Integration: Definition and Hypotheses', in *The Political Dynamics of European Economic Integration*, Stanford University Press.
5   J. M. Grieco, 'Systemic Sources of Variation in Regional Institutionalization in Western Europe, East Asia and the Americas', in E. D. Mansfield and H. V. Milner (1997), pp. 164–86 and S. Haggard, (1997) J. Grieco explains the European exceptionalism by the absence of stable distribution of capabilities and bargaining power of Member States.
6   E. D. Mansfield and H.V. Milner (1997), p.18.
7   Grieco's appreciation is that it is neither necessary nor sufficient. See in Mansfield and Milner (1997), pp.10–11.
8   ASEAN was created in 1967 by five countries (Indonesia, Malaysia, Singapore, Thailand, the Philippines, joined by Brunei in 1984) in the international environment characterized by the Vietnam War and the fears of a communist expansion in the region (see the Bangkok Declaration). The political aspect dominated the first decades of the organization, as shown by the Bali Declaration of 1976. It was only in 1992, after the end of the Cold War, that the fourth ASEAN summit (see the Singapore Declaration) approved the Framework Agreement on enhancing ASEAN economic cooperation focusing on the project of an Asean Free Trade Area before 2002 for six countries, and 2007 for the others. See R. A. Scalapino, S. Sato, J. Wanadi and S. -J. Han, eds (1998), *Asian Security Issues: Regional and Global*, University of California, Berkeley; Rosemarie Foot, 'Pacific Asia: The Development of Regional Dialogue', in Fawcett and Hurrell, ed. (1995). pp.228–49; G. Segal (1990), *Rethinking the Pacific*, Oxford University Press, Oxford; M. Leifer (1989), *ASEAN and the Security of South-East Asia*, Routledge, London; C. McIness and M. G. Rolls eds. (1994), *Post Cold War Security Issues in the Asia-Pacific Region*, Frank Cass, London; Garnaut and Drysdale,eds. (1994), *Asia Pacific Regionalism, Readings in International Economic Relations* Harper, Pymble, Australia; K. Clements, ed. (1993), *Peace and Security in the Asia Pacific Region*, UN, Tokyo.
9   Unfortunately we do not have the space here to go into detail on the hard regional security challenges: from North-East Asia to South-East Asia, without forgetting the turbulent China–Russia relationship and the uncertain normalization between Japan and the People's Republic of China, the issue of Taiwan, and relations between India and China. See D. A. Lake and P. M. Morgan (1997), particularly the Asian chapters by S. L. Shirk and Y. Foong Khong.
10   It was born at the Dakka Summit of 1985 following the Bangladesh proposal of 1980. The Institutions of SAARC: the Council of Ministers, the Standing Committee of Foreign Secretaries, the Standing Committees, the Technical Committees (for example concerning agricultural policy), the Committee on Economic Cooperation, the SAARC secretariat of Katmandu and the Documentation Center in New Delhi. See Kant K. Bhargava (1998), *EU-SAARC: Comparisons and Prospects for Cooperation*, ZEI Discussion papers, Bonn. I express my thanks to Prof. P. Battacharaya (University. of Calcutta) and to Fr. Giri (ISS, New Delhi) for their stimulating observations on this topic.

11 The breakdown of the Soviet Union, on the one hand, drastically limits the external component of the South-Asian crisis and, on the other hand, pushes India to a new dialogue with the USA. One should never forget the impact of the 1962 war with China and its consequences (the partial occupation of Kashmir) as far as India's feelings of insecurity are concerned. In the case of Pakistan, the solidarity of the Muslim international community and of fundamentalism can play a more relevant role. With the exception of some UN conferences (on poverty for example) the common external challenges do not yet bring the SAARC countries together.

12 See the Memorandum of 1996: according to the concept of partnership for development, SAARC can benefit from technical and financial assistance from the EU (on the basis of the 443/92) for the purpose of strengthening regional institutions, infra-regional trade, supporting joint policies among developing countries, networking and communications, research, training, and rural and energy policies. Interregional cooperation between the EU and SAARC already goes beyond previous policies of aid to developing countries: partner countries are helped by adjusting their economies to global competition and expanding trade, but also by building safety networks against social exclusion. The SAARC business networks are increasingly active, including biregional dialogue.

13 The APEC (Asia-Pacific Economic Cooperation Forum) was initiated in 1988 and includes, since 1994, government representatives of eighteen states and entities of the many rims of the Pacific Ocean region: USA, Canada, New Zealand, Australia, the ASEAN countries, Japan, South Korea and China; and also Hong Kong and Taiwan. Mexico, Papua New Guinea joined in 1993. Chile followed and Russia joined two years later. R. Higgott, (1995), S. Haggard, 'Regionalism in Asia and the Americas', in Mansfield and Milner, eds. (1997), pp.43–9 and R. Garnaut and P. Drysdale (1994).

14 Or at least, that portion of deep integration agenda which is in the Americas' interest (S. Haggard, p.46) namely building dispute settlement mechanisms.

15 EFTA was founded in 1960 by the European countries rejecting the pattern of supranational integration characterizing the Rome Treaties of 1957 solely in the name of a free trade area (UK, Scandinavian countries, Austria, Switzerland, Liechtenstein). All but Norway, Switzerland, Liechtenstein and Iceland joined the EC and the EU between 1973 and 1995.

16 Foot p.239. In spite of the first abortive attempt to create an Asian IMF and the remaining closed domestic market (included labour market), Japan is currently coming back to the Asian Pacific region, which is due to be its largest export market, above the American one. For instance, Japan is pushing ahead with a $30 billion Asia Fund to provide low-cost loans. As a consequence, even the theoretical issue of a possible common currency has been discussed at the Forum of the Thirteen Countries in Manila in November 1999 where, among others, China's application for membership in the WTO was supported both by ASEAN and by Japan.

17 Tony Tan (Defence Minister, Singapore), 'Steps for Asia-Pacific security', speech at the Asian Security Conference, Singapore, 17 January 2000.

18 The Andean Community (since 1997 – the Cartagena Agreement – subsequent to the Andean Pact created in 1969), including Venezuela, Colombia, Ecuador, Peru, and Bolivia, shows a remarkable overdeveloped institutional settlement (an Andean Tribunal for internal disputes, a monetary fund, a customs union – including only Venezuela, Ecuador and Bolivia – Presidential Council, Council of Foreign Ministers, a General Secretariat located in Lima). Only since 1990 has infra-regional trade significantly increased up to 14 per cent. See H. M. Lira (1999), *30 anos de Integracion Andina*,

Comunidad Andina, Lima, and E. M. Jimenez (1999), *La relaciones externas de la Comunidad Andina*, Comunidad Andina, Lima.

19 When signing the Asuncion Treaty of 26 March 1991, Argentina, Brazil, Paraguay and Uruguay decided to set up MERCOSUR. It would not formally come into being until 1st January 1995 as a semi-complete free trade area (95 per cent of intra-regional trade is free of customs duties) and as an incomplete customs union (external common tariff covers about 85 per cent of the bloc's products exported to non-member states). Total free trade area and customs union were originally scheduled for 1999/2000 and 2006. However, the financial crisis of 1998/99 caused significant delay. See Haggard, pp.20–48.

20 K. Deutsch, S. Burrell, R. A. Kann, (1957).

21 L. Whitehead (1996), *The International Dimensions of Democratization. Europe and Americas*, Oxford, Oxford University Press, P. Smith, ed., (1995) *Latin America in Comparative Perspective*, Boulder, Westview Press.

22 Grandi, J, Le MERCOSUR en période de transition: évaluation et perspectives in Bibes, *Problèmes d'Amérique latine*, op. cit., p. 80. E. Martinez, Institutional Dynamics and Political Dimension of Europe-Latin America Partnership facing the FTAA Process, draft paper, RCEU/IPSA, Brussels, XII, 1999.

23 European Council, *Conclusions*, Lisbon, 26/27 June 1992, p. 24. European Commission, *Appui de la Communauté européenne aux efforts d'intégration économique régionale des pays en développement*, Bruxelles, COM (1995) 219 final. Report of the European Commission and World Bank Seminar, *Regionalism and Development*, Bruxelles, 2 June 1998. Communication de la Commission au Conseil, au Parlement européen et au Comité économique et social, *Un nouveau partenariat Union européenne/Amérique latine à l'aube du XXIème siècle*, COM (99) 105 final, 9 mars 1999, p. 7

24 J. Dauster (1998), MERCOSUR and the European Union: prospects for an Interregional Association, in *European Foreign Affairs Review*, 3, pp. 447–449 and the papers presented by G. Fonseca; C. Lafer, J. Gama, D. Opertti, M. Soares, R. Lavagna, F. Pena; L. Lampreia, P. Wrobel, R. Altenfelder, A. Valladao, V. Thorstensen, A. Van Klaveren and A. Vasconcelos at the 6th Euro-Latin-American Forum, held under the initiative of the Instituto estudios Estrategicos Internacionais, Lisbon (Lisbon, 25/26 February 2000).

25 The 1999 new programme Avanza MERCOSUR (ahead with MERCOSUR) includes new cooperation in the fields of transports, energy, communications, and the search for foreign investments. In November 1999, according to the *International Herald Tribune*, President Cardoso stated that the WTO's failure in Seattle "showed how much we have to win by strengthening our ties within MERCOSUR", including a coordinated monetary policy, controls on the cross-border flows of money and a common currency, infra-continental negotiations with Chile and the Andean Community and biregional negotiations with the EU. Members of the Argentinean and Brazilian governments support the idea of a Latin American Maastricht Treaty, refounding the association beyond the imbalances provoked by the Brazilian Real's devaluation of early 1999.

26 'Short term' interpretations underline pressures on Uruguay Round for concluding in 1994.

27 Within the political general framework of NTA (1995, including cooperation for trade, global challenges and peace) the Transatlantic Marketplace (TMP) and a set of Mutual Recognition Agreements (MRA) have been established since 1996, while the exclusive inter-regional proposal for a Transatlantic Free trade Area (TAFTA) failed because it was seen by the EU as an attempt to relegate it to one of the many US inter-regional free

trade partnerships (APEC, FTAA, etc.). However, the limited scope of MRAs is to prevent regulations (social, environmental and safety standards) from acting as non-tariff barriers to trade and investment, especially in high tech sectors (see K. Nicolaidis, 1996, Exploring a New Paradigm for Trade Diplomacy: The US–EU MRAs, paper, for ECSA Conference, Brussels). A complementary private initiative was the Transatlantic Business Dialogue (TABD). In 1988, in spite of increasing controversial issues (bilateral trade quarrels, D'Amato and Helm-Burton Laws and so on) a compromise solution has been reached in Birmingham: The Transatlantic Economic Partnership. However, beyond trade disputes, further controversial issues are: since 1999, the transatlantic monetary coordination and, since 2000, the relationship between European Defence Policy and NATO (who will rule strategic planning? Which will be the new command-ment hierarchy? Who will rule peace-keeping operations in Europe?).

28 Mansfield and Milner, (1997) p.16 and the article by Yarbrough & Yarbrough, Dispute Settlements in International Trade: Regionalism and Procedural Coordination, ivi, pp. 134–162.

29 See F. J. Cardoso (1997).

30 The external trade of African countries is mainly (80–85%) oriented to non-African countries.

31 Started in 1980, by Tanzania, Botswana, Lesotho, Zambia, Mozambique, Angola and, later, Zimbabwe, and currently includes 14 Member States. The institutional settlement is intergovernmental: Summits of Heads of States, Councils of Ministers, sectorial Commissions and Coordinating Units led by specific Member States and the Secretariat located in Botswana.

32 The Economic Union of Western African States – CEDEAO in French – founded in 1975, includes French-speaking countries (belonging to the economic and monetary union UEMOA, based on the Franc CFA), English-speaking and Portuguese-speaking West African countries as well. The intra-regional trade is still very weak. On the contrary, political and security cooperation is progressing, as shown by the ECOWAS Monitoring Group, a regional military organization which can intervene (with ambivalent effects) in peacekeeping missions within the region (as it did in Liberia and Sierra Leone).

33 The European aid, though remaining the most important from North to South (14,6 billion Euros from 2000 to 2004), decreased to 50% from the amount of 10 years ago. The imports from ACP to EU decreased in 20 years from 6.7% in 1976 to 3.4% in 1997.

34 The European Fund for Development (for 2001–2006) has been fixed at a level compa-rable with the past budget: 13.5 billion Euro, while the previous 12.9 billion Euro. Moreover, one should add 1.7 billion Euro of loans from the European Investment Bank and also several billion Euro (around 9) remaining from previous funds.

35 The development policy of the EC and EU, already included -under pressure from France -in the Treaty of Rome (part four, art 177–181, ex–130) as complementary to the policies of Member States, has the following goals: a) economic and social development; b) aid for developing countries' access to the global economy; c) fight against poverty; d) consolidation of democracy and the rule of law; e) and consistency with the UN's and international organizations' commitments. The Association's policy towards non-European countries and former colonies (art. 182–188, ex 131–136) adds the purpose of establishing "close economic relations between them and the Community as a whole". The art. 132.2 stresses that associated countries must apply the same trade conditions they apply to the former European colonial power in their trade with each other (and not only for all the EU Member States). That means that increasing infra-regional trade

among developing countries is one of the EC–EU's goals since the 1950s. The Treaty plans to abolish all customs duties on imports from associated countries in no reciprocal way, the EC/EU contributes to investments, creates a European Development Fund, channels aids by Member States, administered by the European Commission (extra budget). This legal background makes the two Yaoundé conventions (1963 and 1968, see Dictionnaire du Marché commun, Paris, July, 1968, vol. 3) and the Lomé convention (1975) particularly stable and oriented towards the long term. The more encompassing perspective of the Lomé convention is due, on the one hand, to the impulses of British enlargement (increasing the numbers of partners to 46) and to the influence of the visions of a new economic international order and the opening of western markets (generalized system of preferences, GSP), particularly asserted by the UN and also by the new German Chancellor W. Brandt, a champion of North–South dialogue. Even if controversial in their achievements, the Lomé conventions were, and remain, a new kind of cooperation between developed countries and 40% of the entire membership of the UN. Africa covers 90% of the population and the economy of ACP countries. The first Lomé convention (1976–1980) has been followed by Lomé II (1980–1984), Lomé III (1985–1989) and by Lomé IV (1990–1999). The main features of the previous conventions were maintained: the central role of the supranational Commission by negotiating and managing cooperation (a comprehensive cooperation concept, including social, economic and cultural dimensions), ACP exports' duty-free access to the EC market (the agricultural products covered by Common Agricultural Policy, were a great obstacle) without reciprocal obligation, and emphasis on – at least formally – equitable and institutionalized relationship. The importance of the development policy of EC-EU has been substantially strengthened by improving trade agreements (even beyond the GSP) and, by increasing the scope of financial and technical assistance "to represent the world's biggest institutionalized link between the developed and developing worlds, worth 46. 5 billion in European Development Fund aid (including EIB loans) from 1958 to 1999" (C. Piening, 1997, p. 176).

During the same period the global development cooperation policy of the EC-EU evolved significantly, to include countries like India and Pakistan and others, which do not belong to the ACP conventions. The budget has gradually increased over the years and adjusted with a view to helping, in a more appropriate way, the poorest countries and including social and environmental goals.

See also G. Edwards and E. Regelsberger, eds. (1990), particularly the chapter on The Lomé Convention. A Model for Partnership, by O. Schmuck. And M. Lister (1998) *The European Community and the Developing World: the Role of the Lomé Convention*, Aldershot, Avebury.

36 K. Arts (2000), *Integrating Human Rights into Development Cooperation: the Case of Lomé Convention*, Vrije Universitat Amsterdam, 2000, particularly chapter 5 on historical developments, chapter 7 on the positive approach to human rights protection, and 8 on the negative approach (sanctions).

37 Already within the previous (IV) Lomé convention (1990–2000) the European Development Fund linked almost 10% of its funding to regional cooperation (the so-called "Programmes Indicatifs Régionaux") in order to support infrastructures, communications, transport and telecommunications likely to increase multilateralism on a regional basis.

38 F. Bergsten (1997) and R. Lawrence (1996).

5. European Union and NAFTA

Alberta M. Sbragia

1. Introduction

As the European Union (EU) continued to forge ahead in fashioning ever more integrative relationships and institutions in the 1990s, its transatlantic interlocutor began to construct a set of new relationships which represented a break with its past. While the Maastricht Treaty, agreed to in December 1991, could be seen as one more step in the institution-building process which had begun with French foreign minister Robert Schuman's famous press conference on 9 May 1950, the American government's decision to negotiate a free trade agreement with Canada and, more dramatically, with Mexico cannot be viewed in such an evolutionary fashion. Although it would be erroneous to see the creation of NAFTA as analogous to the creation of the European Coal and Steel Community or the subsequent European Economic Community, there is no doubt that the United States has significantly changed its foreign policy in the area of international cooperation.

The coming into force of the US–Canada Free Trade Agreement (CFTA) in 1989 opened a new chapter in American foreign economic policy. Once the bulwark of multilateralism and a staunch supporter of multilateral rather than regional initiatives, the United States committed itself to a free trade area with its wealthy northern neighbour. Even more significantly, in 1994 it agreed to extend that free trade area to its poor southern neighbour. Thus was born NAFTA, the North American Free Trade Area. NAFTA represented an important break with not only the American but also the Mexican past. In fact, the relationship between Mexico and the United States (to which, in the Mexican–American War of 1846–8, Mexico had lost the huge territory now known as the American Southwest) historically had been so tense that the president of Mexico turned to the United States only after having been rebuffed by both European and Japanese leaders in early 1990 (Grayson, 1995: 51).

While many analysts assume that NAFTA resembles the EU, this chapter takes as its starting assumption that the EU is so much more institutionalized and integrated than is NAFTA that direct comparisons of the two are not analytically very productive. Although comparison can be very helpful in understanding both the EU (Sbragia, 1992) and NAFTA, neither is a good comparative interlocutor for the other.

At the most basic level of institutional functioning, NAFTA differs from the EU in that it is not a customs union and therefore does not have an external dimension; has a secretariat rather than an equivalent of the European Commission; does not have a permanent institution such as the Council of Ministers and COREPER; has no parliament (whether appointed or elected); has no plans for a common currency or the integration of home and justice affairs; and has no equivalent to the European Court of Justice (ECJ) or the supremacy of European law over national law. Furthermore, NAFTA submits business to national treatment rather than to reciprocity (business is regulated by host country rather than home country rules), does not participate in any international fora such as the OECD and the UN, is not a signatory to international trade or environmental agreements, and so on.

The EU is an evolving system of governance, and that evolution, as seen by the contents of the recently-signed Treaty of Amsterdam, is still in progress. It is, in Helen Wallace's words, 'a part-formed political system' (Wallace, 1989: 205). NAFTA is not in any way a system of governance, and perhaps for that reason the literature about NAFTA has been written primarily by economists rather than by political scientists.[1] This chapter, therefore, highlights those elements found in both the EU and NAFTA which may become typical of preferential trade arrangements around the world, and not those which are unique to the EU and likely to remain so. Economic integration in Europe has been undergirded by the decision to address the German question through integration rather than by the traditional balance of power approach – by the search for a system of interstate relations which would avoid the 'rivers of blood' (to use Winston Churchill's phrase) which characterize European history. NAFTA (and ASEAN and APEC) do not have such political underpinnings, and therefore the degree of institutionalization they will experience is very unlikely to proceed along the lines of the EU. None the less, it may be possible to identify certain similarities in the EU and NAFTA which may be viewed as likely to characterize many preferential trading arrangements organized along regional lines.

This chapter briefly explores why the United States decided to pursue a regional strategy rather than continue to view multilateralism as the only appropriate way to liberalize international trade. It then goes on to describe NAFTA in institutional terms and highlights three elements – asymmetry, the linking of environmental protection and trade, and the unexpected institutionalization of dispute settlement – which have characterized both the EU and NAFTA, although to different degrees. Asymmetry, the environment–trade link and institutionalized dispute settlement may in fact come to be characteristic of international trade agreements in the next century. Certainly, they will characterize the relationship between the EU and the applicants for membership from the east and south; whether they will characterize the Asia–Pacific Economic Cooperation forum (APEC) is a more open question.

2. Multilateralism vs regionalism

The existence of regional blocs is often viewed as a threat to the multilateral trading system institutionalized around the GATT/WTO. Above all, the members of a regional bloc are seen as having fewer incentives to engage in multilateral tariff reduction than they would have if acting unilaterally. In LeClair's words,

> *The formation of a common market eliminates many of the incentives of engaging in meaningful multilateral tariff negotiations. The sheer size of the European Union, for example, makes unimpeded access to the world's markets less crucial ... It is indeed fortunate for the world trading system that the majority of tariff reductions currently in place were negotiated in the 1947 and 1963 sessions of the GATT; that is, prior to the entrenchment of the European Union.* (LeClair, 1997: 9)

Furthermore, in the case of the EC/EU, its own external relations have been, in Raymond Vernon's words, 'explicitly Euro-centric, rather than devoted to the establishment of a trading regime that would eventually have global dimensions'. Those relations have been constructed in an ad hoc fashion and in fact are often 'at odds with the GATT approach' (Vernon, 1991: 546).

   Critics worried about regionalism worry that the resources required to maintain a regional system are likely to be diverted from the maintenance of a global system. As Kahler has put it,

> *The trade and foreign affairs bureaucracy in the [US] government is not large; budgetary stringency and ideological opposition are unlikely to permit substantial growth. A decline in real resources is more likely. Adding responsibility for new regional negotiations that may last for years could soon complicate management of the new dispute settlement mechanism at the WTO and reduce the attention devoted to developing a new WTO agenda.* (Kahler, 1995: 22)

From Europe's perspective, the new American regionalism gives the United States a powerful bargaining chip in multilateral negotiations, enabling it to use 'the threat of a regional option in order to force concessions from Europe in bilateral or global negotiations' (Kahler, 1995: 23). It has already used its role in APEC to gain concessions from the EU in the Uruguay Round. The fact that the United States may be involved in several groupings, and plays a very significant role in all of them, gives it a leverage within the multilateral system different from that enjoyed by the European Union. The asymmetry within these regional groupings can easily work to the advantage of the United States, a point to which we shall return.

   It is not helpful to overstate the importance of regional trading blocs in the world outside of international negotiations and institutions. Business is operating according to a somewhat different logic, as the data on foreign direct investment demonstrate. The emergence of a European–American relationship in which firms are both employers and producers on both sides of the Atlantic cuts across the boundaries of preferential trading areas (Sbragia, 1998). As Raymond Vernon points out, one of the key forces discouraging the emergence of regional trading blocs is the multinationalization of large firms. MNCs operate across regional trading groups and represent a force binding regional groups in a non-governmental framework. The emergence of a 'private transatlantic relationship' (Sbragia, 1998) is an important antidote to the possible regionalization of the world economy.

3. Why NAFTA?

While European integration has been characterized by the understanding that economic integration, along with NATO, would address the security problems of western Europe, the American position on regional integration, by contrast, is based on the decoupling of security and economic integration. The American shift from a position of viewing regional trade agreements as a threat to the stability embodied, in the American view, in multilateral global arrangements has its roots in the changed security environment after November 1989. It is also a response to the perceived success of the then European Community and its magnetic effect on the nation-states of what were once central and eastern Europe. While the United States supported European economic integration in its formative years (Winand, 1993), it has more recently had to react to an integrative initiative which has been far more successful than most would have imagined in the 1950s. The competition between the European Economic Community and the European Free Trade Association (EFTA) was decisively won by the EEC, and the very success of a model based on regional preferential trading arrangements has led the United States to reconsider its own position in support of multilateral rather than regional arrangements.

3.1 The changed security environment

With the end of the Cold War, many of the security concerns which had underlain the American position in favour of multilateral arrangements eroded and became less relevant. It is important to note that the original American position in favour of multilateralism, while undoubtedly compatible with American economic interests, was also formed by the strong conviction that the protectionism of the interwar period had been a leading contributor to the Second World War. From the American perspective, it was imperative that the kinds of protectionism which had marked the 1920s and 1930s be prevented from reappearing, if for no other reason than to prevent the need for American troops once again to engage in combat on European soil.

The link between economics and security was spelled out early in the postwar period, and, although becoming less explicit after that, formed an implicit foundation for the American view of foreign policy (Winand, 1993: 1–5, 112). Multilateralism and security were two sides of a coin, for international trade would promote prosperity which in turn would prevent the emergence of those conditions which lead to devastating war. International trade, of course, was also a necessity for American business; so a position in favour of multilateralism satisfied both those concerned with the potential emergence of military conflict and those concerned with American economic interests. The compatibility of multilateralism (understood as global free trade) and security was stated clearly in Secretary of State Cordell Hull's memoirs:

> *To me, unhampered trade dovetailed with peace; high tariffs, trade barriers, and unfair economic competition with war. Though realizing that many other factors were involved, I reasoned that if we could get a freer flow of trade – freer in the sense of fewer discrim-inations and obstructions – so that one country would not be deadly jealous of another and the living standards of all countries might rise, thereby eliminating the economic dissatisfaction that breeds war, we might have a reasonable chance for lasting peace.* (quoted in Ellwood, 1992: 21–2)

The end of the Cold War and the remoteness of military conflict among the member states of the European Community changed the foreign policy landscape as viewed by American policy-makers. Although the Gulf War represented a major military mobilization for the United States, the lack of a Soviet dimension to that conflict represented a very sharp break with the past. The United States was now operating in a different environment, one in which the link between security and foreign economic policy was much more tenuous than it had been.

3.2 The success of European integration

The American decision to pursue a regional strategy rather than continue to focus exclusively on multilateral options was rooted both in the short-term dissatisfac-tion with the negotiations going on in the Uruguay Round and the longer-term lesson learned from the expansion of the EU (Weintraub, 1997; Boyd, 1997: 151). This latter point is of particular interest. In Sidney Weintraub's words,

> *It was becoming increasingly difficult to persuade the US Congress that the United States should not itself embark on regional trade agreements because of their inherent discrim-ination against non-members in the face of the discrimination exporters from the United States faced in Western Europe. It had become evident that regionalism in Europe would not disappear; if anything, it was expanding to additional countries. Preferential region-alism in Europe, so the argument went, could not be purged by US insistence on multilateralism. This was the ideal context in which to argue that regionalism in Europe is best dealt with by regionalism in North America and that one day – some day – the two regionalisms can come together.* (Weintraub, 1997: 205)

The EU, by its existence and its seeming magnetism to other European countries, was therefore instrumental in changing the long-held American belief in multilater-alism as the dominant strategy. Regionalism was in a sense legitimated by the EU and led American policy-makers to envisage a parallel track in which multilateralism and regionalism could coexist. The symbiotic relationship between the EU and NAFTA is such that the existence of both groupings has led to the current debate on what the most appropriate contours for a global trading system would look like, and whether multilateralism and regionalism can coexist over the long term.

In a feedback loop, the very success of the EU as a customs union with an institutionalized capacity led the United States to change its own international economic policy so as to incorporate a preferential trading area into its portfolio; after NAFTA, it became a member of the APEC group. The United States has thus joined one group in the Americas and one in Asia; so it is not surprising that the notion of a transatlantic free trade area seems to be perennially under consideration in some policy circles.

The success of the EU can be assessed in many ways. Judged by the criterion of whether it has had an impact on American policy, it has been very successful indeed. Interestingly, just as the United States was in a position to support early efforts at European integration, so by the 1990s Europe was organized enough for Miles Kahler to conclude that 'the Commission of the European Union supported completion of NAFTA and found that its trade creation effects were likely to offset any negative economic consequences' (Kahler, 1995: 21). The institutional capacity implied in that statement is of such a magnitude that it is clear that the EU is indeed a system of governance, while NAFTA, albeit the 'most comprehensive free trade pact ever negotiated', is characterized by very weak institutional capacity (GAO, 1993: 8).

4. Institutions

In terms of institutional depth NAFTA is, in comparison with the EU, very thin. There is no equivalent of the European Commission. The NAFTA commission does have headquarters in Mexico City, but does not exist as a continuous organization and cannot make proposals on its own. It is meant to help resolve disputes rather than to propose legislation or provide NAFTA with the administrative capacity so critical to the EU. The lack of institutional capacity, in Weintraub's words, 'was deliberate. The framers wanted to minimize the political content of the agreement' (Weintraub, 1997: 212).

Two commissions do exist: the Commission for Environmental Cooperation, headquartered in Montreal, and the Commission for Labor Cooperation, in Dallas. Furthermore, a North American Development Bank, headquartered in San Antonio, funds infrastructure at the American–Mexican border. Finally, numerous working groups are in place to negotiate some kind of harmonization in a variety of areas, including the safety of trucks moving from Mexico into the north.

Disputes are settled through arbitration rather than a judicial process. There is no equivalent to the ECJ. As we shall argue, however, the dispute resolution process, although very different from that found in the EU, none the less does provide some institutional similarity.

5. NAFTA and the EU: a search for similarities

5.1. Asymmetry

Peter Leslie has recently written that most compound political systems are characterized by asymmetry – that is, some units have more power and/or more privilege than others (Leslie, 2000). A key question has to do with the conditions under which such asymmetry becomes unacceptable to the other units of the system in question.

Clearly, asymmetry does exist within the European Union. EU institutions, however, have deliberately tried to minimize such asymmetry. Although Britain and Denmark, and latterly those two countries plus Ireland, have been allowed to opt out of the Schengen Agreement, in general the *acquis communautaire* has helped promote symmetry. Further, the institutions have attempted to give small countries a degree of power disproportionate to their size. Neither voting weights in the Council of Ministers nor parliamentary representation are calculated strictly according to population, and funds have been allocated to help the poorer members deal with the disruptions inevitably caused by economic liberalization. Most importantly, however, while Germany is the most powerful economy and the largest country in the Union, it does not dwarf the Union's other members.

In NAFTA, by contrast, the United States is the dominant actor in a way very different from the position of Germany within the EU. Simply in terms of trade patterns, trade with the United States dominates NAFTA, whereas trade with its partners is much less important to the United States:

> *Although Canada is the number one trading partner of the United States, and Mexico is number three after Japan, the United States conducts only about one-quarter of its trade with its two North American neighbors. In contrast, more than two-thirds of foreign trade in both Canada and Mexico is with the United States. They have very little direct trade with each other. Put bluntly and somewhat simplistically, foreign trade for Canada and for Mexico means trade with the United States.* (Kehoe, 1994: 7)

Canada was an obvious candidate for a regional partner. It is the largest trading partner of the United States, and US direct investment in Canada is very large. Intra-firm trade is high, as is the incidence of strategic alliances between Canadian and American firms (Weintraub, 1997: 205). When the United States decided to enter a free trade agreement with Mexico, the Canadians decided to join as well (even though Canadian–Mexican trade was small), in order to prevent a 'hub and spoke arrangement ... [in which] the United States would be the hub and Canada and Mexico the spokes and only the United States would have free trade across North America' (Weintraub, 1997: 209).

In some areas, Canada and the United States both enjoy the effects of the asymmetry accompanying the American position. Peter Leslie has recently offered a revision of Belassa's concept of stages of integration (Leslie, 2000). Rather than thinking of a free trade area, a customs union, a common market, an economic union and complete economic integration (*à la* Belassa), Leslie argues we should conceptualize economic union in terms of a trade and investment union (the most basic type), a labour market union, a foreign economic policy union, a monetary union and a structural/development union. Using Leslie's typology, NAFTA is a trade and investment union but is definitely not a labour market union. Neither Canada nor the United States would have approved an agreement which would have allowed the free movement of Mexican workers into the rich economies of the north. Nor is it a foreign economic policy union. NAFTA is not a customs union and therefore has no external dimension. A common external tariff is not in force. Nor is there a common commercial policy. Third parties do not negotiate with NAFTA as they do with the EU; they negotiate with the three member states of NAFTA.

In policy terms, both the United States and Canada had much higher standards of environmental and labour protection than did Mexico. Politically, these two issues came to be associated with the debate over NAFTA in the United States and 'side agreements' in those two areas were negotiated. The North American Agreement on Environmental Cooperation entered into effect on 1 January 1994 along with NAFTA. Under the agreement, both governments and citizens can file complaints if compliance with environmental legislation is weak. Table 5.1 indicates the range of projects which the Commission for Environmental Cooperation (which is funded at $9 million per year) has undertaken to improve environmental cooperation. A bilateral US–Mexican agreement established the North American Development Bank and the Border Environment Cooperation Commission, to help fund environmental infrastructure and community development projects along the border.

Although there seems to be a general view that the Commission for Environmental Cooperation has raised the awareness of environmental issues in Mexico and has led to somewhat greater enforcement, its work has been dogged by complaints from the Mexican government that its wishes are not considered early enough in the process of identifying projects. Understaffing has been severe, with the United States assigning only one staff member to oversee implementation.

In the case of labour, the North American Agreement on Labor Cooperation also came into effect with NAFTA. This agreement is a very visible one, as it is 'the first international agreement to link labor issues to an international trade pact' (GAO, 1997: 27). A Commission for Labor Cooperation was established which for a variety of reasons became operational only in September 1995; in 1996 it was funded at only $1.6 million because of Mexico's financial crisis. One of its major functions is to promote awareness in the NAFTA countries of each other's labour systems. As Table 5.2 indicates, the Commission's work includes the dissemination of information on a variety of labour issues.

Table 5.1   Regional cooperation projects undertaken by NAFTA's Commission for Environmental Cooperation

Work programme area	*Examples*
Conservation	Developing plans to conserve and protect North American birds and monarch butterflies
	Developing plans to establish a North American Biodiversity Information Network
	Developing plans to implement strategies to protect regional marine life
Protecting human health and the environment	Coordinating the completion of regional action plans for PCBs, DDT, chlordane and mercury
	Coordinating the completion of transboundary environmental impact assessment procedures by April 1998
Environment, trade and the economy	Funding and facilitating the creation of an information clearing-house on environment technology and services
	'NAFTA Effects' projects:
	NAFTA intergovernmental institutions study, completed in 1997;
	refining the general framework for assessing NAFTA's environmental impacts by completing a study on the environmental effects of the deregulation of the energy and agriculture sectors, completed in 1998
Enforcement cooperation	Groups established under this programme have met and exchanged information, strategies and expertise on enforcement, compliance and legal trends
Information and public outreach	Enhancements to the commission's website that will provide regional information on the environmental dimensions of physical, socioeconomic and ecological variables

PCB = Polychlorinated biphenyl
DDT = Dichloro-diphenyl trichloro-ethane
Source: GAO, 1997: 20; European Commission website, www.cec.org, 31 Jan. 2000.

5.2 Environment–trade linkage

It is striking that although NAFTA is only, to use Peter Leslie's term, a trade and investment union, it has dealt with environmental protection. Although the inspiration for both the EU and NAFTA was the desire to increase trade and liberalize economies, environmental protection became an important impulse for both groups. In the case of the EU, environmental protection represented the first major policy area added to the Community's reach after a customs union was achieved (Sbragia, 1996), while in the case of NAFTA the agreement could not even be ratified without

Table 5.2   Regional cooperation projects undertaken by NAFTA's Commission for Labor Cooperation

Selected areas of cooperation	*Recent examples*
Occupational safety and health	North American Occupational Safety and Health Week, held May 1999 simultaneously in each country
	Completion of 'Petrochemical Study Tour' on prevention of catastrophic explosions (October 1996)
Human resource development	Workshop on Continuous Learning and Development in the Workplace (April 1996)
Labour management relations	Tripartite conference on 'Industrial Relations for the Twenty-first Century' (March 1996)
Productivity improvement	North American seminar on incomes and productivity
Labor statistics	Report profiling North American labour markets (June 1997)

Source: GAO, 1997: 25; Department of Labor website, 13 Jan. 2000.

an environmental side agreement. The addition of environmental protection to the NAFTA negotiations 'took US and Mexican policymakers by surprise early in the negotiating process' (Gilbreath and Tonra, 1994: 53). Trade negotiators were forced to deal with an issue which often seems alien to them. Whereas environmental policy was incorporated into the EC through the institutional mechanisms of the Community, and was only later incorporated into an intergovernmental treaty (the Single European Act of 1986), in NAFTA the environmental dimension of economic liberalization was accorded such importance that the environmental agreement was negotiated alongside the trade agreement.

The trade–environment link represents an important issue for thinking about the relative costs and benefits of multilateral and regional agreements and groupings. Economists generally argue that free trade is benefited by multilateral rather than regional agreements. Environmentalists, by contrast, are likely to argue that regional agreements are more likely to lead to increased environmental cooperation and environmental protection.

The difference between the fate of environmental protection in global institutions concerned with trade liberalization and in regional cooperative arrangements such as the EU and NAFTA has to do with the relative power of the 'green' states within those groupings. The 'green troika' of the Netherlands, Denmark and Germany has spearheaded the EU's movement in the field of environmental policy and has helped to ensure that southern European countries have a more comprehensive framework for environmental protection than they would have adopted on their own (Sbragia, 1996). Similarly, the pressure on American negotiators from a coalition of environmental groups led the American government to give an importance to environmental protection which clearly the Mexican government would not have given if operating unilaterally. As Richard Steinberg argues,

> *trade–environment rules in the NAFTA are far more developed and environment friendly than in the GATT/WTO, because integration is deeper and green country power more concentrated in the NAFTA ... Unlike the GATT/WTO, which has only the Committee on Trade and Environment to focus exclusively on trade–environment issues, the NAFTA created a broad set of institutions charged with that exclusive focus and with ensuring adherence to specified standards of environmental protection. These institutions perform legislative, judicial and administrative functions ... Like the GATT/WTO, the NAFTA has a dispute settlement process that grants standing only to party governments. But unlike the GATT/WTO, the NAFTA allows environmental NGOs to take formal action that may indirectly initiate a dispute.* (Steinberg, 1997: 245, 247, 248)

The focus on trade–environment issues, and the relatively deep institutionalization of that dimension within an organizational framework characterized by lack of institutional capacity, is a striking example of the 'ratcheting up' effect which takes place when wealthy 'green' countries negotiate with poorer 'brown' countries to liberalize regional trade. Trade and environment are now linked when powerful green countries become involved in regional groupings.

5.3 Dispute settlement

One of the surprising features of the European Community has been the emergence of the ECJ as one of its most important institutions. Although the Court was originally viewed as a means of settling rather technical disputes, it eventually emerged as an institution which actually 'constitutionalized' the Treaty of Rome (Alter, 1998; Sweet and Brunell, 1998). The role of European law is now so important that it is difficult to talk about European integration without incorporating a discussion of the European legal system. Scholars now argue about how best to explain a phenomenon which is so unexpected that it clearly needs to be explained (see e.g. Alter, 1998; Mattli and Slaughter, 1998; Garrett et al., 1998; Mullen, 1998).

Although nothing comparable to the ECJ exists within NAFTA, it is interesting that the dispute resolution procedure has become institutionalized within the Canadian–American framework to a surprising degree. Under the CFTA, either Canada or the United States can request that a binational panel review decisions made by administrative agencies in the areas of anti-dumping and countervailing duties to see if domestic law has indeed been followed. The panel's decision is binding and replaces domestic judicial review. Rather than keep trade disputes within the national bureaucracy – in the US case, the International Trade Administration (ITA) in the Department of Commerce and the International Trade Commission (ITC) – both countries agreed to have trade disputes resolved at the international rather than domestic level. The institutional apparatus agreed to by Canada and the United States was subsequently incorporated into NAFTA (Goldstein, 1996).

The consequences of this dispute resolution procedure have been significant enough to force the American bureaucracy to change the way it handles trade disputes with Canada and Mexico. The decisions have been pro-Canadian and much less protectionist than they would have been if made by the American bureaucracy. Judith Goldstein argues that

> *the FTA and later NAFTA have created a dispute-settlement mechanism that can and has fundamentally altered the behavior of the US bureaucracy. This occurred because binational boards – with more liberal preferences – became the last mover in unfair trade cases, a position previously held by the courts. This enabled importers, frustrated by a decision by the US trade bureaucracy, to choose to petition to a forum in which they had a higher chance of getting their preferred outcome. Binational boards institutionalized their preferences by stipulating acceptable procedures with each remand ... The outcome is what Canada and Mexico had hoped for: greater relief from US unfair trade law.* (Goldstein, 1996: 555)

In this case, we find that administrative agencies and domestic courts – which tended to be deferential to the administrative agencies – were circumvented by the creation of international panels, the decisions of which were binding. The outcome was less protectionist and more favourable to trade than would have been the outcome if national processes had been left to work in their usual fashion.

6. Conclusion

The creation and institutional features of NAFTA reflect the changed international environment in which the United States now operates, its reluctance to institutionalize arrangements which may impinge on its sovereignty, the power of environmental NGOs within the American political system, and the basic fact that its market and international power are such that asymmetry is likely to be an important feature of any regional grouping to which the United States belongs. NAFTA is not the beginning of some kind of integration within the Americas analogous to the integration we have seen in Europe; rather, it is a strategy designed to respond to specific challenges facing the United States in its external environment. It allows the United States to pursue a regional strategy which may, under some conditions, actually increase its leverage within the multilateral framework to which it has long been committed.

One of the domestic factors which will limit the future institutionalization of NAFTA is the power of the US Congress. Far more powerful than any European parliament, and much less constrained by the discipline of political parties, the American Congress stands as a bulwark against the kind of integration which would in any way 'pool sovereignty'. To the extent that institutions are created that could override domestic decisions, they will need to be cloaked in the institutions of dispute resolution. The world of free trade is as likely to be characterized by the judge as by the businessman.

Note

1   I thank Lawrence Graham, University of Texas, for pointing this out to me.

6. Comparison of European and Southeast Asian Integration

Kjell A. Eliassen and Catherine Børve Monsen[1]

1. Introduction

The main aim of this chapter is to investigate how and why regional organizational structures and integrating mechanisms differ between various regions of the world. There exist numerous studies of European integration, and a substantial literature on regional integration in other parts of the world, including Pacific Asia, is now emerging. There are, however, few studies comparing in a scientific way the European and the Asian models of regional integration (exceptions are Holland, 1994; Higgott, 1995; Milner, 1995), although this theme is touched upon more generally in the analyses of regional integration (e.g. Katzenstein, 1996).

The Asian currency and economic crisis of 1997–8 has generated a vast range of scientific literature (Gill, 1998; Henderson, 1998; Montes, 1998; Pape, 1998). Most of these studies focus on both the factors contributing to the crisis and its possible effects; but in their assessments of its impact, few scholars focus explicitly on the future role of regional integration in the difficult situation in which most of the Southeast Asian countries now find themselves. Recent developments show, however, that the crisis has had a profound effect on various aspects of regional cooperation, including the nature of relations between the countries of the region and the degree of institutionalization. One of the main questions to be addressed is whether the crisis will in fact lead to greater integration, and to new forms of multilateral cooperation. Answers to this question will vary according to the time-span under consideration: it is possible to identify certain short- and medium-term trends on the basis of events during the past couple of years, but any assessment of the long-term implications cannot be other than tentative. The persistent instability in Indonesia, which shows no sign of resolution at the time of writing, further complicates the picture.

In this chapter we will study differences in the organizational structure and integrating mechanisms of regional groupings by comparing the development of the European Union (EU) to that of the Association of South-East Asian Nations (ASEAN). An important characteristic of the new regionalism, as represented by, for example, ASEAN, is the very wide variation in the level of institutionalization, with many regional groupings consciously avoiding the institutional and bureaucratic structures of traditional international organizations and of the regionalist model represented by the EU (Garnaut and Drysdale, 1994).[2] On the other hand, Gills (1997) and others have argued that the European economic model and the Asian one are not so different from one another, either historically or in their current forms. 'Institutional' elements, commonly seen as characteristic of the European model, are present in the Asian model; and the 'network' element, seen as more typical of the Asian model, is substantially present in the European system – for example in the practice of lobbying. The tendency has often been to overstate the differences between the forms taken by regionalism in these two parts of the world.

In the first of the sections that follow, we discuss the revival of regional integration. The next two parts of the chapter contain studies of the different mechanisms of regional integration and types of institutional arrangements adopted in Europe and Asia respectively, taking the EU and ASEAN as examples of two quite successful regional cooperating organizations. Having compared the French-inspired EU model of legal and institutional integration with the ASEAN pattern of network cooperation, it is a natural next step to ask why they differ. In the course of an attempt to explain the disparities, we will investigate the main reasons behind regional integration and why different regions produce different logics of integration. We consider whether varying historical, political, economic and cultural patterns have an impact on the differences between the two regional organizations; in this context we give particular emphasis to the economic crisis in Asia, which arguably has had a profound impact on political, social and even cultural patterns in the Southeast Asian countries. The persisting conditions of crisis in the region create both opportunities for and obstacles to greater regional integration. Our analysis will highlight the trends that seem to dominate the current situation, and these will be explained with reference to, among other factors, aspects of state-making in Asia.

Why then, should we compare these two groupings, ASEAN and the EU, rather than any other organizations? ASEAN is perhaps one of the regional organizations most similar to the EU when it comes to the scope and range of the activities covered. We feel that an analysis of similarities and differences between these two institutions of regional cooperation can make an interesting contribution to understanding the role of intergovernmental institutions in various regional responses to the globalization process. Furthermore, regional integration in Europe, it emerges, has in fact been sub-regional integration: the construction of institutional structures to combine the interests of a group of countries within a wider region (Wallace, 1995). Seen from this perspective, the EU is more directly comparable, in global terms, with ASEAN than with, for instance, the Asia–Pacific Economic Cooperation forum (APEC).

Our investigation will be based on a review of existing studies of European and Asian regional integration in general, and of the few attempts hitherto made to compare the EU and ASEAN. However, before embarking on the comparative analysis, it is necessary to consider the revival of regional integration more generally and the principal varieties of regionalism.

2. The revival of regional integration

Economic and political development across the world in recent years has been characterized by both increased globalization and a reduction in the number and significance of borders for trade and commerce. Simultaneously we have seen an expansion of regional integration within every continent, as well as closer cooperation between the different regional groupings.

The period since the late 1980s has witnessed a resurgence of regionalism in world politics. Old regionalist organizations have been revived and new ones formed; and regionalism, coupled with the call for strengthened regionalist arrangements, has been central to many of the debates about the nature of the post-Cold War international order. The revival of political and academic interest in regionalism has been associated with a number of developments, including the end of the Cold War and the erosion of the Cold War alliance systems; the recurrent fears over the stability of the GATT and the multilateral trading order during the long-drawn-out negotiation of the Uruguay Round; the impact of increasing economic integration and globalization; changed attitudes towards economic development in many parts of the developing world; and the impact of democracy and democratization (Fawcett and Hurrell, 1995: 1).

The political salience of regionalism increased significantly as a result of developments within Europe, the successful negotiation and ratification of the North American Free Trade Area (NAFTA), and the increased momentum of cooperative efforts within ASEAN and continuing discussions within the Asia–Pacific region over new economic and security agreements, as reflected in the formation of APEC, the Pacific Economic Cooperation Council (PECC) and the ASEAN Regional Forum (ARF) (Garnaut and Drysdale, 1994). We have even witnessed the development of inter-regional cooperation, as for example in the EU–ASEAN cooperation programme and the EU–Asia cooperation organization (Cho and Chung, 1997).

Since the late 1980s we have observed fundamental changes in the functioning of the world economy and how the multinational companies run their operations, characterized by both increased volumes and increased liberalization of trade, not only within trading blocs but also on a global basis. At the same time, rapid technological development has made the world smaller and altered the conditions for commercial operations. Information, telecommunications and media activity have been crucial in shaping the trading environment, and have contributed to a global restructuring of the companies' production and distribution orders.

In many cases, this evolution has resulted in increasing regional integration. One reason for this may be that globalization and liberalization have led to a diminution of national governments' control over their respective national economies, prompting the industrialized countries at least to attempt to gain compensation through a degree of regional control. The next step will be to exercise control not only within their own region, but also across other regions, in order to retain the political control which the individual countries have lost (Oman, 1994).

The revival of interest in regionalism and regionalist projects needs to be seen within a global perspective (Fawcett and Hurrell, 1995: 3; Higgott, 1997). The fact that regionalist projects have emerged in so many parts of the world suggests that broad international forces may be at work, and that any single-region focus is imperfect. While intraregional dynamics remain important, the resurgence in regionalism needs to be related to changes in the global system, for instance the emergence of an economic system in which state policies are shaped to an ever-increasing extent by the structure and dynamics of an increasingly global world economy, and of a political system in which the boundaries between the 'domestic' and the 'international' arenas have become increasingly blurred.

The return of regionalism to the international agenda has not been universally welcomed; nevertheless, both optimists and pessimists agree that regionalism is on the increase. The end of the Cold War had an important impact on global economic change and the transformation of the international system, and this, together with the passing of the Single European Act in 1986, marked the turning-point in the fortunes of regionalism (Fawcett and Hurrell, 1995: 9). These and other contributory factors have resulted in a proliferation of new regional groupings and a recovery of older regional bodies. What distinguishes this wave of regional activity from others is its truly global nature.

Recent debates suggest that the broad term 'regionalism' is used to cover a variety of distinct phenomena. Rather than trying to work with a single, very broad, overarching concept, it is helpful to break up the notion of regionalism into five different categories: regionalization; regional awareness and identity; regional interstate cooperation; state-promoted regional integration; and regional cohesion (Hurrell, 1995: 39). We will briefly consider what each of these involves.

Regionalization refers to the growth of societal integration within a region and to the often undirected processes of social and economic interaction. Regional awareness and regional identity are inherently imprecise and diffuse notions; it is, however, impossible to ignore them, since they have become more central to the analysis of contemporary regionalism. The emphasis of regional awareness is on language and rhetoric, means by which definitions of regional identity are constantly defined and redefined. Regional interstate cooperation can be of a formal or informal nature; a high level of institutionalization is no guarantee of either effectiveness or political importance. Regional cooperation can entail the creation of formal institutions, but it can often be based on a much looser structure, involving patterns of regular meetings with some rules attached, together with mechanisms for preparation and follow-up. This issue will be discussed in more depth later in this chapter. Regional integration can refer to the legal and institutional relationships within a region in which economic transactions take place, or it can refer to the market relationship among goods and factors within a region (Cooper, 1994: 11). State-promoted regional integration involves specific policy decisions by governments designed to reduce or remove barriers for the mutual exchange of goods, services, capital and people. These policies have drawn a great deal of attention to the processes of integration, on the paths that it might take, and on the objectives that it might fulfil. Regional cohesion refers to the possibility that a combination of the four categories just mentioned might lead to the emergence of a cohesive and consolidated regional unit. It is this potential for cohesion that makes regionalism of particular interest to the study of international relations. These different categories are important aspects of this chapter, and will be used as a general framework for our analysis.

Several different types of regional cooperation exist around the world today. They may be distinguished from one another in respect to how successful they have become, how they are organized and how they operate. The limited scope of this chapter does not allow us to give a full description of the majority of these institutions, or of the way they operate; and it would be impossible to give a general picture of the differences they present. For these reasons we will focus here on the EU and ASEAN, each in its own field a relatively successful example of a particular kind of regional cooperation organization. The EU is based on French-inspired legal and institutional integration models, while ASEAN can be characterized as far more network-based. We will investigate to what extent and how the two organizations differ, both in organizational structure and in integration mechanisms.

There are obviously similarities between the EU and ASEAN; but the focus in this investigation will be concentrated on how the two groupings differ. For example, both are characterized as regional organizations; but the nature of these organizations appears to be different. Again, we can find networks in Europe as well as in Asia; but we will attempt to show here that the nature of the networks is different in the two contexts. Trying to explain these disparities, we will investigate what the main reasons behind regional integration are, and the two regions generate different types of integration logic. We will also conduct an analysis of the varying historical, political, economic and cultural patterns in Europe and Southeast Asia. Before embarking on such an investigation, however, we need to describe the two organizations. We begin in the next section with a description of the European Union.

3. The EU: institution-based integration

There exist various descriptions of the EU, its history, construction, functioning, decision-making processes, etc. Since its birth as the European Economic Community in the 1950s, however, it has mainly been analysed as an example of the *supranational integration* of, or *intergovernmental cooperation* between, (previously) sovereign nation-states (Hix, 1994). Analysis of European integration has been dominated by two contrasting theoretical perspectives on the nature of politics and the process of change within the EC/EU: neo-functionalism and inter-governmentalism (Rhodes and Mazey, 1995).

Many see real movement in the direction of a polity, as individuals, corporations and government actors increasingly identify with, and act according to, European-level institutions and processes (Rhodes and Mazey, 1995). Others view the EU as the site of an ongoing struggle of give and take between member states, where no real European polity has emerged. However, most of these descriptions share the common feature of a focus on the legal and institutional aspects of the EU. In recent years, moreover, there has been a marked shift away from the traditional emphasis by analysts on national governments as the key actors in EU policy-making towards a broader examination of the relative roles of the various actors involved in the EU policy process. The impact of lobbying by organized interests has come under scrutiny (Andersen and Eliassen, 1993; Mazey and Richardson, 1993; Greenwood, 1997), and increasing attention has been paid to the role of policy networks at the European level (Bomberg, 1994; Peterson, 1992, 1995).

In addition, the role played by the European institutions themselves has received growing attention as an 'institutional-matter' perspective on EU policy-making has begun to gain ground (Bulmer, 1994a; Peterson, 1992, 1995). Neo-institutionalist views emphasized institutions as the main actors in European integration. From this perspective, integration is driven by internal institutional logic, characterized by elite predominance. The neo-institutional approach illustrates how deeply divided or segmented societies can remain stable as a result of behaviour and rules that produce 'elite accommodation' (Lijphart, 1984). In the European case, the important new element in regional integration introduced in the Treaty of Rome was the supranational institutions: the European Commission, the European Parliament and the European Court of Justice. This new element meant that, from the outset in the 1950s, the European Community had a potential for taking the initiative that no other regional organization had previously had.

The European Commission acts independently of the national governments and exclusively in the interest of the Union; it has, with very few exceptions, the responsibility for initiating legislation (Edwards and Spence, 1995). The main obligations for the European Parliament are budget, legislation and control authority. Direct contacts between the European Commission and the Parliament are growing, which has created a basis for more autonomous EU decision-making, independent of national interests. The European Court of Justice holds a central position in the overall EU system, its purpose being to safeguard the enforcement of European directives in the member countries. The interpretation of European law, and the final decision on its application, are vested in the Court of Justice (Andersen and Eliassen, 1993: 26).

There are several possible reasons why the priority of supranationalism has been maintained in the EU. A central element is the model of strong nation-states in

Europe which themselves have experienced state- and nation-building processes. Another reason could be the influence of federal models from the United States. Also, the six founding member states can be characterized as relatively homogeneous countries, both politically and economically. However, the existence of supranational institutions has not prevented problems arising, or a lack of dynamism in the development of the EU. That dynamism appeared in the 1980s with another kind of 'supranationality' through majority voting in the European Council.

This points to the other dominant feature of the development of regionalism in Europe: in addition to strong supranational institutions, a major role has been played by nation-states and governments, both in the further development of regional integration and in current policy shaping in the EU. This stands in contrast to other attempts at regional integration. The EEC was established as a result of the Treaty of Rome in 1957, and the legal basis of the Community has continuously been changed as a result of new intergovernmental conferences. At the same time, the European Council functions as the EU's most important executive and legislative authority. Economic and political integration is, thus, first and foremost, a result of nation-state politics.

The first major revision of the Treaty of Rome, the Single European Act (SEA), was signed in 1986 and entered into force in 1987. The SEA settled a plan for the completion of the internal market and introduced majority voting. It is widely considered a turning-point in the integration process in western Europe. In addition to having a major impact on economic integration, the SEA also gave a new impetus to European political cooperation (EPC). 'For the first time in history, political cooperation received a legal basis' (Regelsberger, 1988). The SEA provided the EC with a legal basis for the internal market, rules for majority voting, an outspoken commitment to further social and economic cohesion, a framework for further development of concerted action in the area of foreign policy and, not least important, a new role for the European Parliament through the codecision procedure. This first major revision of the EC's constitutional basis 'brought together in one "single" act a treaty on European cooperation in the area of foreign policy and institutional and procedural reforms' (Nelsen and Stubb, 1994).

The Treaty on European Union signed at Maastricht on 7 February 1992, which came into force on 1 November 1993, created a new European Union based on the European Community, marking 'a new stage' in the process of creating an ever closer union among the peoples of Europe (Duff, 1994). The Maastricht Treaty has further expanded the scope to include education, culture, public health, industry and some other policy areas within the remit of the EU. Much of the treaty followed well-tried precedent, building on past EC treaties and on the corpus of law and policy made by the common institutions over forty years. In addition, the Maastricht Treaty made a division of policy areas into three 'pillars'. The first amends the EEC, ECSC and Euratom Treaties and is formally named the European Community (governed on a supranational level). The second pillar concerns foreign and security policy and is built upon the existing intergovernmental procedures of

EPC. The third covers justice and home affairs. Other provisions of Maastricht were intended to respond to new external challenges, including enlargement.

After the triumph of agreement on the Maastricht Treaty in December 1991, however, the EU was faced with a series of problems concerning its adoption: the ratification process; getting the member countries to cooperate on the foreign affairs front (in the Gulf War and the Bosnian crisis); creating an economic recovery after the worst depression in Europe since the Second World War; and the near-collapse of the European Exchange Rate Mechanism, which was designed to serve as the basis for a European Monetary Union (EMU). All of these things to a greater or lesser extent shows the inability of the EU to live up to expectations. Was this evidence of a failure of European cooperation, or was it just a minor setback in the process of European integration?

Nearly eight years on from the signing of the Maastricht Treaty, during which time it has been followed by the Amsterdam Treaty, we have seen that European cooperation has again progressed in a range of areas. The internal market was, following a few setbacks, put into effect as planned. The Schengen Agreement, which deals with the abolition of border controls, is going to be put into practice in more countries than originally planned. And EMU was activated on 1 January 1999, representing perhaps the most important contribution to a further deepening of the integration process in the years to come.

The EU may be considered quite successful in both the political and the economic arena. Although progress in achieving the objectives of the internal market has varied in line with fluctuations in the world economic cycle,[3] a common European political and economic arena is taking shape. As defined by the SEA, the EU's internal market is 'an area without internal frontiers in which the free movement of goods, persons, services and capital is ensured in accordance with the provisions of this treaty' (Roney, 1995). It is an attempt to remove the physical, technical and fiscal barriers to trade. The Act has increased the importance of the European Parliament, established EU social dialogue, and introduced the qualified majority rule in several political areas that were earlier ruled by unanimity. Although there are difficult policy areas in the EU, for instance employment, energy policy, and matters covered by the second and third pillars, the competence of the Commission has increased within such areas as education, culture, telecommunications, banking, transport, small and medium-sized companies, and the environment (Andersen and Eliassen, 1993: 22). The SEA, the Maastricht Treaty in particular, and to a certain degree also the Amsterdam Treaty have broadened the scope and variety of policy issues which will be influenced by the EU. In the future almost all national policy areas will have a European dimension (Andersen and Eliassen, 1993: 12), based on a strong EU secretariat.

How, then, does this European situation compare to the development of a regional grouping in Asia?

4. ASEAN: network-based integration

In the Pacific Ocean and in most of Southeast Asia we can find a somewhat different pattern of regional integration, as economic integration in the Asia–Pacific region develops in its own very distinctive way. Our argument here will be that unlike in Europe, where governments have played a key role in forging regional frameworks that have served to shape regional business activity, in the Asia–Pacific region it has been the activities of the business community which have to a great extent forced governments to consider ways of regularizing regional relations. Economic integration in Southeast Asia is a result of trade and business operations, which have forced through a minimum of regional economic integration arrangements (Gallant and Stubbs, 1996). Certainly, as one author has noted, the economic interactions we see in the region, including within ASEAN, be they investment choices, trade patterns or capital flows, are not being significantly affected by a regionally based regime (Aggarwal, 1994). This holds true at least for the first part of the 1990s.

As we shall see later, in our analysis of different patterns of regional integration, the theoretical explanations of integration used in the European case do not transfer well to Asia. To some extent, network theory might give the best explanation of the Asian integration process. However, during recent years we have observed an emerging need for institution-building in the ASEAN region in particular.

The foundation of ASEAN, on 8 August 1967 by the signing of the Bangkok Declaration, was the most progressive attempt to date to build a formalized regional integration organization in Southeast Asia.[4] When representatives from Indonesia, Malaysia, the Philippines, Singapore and Thailand established the Association, they held out a bold vision of all countries in Southeast Asia cooperating actively towards peace, stability, progress and prosperity in the region. The ASEAN nations came together with the aim of promoting the economic, social and cultural development of the region through cooperative programmes, safeguarding the political and economic stability of the region against big power rivalry, and serving as a forum for the resolution of intraregional differences (CEC, 1996). However, the Vietnam War and the threat of communist diffusion towards other parts of the Pacific Ocean is regarded as the proximate reason for the establishment of the organization. ASEAN is thus a good example of how economic regionalism can be a mechanism by which broader security and political goals can be pursued, rather than the stress falling on specific questions of economic integration as in the European example (Fawcett and Hurrell, 1995: 4). Political questions totally dominated the first fifteen years of ASEAN's operations, with the progress of economic cooperation largely of a symbolic character. The latter included the declaration of increased economic cooperation at the Bali summit in 1976, the ASEAN industry project plan, the ASEAN industry cooperation plan and the ASEAN preference trade agreement in 1997 (PTA). An example of the symbolic character of such economic cooperation is that even though 16,000 products were listed under the

PTA agreement they accounted for just one per cent of all intra-ASEAN trade (Bernard and Ravenhill, 1995).

After the end of the Cold War and the move towards political normalization in Indochina, ASEAN was able and indeed obliged to outline new projects inside the economic area, which could increase the importance of the organization for its members. At the fourth ASEAN summit in Singapore at the end of January 1992, the heads of government signed a 'Framework Agreement on Enhancing ASEAN Economic Cooperation', which committed the six to the establishment of an ASEAN free trade area (AFTA). The purpose of this agreement was to reduce all tariff rates for intra-ASEAN trade in industrial and agricultural products to zero within fifteen years. AFTA is due to be completed in ASEAN–6 (the five founder members plus Brunei) by the end of 2002 and in Vietnam three years later. Laos and Myanmar will have ten years to complete AFTA, from 1998 to 2007.

In view of the experience of ASEAN's earlier attempts at economic cooperation, it is uncertain how effective AFTA will become. One problem is the lack of bureaucratic preparations inside AFTA. Free trade within a regional organization requires a well-developed administrative apparatus, and ASEAN has only limited administrative capacity. Another problem is the absence of institutions that can enforce the agreement. However, there is potential for the agreement to be successfully implemented in the present political and economic climate in Southeast Asia.

ASEAN also established the ASEAN Regional Forum (ARF), which apart from the ASEAN countries includes several other Asian countries,[5] as well as Russia, the EU, the United States, Canada, Australia and New Zealand. ARF has been assigned the major task that has preoccupied ASEAN since its inception, namely, maintaining peace and stability in the region. In addition, it is helping to ease China's integration into international and regional structures.

After the foreign ministers' meeting in Kuala Lumpur on 24 July 1997, ASEAN – the region's most exclusive club – now consists of nine member states. Two new members were signed up at that meeting: Laos and Myanmar (Burma); Cambodia was not, owing to the *coup d'état* that took place in the month before the meeting. It is possible that this enlargement, and not least ASEAN's new attitude towards the future treatment of Cambodia, namely to monitor political developments and encourage stabilization, will lead to increased institutionalization in the region. It is hard to run crisis-prevention and stabilization work, as well as building confidence, without institutions.

Unlike the EU, ASEAN is an organization with no supranational authority. New members are expected to blend themselves into the membership and adopt the so-called 'ASEAN way' of defence: a positive attitude, quiet diplomacy and goodwill in consultations to achieve consensus and strengthen solidarity (Chalermpalanupap, 1997). ASEAN membership does increase the importance of the regional dimension in the policy-making process of the new members. However, political cooperation in ASEAN, unlike economic cooperation in the region and unlike political cooperation in the EU, involves little or no internal adjustment. Each member still develops its own political system and its own governmental structure. The reality is that national interests and preferences remain a major determinant of the possibilities of economic cooperation within ASEAN (Acharya, 1997).

One major difference between integration in Europe and integration in Asia can be characterized as that between formal and informal integration. Formal integration is described as that which is formalized by the establishment of institutions and common regulations in order to control the relationship between nation-states, as in APEC in Asia and the EU in Europe. Although there are examples of formal integration in Asia,[6] the major form of regional cooperation in this area of the world is informal integration. It is mainly the informal track that distinguishes the Southeast Asian pattern from the patterns prevailing in other regions (Peng, 1997), and for this reason it should be given particular attention. The informal track includes the production networks, sub-regional economic zones (SREZs) and ethnic business networks.

What then, are the reasons for the great differences between the integration patterns of Europe and Southeast Asia?

5. Explaining different patterns of regional integration

After having described how EU and ASEAN differ, with a particular focus on variations in organizational structure and institutional mechanisms, two questions arise: first, what are the main reasons behind regional integration, and why have these driving forces produced different types of integration logic in the two regions? And second, to what extent and how are these differences linked to variations in historical, political, economic and cultural patterns? A further interesting question is why institutionalized cooperation in the Asian region has proceeded so slowly in contrast to the rapidly expanding regional integration in terms of policy cooperation. Why is informal cooperation particularly strong in Southeast Asia?

These are very complicated questions, and there are several relevant elements that have to be taken into account when attempting to answer them. First of all, however, we have to consider the difference between a political and a chronological time perspective when comparing EU and ASEAN. To what extent is it fair to compare ASEAN today with EU today? The EU has both been in existence for longer, and in previous times developed much more rapidly than ASEAN. Perhaps, then, it is more reasonable to seek comparable political time periods, and compare, for example, the EU in the 1970s with ASEAN today. If we do this, then the differences between the two organizations concerning supranationality and organizational development remain significant, but the contrast between a successful versus a slow development of regional cooperation is not so marked.

The motivating forces behind regional integration can be explained in political and economic terms. According to Katzenstein (1996), regional integration is attractive on a number of economic grounds. First of all, relations with neighbouring countries stimulate increased trade and investment relations. Secondly, such economic relations with neighbours do not demand the kind of reciprocity that the World Trade Organization (WTO) usually does. Third, efficiency and ability to compete at a regional level are usually strengthened by global liberalization. Finally, the effects of regional economies of scale and savings in transport costs can create dynamic effects which reinforce economic growth.

We find good examples of the role and importance of these arguments for regional integration in the European case. The revitalizing of the EU through the single market was a direct consequence of a wish to make Europe competitive compared to the United States and Asia. Eliminating obstacles to the free movement of goods, persons, services and capital across country borders is an important way of increasing competitiveness (EIU, 1997: 99). The aim of the single market was to bring about market integration, shrinking the obstacles to trade and creating such a large domestic market that global companies with a base in the EU could be developed. This would imply restructuring industries and companies on the basis of comparative advantage and economies of scale. Both reduced prices and larger profits would result, which also would benefit research and development as well as the competitiveness of the businesses.

The reasons behind and the success of the SEA and the internal market can be explained in economic terms (Balassa, 1961; Kindleberger, 1973; Cooper, 1994; Summers, 1991; Bhagwati, 1993; Krugman, 1993; Young, 1993; Baldwin and Venables, 1994); but it can also be accounted for in terms of political integration theory. The great success of the internal market was seen to confirm the applicability of neo-functionalist theory. From a neo-functionalistic perspective, the Maastricht Treaty represents an integrationist impulse that is likely to strengthen the supranational institutions and responsibilities of the Union. The neo-functionalists state it as a fact that Maastricht was a spillover from the SEA; it followed the logic of the earlier treaty, which made it possible. However, intergovernmentalism has also frequently been used to explain the success of the internal market. From an intergovernmental perspective the EU remains, despite the 1993 initiative, the creation and instrument of national politics and national interests that will continue to constrain integrationist impulses within it.

ASEAN was in 1967 created mainly as a political cooperation organization, with the aim of stopping the further expansion of communism in the region. From the very beginning, however, economic cooperation was thought to be an important part of this defence against revolutionary movements. Gradually the focus of the organization has been turned more and more on to economic and social cooperation. Thus the economic theories of regional integration fit well in explaining the development of ASEAN. One important difference between EU and ASEAN identified above is the lack of supranational institutions in Asian organizations. At the same time, ASEAN does not cover the same policy areas as the EU, and has only a limited degree of free trade among its members. Thus it is difficult to apply the type of political integration theories used in respect of the EU to explain the development of ASEAN.

The ASEAN Free Trade Area (AFTA) attempts to abolish all customs duties among the member countries, which is one step – the first – towards establishing a common market. The Common Effective Preferential Tariff (CEPT) is the main implementing mechanism of AFTA, and provides for member countries gradually to lower tariffs on each other's imports. The aim is to turn ASEAN into a truly free trade area over a fifteen-year period. AFTA involves several areas of cooperation, including the harmonization of standards, the reciprocal recognition of tests and certification, the removal of barriers to foreign investments, macroeconomic consultations, rules for fair competition, and the promotion of venture capital. Nevertheless, the absence within ASEAN of supranational institutions and an ambiguous legislative programme make AFTA more like EFTA than like the EU single market.

In attempting to find a suitable theory of political integration to describe this development, the intergovernmental perspective may offer the best focus. The liberal intergovernmentalist approach assumes that the member states of the EU remain the key actors in determining outcomes in European integration issues. The driving force for these actors is interstate bargaining, concerned with national interests and member states' capabilities. Within ASEAN, it is certainly the case that national interests and preferences remain a major determinant of the possibilities of economic cooperation. As Kusuma Snitwongse (1990) notes, progress in economic cooperation will require a model of development that is acceptable to all because it promises equal benefit, and, at the same time, a greater political will to sacrifice at least some national interests for the welfare of the whole. Yet, as she concedes, in the case of ASEAN, national interests have priority over regional ones.

Increased trade and global liberalization are not the only ways in which globalization can lead to regional integration. Geographical location and functional dependency can create good opportunities for regional economic growth. A geographical concentration of production is to an increasing extent driven by technological clusters and an innovation and production network which offers clear advantages through regional cooperation (Lorenz, 1992). Patterns of cooperation both between and within companies change rapidly. Intra-Asian trade is growing much faster than trade between Asia and other regions. At the same time, these intra-regional adjustments in production are important in enabling the Asian countries to compete in the American and European markets. Globalization and regional integration are processes so closely linked that they cannot be analysed separately.

In the Asian region we witness a kind of regional integration based on trade patterns, business operations and investments, sub-regional cooperation patterns, and informal personal contacts. Business networks – here defined as international business systems formed along ethnic and/or cultural lines, as defined by Katzenstein (1996: 35) – are a particularly important form of non-institutional economic cooperation in Asia. The theory of (business) networks in regional integration is, however, not very well developed, except in a few works such as that by Bressand and Nicolaidis (1990) and Richardson (1995, 1996).

Peng (1997) analyses this form of integration in more detail. He examines three forms of informal cooperation in Asia, including Southeast Asia: (1) production networks based on a multi-tier economic division of labour, which is cooperation along the lines of industrial production; (2) sub-regional economic zones which embody cooperation based on geographical proximity (as for example in ASEAN); and (3) ethnic business networks representing cooperation along ethnic and cultural lines. All three, Peng claims, are usually overlooked as important forms of regional cooperation, although in the absence of formal economic institutions they are actually driving trade and investment within the region. Their importance apparently exceeds that of formal cooperation (Peng, 1997: 13).

To Peng's three types of informal types of cooperation in Southeast Asia may be added the development of policy communities within ASEAN. If we look at the development of ASEAN in the last thirty years, we see that there has been a continuous growth of both formal and in particular informal policy networks or communities. The total number of official ASEAN meetings is now approaching 300 (Chalermpalanupap, 1997: 7) and numbers of informal contacts and meetings are obviously much higher. We assume that this development of more and more arenas for cooperation and ever more frequent contacts is an important source of an even higher level of political and economic integration within this region in the future.

The same kind of multi-level, multi-channel, multi-actor mixture of formal and informal types of activity has also been found within the study of European policy-making. Several authors have introduced the concept of 'policy networks' to describe the linkages between different interests and EU policy-makers (Heclo, 1978; Richardson, 1995, 1996). The concept of policy communities has also been used to underline both the informal aspects of this process (Richardson and Jordan, 1979) and the existence of some kind of continuum of different degrees of formalization of these networks.

We believe that in addition to the more economically based network theory, this idea of policy communities may add to our understanding of the nature and functioning of the decision-making process within the Southeast Asian community, and that to this end the emerging policy communities in the region should be more closely examined. Perhaps this line of reasoning may also help us towards an answer to the question of how to compare the two models of regional integration.

In summary, informal or non-institutional cooperation is the dominant form of regional cooperation in the Asia–Pacific region at the present. It has served the demands of Southeast Asian countries for international economic cooperation relatively well, and in the near future the prevailing East Asian pattern is predicted to persist (Peng, 1997) Through ASEAN, Southeast Asia has set a successful example of a new form of regional cooperation. Until the end of the 1980s, ASEAN had been quite successful as a regional political organization, but in the economic arena its progress has been very slow. In the 1990s, as we have described, both economic and political cooperation have increased considerably.

6. A comparison of European and Asian integration

The second element in our attempt to explain how organizational structure and integration mechanisms differ between EU and ASEAN involves an investigation of how these phenomena are linked to historical, political, economic and cultural patterns. In comparison with Europe or North America, the Pacific region as a whole is a much more heterogeneous region. When looking at varying historical patterns between EU and ASEAN, we will examine two determinants of Asian regionalism suggested by Katzenstein (1996) in his attempt to account for the relative weakness of the formal political institutions of Asian regionalism by a comparison with Europe: namely, power and norms in the international system; and the character of domestic state structures.

American power in Asia after 1945 was relatively much greater than in Europe, and US foreign policy in Asia did not establish the principle of multilateralism there as it did in Europe (Katzenstein, 1996). American diplomacy in Pacific Asia has overwhelmingly been bilateral and not multilateral. This has made it much more difficult for Asian states to develop broad, interlocking and institutionalized political arrangements of the kind that have characterized the European integration process. However, it has been argued (Acharya, 1997) that it is in fact the Asia–Pacific region's extreme diversity, rather than America's extreme hegemony, which might have inhibited the emergence of multilateral institutions in the immediate postwar period; for the Asia–Pacific nations are remarkably different in terms of their political systems, cultural heritage and historical experience.

Katzenstein (1996) notes that the comparative weakness in the institutionalization of Asian regionalism is also attributable to the character of Asian state structures. Some state structures are better suited than others to deal with public law and formal institutions as the preferred vehicle for regional integration. Neither Asia as a whole or any of its sub-regions possesses equivalents of the Europe-wide institutions, foremost among which is, of course, the EU itself. In the establishment of formal institutions, Asian regionalism has during recent decades experienced a series of very slow, or even false, starts. Even the most successful institution of Asian regional integration, ASEAN, has arguably avoided the elimination of tariffs; until recently it was committed only to negotiating some preferential tariff margins for member states on selected goods. One argument advanced in regard to the slow development in Asian regionalism is that 'only the more developed countries appear to accept deeper forms of integration' (Wijkman and Sundkvist Lindström, 1989).

Also, Southeast Asia is greatly influenced by British, Dutch, French, Spanish, and US colonialism. Social forces inherited from the imperial past penetrate these postcolonial states deeply and thus create multiple political connections in intricate network structures. These states have inherited the colonial tradition of 'the rule by law' rather than the west European tradition of 'the rule of law' (Katzenstein, 1996). Southeast Asian countries are constituted legally, but the relation between state and society is governed by social rather than legal norms.

Our discussion of political heterogeneity between the EU and ASEAN is conducted in respect of the *political systems* in the region, related to the definition in most dictionaries and as defined by Hanks (1986): 'Politics refers to the study of the ways in which a country is governed and power is acquired.' The Pacific region is politically highly heterogeneous. The political systems in the ASEAN countries can most appropriately be described as all composed of some form of authoritarian capitalist or semi-democratic system, but with great differences between one another. All the EU member countries are democratic polities, and it could be claimed that the ASEAN countries differ far more in their political systems than do the EU member states. For example, the political difference between Singapore and Vietnam is much greater than the political difference among any two of the European nation-states. These differences obviously constitute a major barrier to institutional economic cooperation. All the free trade agreements previously established have been among countries of similar political systems. This can be explained by the fact that political systems are closely associated with modes of production.

An economy is the system according to which the money, industry and trade of a country or region are organized (Hanks, 1986). We will here examine in particular the *degree of liberalization of the economy* and *differences in per capita income*. The high degree of heterogeneity in the Pacific region makes formal economic cooperation difficult, because it greatly increases the transaction costs of institution-building. By contrast, non-institutional economic cooperation in Asia has functioned well in relation to the progressive liberalization of the Southeast Asian economies, especially in trade and investment, that has been under way since the 1960s, accelerating since the 1980s. The informal, gradual and flexible nature of non-institutional economic cooperation makes this approach highly appropriate as a way to open up economies while minimizing the outside shock accompanying liberalization (Peng, 1997: 14).

Economic disparity is the single most important barrier to formal regional cooperation in the Asia–Pacific region. It reflects the divergence in degree of industrialization, technological level, labour costs, export capacity and several other important factors. Within ASEAN there are enormous differences in per capita income/GNP between, at the end of the 1990s, an average of about $1,086 in Indonesia and $20,400 in Brunei (Poh, 1997). There has been no precedent at any time in world history of a successful free trade agreement among countries with great economic disparity (Peng, 1997: 15).[7] The closest example is the GATT; but GATT is an organization setting rules, rather than a real free trade area.

As we have pointed out above, Southeast Asians have their own way of conducting economic cooperation through informal means. For instance, economic cooperation based on the multi-tier economic division of labour is particularly strong in Southeast Asia. Sub-regional economic groupings (like ASEAN) and business networks are also playing very important roles in Southeast Asian regional cooperation. Strong informal economic cooperation is an important factor propelling regional integration in the absence of effective regional cooperative institutions.

Cultural heterogeneity can also raise transaction costs. Culture is a concept difficult to define, but may for present purposes be said to be a particular society or civilization, especially considered in relation to its ideas, its art, its customs or its way of life (Hanks, 1986). In investigating cultural aspects, we consider *religion* and *language* in the EU and ASEAN respectively.

In the ASEAN countries there are six major religions – Buddhism, Taoism, Hinduism, Christianity, Islam and Confucianism; all the EU countries are Christian. One may argue that within Christianity there are many divisions, but they still fall within one religious creed. Also, language diversity in the Asia–Pacific region is much greater than in Europe. Almost all the EU countries belong to the Indo-European family of languages, the only exception in fact, namely Greece. In contrast, there is a greater diversity among the ASEAN countries, where Thailand and Singapore belong to the Chinese–Tibetan language family, and Malaysia, Indonesia, the Philippines and Brunei to the Malay–Polynesian. Cultural heterogeneity also extends beyond religious and linguistic diversity to much broader categories like consumption behaviour, business practices, methods of management and so on.

The formation of Asian business networks is linked with the strong East Asian cultural tradition (Katzenstein, 1996). Confucianism, which has a strong influence in all the major Northeast Asian societies, Vietnam and the Overseas Chinese societies, has always placed great emphasis on human relations and personal ties. Extensive use of personal networks is an effective way to get around barriers to business in many Southeast Asian countries, both domestically and internationally.

This comparative analysis, comparing EU and ASEAN, can help us to identify elements of Asian and European distinctiveness. It highlights, specifically, the inclusive character of Asian network-style integration in contrast to the continental European emphasis on formal institutions.

7. Impacts of the Asian crisis on the development of regional integration

In a number of articles and books about the Asian currency crisis which have been published recently, it is noted that the two Chinese characters for the word 'crisis', literally translated, mean 'danger' and 'opportunity'(Henderson, 1998; Montes, 1998). In this paragraph, we take this reflection as a point of departure from which to examine the possible short-, medium- and long-term impact of the Asian crisis; in each scenario, one can identify both a set of dangers in terms of negative economic, social and political consequences, and one on the other hand a 'window of opportunity' for reform, paralleled by renewed, sustainable growth. Most authors point at the unique opportunity for increased regional economic cooperation, in a situation where a large number of countries face similar problems. Few, however, have studied in depth both dangers and opportunities resulting from the crisis in relation to the future development of regional integration. In this section we will address this issue in the light of recent events, by pointing at the specific features of the ASEAN countries and of the organizations that are likely to represent opportunities for and dangers to regional integration.

A first point to be highlighted is the expectations among at least a number of Western observers regarding the possibility for reforms in the wake of the crisis. As in the aftermath of the breakdown of the communist system in 1989, there is, albeit on a smaller scale, a perceived opportunity to redress all the inadequacies and the obvious shortcomings of what has been termed Asian 'crony capitalism'.[8] Although each ASEAN country, just like the former communist countries in central and eastern Europe, has its specific constellation of problems and differing abilities to handle the situation, the region as a whole is presented with similar policy recommendations, along the lines of liberalization of financial markets, transparency in transactions, establishment of new regulatory frameworks, and an increase in intraregional trade. The global nature of financial transactions, business and trade makes unilateral action inefficient, if not impossible; countries that tried to cut interest rates unilaterally would face the risk of renewed currency depreciation. The logic of the markets, coupled with the need for reform, thus create 'push' and 'pull' mechanisms, leading in the direction of greater regional integration. An international panel of experts which reports regularly to the APEC forum has recently urged Asian leaders to adopt concerted fiscal and monetary stimulus measures. Institutionalized cooperation in these areas, hardly thinkable before the crisis, is deemed a necessity now.

Secondly, as analysts of the EU integration process have noted, it is sometimes easier to carry out reform when a certain degree of power is delegated to an institution which operates outside of the national framework. If internal pressure can be counterweighted by external commitments, national elites will have more incentive and more scope to carry out unpopular reforms. One need not necessarily talk about supranationalism; greater regional integration in the form of an intergovernmental board of experts, a regional watchdog in charge of monitoring the national economies, will arguably make it easier for other countries to be informed and to exert pressure. The creation of preventive measures was at the core of the discussions among the ASEAN finance ministers in December 1997, which resulted in the establishment of the so-called Manila Framework, whereby member states would partake in the mutual surveillance of each others' economies (Higgot and Reich, 1998: 26). The Manila Framework will operate on an ASEAN-plus basis, to include all the East Asian countries.

The Manila Framework has, however, been criticized for being too vague and inefficient, and disagreement persists as regards to its mandate (Higgot and Reich, 1998). In October 1998 the ASEAN countries announced the creation of another joint surveillance system to provide early warning of future economic risk in the region (see T. Tassell, in *Financial Times*, 7 and 8 October 1998). It will be based on peer review and information exchange in areas such as interest rates, exchange rates and capital flows. On the one hand, this can be viewed as a sign that the drive towards institutionalization of cooperation is taking place in various forums simultaneously; on the other hand, it might be an indication that the former initiative has run into problems and needs to be replaced. Furthermore, even in the new framework, it remains unclear to what extent the participating countries are actually ready to delegate power, and to allow intervention in each other's affairs. In the enthusiasm over new regional initiatives, one should not forget that IMF-based monitoring functioned before the crisis (Henderson, 1998), but that the warnings issued were conveniently ignored by Thailand. Future crisis can only be averted or anticipated if there is a willingness to cooperate with and to follow recommendations from the regional watchdog.

One advantage of regional institutions over the IMF watchdog mechanism which deserves to be emphasized is that the work of the former might be facilitated by a growing sense of regional identity, a so-called 'cognitive regionalism', stemming from the 'all in the same boat' logic. A number of the ASEAN countries, notably Indonesia, Malaysia and to some extent the Philippines, have, by rejecting certain stipulations in IMF packages, focused on the importance of Asian alternatives to what are perceived as Western interventions. Thus the crisis can almost be termed a 'blessing in disguise' if it did indeed lead to a refashioning of a system with inherent flaws under the auspices of a dynamic regional association, based on a stronger sense of a common regional identity. To this end, even the search for a scapegoat such as the IMF or the anonymous 'speculators' might prove useful, as it can rally the populations around certain policies that in the long run have positive effects. One of the stated objectives of ASEAN is to create an 'ASEAN Awareness' that political leaders hope will contribute to social cohesion and political solidarity (Chalermpalanupap, 1997).

A constructed regional identity does not, however, hold a meaning in itself if it is backed by neither an 'imagined (regional) community' (Anderson, 1989) nor successful institutionalization of cohesive forces. The latter has so far been modest in terms of concrete actions carried out. The idea of an Asian bailout fund, launched by Dr Mahathir of Malaysia, has proved extremely difficult to realize at this stage of the process. More realistic projects include regional clearing-houses for domestic and foreign currency denominated bond markets, an ASEAN central bank forum and an ASEAN free trade zone.[9] These alternatives have been discussed by the ASEAN countries, but it is too early to give an assessment of the actual content of the proposed plans. So far, very few initiatives have been put into practice.

The question that remains to be answered is whether this regional identity really exists as a positive and creative force among today's ASEAN countries and political leaders. There is certainly a sense of shared problems and to some extent duties, but joint action does not automatically follow from this. Indeed, the foreign minister of Thailand has acknowledged that, on the contrary, because of the crisis the ASEAN countries have become increasingly prone to conflict among themselves.

In the period after the economic crisis internal conflicts and rivalries, accusations of inappropriate interference and of misconducted policies seemed to multiply, preventing ASEAN members from tackling the most pressing issue of how to revive their economies.

In Asia the strong economic growth of the past twenty years has not, as noted above, produced a high degree of formal, institutionalized cooperation. This can partly be explained by the nature of ASEAN, linked to its original *raison d'être*, namely the desire to create stability in the region by forcing Indonesia into a cooperative framework and constituting a fulcrum to maintain a balance of power. The imperative of stability has always been at the core of the ASEAN regional cooperation, and although economic issues have arguably been higher on the agenda since the mid–1970s, it would be wrong to talk yet of a functional spillover and a consequent real strengthening and deepening of integration. The differences in political structure and economic situation between the countries persist, and these have not been diminished by the crisis; indeed, as instability has increased they have re-emerged.

Tony Tan, Singapore's defence minister, stated that 'if there is instability in Indonesia, it will destabilise the whole region' (*Financial Times*, 16 January 1988, p.5). Destabilization of the region is both translated into, and met by, the inability of ASEAN to act. As evidence of this paralysis it will suffice to mention the huge environmental problems, in particular the destruction of the forests in Indonesia in the summer of 1998; the refugee problem which is damaging relations between Malaysia and Indonesia (and the Philippines); and the acute economic problems in Indonesia, which in addition to creating serious internal turmoil, are also affecting relations between Indonesia, Singapore and Malaysia.[10]

To understand fully both the sources of the tensions among these countries, and the importance of external stability, one has to look, beyond efforts aiming at greater regional integration, to the internal structure of the Asian states. One proposed framework for analysis is the Security–Development–Participation scheme (Ayoob and Samudavanija, 1989), which emphasizes the importance of external stability in enabling political leaders to focus on the more serious internal threats, which usually emanate from grievances of an ethnic, social, economic or political character. The economic development Asia has experienced over the past two decades is based on external stability, and has in turn been used to calm internal tensions, in the sense that certain groups have been rewarded economically for accepting the absence of (or, for the military, a decrease in) political participation and influence. In most cases, political participation is thus overshadowed by security and development, and inversion of this balance has traditionally only taken place through serious internal conflicts and bloodshed. In the circumstances prevailing in the wake of the economic crisis, the political leaders are naturally less able to 'buy' the loyalty of the population, which in turn can result in riots and unrest, as in Indonesia. The balance between external and internal politics is extremely delicate in Asia, in a way different from anything observed in the EU.

A related point to which we would like to draw attention is the existing empirical evidence regarding the behaviour of states in the international system in the wake of an economic recession or crisis. Ever since the Great Depression more than fifty years ago, economic turmoil has created a tendency for states to slow the pace of liberalization and turn to protectionist policies. Integration in the EU slowed down in the difficult 1960s and 1970s, but was fuelled by the economic upturn in the 1980s. In 1992–3 domestic recession, and the need to use monetary policy as an instrument to alleviate it, led the UK to pull out of the ERM, thus slowing the pace of progress towards complete monetary integration. Other European countries accused the UK of a lack of sincerity about the integration project and of giving priority to internal matters over European aims and objectives. In Asia, according to Thailand's foreign minister Surin Pitsuwan, the same trend can be observed: the countries are turning inward, concentrating on fending for themselves, and they are suspicious of outsiders.

This trend is emphasized by a long-standing cardinal principle of non-interference which has shaped the work of ASEAN and the relations between its member countries. The current problem is that certain 'isolationist' policies favoured by some countries have a negative effect on others.[11] Asia's political leaders disagree on the tactics chosen and the policies to be pursued, and they have become increasingly outspoken as they realize that the actions of any one state have an impact on the stability of the region, and thereby on the economic situation of all the countries.

The arrest in Malaysia of deputy prime minister Anwar, and his subsequent trial on charges of sexual misconduct and corruption, has been criticized by other Asian leaders, such as the Philippines' President Estrada and Indonesian President Habibie, who claim that 'our economies are interdependent, and these things affect us internally'. A greater degree of interference by other countries inevitably encourages political activity by the population within the target country: support from Indonesia and the Philippines strengthened the opposition in Malaysia in its protests against the arrest of Anwar. Developments on the intraregional level, between the states, can thus have serious consequences for developments on the national level, and national elites have difficulties in striking the right balance in this delicate two-level game.

Greater regional integration thus presupposes new forms of cooperation, which in fact signify changes in the political culture governing the relations between the political elites in the region. The Thai foreign minister has proposed a new policy of 'flexible engagement' within ASEAN which would allow member states more leeway to interfere in each other's internal affairs in other areas, not only in relation to strictly economic issues. It remains to be seen what form that engagement could take, but it is certain that a new form of cooperation is required. Only a greater ability to intervene in so-called internal affairs can reverse the trend of ASEAN's waning influence.

8. Conclusion

In the light of this analysis, do the changes within ASEAN and within ASEAN countries outlined above suggest that the association will on a long-term basis become more similar to the EU?

We have in recent years witnessed tendencies on several fronts towards more comparable development in the two regions. First, the general tendency, described above, for policy networks or communities to develop in nearly all sectors of society in Southeast Asia, and the increase in the number of summits and formal ministerial conferences make ASEAN more like the intergovernmental aspects of the EU. Still, however, ASEAN is not a supranational body and it does not possess a formal legal identity.

ASEAN involvement in new policy issues, like free trade through AFTA, will strengthen the tendency towards more organized cooperation. One possible hypothesis could be that further development of free trade agreements between countries and regions creates needs for rules and controlling institutions in order to be effective. It is predicted that if AFTA becomes a success, a more institutionalized organization will develop (Westerlund, 1997). ASEAN has already attempted to develop new institutional structures along these lines. Last year it added a protocol for the settling of trade disputes based on a majority voting procedure.

The expansion of ASEAN, with the problems surrounding the membership of Myanmar and the suspension of Cambodian admission, strengthened organizational cooperation. Several new meetings, working groups and procedures have been institutionalized. There are also interesting elements in the ASEAN decision-making procedures which resemble those of the EU, with the use of majority voting and flexible consensus.

The economic, political and social crises currently afflicting the region have both unifying and divisive implications. Our analysis of these factors has emphasized the divisions that seem to dominate at present, partly because national elites have difficulties striking the right balance in the two-level game of coping with internal pressure and external instability. Most of the ASEAN countries have in 1998–9 been turning inward, in several cases to try to calm mounting pressure resulting from the relative deprivation experienced by their populations. This has raised the problem that certain 'isolationist' policies favoured by some affect others negatively. Political leaders have become increasingly outspoken as they realize that the actions of one country have an impact on all the others. In this context, proposals for a policy of 'flexible engagement' have emerged. We see this as the most constructive proposal for reinforcing and strengthening regional integration and regional identity in the post-crisis ASEAN.

The comparative study of the EU and ASEAN highlights the existence of significant differences between the two groupings, on the basis of which a quite unique Asian model is likely to develop. As Paul Evans (1994) has argued, institution-building in the Asia–Pacific region, rather than following the pattern established in

Europe and North America, is instead 'emerging from unique historical circumstances and will likely evolve in its own particular way'. The crisis has made clear the need to re-examine certain traditions rooted in the state-making process of the Asian countries. And although the picture today remains chaotic, the period of transition that the crisis has unleashed may prove to be a key step towards greater integration in the future.

Notes

1   An earlier version of this chapter was presented at a conference on 'Non-state Actors and Authority in the Global System', University of Warwick, 31 October–1 November 1997. The authors would like to thank Solgunn Hoff and Anne Caroline Tveøy who have participated in preparing part of this manuscript, and in addition Pinar Tank and Alice Chamrernnusit for their help in the final editing of the paper, all employed at the Centre for European and Asian Studies at the Norwegian School of Management in Oslo.
2   The term 'new regionalism' has been used by several writers, including Palmer (1991).
3   After rapid initial progress in the 1960s there was a period of stagnation and even retreat from the unified market in the 1970s and early 1980s, before the adoption in 1985 of a new programme to free the internal market by the end of 1992 sparked off a second period of rapid progress (Andersen and Eliassen, 1993).
4   ASEAN today is composed of Indonesia, Malaysia, the Philippines, Singapore, Thailand, Brunei, Vietnam, Laos and Myanmar.
5   China, Japan, South Korea, Cambodia, Papua New Guinea and India.
6   The formal track of the Southeast Asian pattern of integration includes cooperation through regional institutions like APEC, PECC and EAEC (East Asia Economic Caucus), and sub-regional free trade areas like NAFTA, AFTA and the Australia–New Zealand free trade area.
7   This is also evident in the present enlargement process of the EU, where member states are unwilling to take in new members if they fall below an economic standard.
8   In a number of articles published in leading newspapers and magazines, scholars like Jeffery Sachs and Joseph Stiglitz have repeated that the Asian crisis does not bear witness to the triumph of Marxist logic and a coming breakdown of an exhausted capitalist system, but rather shows the need to create an ideal, fully fledged, and in consequence more Western-style capitalist system.
9   The development of the regional free trade area will be accelerated in advance of a 2003 deadline. The ASEAN countries signed a new agreement in October 1998 to speed up regional tariff cuts, according to the *Financial Times* (T. Tassell, 7 and 8 October 1998, pp.5–6).
10 Singaporean banks are heavily exposed in Indonesia and Indonesian refugees represent a burden to the neighbouring countries.
11 Some of the declarations made by Dr Mahathir, for instance regarding bans on foreign exchange trading and investment restrictions, are telling examples.

7. European Union and MERCOSUR

Álvaro Vasconcelos

This chapter sets out to address questions arising from the replacement of the Cold War order by a unipolar order dominated by the United States. For example: must the world resign itself to the continuance of a benevolent US hegemony through the decades to come, or will an alternative means of regulating the international system arise? Will the European Union be capable of producing such an alternative framework? What will be the role of regional integration projects, and in particular, of Mercosur, in this context?

Various models have arisen to describe the international system of the post-Cold War era, from the liberal optimism defended with vigour by Francis Fukuyama in his 'end of history' thesis to Samuel Huntington's pessimistic vision of the 'clash of civilisations',[1] but none has succeeded in explaining the conflictual nature of the modern world. Still less has any produced an adequate explanation of regional integration, a *sui generis* phenomenon capable of transcending the traditional conflictuality between nations and facilitated today by the sheer magnitude of the wave of democratization sweeping, in particular, through Europe and Latin America.

Regionalization, undoubtedly a major trend in the current international system, takes widely different forms. Three main types may, for simplicity's sake, be identified: open regionalism, as embodied in, for example, the North American Free Trade Agreement (NAFTA), the Asia–Pacific Economic Cooperation forum (APEC) or the Euro-Mediterranean Partnership (EMP) initiative; deep integration, as for example in the European Union (EU) and MERCOSUR; and subregional cooperation, as for example in the Southern African Development Community (SADC).[2]

1. Three types of regionalization

Open regionalism may be characterized as the policy generally espoused by defined poles in the international system in order to implement their external economic, political and security relations through free trade agreements. Thus the United States, the EU and today also MERCOSUR multiply their commercial agreements, mainly with neighbouring countries but also with more distant regions. Open regionalism is a vague concept. From the American viewpoint, it means above all the creation of large free trade areas, as for example in APEC or NAFTA; from the European viewpoint, it goes beyond free trade alone to embrace conditionality and political cooperation, as well as development aid.

The processes of deep integration, as for example in the EU and MERCOSUR, are of a different nature. Deep integration differs from open regionalism in that it tends to focus on one core group in the international system. Not only does it go beyond free trade arrangements, it also implies a change in the relations among states, the establishment of common positions vis-à-vis those outside the group – at least in the commercial field – and eventually the creation of supranational institutions. The existing models of deep integration could also be classified as 'open integration' models. This concept refers to 'integration projects which are based on pluralist societies, and defend the values of political democracy, cultural and religious diversity, free competition, citizen participation, associationism and shared sovereignty, projecting and promoting these values in their external relations'.[3]

Most of the European, American and African countries, as well as some in Asia, have made some moves, of varying importance, towards regionalization or subregional cooperation. Projects such as these, however, remain dominated by the participating states as key players, whose voice is decisive in their operation as in their foundation. The EU, the most advanced embodiment of supranational constitutionalism in existence today, was created after the Second World War in recognition of the need for survival and reconstruction in the European states.[4]

Most countries will very probably – and very soon – be participating in open regionalism initiatives of one form or another, particularly those promoted by the United States and the EU. As a general rule, these processes are asymmetrical in respect of both institutional strength and economic development. This trend will reveal ever more strikingly the need for the countries of any given region to engage in deep integration processes if they wish to wield even the minimum of influence within the international system. The regional factor is an indispensable element of the further evolution of the international order.

2. MERCOSUR and its European inspiration

MERCOSUR was founded in March 1991 with the signature of the Treaty of Asunción by Argentina, Brazil, Paraguay and Uruguay. Its motivation lay in the desire to create a common market on the model of the European Community.[5] However, the underlying conditions in the two regions were very different. European integration made its first appearance within the context of a disenchantment with national sovereignty arising from two world wars. Indeed, Raymond Aron claimed that 'the Europe of the nationalists has been killed by wars waged to extreme lengths.'[6] The construction of Europe is also a product of the specific conditions of the Cold War – notably the Soviet threat – which facilitated support and encouragement from the United States, whether at the political or the economic level. The European Economic Community developed under the protection of NATO.

MERCOSUR, by contrast, is an embodiment of integration under post-Cold War conditions. In Latin America, nationalism – including a pan-Latin American feeling – has persisted, especially in opposition to US policies which, in the western hemisphere, are still often considered to be 'hegemonic' or even 'imperialist'. Nevertheless, while the region has not experienced the tragedies of the European wars which delegitimated nationalism, they are emerging from a long period of military dictatorships which has had the same effect on the authoritarian model of governance. Moreover, trends towards globalization have deprived the concept of absolute sovereignty of all meaning. MERCOSUR is considered the first integration project generated by globalization, born as it was from an awareness in Brazil and Argentina that it is very difficult for developing nations on their own to benefit from globalization and to meet the economic and security challenges it brings.

MERCOSUR was set up to answer the need of its members to transform their 'development' policy of the 1960s and 1970s, founded on industrialization by means of import substitution, into a policy of commercial openness and integration into the international market. This new phase coincided with the acceptance by the Latin American states of the policies of structural adjustment and economic stability produced by the Washington Consensus with a view to resolving the burden of foreign debt.[7] As Felix Peña has stated, the four MERCOSUR countries have accepted a common aim of reconverting their economies by creating at the subregional level a habitat favourable to national attempts to improve both structural and business competitiveness.[8]

Implementing these principles in the aggressively neo-liberal atmosphere of the 1990s implied, for the Brazilian and Argentinian governments, the creation as a first step of a competitive platform, a customs union applying a common external tariff to facilitate openness towards the global market. It also required that liberalization between neighbouring countries permit the application of a 'pragmatic liberalism' in relation to the outside world,[9] that is to say a process of gradual and controlled opening and adaptation to the stakes of competition on a worldwide scale.

Awareness that globalization required implementation by states of policies not restricted to the framework of the individual nation-state lent impetus to the creation of MERCOSUR. The customs union brought into being in the Treaty of Asunción stands out as a first step towards a common market and as a move towards clearly defined political objectives.

The MERCOSUR project reflected the internal priorities of the new Latin American democracies as they emerged from the dictatorships and the 'lost decade'

Table 7.1   MERCOSUR exports to leading trading partners (%)

	1992	1993	1994	1995	1996
World	100.0	100.0	100.0	100.0	100.0
EU	31.9	26.8	26.9	25.5	24.5
USA	16.7	17.5	17.3	15.2	15.3
Japan	5.2	5.1	4.8	5.1	4.9
Latin America	25.2	29.9	29.9	31.1	33.0

Source: IRELA.

of the 1980s. Inspired by the success of the European model – which the Latin Americans had been observing and studying closely for some time – it was born when the expectations of the European single market reached their height with the 'Europe 92' programme, which had an international impact comparable only to that of the euro today.

The European single market was seen in Latin America as reflecting a European Community that was 'stronger and more radiant than ever, and much less dependent on the outside world'.[10] It was the image of a successful integration project; but it also brought new difficulties for exporters in the Southern Cone of the South American continent, who feared the 'European fortress', especially European protectionism against Latin American agricultural products. Back in 1992, the EU was already MERCOSUR's main export market, taking almost 32 per cent, and exceeded as a source of imports only by Latin America (see Tables 7.1 and 7.2).

Similar assessments of the impact of the European single market have been made by the American promoters of NAFTA and of the project for a commercial agreement on free trade in the hemisphere, devised in 1990 by President Bush, reflecting concern on the part of Americans faced with the successful consolidation of the EC's trading bloc.

Where MERCOSUR most resembles the European model is in the need felt by the states of South America at the end of the 1980s to consolidate their democratic structures, and in the process to overhaul the security concepts espoused by the military regimes throughout the years of dictatorship. According to Helio Jaguaribe, this amounted to establishing a distinction between internal and external security, and preventing the 'army from being induced into interference in the state's internal affairs, instead becoming converted to protectors of the civil authority'.[11] As in Europe after the Second World War, a post-sovereign political culture sprang up in the newly democratic states, particularly in the academic and industrial spheres – a development made possible only by the liberation of external and internal policy alike from the geopolitical concepts adopted by the military. The success of MERCOSUR has contributed greatly to the consolidation of this new democratic orientation.

Table 7.2   MERCOSUR imports from leading trading partners (%)

	1992	1993	1994	1995	1996
World	100.0	100.0	100.0	100.0	100.0
EU	23.9	23.5	27.7	27.4	26.1
USA	22.3	22.4	20.1	20.3	21.0
Japan	5.4	5.4	5.4	5.7	4.4
Latin America	26.7	25.8	25.8	24.8	26.4

Source: IRELA.

2.1 Integration and democratization

The reconciliation between Brazil and Argentina, made possible by the political transition in these two countries led by Presidents Sarney and Alfonsin, was perceived as being an underlying condition for democratic consolidation. The Treaty of Integration, Cooperation and Development concluded between Brazil and Argentina in 1988 established a focus on the objectives of democratization and development, though not yet at this stage on international competitiveness. The two countries have changed the strategic culture that had hitherto marked their bilateral dealings and which had seen both countries pursuing aggressive nuclear armament programmes. Those programmes have now been abandoned, and the neighbours have stopped regarding each other as enemies.

For Argentina and Brazil, the change in bilateral relations was fundamental in gaining international legitimacy for their fledgling democracies. The creation of Mercosur extended this process to Uruguay and Paraguay, traditionally the buffer states between the 'big two' of the Southern Cone. The establishment by this means of international recognition and credibility was seen as a way of underwriting democracy, and thus represented a convergence of international interests among the four countries.[12] MERCOSUR was thus born from the democratization of the countries of the region, and is based on the twin principles that the success of regional integration depends on the democratic nature of the regimes involved and that the consolidation of democracy depends (in part at least) on the progress of integration. As José Luis Simon has argued, 'If democratic politics and integration are intricately linked in the MERCOSUR, this is all the more true for Paraguay, for which integration is much more than mere trade; indeed, the MERCOSUR created the conditions for the implementation of democracy in Paraguay.'[13]

Democracy is undoubtedly the founding principle of MERCOSUR, and the founder governments are fully aware of this, as was apparent from their concerted response to General Oviedo's attempted *coup d'état* in Paraguay in April 1996. The members made it clear that it was unacceptable for one state in the group to jeopardise the democratic legitimacy of the whole. Shortly after this episode, the fragility of democracy in Paraguay had prompted the MERCOSUR countries to introduce a democracy clause into the constitutional arrangements of the group. The presidential declaration of Potrero de los Funes (in June 1996) not only stated that 'all change to the democratic order constitutes an unacceptable obstacle for the continuation of the democratic process in progress', but made provision for sanctions, ranging from suspension to expulsion from MERCOSUR, to be applied to any country jeopardizing democracy. Following this declaration, the MERCOSUR states have included the principle of political conditionality in their agreements with other countries. Moreover, on 24 July 1998 the democracy clause was extended with the Protocol of Ushuaia to include Chile and Bolivia, countries with which MERCOSUR has association agreements. It is interesting to note that in the EU context a similar democracy clause was introduced only in June 1997, in the Treaty of Amsterdam, in view of the envisaged expansion of the Union to central and eastern Europe.

MERCOSUR, in fact, represents the coming together of two projects: one political, defined by the democratic commitment of the participating countries and lacking any hard structure or well-defined contours; the other economic, aimed at liberalization and commercial openness, both among the member states and towards the outside world. MERCOSUR can thus be described as an 'open pole' model within the international system.[14]

MERCOSUR and the EU embody essentially the same model of regionalism, namely that of 'open integration'. Not only do MERCOSUR and the EU both set the condition that a state must be democratic in order to join; both project through their external relations, especially with their neighbours, the fundamental values that legitimate their own integration processes. Clearly the EU cannot base its international action upon an essentially Hobbesian idea; this reductive view is neither accepted nor understood by its citizens, who consider that its legitimacy resides in its democratic nature. This assumption has been a component of the European Community ever since its creation – in contrast to EFTA, one of whose founder members was the Portugal under Salazar. It was for this reason that neither Portugal nor Spain could initially join the EC; conversely, as soon as the two countries had jettisoned their authoritarian regimes, both considered accession to the Community a fundamental requirement for the consolidation of democracy at home. Mercosur, as its agreements with Chile and Bolivia demonstrate, is conducting its external policy on similar lines.

Since their transition to democracy, Argentina, Uruguay and Paraguay have all attached great importance in their foreign policies to issues relating to democracy and human rights. Brazil, however, was more anxious to distance itself from the US position, and committed itself internationally in this area only with the accession of Fernando Henrique Cardoso to the presidency, in 1994.[15] This commitment was demonstrated by all four MERCOSUR members in their declaration of support for the constitution of the International Criminal Court in Rome in July 1998.[16] However, the controversy over the fate of the former Chilean dictator Augusto Pinochet has come to divide the MERCOSUR countries on the potential conflict between the safeguarding of fundamental rights on the one hand and state sovereignty on the other. Their past experience of dictatorship has influenced the four countries in different ways. With problems similar to those faced by Chile, of military political crimes committed during the dictatorship and not yet brought to court, Argentina, Paraguay and Uruguay echoed the Chilean government's protest at what they called Britain's and Spain's interference in the domestic affairs of Chile. Brazil took a less critical approach. The opposition of the MERCOSUR countries, and indeed of Latin America in general, to the element of extraterritoriality in US policy towards them was made clear in the common declaration on the Pinochet affair made by MERCOSUR, Chile and Bolivia, in which they denounced the 'unilateral and extraterritorial application of national laws, violating the juridical equality of nations and the principles of respect and dignity of the sovereignty of states and of non-intervention in domestic affairs, and threatening their relationships'. At the same time, however, the signatories to the document 'recognize and encourage the gradual development of international legislation dealing with the penal responsibility of a person guilty of committing international crimes'.

2.2 Institutional and economic imperatives

A fundamental difference between the EU and MERCOSUR relates to the latter's institutional shortcomings. Up to now, MERCOSUR has been a purely intergovernmental body, with decisions taken unanimously in the absence of any form of supranational institution. This situation is a result of the sovereignty concept which still dominates diplomacy in the region, and of Brazil's opposition to any system that might put it in the minority. In the EU, by contrast, there exists a complex system of weights and counterweights – the weighted votes system, the provision for blocking minorities, qualified majority voting, a parliament with real (albeit limited) powers – to help balance power across the participating states and protect them from excessively strong leadership by any member or members. MERCOSUR's lack of institutions means a lack of any check on strong leadership, and the consensus rule provides only a limited constraint.[17] In Europe, the France–Germany axis is part of a system of multiple and shifting alliances; in MERCOSUR, the Brazil–Argentine axis is the unchanging core. This asymmetry among the countries involved will continue until MERCOSUR expands. In recent years there has been talk of setting up a tribunal to handle commercial disputes, and this would undoubtedly be an important step; however, the group's institutional weakness will certainly become more marked when Bolivia and Chile become full members, and also under pressure from the free trade zone of the Americas. On this issue President Cardoso remarked in 1998 that 'Brazil must take up this challenge. We are going to have to improve the institutionalization of MERCOSUR.'[18]

MERCOSUR today is a success, a 'trade mark 'as the Brazilian President described it, which has undoubtedly given its member states a new credibility. In the first place, trading relations between the members have changed significantly

Table 7.3   MERCOSUR: distribution of trade among member countries (US$m)

	1990	*1991*	*1992*	*1993*	*1994*	*1995*	*1996*
Argentina							
Total (US$m)	16,431	20,279	16,096	29,891	39,400	38,754	45,844
MERCOSUR (US$m)	2,709	3,715	6,082	7,896	9,950	9,801	11,415
MERCOSUR (% total)	16.5	18.3	37.8	26.4	25.3	25.3	24.9
Brazil							
Total (US$m)	54,121	54,830	57,600	66,951	76,702	96,103	105,251
MERCOSUR (US$m)	3,763	4,725	6,346	8,921	10,505	12,975	14,863
MERCOSUR (% total)	7.0	8.6	11.0	13.3	13.7	13.5	14.1
Paraguay							
Total (US$m)	2,152	2,012	1,894	2,203	2,957	6,336	4,139
MERCOSUR (US$m)	746	656	721	857	1,317	2,451	1,954
MERCOSUR (% total)	34.6	32.6	38.1	38.9	44.5	38.7	47.2
Uruguay							
Total (US$m)	3,047	3,140	3,630	4,022	4,699	4,988	6,404
MERCOSUR (US$m)	1,134	1,214	1,376	1,825	2,269	2,317	2,743
MERCOSUR (% total)	37.2	38.7	37.9	45.4	48.3	46.5	42.8

Source: IMF trade statistics

(see Tables 7.3 and 7.4). In 1996, 25 per cent of all Argentinian exports and 14 per cent of Brazil's were destined for MERCOSUR countries; the corresponding figures for 1990, before MERCOSUR was set up, were 16.5 per cent and 7 per cent respectively. The change has been less marked for Paraguay and Uruguay, for whom Argentina and Brazil were already the leading trade partners. The credibility of MERCOSUR is demonstrated by the significant annual rise in the volume of international investments, up from US$1,284 million in 1991 to US$8,925 in 1996.

The financial crisis of 1998, which particularly affected Brazil, faced MERCOSUR with an important test of its strength. The devaluation of the real on 3 January 1999, in the context of the Brazilian crisis, was a serious bone of contention between Brazil and its partners in MERCOSUR, in particular with Argentina whose products lost competitiveness. Argentina refused to devalue the peso, aware that were it to do so, it would thereby jeopardize the parity with the US dollar which has been the basis of its financial stability.[19] The devaluation of the real led Argentina and Brazil to open intensive trade negotiations, but the resolution of the crisis was a direct result of the Brazilian economic recovery and the stabilization of its currency.

Table 7.4   Trading relations between Argentina and Brazil

	1992	*1993*	*1994*	*1995*	*1996*
Argentina					
Imports					
US$m	3,339	3,568	4,286	4,176	5,327
% total	22.5	21.3	18.7	20.8	22.4
Exports					
US$m	1,671	2,814	3,655	5,484	6,615
% total	13.7	21.5	22.1	26.2	27.8
Brazil					
Imports					
US$m	1,721	2,809	3,662	5,570	7,542
% total	8.4	10.0	11.1	11.3	12.8
Exports					
US$m	3,040	3,661	4,136	4,041	5,170
% total	8.2	9.4	9.5	8.7	10.8

Source: IRELA.

One of the results of the crisis has been an increase in popularity of the idea of a single currency in MERCOSUR, now widely seen as a prerequisite for moving beyond the customs union to create a genuine common market. Added impetus is given to this move towards deeper integration by the risk of 'dilution' of MERCOSUR associated with the proposals for a Free Trade Area of the Americas (FTAA). The credibility conferred on the idea of a single currency by the track record of the euro and the success of the process of economic convergence prior to its adoption, as well as the knowhow being amassed on its operation, should inspire other countries and regions to start examining similar possibilities.

3. The United States and MERCOSUR

The Clinton government, in line with the orientation of the Bush administration at the end of the 1980s,[20] has given priority to free trade agreements as a structural element of the dominant US position in world trade – and as a vehicle for the worldwide dissemination of American interests and values. 'The trade agreements of the post-Cold War era will be equivalent to the security pacts of the Cold War – binding nations together in a virtuous circle of mutual prosperity and providing the new front line of defence against instability. A more integrated and more prosperous world will be a more peaceful world – a world more hospitable to American interests and ideals.'[21] The Clinton administration is actively pursuing a strategy of globalization with the United States as the hub of the world, by means of large-scale agreements such as the FTAA (Free Trade Area of the Americas), APEC or the proposed Transatlantic Marketplace with the European Union. However, in so doing it sometimes runs into opposition from powerful isolationist sectors of American society, and from the labour unions, such as AFL-CIO.[22] Some influential political figures, for example Congressman Gephard (Vice President Al Gore's main rival for the Democratic party presidential nomination) are in favour of a more isolationist stance, perhaps rightly believing it to be closer to the instincts and preferences of most Americans. It is this political sensitivity that caused Congress to deny President Clinton the 'fast track' option that would have enabled him to negotiate free trade agreements directly, particularly with the Latin American countries.[23]

For the United States, MERCOSUR is a trading detour, an optional step in the regionalization of the Americas. In the run-up to the Second Americas Summit held in Santiago, Chile on 18–19 April 1998, there was noticeable tension between the Brazilian and American delegations, particularly over the creation of a free trade zone for the Americas before 2005, a schedule which does not give MERCOSUR the time it needs to consolidate. Some commentators, such as the eminent Brazilian sociologist Helio Jaguaribe, go so far as to assert that MERCOSUR must say no to the FTAA because 'constitution of the FTAA implies, in practice, the disappearance of MERCOSUR as it would lead to the elimination of customs frontiers between all the countries of America and, as a result, of the common external tariff, which is one of the fundamental characteristics of MERCOSUR.'[24] For its part, the United States sees MERCOSUR as one of a number of small trading units, each with its own system of regulations and obligations, which stand in the way of the American leadership and its vision of open regionalism.[25] On the eve of President Clinton's visit to Brazil and Argentina in October 1997, the US administration declared that the FTAA did indeed imply the disappearance of MERCOSUR; but the President himself, during his visit, publicly recognized the political importance of MERCOSUR in cooperative relations between Brazil and Argentina and declared that it was compatible with the FTAA.

US negotiators dislike the fact that MERCOSUR participates as a bloc in the FTAA talks. Many US politicians see Brazil as the Latin American country that is most independent of US foreign policy and the only real opponent of the US position on the free trade area. Some even take the view that MERCOSUR, working towards a strong relationship with the EU, is part of a Brazilian strategy of independence, and that Brazil is setting itself up as a kind of Latin American France. Argentina, by contrast, has been more closely aligned with US international security policy. Unlike Brazil, Argentina has participated in military operations led by the United States, such as the 'Desert Storm' campaign during the Gulf War in 1991; and, by way of thanks for this support, President Clinton has granted Argentina the status of leading ally outside NATO, a rank already conferred on Israel, Egypt, Japan, South Korea, New Zealand and Jordan.

Nevertheless, despite these divergences the MERCOSUR identity has been confirmed in the context of the FTAA negotiations, during which the four members spoke with one voice. This cohesion derives not just from the fact that MERCOSUR is a customs union in the process of being set up, but from the recognition of all its members that it is in their mutual interest that it continues to exist. With each of them aware that MERCOSUR could be dissolved within the FTAA and none daring to question the importance of a form of free trade with their great northern partner, all want to participate in the Americas initiative while simultaneously maintaining and strengthening MERCOSUR. This sense of common purpose enabled Mercosur to carry the day at the Santiago Summit in pushing the deadline for the FTAA negotiations out to 2005.

There exists in relation to Latin America an element of competition between Europe and the United States which MERCOSUR is attempting to turn to its advantage. During the debates in Congress on the authorization of the presidential 'fast track' in negotiating trade agreements, the Clinton administration insisted on the need for approval in terms reminiscent of the Monroe Doctrine, and with explicit reference to the threat posed by Europe to US interests: 'While we debate, Europe is negotiating free trade agreements in our own hemisphere which we cannot. That is a bad deal for the United States.'[26] The House of Representatives was also reminded that 'between 1993 and 1996, US exports to MERCOSUR increased by an impressive 51% – but the EU's exports grew even faster at 62%. This has been a tough competitive battle, but without an FTAA it may soon be all but over – not because of the quality of our products or the competitive edge of our firms, but simply because of a failure of our political resolve.' The administration was convinced that 'MERCOSUR would not survive if the President had fast-track and, therefore, the leadership initiative in the Americas to implement his vision.'

The administration's failure to win the fast-track option has created conditions favourable to the consolidation of MERCOSUR, giving it the scope for a more gradual opening up of its economies and the establishment of a more balanced relationship with the United States and Europe. One possible path of evolution could lead to its becoming a focus of integration for the whole of South America. The negotiations aimed at establishing a free trade agreement between MERCOSUR and the Andean Community[27] are a step in this direction.[28] However, there are enormous obstacles down this path, for the Andean Community includes member states with unstable conditions, such as Colombia and Ecuador, as well as others, such as Peru and Venezuela, which do not meet the conditions for membership of MERCOSUR stipulated by the democracy clause.

Both MERCOSUR and the EU look upon free trade and globalization differently from the United States, which sees these processes fully corresponding to its own interests. For the EU and MERCOSUR the continental and global free trade projects, accompanied by the deregulation and privatization measures set in train in the Thatcher and Reagan years, may jeopardize cohesion among member states and lead to a loss of the identity conferred by projects that go beyond the establishment of free trade arrangements, whether in the shape of a customs union (as in MERCOSUR) or in the more ambitious form of economic and monetary union (in the EU), especially in respect of the social model on which these groupings are based.

4. MERCOSUR as a strategic partner of the EU

Despite its limited international influence, MERCOSUR is a strategic partner for the EU in building a new multilateralism based upon a more balanced relationship with the United States; accordingly, relations with MERCOSUR have a high priority in EU foreign policy. This view is strong in Portugal, Spain and Italy for historical reasons, and in Germany because of its large investments in the countries of the region. It is also espoused officially by France since the visit of President Jacques Chirac to Brazil in 1996, but it is true that of the major EU countries France has the most difficulty in maintaining a coherent political line towards MERCOSUR, torn as it is between pacifying its agriculture lobby, its particular regard for certain individual Latin American countries, such as Mexico, and its recognition that MERCOSUR has a place in a multipolar vision of the world. Nevertheless, while in Brazil President Chirac stated that 'the future of Latin America does not lie with the North–South axis. It is with Europe, on account of historical and cultural reasons, because we have the same values, the same type of humanism, and also the same economic systems.'[29]

For many European countries, MERCOSUR 's importance lies only in the part it plays in their foreign trade. If Europe were only a trading region, then MERCOSUR would be reduced to a 'backyard' of the United States, in a version of the Monroe Doctrine by which South America was prevented from engaging in political dialogue with partners other than the United States.[30] But even from a strictly economic viewpoint it would be a mistake to overlook the importance of MERCOSUR for the EU – an importance amply demonstrated by the fact that 56 per cent of all EU investment in Latin America and the Caribbean between 1990 and 1996 was in MERCOSUR countries (see Table 7.5); and the proportion is still growing.[31]

A fresh boost was given to relations with Latin America when Portugal and Spain joined the Community in 1986. Indeed, a declaration about those relations was annexed to the membership treaty. This impetus was reinforced on the Latin American side by the successful consolidation of democracy in the region and to the appearance of regional groups – the Andean Community and the Central American Community as well as MERCOSUR itself. The European Commission, under the influence of Portugal and Spain, has attempted to promote relations with these groups and with Mexico, taking advantage of Mexico's role as a member of NAFTA and of the Iberian countries' turns to preside over the Council of Ministers. It was in 1992, during the Portuguese presidency, that the first informal ministerial

Table 7.5   MERCOSUR: foreign direct investment by the EU, United States and Japan, 1990–1996

	Europe		*United States*		*Japan*	
	US$m	*%*	*US$m*	*%*	*US$m*	*%*
Argentina	4,954	19.1	5,853	10.3	188	5.9
Brazil	8,859	34.2	18,720	32.8	1,553	48.5
Paraguay	43	0.2	45	0.1	1	0.0
Uruguay	544	2.1	235	0.4	−1	0.0
MERCOSUR	14.4	55.6	24,853	43.6	1,741	54.4
Latin America and Caribbean	25,889	100.0	57,064	100.0	3,201	100.0

Source: IDB/IRELA

meeting took place between the twelve members of the European Community and the four of MERCOSUR, and in 1995, during the Spanish presidency of the Union, that the EU-MERCOSUR framework agreement and the project for an interregional free trade area were launched. At the same time political talks with the Rio Group and the San José Group have been continuing.[32]

The political convergence between the European Union and MERCOSUR derives above all from the similarity of their open integration processes and their shared need for a more balanced international system in which they will depend less on the United States for their stability. However, it must be emphasized here that MERCOSUR does not undermine either pan-Americanism or the European Union's solidarity with the United States through NATO and transatlantic dialogue. What both the Europeans and the 'Mercosureans' must do is build a system regulated by international rules that are as widely accepted as possible, not only in relation to international trade but also in the spheres of security, human rights and the environment. In today's world, where the United States is the only well-defined pole, most security crises require North American military intervention – as was made clear in the Gulf, in Bosnia and in Kosovo. What, then, is the alternative to unipolarity and American unilateralism? The traditional multipolar perspective assumes that the EU could become a traditional power, like an enlarged France; but this possibility is not universally favoured. The model projected by the EU in the international order is not that of a traditional multipolar system with ephemeral alliances, possibly formed by the five continental superpowers (EU, United States, China, Japan, Russia), which would reproduce the nineteenth-century European balance of power system on a world scale and which India and Brazil (or MERCOSUR) could join later. What is needed is a different kind of system which, in the words of Jean-Marie Guéhenno, 'would be based neither on the indefinite supremacy of the United States, nor on the pursuit of independence and sovereignty as the ultimate goal of a political entity,'[33] but would be a kind of institutionalized interdependence organization. Jacques Chirac, on his visit to Brazil in 1997, said: 'The unstoppable progress towards a multipolar world would, however, risk slipping progressively towards the affirmation of antagonistic poles, if some of today's leading actors attempted to oppose this evolution rather than participate in organizing it.'[34] We must go further: the European model assumes that the Union will not be transformed into a superstate, but will be able to influence the creation of international rules, based on a fabric of interdependent multilateral economic and political institutions, such as the WTO or the recently founded International Criminal Court, testimony to the growing role of international law. In short, a multilateral system based on multiregionalism must be created.

For this to occur, it is important that the new supranational European pole gains a greater capacity for political intervention, and that similar new poles are consolidated. To this end, the EU must resist the diminution of MERCOSUR into a free trade area or even its dissolution into the world market, and must defend its consolidation as an open, supranational pole of multiregionalism and multilateralism. It is essential, moreover, that this political objective be translated into an interregional trade agreement. Such an agreement between the EU and MERCOSUR would represent a significant stage in the process of mutual identification as open poles of the new international system. It is important for the EU that the MERCOSUR pole be defined with as much precision as possible, and that other potential such poles, for example in South-East Asia with the democratization and enlargement of ASEAN, and in southern Africa with the development of the SADC, are fostered.

The European Union's aim is to see the emergence of a world that would not rely on the leadership of a superpower to govern it; a world where the traditional loci of power would be diminished and lose legitimacy. The poles it would like to see built are not traditional power poles but open poles equipped with a capacity for military intervention resulting from cooperation between states and legitimated by multilateral institutions, especially the United Nations. On this subject, one of the conclusions of the Fifth Euro-Latin American Forum is that:

> *The European Union and MERCOSUR have a common interest in the promotion of a multipolar world governed by multilaterally determined and universally applicable global 'game rules'. They have a mutual interest in that all actors, both powerful and weak, work towards a 'pact of mutual trust', based on the participatory creation of a new global agenda and regulations. In sum, they have a shared interest in replacing a pax americana with a pax interdemocratica.*[35]

The United States is more at ease than the EU with the idea of building a global market within which it would be the only superpower, one in which its role of 'good cop', of indispensable nation, of domination could not be contested. Paradoxically, the EU and MERCOSUR, though they may fear the consequences of market globalization, are in a very favourable position themselves to lead the way in the globalization of law, the building of a system of multilateral regulation which sets limits on the sovereignty of states and the unilateral use of force. The two groups have been united in their condemnation of unilateral US measures such as the Helms–Burton and D'Amato acts, and in respect of the need for an internationally legitimated line of action towards Iraq. Nevertheless, the United States remains essential to the success of any international project, and especially to that of a multilateral system of laws and regulation. Also, as the authors of the RAND Corporation study on Euro-American relations have emphasized, the United States needs allies in order not to slip into a tendency towards unilateral action.[36]

The Rio de Janeiro summit of June 1999 between the European Union and the countries of Latin America and the Caribbean is a sign that the EU wants to give its relations with Latin America a new visibility as part of a diplomatic programme of talks at the highest level, following on the Euro-Asian summit in London in 1998 and preceding the Euro-African summit held in March 2000 in Cairo, and in parallel with continuing transatlantic talks with the United States and Canada. Relations between the EU and Latin America have changed considerably in recent years with the accession of Mexico to NAFTA, the setting up of the Andean Community and, above all, the progressive consolidation of MERCOSUR. In other words, relations are being deepened not with individual countries or with all the countries of the region as a bloc, but with established regional groups. The summit diplomacy will remain no more than a theoretical exercise unless it is accompanied by firm agreements between the EU and these different regional groups, in particular MERCOSUR. If negotiations towards such agreements are to be undertaken, resistance in certain countries needs to be overcome, especially in those most sensitive to pressure from agricultural interests. A free trade agreement with MERCOSUR that did not cover agricultural products is inconceivable. In this field, account must be taken of the interests not only of the farming community, but also of the industrial and financial sectors; and of the Union's political interests as well as its economic interests.

The US–EU– MERCOSUR relationship is still an unbalanced one. The US–EU axis is certainly the strongest one; but the United States is also an important strategic partner for the Latin Americans, all members of the OAS (Organization of American States). To balance the triangle, the EU–MERCOSUR axis must be strengthened; but this does not imply the establishment of a three-way relationship, a powerful alliance of the democratic Western world, directed by the United States. Such an alliance would be perceived as excluding and opposing the non-Western world, and would thereby encourage instability.

To sum up, the European Union's multilateralist project is not a throwback to the traditional multipolar system, characterized by an unstable equilibrium among the powers and the frequent dissolution and reversal of alliances. Western Europe has put an end to this system of permanent rivalry through integration. The European vision of regionalism implies the consolidation of the poles of integration, such as MERCOSUR, and in this differs from the North American vision of 'open regionalism' which pulls in the opposite direction to projects of deep integration in Latin America. The United States, often identified with the phenomenon of globalization, is thus the external factor of identification, a contrasting model which enables definition through difference for Mercosur – and, increasingly, for the European Union too.

The international project of the EU consists in building a new multilateralism based on areas of regional integration and on experience of supranational regulation of the relations between states: in other words, in turning the international system into a 'community' on the basis of the success of its own model, which is then extrapolated into the wider world. This may be a utopian vision; but it is the only vision of the world that can make sense of the common foreign and security policy of the civil power that is the European Union. Only this vision can answer the specific security concerns of its members and unite their diverse interests in a common project. Today, there are three essential elements to this project: integration of the countries of the European continent, from Portugal to Russia, in a single community of destiny in a common project of democracy and social justice; in the long term, the extension by inclusion and prosperity of this security area to North Africa and the Middle East; and the formation, with MERCOSUR, of the first link in the chain of interregional agreements.

Notes

1   Francis Fukuyama, 'The End of History', *The National Interest*, Summer 1989; Samuel P. Huntington, 'The Clash of Civilisation?', *Foreign Affairs*, vol. 72, no. 3, 1993, pp. 22–49.
2   The EMP, comprising the fifteen EU countries and the twelve Mediterranean states, is an open regionalism project that could lead to the creation of a vast free trade area in 2010. The SADC was formed in 1992 from the former SADCC (South African Development and Coordination Conference), founded in 1980. It includes Angola, Botswana, the Democratic Republic of the Congo (1997), Lesotho, Malawi, Mauritius (1995), the Seychelles (1997), South Africa (1994), Mozambique, Namibia, Swaziland, Tanzania, Zambia and Zimbabwe.
3   See Guilherme d'Oliveira Martins and Álvaro Vasconcelos, 'A lógica da integração aberta, base de um novo multiregionalismo', in *Integração Aberta*, Lisbon: Euro-Latin American Forum, Institute for Strategic and International Studies (IEEI), 1995.
4   See Marie-Françoise Durand and Álvaro Vasconcelos, *La Pesc – Ouvrir l'Europe au Monde* (Paris: Presses de Sciences Politiques, 1998).
5   Monica Hirst, 'A dimensão politica do Mercosul: especificadades nacionais, aspectos institucionais e actores sociais', in *Integração Aberta* (Lisbon: Euro-Latin American Forum/IEEI, 1995), p. 193.
6   Raymond Aron, 'L'Europe face à la crise des sociétés industrielles', in *L'Europe? L'Europe*, texts collected by Pascal Ory (Paris: Omnibus, 1998).
7   The Washington Consensus emerged from a seminar promoted by the economist John Williamson in 1989, organized to discuss the reforms needed to resolve the Latin

American debt crisis. It consisted of a set of economic, financial and social policies and reforms, recommended by multilateral institutions such as the IMF and the World Bank, the application of which set the conditions for the grant of loans, renegotiation of external debt and, ultimately, the reinsertion of Latin America in the international financial system.

8 Felix Peña, 'America Latina, el Mercosul y la Comunidad', in *Convergência Natural* (Lisbon: IEEI, 1993), p. 96.

9 Hélio Jaguaribe, speech delivered at the Fourth Latin American Forum, Institute for Strategic and International Studies (IEEI), Rome, 1996.

10 Geraldo Holanda Cavalcanti, 'As opções da América Latina face às transformações de hoje', speech delivered at the First Euro-Latin American Forum, Federação das Indústrias do Estado de São Paulo (FIESP) and IEEI, São Paulo, 1990.

11 Hélio Jaguaribe, 'Uma nova concepção de segurança para o Brasil', *Estrategia: Revista de Estudos Internacionais* (Lisbon), nos 8–9, 1996.

12 Hirst, 'A dimensão política do Mercosul'.

13 José Luis Simon, 'Lessons from Paraguay', *Open Integration Newsletter* (Lisbon: IEEI, 1998).

14 For a more detailed analysis of MERCOSUR as an open pole in a system of undefined polarities, see: Celso Lafer and Gelson Fonseca, 'A problemática da integração num mundo de polaridades indefinidas', in *Integração Aberta* (Lisbon: Euro-Latin American Forum/IEEI, 1995).

15 Alexandra Barahona de Brito, 'Condicionalidade politica e cooperação para a promoção da democracia e dos direitos humanos', in *Além do Comercio* (Lisbon: IEEI, 1997).

16 At the Conference of Rome in July 1998, 120 countries out of 148 were in favour of the creation of an International Criminal Court. This permanent court will have the authority to try individuals accused of major violations of international human rights law.

17 Guilherme d'Oliveira Martins, *O enigma Europeu* (Lisbon: Quetzal Editores, 1993).

18 Speech by Fernando Henrique Cardoso, delivered at the closing session of the Fifth Euro-Latin American Forum, IEEI, Lisbon, 1998.

19 See *Latin America at the Brink? Effects on the Global Finance Crisis*, IRELA, 1998.

20 See Alfredo Valladão, *Le XXIe siècle sera américain* (Paris: La Découverte, 1993).

21 Stuart E. Eizenstat, 'Our Future Trade Agenda', remarks before the House of Representatives, 24 September 1997.

22 See Riordan Roett, *The EU and MERCOSUR: US Perspectives*, text prepared for the Fifth Euro-Latin American Forum, Lisbon, May 1998.

23 Before the 'fast-track' option was put in place in 1974, US law already allowed the President to negotiate, within certain stipulations and time limits, commercial agreements and reciprocal tariff reductions with trading partners. The 1974 bill confirmed the power of Congress to delegate authority to the President to negotiate commercial agreements and tariff reductions subject to a consultative mechanism between the President and Congress during the negotiation procedure, establishing fixed objectives and including a number of procedures enabling agreements to be established on non-tariff barriers.

24 Helio Jaguaribe, *Mercosul e as alternativas para a ordem mundial* (Rio de Janeiro: Instituto de Estudos Politicos e Sociais, 1998).

25 Roett, *The EU and Mercosur*.

26 Eizenstat, 'Our Future Trade Agenda'.

27 On 16 April 1998 the member countries of the Andean Community and of MERCOSUR signed a framework agreement for the creation of a free trade area between the two

blocs. In April 1999, the Andean Community signed an Agreement on Economic Complementarily of Tariff Preferences with Brazil, as a first step toward the creation of a free trade area between the Andean Community and Mercosur. A similar process was launched between the Andean countries and Argentina on 29 October.

28 The Andes Pact, consisting of Bolivia, Colombia, Ecuador, Peru and Venezuela, was instituted by the Cartaginia Agreement in 1969. In March 1996, with the Trujillo Protocol, the Pact became the Andean Community of Nations.

29 'Jacques Chirac sets off to reconquer Latin America', *Le Monde*, 12 March 1997.

30 The Monroe Doctrine, announced in a presidential declaration in 1823, aimed at keeping European powers away from the western hemisphere by proclaiming the end of colonialism in the New World and non-intervention by the United States in European matters, and encouraging Europe similarly to remain detached from American affairs.

31 *European Direct Investment in Latin America*, IRELA briefing, November 1998.

32 The Rio Group, formed on 18 December 1986 by Argentina, Bolivia, Brazil, Chile, Colombia, Costa Rica, Ecuador, Mexico, Paraguay, Peru, Uruguay and Venezuela, constitutes a forum for Latin American political coordination and dialogue with the EU. In September 1984 the foreign ministers of the European Community, Portugal and Spain met in San José, Costa Rica, with the representatives of the countries of Central America, with a view to re-establishing peace in the region and discussing democratization measures throughout the continent. This was the first of a series of meetings that led to the institutionalization of a political dialogue between the EU and Central America, known as the San José process. The last meeting took place in the Algarve from 21 to 24 February 2000, during the Portuguese presidency of the European Union.

33 Jean-Marie Guéhenno, 'The Impact of Globalisation on Strategy', paper delivered at the 40th Annual Conference of the International Institute for Strategic Studies, Oxford, 3–6 September 1998.

34 Speech by Jacques Chirac, delivered to the Congress of the Federal Republic of Brazil, Brasilia, 12 March 1997.

35 Report of the Fifth Euro-Latin American Forum, *Setting Global Rules* (Lisbon: IEEI, 1998).

36 David C. Gompert and F. Stephen Larrabee, eds, *America and Europe: A Partnership for a New Era* (Cambridge: Cambridge University Press/RAND Corporation, 1997).

8. African Regionalism and the SADC

Carolyn Jenkins and Lynne Thomas

Regionalism is not a new phenomenon in Africa.[1] Indeed, the world's oldest customs union exists in southern Africa, and the list of both past and present multilateral economic agreements is probably longer than that of any other continent. However, while some successful examples of regional cooperation do exist,[2] Africa's record of creating and sustaining regional frameworks is generally poor.

Almost all regional trade initiatives in Africa have achieved very little, in spite of their political appeal. A range of studies indicates why this is the case.[3] Many schemes were designed without regard for members' incentives to comply; implementation has sometimes not been feasible, as countries have overlapping and incompatible membership of different regional arrangements; and members have frequently substituted non-tariff barriers for tariffs against each other. Domestic economic policies have also undermined the effectiveness of African trade integration schemes. Moreover, the structure of demand and production is too similar across African countries to generate substantial trade creation. This suggests that any union – except, possibly, one involving South Africa – will be too small for economies of scale to be realized.

Nevertheless, African policy-makers continue to pursue broader economic cooperation as a potential solution to small markets and generally weak economies. Political interest in regionalism has received added impetus in recent years as a result of growing fears that Africa may be marginalized. The potential expansion of the European Union to encompass east European states and the increasing integration of the Americas, for example, have created the perception that Africa risks being left behind in the formation of regional economic blocs, with adverse consequences for trade and investment.

At present, several regional integration initiatives are being pursued across Africa, aimed at promoting economic growth. The Southern African Development Community (SADC) is, arguably, more likely than some others to provide the basis for successful economic cooperation due to the participation of South Africa, the continent's largest economy (accounting for nearly one-quarter of total African GDP). Part of the problem facing most African regional groupings is the lack of a

Table 8.1   SADC members and other regional groupings

SADC	COMESA	SACU	CMA	CBI
Angola	•			
Botswana		•		
DR Congo				
Lesotho		•	•	
Malawi	•			•
Mauritius	•			•
Mozambique				
Namibia	•	•	•	•
Seychelles	•			
South Africa		•	•	observer
Swaziland	•	•	•	•
Tanzania				•
Zambia	•			•
Zimbabwe	•			•

SADC: Southern African Development Community
COMESA: Common Market of Eastern and Southern Africa
SACU: Southern African Customs Union
CMA: Common (Rand) Monetary Area
CBI: Cross-Border Initiative

large, more developed partner to provide both a significant regional market and a source of external capital and expertise, particularly in regionally integrated production processes. The involvement of South Africa in SADC (representing around 70 per cent of SADC's GDP – has alleviated this constraint to some extent by improving the potential for cross-border trade and investment with a relatively large and more developed neighbour.[4]

SADC is not the only regional integration initiative in which southern African countries currently participate (see Table 8.1). Many are members of the Common Market of Eastern and Southern Africa (COMESA); others are involved in the Cross-Border Initiative (CBI); and a small subset of SADC members are involved in the long-standing Southern African Customs Union (SACU) and the Common Monetary Area (CMA). The existence of overlapping membership of regional initiatives is common across Africa and provides a confusing picture of priorities. This is one reason why some of these initiatives have not been sustainable.

In this chapter, we focus on SADC as an example of regionalism in Africa with the potential to create a sustainable framework for economic growth and development. The Community's history, current structure, membership and key economic indicators are briefly reviewed. The impact on the region of the trend towards globalization is discussed, and the importance of regional trade integration in southern Africa is examined, together with SADC's possible role in broader trade initiatives. Finally, some of the potential barriers to continued economic cooperation in southern Africa are highlighted. We conclude that the achievement of policy coordination and an outward orientation are key challenges facing SADC in promoting growth in the region.

1. An overview of SADC

SADC evolved out of the Southern African Development Coordination Conference (SADCC), established in 1980 with the objectives of promoting self-reliance in the region and encouraging regional cooperation in development projects. The original members of SADCC sought to reduce their dependence on the rest of the world and in particular on their then hostile neighbour, South Africa. SADCC worked rather well in bringing regional political leaders together, and as a means for procuring foreign aid, although it failed to achieve its broader objectives.

In 1992 the SADCC broadened its concerns to facilitating regional economic integration and became the Southern African Development Community, laying out its aspirations for regional cooperation in the Windhoek Treaty of that year. Integration initiatives were to be given content in a series of protocols, which would provide a framework for the negotiation of specific programmes for greater cooperation. The overarching aim was to build a community which could compete globally, with regional integration yielding balanced economic growth and development for the member states.

SADC operates through a variety of institutions. The Summit, made up of heads of state or government, is the ultimate policy-making body. A Council of Ministers, comprising (usually) those ministers from each member state with responsibility for the economy, monitors the progress of SADC and the appropriate implementation of regional policies. Much of the work of SADC is carried out through sectoral commissions and coordinating units, which are led by specific member states and operate through government institutions. For instance, the Finance and Investment Sector Coordinating Unit is located in South Africa's Department of Finance; the Industry and Trade Coordinating Division in Tanzania's trade ministry. These institutions cover a wide range of sectors, reflecting SADC's objective of widespread regional cooperation, as illustrated in Table 8.2. SADC also has a Secretariat, located in Botswana, which is the principal executive institution of the organization.

The current membership of SADC is set out in Table 8.3, together with key economic indicators. The original nine members were joined by Namibia in 1990, by South Africa and Mauritius in 1994, and by the Democratic Republic of Congo and Seychelles in 1998.

The size of the SADC economy amounted to US$198 billion in 1997. The figures presented in Table 8.3 highlight the large disparities which exist across the region's economies, in terms of both size and relative well-being (as measured by

**Table 8.2   Sectoral responsibilities in the Southern African Development
Community**

Member state	*Sectoral responsibility*
Angola	Energy
Botswana	Agricultural research
	Livestock production and animal disease control
Lesotho	Water
	Environment and land management
Malawi	Inland fisheries, forestry and wildlife
Mauritius	Tourism
Mozambique	Culture and information
	Transport and communications
Namibia	Marine fisheries and resources
South Africa	Finance and investment
	Health
Swaziland	Human resources development
Tanzania	Industry and trade
Zambia	Mining
	Employment and labour
Zimbabwe	Food, agriculture and natural resources
	Crop protection

Source: Website of the Southern African Development Community: http://www.sadc.int

GNP per capita). More than two-thirds of the regional economy is accounted for by
South Africa, which contains just over 20 per cent of the SADC population. The
next largest economy is the Democratic Republic of Congo at 10 per cent of the
total (although it has the largest share of the population at around one-quarter),
then Zimbabwe at 4 per cent. These economies contrast with Lesotho, Malawi,
Mozambique and Swaziland, each of which represents around 1 per cent or less of
the SADC total. Mauritius enjoys the highest GNP per capita which is, in purchasing power parity terms, 18 times that of the poorest economy, Mozambique.

The disparities in economic welfare which are evident in Table 8.3 are accompanied by a considerable divergence of macroeconomic policy frameworks and
performance, with stronger performances apparently linked to more liberal trade
environments and more conservative economic policies.

Table 8.4 contains summary information on economic performance and macroeconomic policy indicators in the first half of the 1990s, comparing economies that
engage in more external trade with those that are comparatively closed to international trade.[5] Eight member states are classified as 'more closed' to trade and
generally display weaker policy indicators,[6] while six are 'open' and tend to have
more conservative macroeconomic policies.[7] The relative importance of foreign

Table 8.3   SADC indicators

Country	GDP 1997 (US$m)	Population 1997 (m)	GNP per capita 1996 purchasing power parity (US$)
Angola	7,785	11.6	1,030
Botswana	5,238	1.5	7,390
D. R. Congo	19,828	48.0	790
Lesotho	953	2.1	2,380
Malawi	2,326	10.1	690
Mauritius	4,136	1.1	9,000
Mozambique	2,270	18.3	500
Namibia	3,159	1.6	5,390
Seychelles	521	0.1	n/a
South Africa	132,646	42.3	7,450
Swaziland	1,138	0.9	3,320
Tanzania	5,358	31.5	n/a
Zambia	5,115	8.5	860
Zimbabwe	7,905	11.7	2,200
Total	198,378	190.1	

Source: African Development Bank, *African Development Report 1998*; World Bank, *World Development Indicators 1998*.

trade is measured by the ratio of average two-way trade (exports plus imports) to GDP over the period from 1990 to 1995. Countries are judged to have a more open trade regime when this ratio exceeds 1. The table illustrates that maintaining openness to international trade is generally consistent only with a more stable macroeconomy, where trade policy is less likely to be subordinated to the imperatives of internal and external balance.

The more trade-reliant economies, on average, grew significantly faster than the closed economies in the first half of the 1990s. Average annual growth in this period was 4.2 per cent for the more open economies, compared to 1.5 per cent in the closed economies (excluding the Democratic Republic of Congo, which is a significant outlier). This is entirely consistent with recent findings for developing countries generally and Africa specifically (reviewed in Collier and Gunning, 1999). At the same time, inflation rates were higher in the more closed group of economies, corresponding with larger government deficit ratios and higher money supply growth. Average savings rates were very similar in both groups, but the average investment ratio was higher in the group that trades more (Lesotho is a notable outlier in both cases). Aid dependence was high in all but one of the relatively closed economies.

Table 8.4   Economic performance and policy frameworks in SADC, average 1990–1995

Country	Real GDP growth (%)	Consumer price inflation (%)	External debt to GNP	Investment to GDP	Savings to GDP	Aid as % of imports	Exports+ imports to GDP	Money supply growth (%)	Real lending rates (%)	Budget deficit (excl. grants) to GDP
More open										
Botswana	5.0	12.5	17.2	33.1	31.5	5.4	124.8	8.7	0.3	5.7
Lesotho	5.4	12.9	42.2	82.3	−26.7	15.4	147.4	13.5	3.7	−4.5
Mauritius	5.3	8.2	38.8	29.6	24.3	3.5	126.7	13.6	9.4	−2.9
Namibia	4.2	11.8	12.9	20.1	13.3	9.1	119.7	25.0	6.9	−6.9
Seychelles	3.2	2.0	43.0	23.5	22.3	9.9	116.9	7.7	13.4	−6.0
Swaziland	2.3	12.7	25.8	19.9	12.0	7.4	172.6	13.9	2.5	−0.5
More closed										
Angola	−0.4	870.3	250.1	14.0	30.1	21.1	80.3	...	...	−25.7
DR Congo	−7.3	5,444.5	190.6	6.5	7.1	24.7	43.7	2,530.0	–	–
Malawi	3.5	30.8	113.2	16.4	2.9	79.2	62.0	31.1	0.0	−13.3
Mozambique	4.9	47.5	431.5	49.4	7.6	143.4	86.5	–	–	−25.5
South Africa[a]	0.6	11.8	16.5	16.2	19.7	1.1	44.9	16.3	5.8	−6.5
Tanzania	3.5	28.9	185.4	32.8	4.0	68.3	65.8	31.1	6.8	−6.5
Zambia	−0.4	117.7	222.0	12.9	10.5	95.2	64.6	61.0	−33.8	−12.4
Zimbabwe	0.5	25.9	70.4	22.1	18.2	21.4	83.3	37.0	0.0	−10.0

Note: [a] South Africa is defined as a closed economy according to the criteria used. However, it has a conservative, 'investor friendly' macroeconomic stance and probably fits more comfortably in the group of 'more open' economies.
Source: Based on Jenkins and Thomas (2000); *World Data CD-ROM, 1995*; *African Development Indicators*, various issues; World Bank, *Global Development Finance, 1997*; International Monetary Fund, *International Financial Statistics Yearbook, 1997*, *Staff Country Reports*, various issues; OECD, *Geographical Distribution of Financial Flows to Aid Recipients*, various issues; Economist Intelligence Unit, *Country Reports*, *Country Profiles*, various issues; various central bank publications from Botswana, Swaziland, Lesotho, South Africa and Zimbabwe.

There is evidence of considerable variation in domestic economic policies. More conservative policies and greater stability have tended to be evident in the group of economies that engage more in foreign trade. This is also true of South Africa which is classified as comparatively closed. Very few southern African countries managed to keep their deficit-to-GDP ratios below 5 per cent in the period considered, although there have been notable improvements for some countries in recent years. The problem has been particularly acute in those economies exhibiting evidence of macroeconomic instability – in these countries, the external debt-to-GNP ratios are high and, in many cases, rising. For these economies, a weak fiscal stance has undermined the goals of monetary, financial and trade liberalization. However, these problems are not true of all countries in the region, some of which are liberalizing successfully in the context of falling public-sector deficit ratios. Here, inflation rates are falling, and economic growth, while not spectacular, is positive and steady.

2. SADC and globalization

In recent years, globalization has arguably been the most important feature of the world economy, driven by a combination of technological advances and the liberalization of trade and financial flows. This has brought both considerable benefits in terms of increased trade, investment and growth, and new challenges for governments, especially in the developing world, through heightened vulnerability of domestic economies to external shocks.

SADC represents less than 1 per cent of world GDP and contains around 3 per cent of the world's population. The region, along with the rest of Africa, has been less affected by the trend towards globalization than other developing regions.

2.1 Trade and international capital flows

Africa's share of world exports fell between 1990 and 1996; SADC's share also declined in the early part of the 1990s, although by 1996 it had almost recovered to its 1990 level. SADC currently represents around 1 per cent of total world exports – with the South African-dominated Customs Union accounting for more than half of this share.[8]

Perhaps of greater significance is SADC's apparent lack of access to international capital flows. According to data from the World Bank,[9] total capital flows to the developing countries increased (in nominal terms) from US$98 billion in 1990 to around US$300 billion in 1997, with private capital substantially replacing aid in the composition of external capital resources. This increase has been far from evenly spread across the developing regions. The share of total net long-term resource flows to the East Asia/Pacific and Latin America/Caribbean regions increased respectively from 27 per cent and 22 per cent in 1990 to 37 per cent and

32 per cent in 1997. By contrast, sub-Saharan Africa has seen a decline in its share of total net resource flows from 17 per cent in 1990 to just 6 per cent in 1996 (a comparable figure for SADC as a region is, unfortunately, not available).

Available data indicate that the experience of SADC countries in attracting capital flows have been mixed. Angola and Mozambique have recorded large net inflows (relative to their GDP): for Angola, this has been driven by foreign investment in the offshore oil sector; for Mozambique, these inflows are largely explained by aid. Moreover, South Africa became a major emerging market destination for portfolio investment following political reform and the reintegration of the country into global capital markets. However, for most other countries in SADC, the US dollar value of net resource flows fell in the mid-1990s.

Furthermore, SADC has attracted less than 2 per cent of the total flows of foreign direct investment to developing countries in recent years (Hess, 2000). In 1997, direct investment flows to the developing countries were five times the 1990 level – and the top 10 recipients of these flows (amounting for 72 per cent of the total) were almost all in Asia and Latin America, with one east European exception (World Bank, 1998). The benefits of foreign direct investment go beyond the simple notion of capital inflows supplementing domestic savings in the financing of investment. Such flows are usually accompanied by the transfer of technology and skills and are often associated with expanding trade opportunities. For these reasons, they are generally considered to be the most desirable form of capital flow.

Creating a more attractive environment for foreign direct investment and addressing the seemingly poor perceptions that foreign investors have of the region is probably the most important challenge facing SADC if it is to take advantage of globalization. Policies to achieve these aims will be wide-ranging. For example, sustained fiscal and monetary discipline is critical for economic stability, while greater stability of the policy environment generally is crucial for domestic as well as foreign investment; at the microeconomic level, greater flexibility in labour markets, higher levels of skills and improved infrastructure are important; and, institutionally, improvements in the bureaucratic process of investment approval and greater transparency will also be necessary (Jenkins et al., 2000).

2.2 The potential adverse consequences of globalization

While there are considerable benefits to be gained from attracting increased international capital flows, there are also potentially adverse consequences. The experiences of Mexico in 1994–5 and throughout Southeast Asia in 1997–8 demonstrated the vulnerability of many emerging markets to periodic exchange rate crises. Such experiences demonstrate the need for countries with increasingly open economies to develop appropriate policy responses to volatile swings in capital flows and other forms of external shocks. This will be an important challenge for SADC governments as they seek to become more integrated in the global economy and as financial markets in the region become more sophisticated.

Within SADC, South Africa, with its relatively sophisticated financial markets, has been particularly exposed to volatile capital flows, experiencing surges in capital inflows in 1995 and 1997, followed by exchange rate crises in 1996 and more recently in 1998 – at least in part in response to the general crisis in emerging markets. Zimbabwe has experienced large outflows, severe exchange-rate depreciation and high rates of inflation in 1998 and 1999, although these were driven more by domestic political and economic factors. The underdeveloped nature of financial markets in the rest of SADC has, at least to date, meant that the region has largely been insulated from emerging market trends. However, to the extent that financial crises in other parts of the world impact on world economic growth (and, therefore, trade) and direct investment flows, the effects of 'crisis contagion' on southern Africa may be more subtle and long-term (see e.g. CREFSA, 1997).

3. The SADC free trade area

In order to overcome the problems of small markets coupled with marginalization in the world economy, SADC member states are currently negotiating the terms of a regional free trade area (FTA). This is perhaps the most important initiative being undertaken by SADC. A trade protocol has been drafted which calls for the establishment of an FTA within eight years of ratification, with the gradual elimination of tariffs and non-tariff barriers to trade over this period. Following the adoption of the protocol in 1996, SADC trade ministers and officials have been working towards a programme for the implementation of the FTA. The establishment of the FTA is expected to mean the freeing of around 90 per cent of intra-regional trade, in line with the rules of the World Trade Organization which state that 'free trade' should cover 'substantially all' trade.

As shown earlier, at least half of SADC members have been relatively closed to international trade. In part, restrictive trade policies have been driven by a perceived need to protect weak domestic industries, but they have also been used as an instrument for balancing otherwise unstable macroeconomic regimes. Since the beginning of the 1990s, extensive unilateral trade liberalization has occurred across southern Africa – either through aid-supported structural adjustment programmes or, in the case of SACU, through agreement with the WTO. More recently, attention has turned to the role of regional trade liberalization in encouraging faster economic growth across southern Africa.

3.1 The importance of trade openness for growth

Over the past 30 years, economic growth in Africa has compared poorly with that of other developing regions. During the 1980s, average annual growth in sub-Saharan Africa was just 1.7 per cent compared to an average of 3.1 per cent for all developing countries; in the first half of the 1990s, this gap narrowed slightly (to

2.0 per cent versus 2.9 per cent), but economic growth has generally been insufficient to generate substantial improvements in well-being across the region.[10] Regional trade liberalization is seen as an important step in efforts to improve growth rates in southern Africa – in the long term, liberalization is expected to generate a significant increase in intra-regional trade and cross-border investment.

The importance of an open trade environment in explaining economic growth performance has been demonstrated in a variety of studies covering both developed and developing countries. One conclusion to emerge from the literature is that openness to trade is associated with higher rates of economic growth, or, conversely, that a lack of openness to trade is correlated with poor growth performance.[11]

International trade facilitates technology transfers, the exchange of information, and opportunities to realize economies of scale, and trade agreements provide greater certainty for trade policy generally, especially in countries which have a history of reversing moves towards unilateral liberalization. As all of this reduces the risks of – or raises the returns to – investment, greater volumes of investment provide one of the reasons for the observed positive relationship between openness to trade and economic growth. This has been found to be the case in several studies which are concerned with investment in Africa.[12]

Clearly, a more liberal trade policy does not explain everything about a country's economic growth rate. There are a variety of other important explanatory factors, like human capital (education and health), the type of investment undertaken (not only the volume), political stability, the presence or absence of market distortions, diversification away from a dependence on primary (especially non-mineral) exports, and location. In Africa, the magnitude and persistence of external shocks, deficient public service provision, and political and economic instability have also been found to correlate negatively with growth. For trade liberalization to yield higher economic growth, a broader range of policies are needed to create an accommodating environment for growth (Jenkins et al., 2000).

3.2 Regional integration and economic convergence

Regional trade liberalization enables members – especially those which are poorer – to reap some of the gains from trade via larger markets and improved efficiency, without exposure to non-regional competition.[13] There is evidence that regional trade groups form convergence clubs, where poorer members catch up with (converge on) richer ones through the process of trade (Ben-David, 1995; Barro and Sala-i-Martin, 1991; Dowrick and Nguyen, 1989). It has been argued that all countries which are open and integrated in the world economy are, in fact, members of a convergence club (Sachs and Warner, 1995: 41).

There is evidence that, as elsewhere, trade among African countries promotes convergence. There are problems attached to measures of macroeconomic convergence, but two of the simpler measures are set out below in order to illustrate SADC trends.[14]

The most simple measure is σ-convergence, when the dispersion of income levels across countries diminishes over time, with dispersion typically measured by the deviation of each country's per capita income from the average for the group. If countries which are initially very different are converging, it is expected that this deviation will be growing smaller.

Consider the European Union as a point of reference for comparison. Since the formation of the Common Market in the 1950s, the dispersion of per capita income of all EU members has fallen, as shown in Figure 8.5.[15] There was some interruption to this trend in 1982–3, when a degree of divergence occurred, but this was subsequently reversed.

The calculations for SADC members are plotted in Figure 8.6. In contrast to the downward-sloping pattern of convergence that is evident in the data for EU countries, the pattern for SADC countries is essentially flat – indicating that no convergence in per capita incomes has occurred over the 30-year period. Indeed, the degree of dispersion was marginally higher at the end of the period than at the beginning, which suggests that the countries have, if anything, *diverged* slightly. The absence of convergence among the SADC countries may be due to several factors, including different responses to the oil and exchange-rate shocks of the 1970s, and different problems with indebtedness, but there are also uniquely domestic policy issues which have promoted or slowed growth.

If, however, the sub-sample of SACU member countries is examined separately, as shown in Figure 8.7, a strikingly different pattern emerges. Although the intra-SACU dispersion of per capita incomes held roughly constant through the 1960s, it dropped steadily in the 1970s and 1980s. The result of this downward trend was that the dispersion at the end of the period was little more than half what it had been at the beginning – a degree of convergence that slightly *exceeds* that evident in the EU countries over the same period. It is particularly interesting that neither the oil price shocks of the 1970s nor the gold price shock of 1980 – both of which would have had asymmetric effects on the SACU countries – caused any significant interruption to this pattern of convergence.

The second measure of convergence is β-convergence. This occurs when countries which are initially poorest grow faster than those which are richer, 'catching up' with richer economies. A downward-sloping plot of average growth rates on initial GDP will indicate possible β-convergence: if the hypothesis of convergence is supported by the data, then those countries whose per capita income was below the average for all countries at the beginning of the period should have higher average growth rates subsequently.

In Figures 8.8 and 8.9, time-averaged growth rates (average growth between 1960 and 1990) for members of the EU (Figure 8.8) and SADC (Figure 8.9) are plotted against initial (1960) GDP per capita relative to the regional average.[16]

In 1960, the poorest country in Europe in per capita income terms was Portugal, whose income per head was 64 per cent below the European average at that point. Portugal grew by an average of 4.8 per cent in real terms annually over the next 30

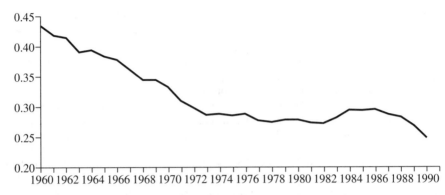

Figure 8.1   Standard deviation of log of per capita income: EU

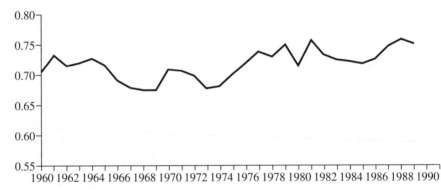

Figure 8.2   Standard deviation of log of per capita income: SADC

Figure 8.3   Standard deviation of log of per capita income: SACU

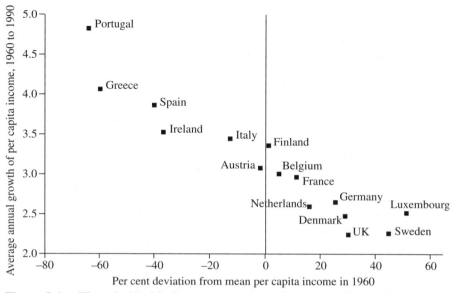

Figure 8.4 **The relationship between per capita income in 1960 and subsequent growth (EU)**

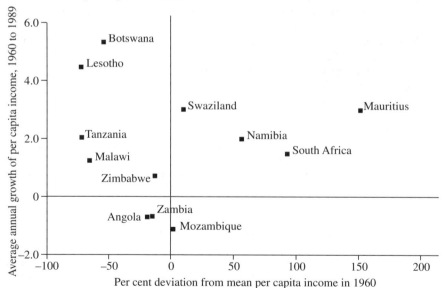

Figure 8.5 **The relationship between per capita income in 1960 and subsequent growth (SADC)**

years. On the other hand, Sweden and Britain, with per capita incomes 45 and 30 per cent above the average respectively in 1960, grew most slowly over the decade.

Figure 8.9 shows that, using this second measure, there is no pattern of convergence among southern African economies over the period. Almost all of the below-average economies in income per capita terms had below-average growth rates over the period, while Mauritius began best-off in 1960 and grew on average 3 per cent each year (in terms of real income per head) over the 30 years which followed.

However, if one looks at the subset of SACU countries, there is again a very clear trend of convergence, with initially low-income Botswana and Lesotho converging on Swaziland, Namibia and South Africa, but diverging from Malawi and Tanzania which began with similar levels of income per head.

Both measures of convergence demonstrate that SADC countries have, if anything, diverged over the 30 years between 1960 and 1990. This implies that the relatively rich have been getting richer, while the poor have been getting poorer. It should be noted that there is no reason to expect that the SADC countries should have converged, as free trade in the Community is a very recent ideal. However, within the Customs Union movements of goods have been free for most of the century and smaller members have grown rapidly, particularly since the early 1970s.

The possible reasons for convergence in SACU include:

1 free trade between SACU members;
2 transfers from South Africa to other members under an enhanced customs revenue formula;
3 the existence of a currency union (Botswana is not a member of the Common Monetary Area, but the pula largely tracks the rand);
4 similar (comparatively conservative) macroeconomic policies;
5 country-specific factors which have little to do with regional arrangements (Jenkins and Thomas, 1998).

These explanations are not mutually exclusive: cases 2 to 5 do not rule out the importance of international trade in driving convergence in SACU. Although this evidence is not conclusive, it seems likely that access to the South African market has allowed smaller members to escape the limitations imposed by small domestic markets and this trend is at least consistent with that of other regions, both developed and developing.

3.3 Implications for SADC: the potential benefits of the FTA

The existence of one convergence club in southern Africa provides some grounds for optimism that 'catch-up' convergence could also occur in a more closely integrated SADC. Smaller members of SADC stand to gain from regional integration in a variety of ways:

1 South Africa is more than twice the size of the *sum* of the economies of the other SADC members, each of which therefore stands to increase its export markets substantially, with the potential for reaping economies of scale in domestic production.
2 While exposure to South African competition will inevitably eliminate some production, more efficient firms will improve productivity and output, and diversification into products for the comparatively large South African market can be expected.
3 Exposure to South African competition will help prepare smaller countries for greater integration into the world economy, by enhancing both quality and productivity and thereby competitiveness.
4 Countries undergoing donor-funded structural adjustment programmes (SAPs) will find the credibility of their trade liberalization enhanced, because the policy lock-in mechanism of a regional FTA should be more effective than liberalization under SAPs has proved to be. If SADC develops an effective enforcement procedure, the costs of reversal of the SADC process could be high for a defaulting member, making it more likely that policy changes will be sustained.
5 Outward investment from South Africa will both increase resources (access to savings and foreign exchange) and provide opportunities for technology transfers and better integration with South Africa's more sophisticated financial markets.
6 Greater two-way trade together with foreign (mainly South African) investment should generate industrial development and help the diversification of production into non-traditional exports.

South Africa also stands to benefit from the regional FTA in various ways:

1 There should be some market expansion, particularly for manufactured output, as the SADC countries are an important destination for South Africa's manufactures. There are two caveats to this: first, in aggregate the SADC market is considerably smaller than South Africa's total (formal) domestic market; and second, market penetration by South African exporters will probably occur anyway, even without a SADC FTA.
2 The FTA will increase opportunities for profitable cross-border investment, not least by improving the flow of information.
3 South African investment in the region will generate additional demand for South African goods, with second-round growth effects for existing firms.
4 There should be slower inward cross-border migration if the neighbours are expanding their economic – and especially industrial – capacity. Higher rates of economic growth from increased trade and greater investment should create jobs in the smaller countries, some of which are exporting labour both legally and illegally to South Africa.

However, regional trade liberalization is not in itself a solution to creating economic growth in the region. There are three important points that need to be considered.

First, South Africa should not be tied to the region at the expense of pursuing wider economic opportunities; second, regional integration should be viewed as a first step in the process of wider trade integration; and finally, SADC governments need to adopt macro- and microeconomic policies that are consistent with promoting trade and investment. These issues are explored below.

3.4 Implications for SADC: regional integration will not be enough for South Africa

One of the implications of the notion of convergence clubs is that there may be limits to the extent to which growth performance via regional arrangements can be enhanced: 'catch-up' implies that the benefits in terms of economic growth are greater the lower the initial level of income. In other words, the richest member is constrained in the extent to which economic growth can be accelerated by the forces driving catch-up. This suggests that, if South Africa is to improve its own growth performance, it will need to look beyond the region.

Securing higher future rates of economic growth in South Africa and in the region as a whole requires that South Africa expand its trade agreements beyond that with SADC. There are three reasons for this. First, South Africa does not reap significant dynamic gains from regional trade: on average it has superior technology, is the source of most of the region's investment, gains no enhanced credibility, and has limited opportunities to reap economies of scale. Second, many of the non-SACU members of SADC are instinctively protectionist, and regional integration is seen by some of them as an *alternative* to unilateral liberalization. A frequently raised motivation for regional integration in Africa is a lowering of dependence on OECD economies. In this way, their agenda is different from that of South Africa (and the other SACU members) which has embarked on a process of closer integration into the world economy via unilateral liberalization under its WTO agreement. Finally, South Africa needs to be in a position where it will have the opportunity to converge on both high-income and fast-growing economies. Jenkins (1997) thus argues that South Africa should look to establish a network of reciprocal FTAs with regions such as the EU, NAFTA, East Asia and possibly Australasia. It is argued that it is in the interests of SADC as a whole for the dominant partner to accelerate its growth through expanding trade with the rest of the world. The agreement between SACU and the EU is highlighted below.

3.5 SADC and global integration

For all SADC members, regional integration should not be perceived as an alternative to more general trade liberalization, which is crucial if African economies are to grow, but rather as one step in a process of greater integration into international markets. Regional integration is complementary to global integration: it can play an important role in facilitating trade and investment through creating larger markets, which could ultimately enable SADC to compete in the global context.

Continued progress in liberalizing *vis-à-vis* the rest of the world is important for the entire region. Two interrelated initiatives are of particular relevance: the free trade agreement between South Africa (and the other members of SACU) and the EU; and the negotiations on the successor to the Lomé Convention, through which SADC members (with the exception of South Africa) have preferential access to the EU market.

In June 1995 negotiations commenced between South Africa and the EU over trade preferences. South Africa's initial request for Lomé status was rejected, but the country was offered a free trade agreement, with immediate access to Europe for most exports in return for phased exposure to European exporters. The FTA was expected to offer potential benefits both for South Africa and the region, although, as with any trade liberalization, there were concerns about the short-term impact on domestic producers. For South Africa, it offered the potential (long-term) opportunity for stronger growth and convergence with higher-income economies; and stronger growth in South Africa would also provide a stimulus to other regional economies.

The negotiations between the EU and South Africa have been drawn out and difficult. It became apparent at a fairly early stage that the agreement would be modest in its scope, with only a small percentage of SACU's current exports facing a material improvement in terms of access to the EU (see e.g. Stevens, 1997). The EU's negotiating mandate was unattractive to South Africa in its early insistence that fishing rights be tied to trade negotiations and its exclusion of certain agricultural products from discussion, a factor which reduced South Africa's ability to exchange concessions with the EU. In addition, South African manufacturers were wary of greater exposure to foreign competition before the WTO commitments had been fully discharged, and were consequently ambivalent about the process. South Africa was also under pressure from its partners in SACU and in SADC, which were (and continue to be) concerned about the implications of the free trade agreement for their economies, in terms of exposure to European competition.

A trade, development and cooperation agreement was finally signed at the end of 1999, amid disputes over the naming of fortified wines and the position of canned fruit exports. Subsequently, implementation has been further complicated by objections from some EU governments on the naming of spirits. At the time of writing, these issues were yet to be resolved, despite the fact that the agreement was due to be implemented at the beginning of 2000.

In essence, the proposed agreement allows for tariff phase-down by the EU over a maximum of six years (with the exception of certain agricultural and fisheries products), while South Africa has up to ten years to eliminate tariffs on most of its imports from the EU. A special safeguard is written into the agreement to cover 'disruption' of agricultural markets by exports of one party to the other; and a review within five years of the entire agreement is also included. The treaty also includes specific provision for developing and promoting cooperation not only between the parties to the agreement but also with the rest of southern Africa. Areas specifically noted for the development of regional linkages include small enterprise development, telecommunications and information technology, energy, mining, transport and tourism.

Ultimately, the conduct of the negotiations between the EU and South Africa has sent negative signals to other developing countries as they begin to negotiate the successor to the Lomé Convention. At the time of writing, the existing Lomé arrangements had been extended for a period of seven years, during which time negotiations on a fundamentally different form of trade and aid agreement would take place between the EU and the group of 70 African, Caribbean and Pacific (ACP) countries, to be phased in over a further 12 years. The EU appears to favour the establishment for all but the least developed of the ACP group of regionally negotiated trade agreements that would be based on the principle of reciprocal but asymmetric access to markets. These proposals face considerable opposition within the ACP group.

The EU's agreement with South Africa was widely regarded as a test case for the post-Lomé arrangements. The obstacles created by the EU in concluding the agreement with South Africa has reinforced the view that the EU will not compromise on its remaining protectionism. This is likely to have increased the reluctance of the ACP countries to consider alternatives to the existing Lomé arrangements.

3.6 Making the FTA work

Regional trade policy is just one element of the overall economic policy framework, each component of which needs to be consistent with the others if the goals of trade liberalization are to be realized.[17] Although much of the work needed to make regionalism successful in southern Africa is in the hands of domestic governments, there is scope for regional initiatives to support the FTA – for example, there is potential for improving transport links through regional networks and for developing multi-country initiatives to attract investment.[18] Moreover, the perceived need for sharing the potential gains from regional trade will inevitably require some mechanism for ensuring balanced development in the region. One alternative that is currently being explored is the creation of a regional development fund, financing investment in infrastructure, which could accompany the establishment of the FTA.

The potential role of supporting regional initiatives suggests that it will be vital for the various sectors of SADC (as illustrated in Table 8.2 above) to coordinate their activities. For example, while the regional FTA is the responsibility of the industry and trade sector in Tanzania, a regional development fund would more naturally fall under the remit of the finance and investment sector in South Africa. Development corridors and spatial development initiatives could require coordination across several sectors, depending on the nature of the projects envisaged. Such coordination will be important to reduce duplication of effort and to ensure an appropriate targeting of limited resources. Political rivalries, however, may make such cooperation difficult in the foreseeable future.

4. Political barriers to regional integration

Previous sections of this chapter have argued that trade liberalization is not a panacea in itself. SADC member states must implement consistent macroeconomic policies together with micro measures to improve the environment for investment if regional integration is to deliver the long-term goal of stronger economic growth.

Nor is policy implementation the only barrier to successful regional integration in southern Africa. There is also evidence of political tensions in SADC. These tensions surfaced during 1998 following the direct intervention by some member states in the war in the Democratic Republic of Congo, while other members attempted to pursue resolution through talks. This conflict, together with the continuing civil war in Angola, has had significant economic and security implications for some SADC member states. At the time of writing, there was no clear resolution in sight for these conflicts. While political instability remains in parts of the region there is a continuing risk that political divisions may undermine the fragile process of regional integration in southern Africa.

Underlying many of the political tensions in southern Africa is a fear of the dominance of South Africa. As already noted, South Africa represents more than two-thirds of the regional economy and is expected to benefit the most, at least in the short term, from any regional trade integration initiative. There is a clear need for South Africa to be seen to be taking the concerns of its smaller neighbours seriously, although, as argued above, this should not occur at the expense of a more outward-oriented focus. South Africa has shown its willingness to make concessions – such as opening its markets to regional partners more rapidly than called for as part of the proposed SADC FTA. It is yet to be seen whether this will be enough to allay fears of polarization of industry in South Africa as a result of integration. In the longer term, the development of regionalism in southern Africa will prove politically sustainable only if cooperation is seen to benefit each of the participating countries.

5. Spillover effects and macroeconomic policy coordination

Within southern Africa, there has been some debate on the need for more general economic policy coordination among member states, in particular in the form of monetary integration. International interest in policy coordination is driven in part by the spillover (cross-border) effects of macroeconomic policy, which are particularly acute when small countries are closely linked to larger economies. This is at least one motivation for the concern within SADC over this issue: it arises both because of South Africa's dominance in the region and because of the cross-border impact of uncoordinated structural adjustment programmes.[19]

Monetary cooperation usually takes the form of fixed exchange rates, where the smaller country makes a one-sided commitment to fix to the currency of the dominant country, which sets policy freely. However, few fixed rate regimes have remained intact, as reserves available to support exchange rates are frequently dwarfed by potential short-term capital flows which magnify weaknesses in the commitment to the fixed exchange rate. Experiences in Europe (1992), Mexico (1994–5) and Asia (1997–8) have shown that a fixed or pegged exchange rate regime can be costly to maintain when there is a lack of credibility or where the regime is perceived as unsustainable. It is worth noting, however, that the Common Monetary Area, encompassing South Africa, Lesotho, Namibia and Swaziland, has been sustained over a period of many years and has, arguably, yielded benefits for the smaller economies in terms of macroeconomic stability, in comparison to many of their southern African neighbours.

Monetary union is optimal among economies that are very similar. If participants exhibit marked differences, it is imperative that one or a combination of conditions holds: there is wage flexibility; there is mobility of labour; politically acceptable transfers are possible; and/or countries react similarly and flexibly to shocks. On the other hand, in a group of countries marked by rigidities and immobility a degree of real economic convergence is necessary for exchange-rate/monetary policy coordination. Moreover, in practice, any group of countries contemplating a policy union will require convergence in macroeconomic stability indicators, like inflation and debt ratios, as a prerequisite for admission in order to protect other members from adverse policy spillover effects.

Many of the SADC economies are characterized by rigidities and immobility. Moreover, members react differently to external shocks; and, as shown earlier, there is divergence in policy and stability indicators. Jenkins and Thomas (1998) conclude that the apparent lack of macroeconomic convergence of the SADC countries (as illustrated above) and the significant divergence of policy and stability indicators suggest that southern Africa is not yet in a position to establish and maintain regional monetary integration.

Premature attempts at policy coordination could have political costs that weaken the prospects for cooperation in areas such as trade and infrastructural development. Feldstein (1988) argues that an attempt to pursue coordination in a wide range of macro variables is likely to result in disagreements and disappointments that reduce the prospects for cooperation in the more limited areas of trade, defence and foreign assistance where cooperation is necessary. Moreover, the mechanisms for consultation and agreement may slow down the implementation of painful policy decisions.

It would appear that it is premature for SADC to attempt macroeconomic policy harmonization, even in the face of real problems of unbalanced economic power and spillover effects. Instead, by concentrating on issues that are of most immediate concern – and that are more likely to 'work' – SADC may successfully build a platform from which to embark on more ambitious regional integration initiatives in the longer term.

6. Concluding comments

This chapter has argued that SADC has the potential to become a sustainable regional institution promoting economic growth in southern Africa. However, it is important that the underlying political tensions in the region are addressed so that they do not become a destabilizing factor in the process of integration.

The Community as a whole needs to adopt an outward-looking focus rather than a narrow regional view. For South Africa, this is particularly important for accelerating its own economic growth. Regionalism in southern Africa should be seen as a step towards increased participation in the global economy. In particular, the SADC FTA could become a means for pursuing trade agreements with a range of developed and developing regions.

Finally, coordination of activities within the institutional divisions of SADC will be of increasing importance as the region becomes more integrated. Regional cooperation across a wide range of sectors could contribute to creating consistent policy frameworks for increasing trade and cross-border investment. However, much of the responsibility in this area will ultimately lie in the hands of the individual countries' governments themselves.

Notes

1　Parts of this chapter draw on Jenkins et al., 2000.
2　For example, the southern African Customs Union; the (rand) Common Monetary Area; and the CFA franc zone. It is interesting to note that these relatively successful initiatives involve links with a more developed partner – in SACU and the CMA, the partner is South Africa; the CFA franc was previously linked to the French franc and is now linked to the euro.
3　See Berg, 1988; Collier and Gunning, 1996; Decaluwé et al., 1995; De Melo et al., 1993; Elbadawi, 1995; Fine and Yeo, 1994; Foroutan, 1993.
4　It is not suggested that the relief of this constraint necessarily confers success: SADC has shown evidence of political divisions (see below), while other regional groupings, notably COMESA and the new East African Community, are showing considerable political commitment to closer integration.
5　This section draws on Jenkins and Thomas, 2000.
6　The exception is South Africa, which is defined as more 'closed', but which has a conservative, 'investor-friendly' macroeconomic policy stance.
7　It is possible to group SADC countries by a range of different criteria: for example, SACU and non-SACU members, or open and closed economies, or those that export mineral or agricultural products. The distinction chosen here is between those that have a more conservative policy stance, and those which have struggled to liberalize their economies. Some of these economies significantly improved their economic performance in the late 1990s.
8　*Direction of Trade Statistics Yearbook*, International Monetary Fund (various years).
9　World Bank, *Global Development Finance 1998.*

10 There is significant variation in the economic growth of countries in the region. In the 1980s growth rates ranged from 10.3 per cent in Botswana to 0.8 per cent in Zambia; in the first half of the 1990s, growth was 7.1 per cent in Mozambique compared to −6.6 per cent in the Democratic Republic of Congo.

11 See e.g. Edwards, 1993; Sachs and Warner, 1997; Sala-i-Martin, 1997. These findings are not wholly undisputed, however; see e.g. Rodriguez and Rodrik, 1999 and Krishna et al., 1998. In a review of African growth performance, Collier and Gunning (1999) point out that Africa is less open than other regions to trade, partly due to policy and partly due to natural barriers, for example in the case of landlocked states. Almost all of the studies of Africa find that impediments to trade have been detrimental to African growth performance, reducing the annual growth rate by 0.4–1.2 percentage points.

12 Sachs and Warner, 1995; Bhattacharaya et al., 1996; Collier and Gunning, 1996.

13 This section draws on Jenkins and Thomas, 1998.

14 For a third, more technical measure, see Jenkins and Thomas, 1998.

15 Data are from the Penn World Tables, Mark 5.6. Figures 8.5–8.7 are from Jenkins and Thomas, 1998.

16 Data are from the Penn World Tables, Mark 5.6; see Summers and Heston, 1991. Figures 8.8 and 8.9 are from Jenkins and Thomas, 1998.

17 A recent study by Jenkins et al. (2000) considers a broad range of policies that could be implemented to support the proposed SADC Free Trade Area. This study finds that in several areas, current domestic policies in SADC are incompatible with the aims of regional trade liberalization.

18 There is growing interest in the concept of cross-border development corridors in southern Africa and, in South Africa, the government is promoting the similar concept of spatial development initiatives. Such projects generally involve government, local and foreign businesses and multilateral agencies and are aimed at promoting the development of infrastructure and investment across several sectors within a particular (cross-border) area. For example, the Maputo Corridor runs between the industrial Witwatersrand–Pretoria region of South Africa and the port of Maputo in Mozambique, passing through areas of mining, industry, agriculture, forestry and tourism. (Maasdorp, 2000.)

19 For example, Zimbabwe's devaluation was argued to have negatively affected Botswana's regional exports.

Part III
European Union as a New
Civilian Power in the Making

9. The European Union and the Challenges of the Near Abroad

Mario Telò

A distinctive feature of this book is the consideration of possible tensions between the EU's increasing global actorship and its relations to the near abroad. The two dimensions, regional and global, are not always easy to reconcile. Global responsibilities demand further integration, by representing the EU worldwide and also more centralized and efficient decision-making. The regional dimension however entails both issues, deepening and widening; enhanced ability to act at continental and Mediterranean level, but also a pressure for wider membership, up to now without any strategically defined borders. Since the size matters and the very nature of a regional organization interacts with the balance between deepening and enlarging, we will commence by analysing the evolving relationship of the EC-EU with the "near abroad", namely with the Eastern/continental dimension and with its southern neighbours.

The evolution of European regionalism is confronted with very complex challenges coming from the so-called arch of the crisis, from the East to South of the EU. R. Seidelmann and G. Joffé both contribute to this volume, respectively considering Eastern Europe and the Mediterranean. A common problem concerns the complex interrelationship between the economic and political dimension of partnership, and the changing balance between the military dimension and the other issues. In both cases, even if during the last decade we witnessed a shift towards dramatic military and civilian crises, a new kind of threat is emerging, i.e. ethnic fundamentalism, refugee flows and so on. Secondly, in both cases, even if for different reasons, the original kind of Western European regionalism is being challenged because of the implications of multiple demands of full membership.

1. European Union and the challenge of a continental Europe

Ten years after the fall of the Berlin Wall we are witnessing a new situation as far as continental Europe is concerned.[1] On the one hand, we see Western-centred

East–West cooperation. In spite of domestic instability, Russia's step by step integration into Western international organizations and a change in Russian priorities are making a military conflict between East and West unthinkable. "In comparison with the past, the new East–West relations in Europe are basically demilitarized, based on economic and political cooperation and on a Western-dominated power formula" (Seidelmann). On the other hand, as confirmed by the Kosovo war, nationalism, ethnocentric movements and economic backwardness, in one word, "Yugoslavization", make the design of a new European peace order not yet credible, by highlighting the political limits of the EU. Moreover, one must not underestimate the collapse of Eastern European subregional cooperation[2]: "Visegrad", "Black Sea community" and "Community of Independent States". Last but not least, the new pan-European institutional architecture, shaped after 1989 (the institutionalization of the Organization for Security and Cooperation in Europe, 1990 "Charta of Paris" and revival of the Council of Europe), is largely disappointing as far as the governance of the continent is concerned. Certainly, the EU and NATO are the major actors at continental level and they dominate political and economic developments in Eastern countries. However since their strategies and interests present both similarities and differences, the first question is to what extent and how is the EU strengthening its role as a regional engine, and to what extent is its role submitted to the leadership of others. It is a matter of fact that such huge regional problems already changed from an inter-bloc issue to a major challenge for the EU, and constitute a global issue, concerning also the main world power.

Let us turn to the second question. The EU is becoming more and more of an attraction from an economic and civilian point of view. Among the twenty-four applications for membership during the history of European integration, ten were from Central and Eastern Europe and some more will come. This proves the significant regional influence of the EU and its impact on both domestic policy and the external relations of Eastern neighbouring countries.[3] History, security, economy and social links create a high degree of interdependence between the two parts of Europe. Since part of Eastern Europe still faces obstacles and difficulties regarding democratization, growth and peace, if the EU proves itself unable to manage, control and solve these problems, they will consequently have an impact on the EU's inner democracy, legitimacy and political support. The integration process itself would likely be put in question as a result.

The EU is being challenged to cope with its pan-European responsibilities. On the one hand, if the EU, as an organization, fails in the present rivalry with NATO (enlargement and partnership with Russia) and with the larger Member States (in the logic of national spheres of influence), it will lose the political support of European public opinion. This would threaten the basic idea of the EU as a community for peace, wealth and democracy building. On the other hand, the huge political, financial, institutional, social and cultural implications of the next Eastern enlargement have no precedent in the history of European construction.

The current situation shows dramatic weakness, as far as EU regional action is concerned, regarding enforcing and settling peace agreements, defending national minority rights and implementing a so-called "Marshall Plan " for Eastern Europe. Seidelmann's paper underlines three major limits of the EU as far as a regional actor is concerned:

- In spite of the "Stability Pact" and the new "common strategies", approved in 1999 by the Cologne European Council (regarding Russia) and by Helsinki (regarding Ukraine),[4] the EU still lacks a comprehensive, cost-efficient, and cohesive political-economic "grand" strategy towards Eastern Europe, the Balkans and Russia in particular.
- The Maastricht CSFP project, in spite of the improvements approved in Amsterdam (new Treaty provisions) and in Helsinki (new military means for "Petersberg tasks" and defence policy) still lacks a satisfying degree of institutionalization and policy implementation.
- The EU shows clear limits regarding its diplomatic power in relation to inter-governmental bodies (the "Contact group " for instance), to Nation States' power and to the American role in Europe.

As a consequence, in terms of power, the EU shows its dramatic deficits in the case of the remilitarization of local conflicts (as shown by the former Yugoslavia and former USSR experience), particularly in comparison with the enhanced NATO role in Eastern European security challenges.

Ten years after 1989, instead of a homogeneous trend, we are observing not one, but instead many "Eastern Europes". There is a "winners group" (such as Poland, the Czech Republic, Slovenia and Hungary), where relative success in economic and democratic transition is making EU enlargement possible, in the medium term.[5] There is a "losers group" (Russia, Ukraine, Belarus, but also some of the Balkan countries). Here, the failure of economic and political reform has provoked a vicious circle of dependence on the West. Economic crisis, domestic turbulence, foreign and domestic malevolence and the real threat of regional instability and anti-West movements have aggravated this. After the Kosovo war, a new group was born, including Albania, Macedonia, Yugoslavia, Croatia, Bosnia, Serbia, Montenegro and Kosovo, where *ad hoc* plans and new priorities have been agreed, because of political and humanitarian criteria. In conclusion, the general picture is still very ambiguous concerning the feasibility of a new peace and democratic order at pan-European level.

As far as the foreseeable future is concerned, two developments are possible, since the Yugoslavian tragedies of the 1990s definitely shattered the rhetorical idealistic approach of a general benevolence and a final victory for democratic values. Either one can conceive the Eastern European problems as marginal for the global governance of the world economy and security, or one can emphasize the threat coming from pan-Slavonic fundamentalism, both in the Balkans and in the former Soviet Union. The first vision takes into account the dramatic decline of the former USSR as a superpower, the end of the nuclear threat and the transformation of Eastern Europe as part of a growing and encompassing EU, becoming a soft hegemonic regional power, organizing the continent in concentric circles, integrating norms and interests. In the second vision, nationalism, fundamentalism and ethnic conflicts will increase regional wild instability, even if not in the civilization's clash picture. The attempt to build collective security institutions in Europe was formerly conceived as a step between traditional defence institutions and cooperative security institutions.[6] But one of the problems is that, in case of military conflict, the EU needs to be complemented by its competitor: the enlarging NATO's more effective parallel role.

The issue of the political role of the EU interacts with the challenge of enlargement. Regarding the future of West European regionalism in the new pan-European environment, 1989–91 was a historical turning point. The small-sized, economic and functional European Community has gone. The consequences of continental change are contradictory and potentially conflicting. On one hand, the new European Union, including a political union, needs deepening and strengthening in order to cope with external responsibilities and challenges. On the other hand, the external demands of a huge expansion process force the EU to increase internal differentiation and consequently to set a new regional integration model. The large array of instruments and the fluctuation of EU-Ost-Politik of the past decade, from President J. Delors' project of "concentric circles", to the Copenhagen European Council setting the criteria for Eastern enlargement (1993), to the "Agenda 2000" (1999), to the Helsinki Council's openness, show a lack of strategy. However, the acceptance of the principle of thirteen candidates, with the as yet unclear issue of the final Eastern border, raises the question of the institutional settlement in a wider Europe and interacts deeply with the hard process of Treaty revision. The debate on hard core, flexible integration and "enhanced cooperation" has to be seen as a reaction to the growing uncertainties of regional integration within the new geopolitics of a continental Europe. Later on, we will explore the alternative scenarios. The crucial Balkan challenge has clearly shown that only an efficient, legitimized internal political differentiation, included within the institutional framework of the European Treaties, could overcome opposite (even if not entirely contradictory) trends, either towards a kind of Voltairean "Candide Europe" or towards an unaccountable directorate of major states (according to the path of the "Contact group").

2. European Union and near abroad: Mediterranean

The second important chapter of the near abroad is the Mediterranean region. At first glance, there are important similarities with the relationship of the EU to Eastern Europe:

• First, European policy is ambitious but ambiguous, including both duality (EU openness to external partners belonging to its periphery) and, as far as some countries are concerned, a promised deeper linkage, namely the Union's enlargement (regarding Cyprus, Malta and Turkey);

- Secondly, after the end of the world's bipolar structure, increasing differences emerged between the USA and the EU as far as interest and security perceptions in that area were concerned. The EU is not only the dominant trade and economic partner with northern African and southern Mediterranean countries (see tables in Joffé's chapter). What is more, the interdependence between Western Europe and northern Africa regarding energy provisions (more particularly since gas pipelines are partly substituting oil) is crucial and symbiotic. The USA has mainly strategic security concerns (plus price stability) in that area.[7] Furthermore, almost every EU State is also seriously concerned with regulating immigration, in preventing crime, illegal traffic and terrorism.[8]

Beyond the historical colonial and post-colonial links, this important background explains the EU's interest in the success of the "Barcelona process", which started in 1995 and brings together the northern and southern rims of the Mediterranean (fifteen EU countries plus twelve southern Mediterranean countries). It excludes the US while the OSCE does not. However, the "Euro-Mediterranean partnership" is particularly asymmetric as regards the respective main concerns and expectations of the two rims: multiple security issues on the one hand, and economic development on the other. The so-called "European methodology" had been applied again, in order to increase economic interdependence as a means towards a pacific settlement of security issues in the long run.

As far as the impact of the European-Mediterranean process in general is concerned, we are still witnessing a rather modest result. The EC and the EU can be seen as successful past democratizers of the European rim of the Mediterranean region from the very beginning of the integration process (taking the example of young post-fascist democracies like Italy, Spain, Greece or Portugal). However, in the countries where no promise of full membership is possible, "democratic conditionality" hardly works.

For the coming decade, though more external, new Mediterranean candidates, namely Malta, Cyprus and particularly Turkey, raise hopes of a successful gradual replication. But very little is happening regarding the democratization of other southern Mediterranean countries.

Past common statements and actions, concerning the Middle East and North Africa, have largely been failures. The "Venice statement" of 1978, the ECP, the Euro–Arab dialogue, the Lisbon European Council's 1992 conclusion (which declared the Middle East a zone of common interest) and finally the CFSP joint actions in the Middle East since 1993, were not particularly successful. This underlines the fact that the "Barcelona process" challenge is very tough.[9] The 1995 Barcelona Declaration expresses the common consciousness of EU Member States, that geographical proximity and European interests in the region demand a more encompassing and long-term strategy than previously. These should bring together all dimensions of a very complex relationship, and reject the catastrophic scenarios regarding intercultural dialogue. It has been structured in accordance with the "CSCE-OSCE" model (Helsinki process), underlining, even by such formal parallelism, the request of many Member States, to balance the Eastern commitment with a Southern commitment, facing simultaneously the other side of the "arch of the crisis" almost surrounding the EU.

The "Barcelona process" firstly entails cooperation in security matters, linking peace and domestic democratization, respect for human rights and the common fight against terrorism. The second basket supports a sustainable and balanced economic and social development, largely based on IMF prescriptions, but corrected by pressures for a move towards a common market of EU partners. The third supports a promotion of better understanding between northern and southern cultures and the development of a civil society within the southern Mediterranean States.

As for the poor achievement and the huge deficits of the first basket. They are well illustrated by indifference to the killing of 60,000 Algerians during the past years, the lacking energy security policy and poor foreign policy in the – indirectly linked – Gulf area, the lack of cooperation in the fight against terrorism, drug trafficking and crime and also the marginal role played in the Middle East peace process, in spite of huge financial commitment and effort in implementing a new Palestinian democracy. Joffé's chapter mentions two explanatory factors:

- The southern Mediterranean states' opposition to the EU interfering in their domestic affairs. Even if symbolic, national sovereignty is very important for authoritarian or semi-authoritarian regimes.
- The political weakness of the EU, not only when military conflicts within the region might tend to affect high-level politics and as such, demand the intervention of the USA, but also as a mere mediator.

The realistic forecast by Joffé, regarding the economic basket of the Barcelona process, is that the process will continue, despite the huge challenges, for the simple reason that the Southern partners of the very near economic giant, the EU, "do not really have a big choice". The problems are not limited to the relatively restricted parallel EU funding (including the next MEDA II) and EU agricultural protectionism. They include the huge destabilizing impact of deregulation and liberalization, which threaten non-competitive companies and branches, have relevant direct socio-political consequences and interfere with the other baskets of the process.

However, such an "imposed nature" of the Barcelona partnership gives the third basket cooperation a new light. On one hand, new communication technologies and relevant foreseeable political implications of strengthened civil societies are making pluralistic and participatory democracy both more possible and more necessary than in the past. On the other hand, a failure in constructing better cross-cultural understanding would potentially have disruptive consequences, even as far as the other baskets are concerned.

There is another aspect to be explored. The EU's strategy to encourage partners to cooperate regionally seems to be particularly unsuccessful in the Mediterranean. The main question is as follows. Is the desired subregional cooperation community a matter of voluntary association or rather of a mere external coercion? Of course, there were many previous regional attempts in the Maghreb and the Arab world, independently from any EU pressure. However for different reasons, they all failed. Should the attempt to create a common market succeed now, because of the new EU support?

3. The near abroad and the future of deep regional integration

The Euro-Mediterranean relationship suggests two interesting theoretical developments concerning analogies and differences between deeper regional integration and softer regionalism open to the near abroad. The comparison with the EU-Eastern Europe process is useful, even if, similarities cannot be overemphasized. For example, it is true that, as far as central Europe is concerned, the EC-EU policy to support the creation of an autonomous "Visegrad" common market, as an alternative to EU enlargement, though formally established, was fragile. This is because the new post-communist democratic leaderships never welcomed it. They openly desired full membership. However obviously the expectations held outside of the continent, namely those of the North -African and Euro-Asian countries, to become an active and direct part of the EU decision-making process, cannot have the same legitimacy. Art. 49, ex-Art. O, of the TEU, states that "every *European* State can apply to become a full member of the Union".

The comparison with the US–Mexican relationship is also very stimulating, even if analogies must not be exaggerated. Although they are very "distant neighbours", they are united by soft regionalism within NAFTA. By contrast, the North-South relationship established within the "Barcelona process" is as yet much less linking than NAFTA. But this occurs between countries which belong to different continents, a fact which obviously not only limits possibilities of deep integration but also gives another meaning to Mediterranean "soft regionalism", being closer to the APEC intercontinental example.

This does not mean that multilateral regional intercontinental cooperation has realistic chances of success, on the limited basis of the security needs of the stronger side and economic needs of the weaker side. However, Euro-Asiatic Turkey's success in becoming an official candidate (and the Morocco application) on the one hand, and the Ukrainian-EU relationship on the other, legitimate the final question raised by Joffé's chapter, not only regarding the Southern border but also the Eastern border. Will the relationship between the EU on one side, and Southern and Eastern partners on the other side (the duality model) be able to cope with such moving boundaries? Or is the model due to be overcome sooner or later by new and more encompassing institutional paths as far as the whole pan-European/Mediterranean architecture is concerned?

An answer to this crucial question must be divided into two parts:

- There are limits to a positive trade-off between widening and deepening regional organizations. Too broad an enlargement improves geopolitical legitimacy but dramatically weakens efficiency and effectiveness when acting at regional and global levels. Too wide an Eastern enlargement, parallel to a Mediterranean enlargement of the EU, would not only dilute the European integration process. Such an enlargement would also seriously jeopardize the EU's ability to play the role of both regional and global actor, providing governance and stability within the continental and world economic and political systems.

This is one of the main differences with NAFTA, as an open regional agreement centered on a superpower. Of course, new structures can be created around the EU, in order to strengthen the feeling of solidarity and common interests between the two rims of the Mediterranean region and between a wider EU and Russia. Furthermore, independent and endogenous federative processes among more democratic southern Mediterranean countries and within the boundaries of the former Soviet Union (and the current Commonwealth of Independent States) would help to create a true partnership with the EU. This is in contrast to the centre–periphery dual path, which would inevitably deepen divisions and provoke long term regional and global instability.

In case of the EU's failure to reach a greater institutional ability to clearly set and implement more consistently its common goals and regional strategy, the main engine for the whole process would break down. It would probably be substituted by informal intergovernmental and hierarchical bodies, for example, an intergovernmental directorate, or by the sole global superpower.

- The second answer is theoretical: the relationship between the EU and the near abroad will be obliged to evolve dramatically within next few decades on the one side, towards a deeper and a wider European Union, and, on the other side an improved continental and interregional partnership. In conceiving these scenarios, we need to question the concept of "open regionalism". To clarify and stress this distinction at the conceptual level is not only important regarding that part of the world, but also regarding the whole framework of the above-mentioned theoretical discussion on new regionalism.

Notes

1   For a contrast, ten years after the fall of communist regimes, see M. Emerson (1998), M. Lavigne (1999); A. Mayhew (1998); M. Nuti (1999) ed, *Dieci anni di transizione postcomunista in Europa centrorientale, Europa/Europe*, Rome, n. 4.

2   M. Lavigne, *L'intégration des pays d'Europe centrale dans l'économie mondiale: régionalisation et mondialisation*, paper, Universite de Pau. 1998.

3   The Helsinki Council of December 1999 modified the schedule introduced by the Commission Paper of 1998 "Agenda 2000". The division between the first group of six candidates (Poland, Hungary, Czech Republic, Slovenia, Estonia, and Cyprus) and a second group (Bulgaria, Rumania, Slovakia, Latvia, and Lithuania) has been overcome. Malta and Turkey have been added to the list of official candidates. Secondly, developments in the former Yugoslavia foresee Croatia and Serbia as future candidates, as well as special association agreements with Macedonia, Bosnia and Albania. Finally, Ukraine would like to join the list of associated countries and later on be a candidate. When possible, Belarus and Moldova could like to do the same.

4   The Amsterdam Treaty provision of "common strategies" (to be decided by the European Council by unanimity procedure) allow the Council to adopt Qualified Majority Voting by "common actions" (Art. 13 and 14, TEU).

5   Alan Mayhew (1998) and European Commission (1997), *Agenda 2000*, Brussels .

6   See C. Kupchan, Regionalizing Europe's Security, in Mansfield and Milner, eds (1997), p.16.

7   R. Aliboni, ed. (1990) *Southern European Security in the 1990s*, Pinter, London.

8   R. Bistolfi (1995), *Euro-Méditerranée: Une région à construire*, Paris, G. Joffé (1995), Europe and North Africa, in *Cambridge Review of International Affairs*, Winter /Spring, n. 2, pp. 84–103; B. Khader, ed. (1994), *L'Europe et la Méditerranée. La géopolitique de la proximité*, L'Harmattan, Paris; E. Rhein (1996), Europe and the Mediterranean: A Newly Emerging Geopolitical Area, in *European Foreign Affairs Review*, vol. 1, n. 1 July, pp. 79–86; G. Edwards & E. Philippart (1997), The EU Mediterranean Policy: Virtue Unrewarded, in *Cambridge Review of International Affairs*, Summer/Fall, vol. XI, n. 1, pp. 185- 206.

9   *Barcelona Declaration adopted at the Euro-Mediterranean Conference* (27 and 28 November, 1995) Barcelona; European Commission (1997), *Progress Report on the Euro-Mediterranean Partnership*, Communication to the Council and the European Parliament, Brussels, 19 February.

10. European Union and Eastern Europe

Reimund Seidelmann

Both in the academic as in the political debate the expression "Eastern Europe" has become a synonym for an intellectual as well as a political problem and challenge. For the political scientist, the Eastern European problem is not only a specific area or country issue but has revitalized and refocused transformation studies,[1] has become a major issue for theoretical as well as applied democracy studies,[2] has given new thoughts for peace and conflict studies,[3] and finally has emerged as an important issue for integration studies.[4] For the politically concerned, Eastern Europe means on the one side a long-sought and peaceful change for the better and on the other side specific political challenges such as the Yugoslavian conflicts and the deterioration in Russia to which the European political community has not found adequate and effective prevention, control and solution yet. But although the management and solution of the Eastern European problem constitutes an important issue for Europe and specifically for the EU's political agenda, this also has a general and global dimension as well. The decline or the implosion of the superpower USSR, the reorganization of the European power constellation, and its effects on EU–US and other relations demand a definition of the notion, Eastern Europe as a regional but also as a global issue. Therefore – and in contrast to other views – it is seen as both politically legitimate as well as analytically necessary to regard the Eastern European problem not only as a European problem but as subject and object of the general formula not of globalization but of a dialectic interrelation between globalization, regionalism, and the nation-state. In order to do so, both the substantial as well as the theoretical dimension of the problem will be discussed with the aim to broaden both the debate on the Eastern European problem and on globalization.

1. Defining the problem as a historical one

To define the problem of Eastern Europe one can start with a historical comparison between the situation during and after the East–West conflict. This not only follows an understanding of political processes as historical ones but allows us to define the Eastern European problem as a new historical challenge as well.

Both regarding the structure of the pan-European state system as well as of Western and Eastern Europe, the end of the East–West conflict has led to fundamental and far-reaching change. Despite all advances in conflict management through detente policies, the European state system was dominated by the East–West conflict – i.e. military confrontation, political power rivalry, and division into two blocs. The dynamic of bloc-confrontation and bloc-integration dominated East–West relations in Europe and constituted an essential, costly, and high-risk problem for the European system as well as a structural, vital, and dominant destabilization of its security order. The end of the East-West conflict has downgraded this old security problem in the political agenda of the European state system; in today's Europe, military security problems only have a subregional character, are limited in horizontal and vertical terms of escalation, only have minor military effects, and constitute a politically important but not a vital problem for the regional order as such. But after and with the end of the East–West conflict Eastern Europe still constitutes a problem for the whole region as well as for its main national, multinational, and supranational actors. Two wars in Yugoslavia, still-existing conflict potentials between Russia and the newly independent nations of the former USSR are illustrations. Although the new Eastern European problem results more from the past and reflects more the present structural deficits of the emerging new European order, it differs from the old one in terms of quality, dynamic, and political relevance. This is both due to the structural change in the regional system in general and its power constellation in particular. In the period of the East-West conflict, the confrontation with the Eastern bloc constituted not only a, but the most important, regional problem and while the Eastern bloc was poor in economic power, it nevertheless commanded a military power of equal relevance[5] to the Western one. Disarmament, collapse of the Warsaw Treaty Organization, disintegration of the USSR, and the many problems of transition not only downsized but marginalized the military ability of Russia as the successor of the USSR to threaten Western Europe. The new asymmetric or Western-dominated East-West cooperation, Russia's stepwise integration into the Western institutional and power formula underlined by its association to NATO and the change in Russia's political priorities created a constellation in which political will to militarizing conflict with Western Europe became unthinkable or counter-productive.[6] In comparison to the past, the new East-West relations in Europe in general and the Russia–West in particular are basically demilitarized,[7] are based on economic-political cooperation, and on a Western-dominated power formula. However, this new power formula includes military policing by or through Western, i.e. NATO's use of military force as in the case of the two Yugoslavian wars.[8] Military policing through NATO as well as political actions of EU against non-democratic forces[9] – even when they are part of the national governments – are based on an understanding of the new European order not as a permissive but as an actively self-defending one.

They not only constitute important elements of Europe's new identity but also are a clear message to Eastern Europe. In addition, the Eastern European subregion proved unwilling and unable to develop effective subregional structures to shield against or limit EU dominance. While the Visegrad and the South-Eastern Europe/Black Sea as well as other projects failed to materialize, the CIS project has been stalled because of the old and new Russian problem – i.e. the potential revitalization of Russian power projection towards former Soviet republics or within CIS.[10] Thus, the demilitarization or re-politization and further economization of East–West relations together with the collapse of Eastern European subregional cooperation resulted not only in downsizing and downgrading the old East–West problem but also in establishing a revitalizing, enlarging, and deepening EU as the dominant pan-European actor, which, together with an enlarging and re-legitimized NATO and supplemented by the new Stability Pact in the Balkans, directly and indirectly controls political and economic developments in Eastern Europe. While recent EU steps towards materializing the new European Security and Defence Identity (ESDI) open a perspective for a more comprehensive EU power projection mainly towards Eastern Europe in general and the Balkans in particular, the establishment of the European Monetary Union (EMU) has illustrated again the interrelationship between the EU's integration process, power projection towards Eastern Europe, and redefinition of the EU's global role.

But the disappearance of the old Eastern threat problem and the emergence of a new and EU-dominated pan-European power constellation did not mean the establishment of a new order without structural problems in and with Eastern Europe. Socio-economic transformation, redefining national sovereignty and dynamics of nation-building, and the many unsolved ethnic, political, and economic conflict potentials within and between Eastern European states have resulted in cumulating and mutually reinforcing problems, of which the most important are socio-economic crises, political instability, ecological disasters, and the "Yugoslavization" – i.e. the militarization of domestic and neighbour-to-neighbour conflicts.[11] With the dissolution of the Eastern bloc and the disappearance of a politically unifying, pacifying, and economically supportive Soviet Union as well as *vis-à-vis* the lack of efficient subregional control, these problems turned from intra-bloc to regional ones and also have "Europeanized" issues such as the Balkans, which traditionally had been marginalized and neglected by Europe's major actors. And with an enlarging and politicizing European Union, which turned from second range to central actor of European affairs, such regional problems turn into a major problem for the European Union and constitute a global challenge as well, which will be discussed hereafter.

1.1 The EU view

Following an understanding of politics as a matter of norms, interests, and power in the view of the European Union the new Eastern European problem has three aspects. First, in terms of interests, it constitutes an economic, socio-migratory, ecological, and still-existant but limited military threat,[12] and a major challenge for peace and security policing to the EU as such, to some of its member nations in particular. However, a serious evaluation of probability and expected damage of the specific threat dimensions as well as its cumulated effects on EU interests can lead to the conclusion that these threats are not vital but limited and are presently under relative political control – even if this control seems inadequate and questionable as cost-effectiveness is concerned. All worst-case events of the past like the ecological problem of Chernobyl, continued migratory pressure from the East towards the West, the past and potentially future conflicts in Yugoslavia, and the many financial and political crises in Russia proved to be of limited political weight, to be containable within the existing structures and mechanisms, and of important but nevertheless not vital relevance for the European Union. This does not mean to discount the problem in absolute terms in regard to the Eastern European states in which they occur. But with regard to EU interests, it means that in contrast to the old Eastern problem the new one is limited in relative terms, is second-rate in terms of EU's present political priorities, and competes in the setting of the political agenda with many other problems.

Second and in terms of norms, the new Eastern European problem is a problem of domestic as well as of subregional political order. It constitutes a problem for democracy, which concerns EU interests as well as its character as a value- or democratic community. Both the EU's definition of democracy as well as its normative mission towards Europe are threatened if the socio-economic crises and the specifics of nation-building or power-formation in Eastern Europe lead to limit, block, or even reverse the dynamic of democratization or democratic consolidation. Or – as in the case of Yugoslavia – malevolent actors in Eastern Europe turn to military aggression either to the inside as in the case of Kosovo or the outside as in the case of Bosnia-Herzegovina. This is not only a problem of outside image and international credibility but is of important but often overlooked inner political relevance for the EU and the integration process in general. In addition to the problem of democratization, parts of Eastern Europe still show a problem of peace. Although peace-building or the "civilization" of interstate relations can be regarded primarily as a result of – as well as a condition for – democratization or the development of the "civic society" it nevertheless depends on the regional pattern, interaction mode, and institutional framework being able and willing to stimulate, support, and secure this peace-building process. Like democratization and socio-economic reforms, peace-building efforts in Eastern Europe show different stages of development and reach. Policies of Eastern European candidates for EU-enlargement prove that true democratization leads to such foreign effects and that EU's and NATO's strategy of incentives has been effective. Russia, however, shows mixed results. While showing an impressive record of peaceful solutions of conflicts with neighbour states like the Baltics, Ukraine, and the Caucasus states, Russia's unsuccessful policy for solving the Chechnya-problem with military means shows that the "pacification" of Russian politics has not been completed. Finally, the past and eventually future wars or semi-wars in Yugoslavia illustrate that old mechanisms of nation-building, power formation, and militarizing conflicts are still in effect. This means, in other words, that the newly emerging pan-European security system has on the one side led to a remarkable state of demililtarization and peace- and security-building but has on the other side to cope with some important structural deficits or cases of political regression. If one defines the EU as the only effective responsible pan-European actor, such deficits in democratization and peace-building are not only a problem of the countries directly concerned but of the EU as well. The EU's inner democratic legitimacy and political support, which are essential not only for the present state of integration but also for the future integration process, are put into question, if the EU proves unable and unwilling to manage, control, and finally solve the democracy and peace problem of Eastern Europe. And this is not only an abstract problem of the better order but might turn into a structural problem of EU integration as well. If in the present political competition between EU, NATO, and major nation-states the EU fails to fulfil such a role,[13] in the long run political elites and the public alike within and outside the EU will limit and even withdraw their support for the EU and European integration in general and might finally put the basic idea of the EU as a community for democracy-, wealth-, and peace-building[14] into question. Thus, both the idea of understanding the EU's role as not only an intra-EU but an all-European peace and security maker as well, as the EU's recent steps towards establishing common will and military ability for the projection of its democratic and civic order to the rest of Europe and its neighbouring regions,[15] have opened important perspectives for Eastern Europe.

Third, the new Eastern European problem is a problem of as well as an opportunity for EU power politics. It constitutes a major challenge or test to the EU's willingness and ability to fulfil its new role as the European actor – both to the inside as well as the outside. While this seems relatively easy with cooperation-, benevolence-, and democracy-oriented Eastern European actors, the cases of Yugoslavia, Chechnya, Caucasus have shown the EU's limitations in projecting power to the malevolent, in keeping or re-establishing its type of democratic and peaceful order, and to fulfil its political mission or responsibilities towards the region. Worst cases – e.g. that of Russia socio-economically further deteriorating, de-democratizing, and re-militarizing its foreign policy – are still conceivable and would put on EU willingness and ability to a new and more far-reaching test than in the case of Yugoslavia. Present EU policies of limited political management – or mostly containment, symbolic politics, and internationalizing – or Americanizing or UN-izing of Eastern Europe or the Eastern European problem – should not be mixed up with long-term effective solutions or the establishment of a pan-European democratic growth- and peace-community, which are the objectives behind the EU's post-Maastricht efforts in regard to CSFP, ESDI, and enlargement policies. Again, this is not only a problem of legitimacy and concrete interests, but creates a long-term problem for political willingness to turn to the EU – and EU integration – in continuing to establish a new regional order and to define the democratic and integrative project as an attractive model to solve regional problems.

While on the one side the end of the East-West conflict created a historically unique opportunity for widening, deepening, and projecting EU power towards the East, the EU's will and ability to make use of such opportunity has been limited in the past in three aspects. First, although economics, i.e. the EU's traditional source of power, has been used to promote and smooth socio-economic transformation, democratization, and de-militarization, the EU still lacks a comprehensive, cost-efficient, and cohesive economic-political strategy towards Eastern Europe in general and towards Russia in particular.[16] Second, the CSFP-project in general and concerning the issue of a common, coherent, and effective policy towards Eastern Europe – including Russia, Yugoslavia, etc. – in particular has shown little progress both in terms of institutionalization as well as in terms of implementation of common policies. EU member-states' idea to supplement EU efforts in South-Eastern Europe through the establishment of the Stability Pact are still far from being effectively realized. Thus, EU political-diplomatic power is still limited both in absolute terms as well as in relation to nation-states' power such as Germany's, France's, and others. Third, military power of the EU as EU-power in terms of hard security guarantees, peace-keeping, and peace- and democracy-re-establishing, is despite all ESDI-rhethoric still not only marginal in absolute terms but suffered relative marginalization because of NATO's role in and for Eastern Europe in general and Yugoslavia in particular.[17] Again, the EU lacks both effective and sustained political will and military ability to overcome such deficits; finally accepting an anachronistic US responsibility for European affairs seems an easier way to manage Eastern European security problems than pursuing the build-up of a comprehensive EU power potential.[18] In the absence of a potent competitor for power in Eastern Europe and *vis-à-vis* the fact that the new Eastern European problem is primarily an economic-political and less a military-political one such limited and sometimes incoherent and unconcisive power projection nevertheless propelled the EU into dominant power player in the region – challenged less from the outside but more from its major nation-state members from the inside. Whether the EU is willing and able to effectively complement its economic power through a truly common foreign and security policy plus an integrated and effective military capacity is still an open question. Here, the problem is not only to reach break-throughs but to secure sustainability.[19]

If one finally looks at Europe in a normative and Western European oriented understanding of history based on the idea of enlightenment, the new Eastern Europe not only poses a problem for EU interests, norms, and regional power, but at the same time a challenge and an opportunity to further develop as a civic order. In principle, the EU – as the main product, mean, and source of the European integration process – might develop both will and ability to establish, maintain, and develop a new pan-European order not despite but because of this new and structural problem. But in contrast to the period of the East-West conflict the new Eastern European problem constitutes more a political challenge for order projection towards the East than a forceful external integrator plus policy-stimulator because it does not pose a vital threat to EU interests and power, as discussed above. This means that the objective necessary for a cohesive policy of enlargements, of developing an efficient grand strategy towards a neighbouring subregion, and to establish or gain common control of the necessary political-diplomatic, economic, and military means does not translate into a political top priority, does not produce the sort of comprehensive political willingness, and does not demand that kind of political ability which characterized the European order during the East-West conflict. This, however, does not discount the concept of historical learning through challenges and the concept of the responsibility of power. But given the new constellation of factors, which stimulate and block further integration as well as political will to solve the Eastern European problem, and given the general weight of Eastern Europe in the European political agenda, this means the search for new actors, mechanisms, and dynamics in order to continue – and implement – Maastricht's redefinition of integration and unionizing, to project its historical successes towards Eastern Europe, and to benefit in a common way from newly established growth opportunities, social stability, environmental and military security, which result from a solution – and not from a management – of the new Eastern European problem.

1.2 The Eastern European View

Although the far-reaching "Westernization" of Eastern European societies and politics as well as EU and Western European agenda-setting for control and solution of the new Eastern European problem create the temptation to define the Eastern European problem as predominantly, perhaps even as, a Western problem only, a normative as well as a functional approach demand to define the new Eastern European problem in fact as *the* Eastern European problem. This means in analytical terms looking at the Eastern European problem not only from a Western but from an Eastern European view as well; in political terms this means to state that Western European nations, EU, NATO, OSCE etc. can only complement but not substitute Eastern European efforts to solve the problem.

To understand Eastern Europe, one has to underline the far-reaching political change in terms of norms, interests, and power. Prepared and sometimes already introduced during detente, Eastern European societies regarded the Western model as superior compared with their own former Communist model in terms of values and order, socio-economic performance, and peace and security services. When the end of the East-West conflict allowed a fundamental re-orientation and at the same time had fully discredited even a reformed Communist model, "Westernization" in general and democratization, socio-economic transformation towards market economy, and participation in Western institutions like EU, NATO, and the Council of Europe seems to be the only alternative to the present crises, the only model for nation-building, -rebuilding, and -redefining.

But besides these common experiences and this common re-orientation, Eastern Europe did not define itself as a sort of regional entity with common problems and goals to be solved through common politics and common institutions but primarily as individual nations on the way towards Western Europe. This means that in respecting the newly emerged and emerging political identities in Eastern Europe one has to give up the perception of a more or less homogeneous Eastern Europe. And this is not only the result of the new thinking in Eastern Europe but results from empirical realities as well. In other words, there are many Eastern Europes; domestic transformation and foreign re-orientation of Eastern European states show some patterns and qualities, which vary more than structures, patterns, and modes of Western European policies. Regarding the relation between EU and Eastern Europe and referring to EU strategy towards Eastern Europe, one can classify at least three different types of Eastern European nations: the "winning", "losing", and "in between" Eastern European countries.

For the "winners" such as Poland, Czech Republic, and Hungary, socio-economic transition, democratization, and foreign orientation to the West meant to adapt to the Western model of a civic democracy, which promises individual freedom and political participation, social market economy, which promises economic wellbeing and social fairness, and "civic" foreign policy, which promises both security and peace. Orientation to the West as well as a policy of more or less unconditional integration in Western institutions like EU, NATO, and the Council of Europe resulted from a strategy combining new norms, traditional interests, and a policy to seek new net power advantages through integration in EU and NATO. Despite the problems in the first years, the strategy of combining transformation, modernization, and integration, or of "the return to Europe" through adaptation produced substantial success, political acceptance, and inner and outer legitimacy which the old Communist elites could never achieve. It is not by chance that these "winners" are not part of the Eastern European problem. On the contrary – they benefit from the problem in portraying themselves both to the inside as well as the outside as the "no-problem"-countries.

One of the most prominent "losers" of the end of the East-West conflict and the resulting changes is Russia.[20] Socio-economic transformation did not solve but aggravated the economic crises; political change led to the typical "Oblomov"-stalemate, and orientation to the West plus association with NATO revitalized the old dispute, whether Russia is European, Eurasian, or something different.[21] While in countries like Poland the combination of transformation, modernization, and integration reinforced each other and resulted in political success, Russia's transformation into two economies, societies, and political camps together with the inner and outer effects of its general decline in power[22] and dependence on the West resulted in economic and political deterioration and a far-reaching crisis of political identity and culture. This, however, creates not only a new inferiority complex in security policies but constitutes a major concern in Russia's neighbours and beyond, which translates such a lack of domestic stability and predictability into a political-military threat.[23] Thus, domestic instability turns into regional instability, which has been illustrated by Russia's military intervention in Chechnya. In fact, Russia has to regard itself as one of the major losers of the post-East–West-conflict period in all aspects and constitutes therefore a source of instability for Eastern Europe and the CIS.[24] While special cooperation with the West in general and the EU in particular has been a way to manage these structural problems, Russia's association with NATO[25] has opened a perspective for containing the effects of the Russian problem towards her Eastern European neighbours. It has to be kept in mind that both management and containment, however, do not constitute solutions for the structural problems of such a "loser" country; this limits the outer effects but leaves Russia because of its size, its military and in particular nuclear, power potential, and geographic position as the most relevant Eastern European problem.

Between "winners" and "losers" one has to mention those countries which on the one side have tried to follow some of the models, concepts, and strategies of the "Western" Eastern European countries but tried, partly intentionally and partly for lack of political will and ability, to preserve some of the old patterns and structures or to pursue a third way. The Slovak Republic of the past[26] – i.e. until 1998 – is a perfect example of such a mix of Westernization, preserving previous formulas, and searching for a political model of its own after separating from the Czechs. Caught between new and old policies, Western and Eastern orientation, and nation-building and solution of political and economic problems, the Slovak Republic faced a no-win situation. Domestic acceptance was limited, cooperation with Russia did neither solve the security problems of the newly independent nation nor constituted a viable alternative to integration in Western institutions, and NATO as well as the EU dropped Slovakia from the first round of Eastern enlargement.[27] The case of Croatia reveals a similar dynamic under different conditions. While subscribing to a regressive, i.e. militant-chauvinistic-authoritarian formula to reach independence and to pursue nation-building under the "old" Croatian regime, political elites as well as the population in general used the elections of 2000 for introducing far-reaching political, economic, and foreign policy change. Making "Westernization" the main priority meant to subscribe fully to EU standards and to use preparation for EU- and NATO-membership for the structural modernization of the political system, society, and economy as well as fully adapting to the idea of Europe in general and of the Balkans in particular as a peace-in-security order.

Thus, both the "in-between" strategy of the old Slovakian governments as well as the regressive character of the old Croatian government proved as counter-productive, unacceptable both for the domestic as well as the foreign players, and anachronistic because ignoring the current dominant structures and dynamics. While thus producing irritation towards the inside as well as the outside, these "in-between" nations constituted only a limited problem to the region. With no major military power projection and a policy which would sooner or later turn to the EU and NATO for support and eventually integration, even problems like a minority policy unacceptable to neighbours and European standards could be regarded as interim ones with no major effects on the general trends, patterns, and structures set by NATO and the EU.

Introducing the distinction between successful policies of consequent Westernizations of the "winner" countries, which become more Western than Eastern European countries, the "in-between" countries as countries, which have not yet found the way towards Westernization, and the "loser" countries follows the basic assumption, that the Western and only the Western model offers the best – i.e. cost-effective, accepted, and legitimatized – solution for basic problems of the European region and its nation-states. Again, this follows European understandings of history as a process of successful learning, political responsibility, and participation in progressive "civilization", which includes democratization. In addition, introducing the terms anachronistic, counter-productive, or not rational means to follow conceptual traditions which were cultivated in Western Europe. But the ongoing conflict in Yugoslavia, the political debate in Russia as well as developments outside of Europe and in the international system as such, however, should remind the supporter of such a European understanding that this is one but not the generally accepted and pursued concept. Further – and as the history of the old Europe proves – such concepts of general benevolence, enlightened learning, and communality fall short if confronted with the malevolent. While Western Europe in general and EU-Europe in particular was willing and able to not only manage but solve the problem of malevolence within its boundaries, while the Westernization of Eastern European nations widens these boundaries to the East, and the combined economic and military power of EU plus NATO creates optimal conditions to limit, contain, and overcome malevolence beyond these boundaries, malevolence as well as political dynamics, in which structural crises lead to domestic and foreign malevolence, are both an existing as well as a potential option for Eastern Europe. While despite all limitations and restraints the EU has developed a grand strategy for political and socio-economic transformation in Eastern Europe, EU definition and implementation of a pan-European order, which provides both peace and security to the inside as well as the outside, which introduces, stimulates, and honours civic cooperation within and between European nations, and which effectively deters political and military malevolence and – if this fails – re-establishes peace through military policing, is not only at a very initial stage but also meets significant dissent within the old EU, the applicant countries and in the US.[28]

The historical approach leads to ambivalent results concerning the question of how to cope with this challenge. On the one side, Western and EU-Europe constitute the proof that the creation of a democratic peace- and growth-community is feasible. On the other side, the new problems of Eastern Europe and in particular the re-emerging of the old Eastern European problems in Yugoslavia etc. prove that malevolence, however anachronistic in historical terms, irrational in rational choice terms, and unacceptable in terms of democratic legitimacy it is, still exists both as a political option as well as a political reality. Now, one can turn to the structural approach to see, whether it assists in finding a solution to this problem.

1.3 The global view

From a global viewpoint the end of the East-West conflict and the disappearance of the mutual military threat with all its consequences for the international system as such had and has different effects in all three dimensions of politics.

First and in terms of economic and military interests, the marginalization of the Soviet military threat meant a structural change in the agenda of the international community. While the mutual military threat of the East-West conflict not only threatened the survival of the global community as such but structured international politics including North-South, West-West, South-South, and other relations, the end of the East-West conflict eased the military burden, significantly reduced nuclear risks, and allowed kinds of multipolarity and regionalism. In general, the relative demilitarization of the international system, improvements in peace- and security-building regimes, and peace-keeping introduced a new quality of harmonized international control, while at the same time increased "economization" of international politics including better management and even governance of economic, financial, and monetary globalization and "civilized" international relations, i.e. made military means less relevant for pursuing long-term political interests. In particular, the Soviet Union and then Russia disappeared as a source of global military destabilization, Soviet/Russian economic transformation did not disrupt supply of raw materials to the global market, despite all economic and financial problems Eastern Europe including Russia and the CIS did not turn into a major threat to the world economy, and Eastern Europe's integration and association to the EU as well as NATO did not cause structural change, instability, or disorder to the existing global economic and military structures. In addition, the new Eastern European problems did not cause disruption or structural change but constituted only a marginal problem for global control and governance of the world economy and global security. While in sum the end of the East-West conflict constituted significant progress in terms of both technocratic control of international affairs and a better, i.e. more civic global order, the new Eastern European economic, military, and political problem seems of minor relevance in terms of global interests in manageability and governance.

Second and in terms of power, the end of the East-West conflict caused two structural global changes. First, the disappearance of the USSR as military superpower and the monopolarization of global military power projection in the hands of the US established or renewed on the one side military-political unipolarity and on the other side more predictable, effective, and controllable security governance through US-led regime-building, US and NATO efforts in peace-keeping, and use of US military-political power for maintaining global control. Eastern Europe including Russia in particular turned from a regional bloc led by a superpower into integrated and associated parts of the EU and NATO, which meant not only a far-reaching downgrading of power status but an equally far-reaching limitation of will and ability for Russian military power projection. Second, the disappearance of the Soviet threat plus the collapse of the Eastern bloc marginalized Western European dependence from US security guarantees. Together with the projection of EU direct and indirect power towards the East and the economic-political nature of most of the new Eastern European problems, which ask for economic-political strategies only the EU could pursue, the power equation between Europe and the US underwent structural change. Despite all limitations in day-to-day operations of the EU and all US symbolic politics and rhetoric of leadership towards and in Europe, the new developments allow, favour, and stimulate both European regionalism as well as the EU to become the pan-European power. Further, EU realization of Maastricht's EMU project illustrates EU willingness to complement its existing economic power projection capability with a significant and supranational monetary power base, which restructured the global monetary system and ended US hegemony. While these two structural changes had and still have major effects on the intra-European as well as the Atlantic power balance, from a global view of political control and better governance they nevertheless did not only pose no major problems but led to more stability and made global control even easier.

Third and in normative terms, the end of the East-West conflict, the integration and association of Eastern Europe to Western Europe, EU, and NATO, and the new Eastern European problem constitute the most interesting as well as challenging developments. First, the end of the East-West conflict allowed in principle a feasible search for a new and better global order including a reform of global control and governance. It was not by chance that the US, following its idealistic traditions, asked for a New Global Order after ending the Second Gulf or the Kuwait War and the concept of good or better global governance was revitalized after the end of the East-West conflict. Second and as it has been outlined above, both the transition process as well as the new problems of Eastern Europe posed the interrelated political challenge of national democratization and a more peaceful regional and global order. As a test case for these two political challenges, Eastern Europe – because of its Westernization, Europeanization, or integration and association towards EU-Europe – proved that revolutionary domestic and regional transition can be pursued peacefully, that the integration-based EU model of a democratic growth- and peace-community worked not only under regionally limited conditions but is extendable in principle to neighbouring areas, and the specific European strategic mix of democratic values, socio-economic progress, and common peace and security seemed successful in technocratic terms as well as in terms of enlightened learning. The many deficits of EU's day-to-day operations as well as its structural shortcomings both within the integration process as well as concerning the establishment of the new and better pan-European order are both conceptual and operational problems. This means in other words, that the model as such seems not only feasible in historical terms but adequate to produce structural progress in terms of long-sought better order. Although one has to warn against a simplistic transformation of the European model towards other regions and regionalization processes as well as towards globalization and global control, the model itself and the underlying idea of implementing the better order through integrated structures, introduction of common goals, and linking normative approaches with interests and a new definition of power seems an adequate starting point for continuing and revitalizing ideas of better global governance and a new democratic global community. Thus and despite the many shortcomings, deficits, and failures, the model and political approach which underlies the relations between the EU and Eastern Europe have a major significance for policies of global change.

2. Defining the problem in systematic terms

After having looked at the interrelation between the EU and Eastern Europe in a more empirical-analytical way, one can now ask the question: how such an analysis can contribute to the ongoing general theoretical debate in international relations in general and to the discussion on globalization in particular. To start with, one has to refer to two basic assumptions of the past argumentation. First, that politics is a matter of norms, interests, and power; second, that present international politics are object and subject of globalization, regionalism, and the nation-state. It has to be recalled, that such an understanding of politics is not in line with a school of thinking which reflects the present debate in the US but explicitly seeks its roots in the European traditions of social and state philosophy.

As a first step this means – and this has been already outlined – redefining the new Eastern European problem in systematic terms as a problem of norms, interests, and power and that this is not a cumulating but an integrating formula. This implies on the one hand that neither an idealistic approach of general benevolence nor a realistic approach of power politics is able to explain and to outline adequate solutions. It means on the other hand that a solution of the problem must be based on a grand strategy, which uses power – including military power – in a qualitatively new way – to establish, maintain, and secure a better order, i.e. an order, which is based on the idea of common interests to secure domestic support and regional consensus, and which at the same time establishes both democratic norms and peaceful solution of conflicts. In this view, it is important to underline that although of fundamentally different nature these three elements do not necessarily compete with or contradict each other – or in other words that an idealistic approach does not necessarily contradict a realistic solution. The new Eastern European problem is a typical case, where – at least for countries like Poland, the Czech Republic, and Hungary – these elements can and have reinforced each other. This evaluation is based on three hypotheses, verified in the Eastern European case. First, democratic structures not only allow better solutions of socio-economic crises but are conditions for the development of the civil society, which seeks demilitarization of its foreign policy and peaceful solutions of conflict. Second, a policy of integration, i.e. common economic, ecological, military, and other interests, from which everybody benefits, legitimizes and stabilizes the establishment of a new European order or EU expansion as a democratic growth- and peace-community. Third, such a policy, based on norms and common interests, not only defines but legitimizes the EU's "soft" power politics, secures acceptance, and further establishes this specific historical momentum which has characterized EU integration in the past despite its shortcomings, deficits, and set-backs.

In a second step, the new Eastern European problem can be regarded as a problem of two basic dimensions of politics – the historical or the dimension of time in political calculation, and the concept of political responsibility. Like the demand to interrelate norms, interests, and power for achieving "better" politics in terms of norms and rational choice, the idea of historical learning and political responsibility aims to improve political thinking by broadening the horizon in terms of time and social approach. The introduction of historical learning in reference to traditional ideas of "civilization" or "progress through democracy" in the theory of democracy or enlightenment as well as the idea of "responsible" policy in reference to an understanding of politics as a part of the "*vita activa*" concept in Western philosophy and religion defines a basic attitude towards policy which differs from the strategy of pragmatism in two aspects. First, the notion of historical learning and political responsibility is based on cost-benefit calculations which ask not only for the short- but for the long-term benefits and weighs the costs of structural reforms against the costs of pragmatic adaptation, to be cumulated over a time period, which exceeds the traditional election terms of democratic political life. Second, the notion of responsibility complements political cost-benefit rationality with the even disadvantageous burdens and risks of structural reforms or policies to overcome the causes and not the phenomena of problems. Both dimensions, i.e. the time and the social dimension, become important when interrelated. Negatively speaking, policies of giving priority to short-term opportunity costs and placing burdens on the shoulders of others seem to win easier public support – in particular in and through modern media. Positively speaking, only long-term and responsibility-oriented policies are able to shape, correct, and re-establish order, create willingness for necessary but unpopular structural reform, and lead to qualitatively better levels of democratic development or civilizing.

This reference to the idea of historical learning aims not only at the theoretical debate but has important political connotations. It allows the contrast of present "pragmatic policies" not only with norms but with a historical interpretation of responsibility, which means to call for political will and the creation of adapted political structures and institutions to solve problems like the new Eastern European problem instead of muddling through and referring to US leadership if things get worse. Concerning EU policies and EU integration in general, this means to revitalize the spirit of Maastricht or to learn from the grand designs of Europe-building of the late 1940s and early 1950s. Historical learning *vis-à-vis* the new Eastern European problem instead of "realistic" pragmatism is not only an opportunity but – as it was outlined already – a political necessity as well. Although the new Eastern European problem is tolerable in terms of EU interests, EU's power position or its role as the dominant actor in European affairs is at stake. In the last years, NATO as EU's main competitor has proven more effective as well as politically convincing in high-profile aspects of the Eastern European problem – establishing institutionalised association of Russia to Western structures, speedy enlargement to the East, and managing the Yugoslavian problem. If NATO and EU could be regarded as comparable in terms of basic political formula, goal-means-profile, and way of power projection, such a competition in general and political formulas like division of labour through interlocking institutions in particular could be welcomed. But the competition between NATO and EU is not between equal or complementing actors but between qualitatively different actors. NATO is still based on the Atlantic political formula – including US leadership – which conflicts with the EU's Europeanistic understanding of regionalism. NATO still defines power and security as a primarily military matter, which conflicts with the EU's traditional view and Maastricht's vision of "demilitarizing" European affairs in general and security in particular. Although integrated in military terms, NATO's political rationale is that of an alliance of nation-states led by a global superpower and not a supra- and supernationalizing actor based on the federalist or unionist model. And NATO's formula of solving the new Eastern European problem focuses selectively on the military dimension and not on the interrelation between economic growth, environmental rehabilitation, security, and democratic development, which exactly defines the problem. As the case of Yugoslavia documents, the policy of parallel support of EU and NATO constitutes a pragmatic approach of conflict management and conflict containment but excludes a solution of the new Eastern European problem in general and the Balkan problem in particular and, in addition, ignores the qualitative competition between NATO and EU.

The third aspect of the new Eastern European problem results from the thesis that globalization first is no more than only a development in international politics and second that it is part of a dialectic equation of globalization, regionalism, and the nation-state's willingness and ability to continue, increase, or re-establish control of international politics. On the one hand this understanding recognizes the relevance of globalization and at the same time disagrees with the idea that globalization is the dominant trend and the only problem of international relations. When in recent years the debate in international politics turned to the problem of structural change of the international system and declared globalization as the most important factor of change, and suggested better global governance might be the only way to control it, it revitalized two important insights. First, it re-emphasized that international relations have to deal with the structural change of the system in general. After decades of focusing on the East–West, North–South, and regional conflicts with its implicit exclusions and partial views of the global system, the new debate follows a more integrative or "global" approach. This means to understand globalization as a phenomenon which afflicts all actors in the international system and which conditions the behaviour of even those actors who ignore, try to escape, or dissociate themselves from the system. Second, this system-oriented view leads to the question of how to control structural change like globalization. Thus, the integrated approach of the analysis, which underlines the global quality of the international system, leads to the question how such processes of structural change can be controlled or politically mastered. Following the analysis such a control actually is not so much a matter of foreign policy of a nation-state, supra-, or supranational actor but of ability and willingness of the global actors to establish good or better political common governance of such a globalization.[29]

In general, this new emphasis on structural global change and its political control rightly responds to objective necessity and subjective political will. In particular, however, there are trends in the current debate about globalization which unnecessarily limit both its reliability and validity and lead both to a distorted view of global change and of necessary politics. First, globalization is often regarded as a new phenomenon although it has characterized international relations since decades. Global or globalizing interdependencies both in structures as well as in behavioural patterns can be found in early and later colonialism from the 15th to the 19th century, in nuclear arms races of the East-West conflict, and in today's peace-keeping missions as well; they differ only in the ways but not in the basics. And while the ways and means of global actors to control such developments have changed, the political message about the limits of the nation-state to control such dynamics has remained the same. Second, globalization is not only an economic, financial, and monetary but a political and military affair as well. International relations have often been subject to economistic views and theories and such a reductionism seems understandable in periods where military threats are perceived as of less importance and political stability as guaranteed. But a truly systematic and historical approach to structures, mechanisms, and patterns of international relations shows that on the one side global change has never been mono-dimensional and on the other side that there is no primacy of economics and that there still exist issues, segments, regions, and periods in which political and security needs outplayed all economic rationality.

In order to overcome such self-inflicted analytical restrictions globalization has first to be defined as a phenomenon with an economic, military, and political – and even a socio-cultural – dimension. These dimensions can show different patterns and dynamics of globalization, different underlying power patterns, and different rationalities for political control or its absence. Second, globalization has to be seen in historical perspective as well. As a historical and crucial phenomenon of the international system, globalization underlies change; in other words there are periods of globalization, de-, and re-globalization. Third and returning to the beginning, globalization must be interrelated to regionalism and re- or continued nationalization. Regionalism such as the EU constitutes is both result as well as cause of globalization. The idea to integrate in order to create better conditions for realizing interests, power, and norms *vis-à-vis* a globalizing world is a well-known strategy in international politics and economics as well as to globalize in order to overcome regional protectionism etc. Both globalization and regionalism demand from nation-states to transfer sovereignty, to accept outer limits of their realization of interests and power, and to downgrade its role as dominant actor in international politics. Thus, both developments depend on the nation-state's ability and willingness to accept, promote, and control regionalism and globalization – in other words both globalization and regionalism result from nation-state behaviour or non-behaviour as well as they shape it.

If one finally introduces the idea of a historical responsibility for the better into this debate one has first to discuss models for better global order and governance. Here, one could discuss the thesis, which was presented earlier, that the European model seems in principle a feasible and progress-producing model not only for Western and pan-Europe but for global community-building as well. But understanding politics as part of a *"vita activa"* approach or as a responsibility, as it was done in this argumentation, means to complement the search for the best model with the search for strategies of how to create the necessary sustainable political will in and between the relevant actors to define themselves not only as an object of globalization, regionalism, and re-nationalization but to become subject of this dynamic. What is needed is not only the best model for a new global order as well as new regional orders but the political will to re-introduce and revitalize the idea of common active political governance or to refer to the politicians' responsibility to establish, secure, and improve order.

Notes

1   See, for example, Russell Bova, Political Dynamics of the Post-Communist Transition: A Comparative Perspective, in: *World Politics* 44 (1994), pp. 113–138; Samuel Huntington, The Third Wave: Democratization in the Late Twentieth Century, Norman 1991; Philippe C. Schmitter/Lynn Terry Karl, The Conceptual Travels of Transitologists and Consolidologists: How Far to the East Should They Attempt to Go?, in: *Slavic Review*, Spring 1995, pp. 111–127.

2   See, for example, Jan Zielonka/Alex Pravda (Eds.), Democratic Consolidation in Eastern Europe: International and Transnational Factors, in press, Dieter Nohlen, Demokratie, in: Dieter Nohlen/Peter Waldmann/Klaus Ziemer (Hrsg.), *Lexikon der Politik*, Vol. 4: *Die östlichen und südlichen Länder*, Beck Verlag, München 1997, pp.118–127 and 122; Philippe C. Schmitter, The International Context of Contemporary Democratization, in: *Stanford Journal of International Affairs* 2 (1993), pp.1–34; Dean McSweeney/Clive Tempest, The Political Science of Democratic Transition in Eastern Europe, in: *Political Studies* XLI (1993), pp.413 and 417; G. V. Hyde, Adrian Price, Democratization in Eastern Europe: the External Dimension, in: Geoffrey Pridham/Tatu Vanhanen (eds.), *Democratization in Eastern Europe*, London/New York 1994; Wolfgang Zellner/Pal Dunay, Ungarns *Außenpolitik 1990–1997*, Nomos-Verlag, Baden-Baden 1998; and

Mario Telò (ed.), *Démocratie et construction Européenne*, Editions de l'Université Libre de Bruxelles, Bruxelles 1995.

3   See, for example, Eric Remacle/Reimund Seidelmann (eds.), *Pan-European Security Redefined*, Nomos-Verlag, Baden-Baden 1998; Emil Kirchner/Kevin Wright (Eds.), Security and democracy in transition societies. Conference Proceedings, University of Essex 1998, and *Journal of European Integration*, Special Issue *Problems of Eastern Europe*, No 2–3/1997.

4   See, for example, Mario Telò (ed.), Un défi pour la Communauté Européenne: Les boule-versements à l'Est et au centre du continent, Editions de l'Université de Bruxelles, Bruxelles 1991, Mario Telò (ed.), *L'Union Européenne et les défis de l'élargissement*, Editions de l'Université de Bruxelles, Bruxelles 1994; and Mario Telò/Paul Magnette (Eds.), *Repenser l'Europe*, Editions de l'Université de Bruxelles, Bruxelles 1996.

5   There is no need to go into the discussion, whether the military capability of the WTO was equal to that of the West. Using the term relevance means that despite all asymme-tries in military capability and because of mutual assured nuclear destruction the USSR constituted an "equal" power in military dimension.

6   Such calculations are based on the assumption of rational cost-risk-benefit calculations. Although Western-Russian relations have a broad range of measures to secure and re-establish such rationality, it cannot be taken for absolutely granted.

7   See, for example, the process of "re-civilizing" or "de-militarizing" Soviet/Russian foreign policy underlined by Russia's policies towards the second Yugoslavian war.

8   Military policing should not be confused with military aggression because of its special legitimacy, its goal-mean limitation, and its explicit reference to agreed political formu-las. This concept of military policing as a legitimate mean to keep, to enforce, and to re-establish peace and security has been applied in peace-keeping in Bosnia-Herzegovina and in ending violations of the basic European consensus on democracy, minority rights, etc. in Kosovo.

9   Such as in the recent case of the participation of the FPÖ in Austria's government.

10 A recent case is Russia's military intervention in Chechnya.

11 For an overview see Reimund Seidelmann (Ed.), *Crisis Policies in Eastern Europe*, Nomos-Verlag, Baden-Baden 1996.

12 Think, for example, of the remaining nuclear weapons and nuclear material.

13 For a detailed analysis of the European security architecture and its problems see, for example, Reimund Seidelmann, NATO's Enlargement as a Policy of Lost Opportunities. In *Journal of European Integration* No 2–3/1997, Special Issue on *Problems of Eastern Europe*, pp.233–245, simultaneously published in Cicero Paper Paris/Maastricht, No 3/1997, S. 41–55.

14 See, for example, Panos Tsakaloyannis, *The European Union as a Security Community*, Nomos-Verlag, Baden-Baden 1996.

15 See, for example, EU's activities towards its Mediterranean south.

16 See Reimund Seidelmann, The Old and New Soviet Threat: the Case for a Grand New Western Strategy towards the Soviet Republic in the 1990s in: Peter Ludlow (ed.), *Europe and North America in the 1990s*, CEPS Paper No 52, Brussels 1992, pp.69–88.

17 See Reimund Seidelmann, Amsterdam e la sicurezza europea. Un' opportunità nuova o perduta in: *Europa/Europe* No 1/1998, pp.66–86.

18 For a recent example of such a political ambiguity see Tony Blair, Time for Europe to Repay America the Soldier, in: *International Herald Tribune*, November 14–15, 1998, pp.8.

19 The establishment of an effective and integrated military power projection capability is a matter of 10–15 years.

20 Another example but under different specific conditions is Ukraine; see, for example, Oleg Strekal, Nationale Sicherheit der unabhängigen Ukraine (1991–1995). Zur Analyse der Sicherheitslage und der Grundlagen der Sicherheitspolitik eines neu entstandenen Staates, Nomos-Verlag, Baden-Baden 1999.

21 For details see Jens Fischer, *Eurasismus*, Nomos-Verlag, Baden-Baden 1999.

22 Compare Irina Zviagelskaia, Russia's Security Policy and Its Prospects, in: Eric Remacle/Reimund Seidelmann (Eds.), *Pan-European Security Redefined*, Nomos-Verlag, Baden-Baden 1998, pp. 305–318.

23 See, for example, the discussion in Janusz Golebiowski (Ed.), *Poland, Germany, Russia: Perspectives on Collaboration*, University of Warsaw, Warsaw 1995.

24 See, for example, Michael R. Lucas, The CIS and Russia, in: Eric Remacle/Reimund Seidelmann (eds.), *Pan-European Security Redefined*, Nomos-Verlag, Baden-Baden 1998, pp. 319–351.

25 For a new analysis see Günther Trautmann, Russia and the Euro-Atlantic Community, in: *Journal of European Integration* No 2–3/1997, pp.201–232.

26 For details see Ivo Samson, *Die Sicherheitspolitik der Slowakei in den ersten Jahren der Selbständigkeit. Zu den sicherheitspolitischen Voraussetzungen der Integration der Slowakischen Republik in die euroatlantischen Verteidigungsstrukturen*, Nomos-Verlag, Baden-Baden 1999.

27 In addition to these developments tactical aspects played a role. Germany, which promoted Eastern enlargement, offered to drop Slovakia to overcome reluctance in other EU countries and to demonstrate German willingness to compromise.

28 See, for example, the "Trojan-horse" dispute about countries like Poland, which are accused to be more US than EU-oriented and to use EU membership as a mean to limit further "Europeanization".

29 The political perception of globalization ranges from ignorance over highlighting the negative effects or the "threat" of globalization to uncritical praise of the new opportunities.

11. European Union and the Mediterranean

George Howard Joffé

Since the end of the Cold War, with the disappearance of the stability inherent in the antagonistic balance of power between the Soviet Union and the United States, profound changes have been taking place within the international system. This has been particularly true of the Mediterranean region which used to serve as a surrogate arena for superpower competition. The old superpower regional system was based on confrontation between the superpowers (and their clients), together with the non-aligned world which, in the Mediterranean and Gulf, at least, also set the superpower balance off against regional associative arrangements designed to achieve a similar level of stability through tension by mimicking the superpower divide (Little, 1989). While the structures that have begun to take shape in place of the old system in the period since 1989, during which this transition has been taking place, cannot yet be assumed to be stable elements of a new international order, some elements of durability do seem to be emerging.

This change in systemic regional structures has had profound implications for the states of the Middle East and North Africa, particularly in their relations with the European Union. It may not yet be clear whether the outcome, in the Mediterranean or elsewhere, will be an aspect of a system best characterized as 'international' or 'global', but it is clear that zones of regional integration are beginning to emerge and that they have considerable implications for the future evolution of state and nation, the two primordial elements of the international system for the past two to three centuries.[1] How this process unfolds will perhaps be the most important outcome of the Euro-Mediterranean Partnership Initiative (EMPI), the European Union's Mediterranean policy introduced in the Barcelona Declaration of November 1995 that is now the formal framework for regional change.

The problem for the political analyst is to identify and understand the real nature of the regionalist system being created in the Mediterranean. Superficially, at least, it appears to be part of a dualism, bringing together the structured integration of the European Union itself and the 'open regionalism' (see Chapter 7 by Vasconcelos in this volume)[2] which is said to characterize the Barcelona process, the name usually given to the implementation of the policy outlined in the Barcelona Declaration.

Yet the introduction of states in the region not previously considered to be an integral part of Europe – Cyprus, Turkey and Malta – as future EU partners at the Helsinki Summit of December 1999 raises questions about the rationale behind the Euro-Mediterranean Partnership Initiative and whether it is itself now no more than a transitional stage in an expanding process of regional integration, or 'closed regionalization' (Thomas, 1998: 63), rather than open regionalism. Such questions are rendered even more acute by the security dilemmas presented by the Mediterranean and the ways in which they will be addressed, as the Maastricht Second Pillar is given substance through the evolution of a common foreign and security policy alongside new European intervention force structures.[3]

1. A problem of definition

As Stephen Calleya (1997: 15) has pointed out, the subject of regionalism has received relatively little analytical attention in recent years, not least because of the dominance of neo-realism in theoretical studies of international relations, in which the state and the international arena have been the primary referents. None the less, the growing effects of multinational organizations and transnational corporations on the international scene, together with the implications of the phenomenon of globalization (however defined) has begun to alter these assumptions (Mittelman and Falk, 1999). In addition, the experience of the European Union and its relationships with peripheral and semi-peripheral states and regions (Buzan, 1991: 431–451) has thrown the issue into sharp relief within the world of practical politics and diplomacy.

A major problem, however, is to establish precisely what the term 'regionalism' means. Neither a geographical nor a systemic definition alone provides a comprehensive mechanism for the conceptualization of the term. Geographical contiguity is clearly an essential component but does not, of itself, provide any insights as to what regionalism actually is, although it does imply that a plurality of states is involved. Indeed, other than for the purposes of geographical or economic analysis, the term 'regionalism' is meaningless unless defined in social or political terms as well. In short, the concept essentially relates to a process of political, cultural or social interaction between entities within its geographical bounds, and it is that process of interaction that gives it meaning.

This interaction is not a purely reactive process; it also involves purpose and action to prioritize the key elements that animate the concept. It is, in essence, a constructed sociopolitical reality, often involving a shared economic dimension, within a geographically contiguous international region (Calleya, 1997: 35–6). This is important, because although the Euro-Mediterranean Partnership is articulated at present in largely economic terms, the Barcelona Declaration makes it clear that its signatories recognized the underlying social, political and security realities on which it will impact.

Several further questions arise, not least about the taxonomy of the regionalism concept itself, particularly in the Mediterranean context. What are the drivers of interaction? Why should they become important now, in the wake of the Cold War, rather than having a far longer historical reach? What are the bounds of a region and what is the effect of the external world upon it? To what extent is there competition between states and regions, and how do the concepts inter-relate? Is there an alternative inter-relation between nation and region that has greater significance than that involving the state, or do state and nation complement each other in this relationship? How should the linkages between an integrated region, such as the European Union, and states to which it relates in a form of open regionalism be conceptualized? Is this a relationship of a centre–periphery/hub–spoke nature, or are there more substantive, egalitarian connections involved, of the kinds implied by the Barcelona Declaration's objective of a 'shared zone of prosperity and stability'? And what of the relationships among the states of the southern Mediterranean shore in this context? Are these to be static or evolutionary – and, if the latter, what is the outcome likely to be? Indeed, as suggested above, is not the concept of 'open regionalism' merely a transitional stage towards a more profound regional relationship? If so, what will this be and how will it, in turn, relate to the wider concepts of globalization and internationalization (Thomas, 1998: 59–74)?

2. Formal rationales

The most obvious justification for the conscious creation of a system based on open regionalism in the Mediterranean area is the economic rationale. There is little doubt that the European Union is of prime importance for the Middle East and North Africa (MENA) region, since it is the dominant global trading partner by far, being involved in over 30 per cent of regional commerce (see Table 11.1). When the North African region is taken alone, this percentage rises towards a staggering 68.3 per cent. For the EU, however, the MENA region generates only around 3 per cent of total trade, although, once intra-European trade is excluded, this figure rises towards 10 per cent. In short, the Union is an extremely important

Table 11.1   Europe's role in Arab world trade, 1997

Trading partner	% total Arab world exports	% total Arab world imports
European Union	26.0	45.6
Japan	16.3	6.4
United States	8.8	13.4
Arab countries	8.5	9.6

Source: Middle East Monitor, December 1999, p. 2.

trade partner for the MENA region, but the MENA region itself is of minor importance to Europe. European interest towards it must, therefore, be motivated by other factors, such as European perceptions of security intermeshed with the economic relationship; and this is indeed the case, as I discuss below.

2.1 The role of trade

Among the world's regional groupings trading with the European Union, the Mediterranean is third in importance to NAFTA and the DAE (see Table 11.2) – although here it should be noted that the term 'the Mediterranean' comprises both the MENA states and the states of southern Europe, which inevitably predominate in the overall trade picture. The Middle East alone, for example, accounts for 3.98 and 2.69 per cent respectively of Europe's imports and exports.

Within the overall levels of Middle Eastern trade, incidentally, Israel absorbs 0.79 per cent of European exports and generates 0.42 per cent of European imports (IMF, 1997). Israeli imports from Europe, by contrast, were 23.72 per cent of total exports to the Middle East from Europe in 1994, but generated only 17.66 per cent

Table 11.2   European Union: main trading partners, 1995

	Exports		Imports	
	%	bn ECU	%	bn ECU
Extra-European Union	100.0	569.0	100.0	544.7
United States	17.8	101.0	19.0	103.6
Japan	5.8	32.9	10.0	54.3
EFTA	12.2	69.5	12.9	70.4
CEEC	10.2	58.3	8.6	47.1
CIS	3.7	20.8	4.7	25.3
Africa	9.1	51.6	8.8	48.2
Latin America	5.6	31.9	5.5	30.2
DAE[a]	11.5	65.6	10.0	54.4
China	2.6	14.6	4.8	26.3
Asia[b]	10.9	61.9	8.5	46.3
Oceania	2.4	13.5	1.4	7.4
ACP	3.1	17.5	3.7	19.9
Mediterranean	11.3	64.4	8.5	46.3
ASEAN	6.5	36.9	6.3	34.5
OPEC	7.0	39.7	7.4	40.2
NAFTA	20.3	115.6	21.8	118.6

Notes: [a] DAE = Korea, Thailand, Taiwan, Malaysia, Singapore, Hong Kong.
[b] Asia = Middle East, Afghanistan, Indian subcontinent and other Asia, excluding DAE.
Source: Eurostat Comext, II.

of the region's exports to Europe. Israel is, therefore, a major component of Middle East trade, even if it is of minor importance to Europe.

The European role in trade with the individual Maghrib states is striking (see Table 11.3). The European Union generates 64.9 per cent of the region's imports and absorbs 71.0 per cent of its exports. It is not surprising, therefore, that, since 1990 and the end of the Cold War, all the Maghrib states have been primarily concerned with their economic relationships with Europe; although support may have been accorded to the American-inspired MENA Economic Summit process in 1999 – particularly by Morocco and Tunisia – this was for wider national strategic concerns than because of perceived economic advantage.

2.2 The oil equation

The major European imports from the Middle Eastern and North African region tend to be hydrocarbon-based energy sources. In the past, oil dominated; but this is now changing as natural gas begins to take over the major role. In 1995, out of the Middle East's total oil exports of 16,651 million barrels per day, Europe, defined in its widest (geographical) sense, imported 3,430 million b/d – with central Europe absorbing 348,000 b/d. Europe also imported 2,117 million b/d of North Africa's total exports of 2,696 million b/d, with central Europe taking 100,000 b/d. Table 11.4 shows clearly how dependent Europe is, in comparison to other major energy-consuming regions, on the MENA region. Gas imports are, however, increasingly important, and a fifth of Europe's natural gas imports already come from North Africa. This energy dependence on the Mediterranean rim will grow as gas from Central Asia and even from the Gulf or Nigeria becomes available, and as gas continues to grow in importance as a preferred, environmentally clean fuel. Furthermore, such gas imports will increasingly be delivered through fixed pipeline systems, rather than by liquefaction and maritime transport. This suggests that Europe's security concerns over the region will increase, both in nature and in intensity, as its energy dependence on the MENA region increases.

In 1995, Europe obtained 23 per cent of its gas from North Africa – 15.2 billion cubic metres as liquefied natural gas and 17.8 bn cu metres through the Trans-Med pipeline, out of a total import level of 157.5 bn cu metres over the year, mainly from Russia (117.4 bn cu metres). Algeria generated 17.7 bn cu metres of liquefied natural gas and 17.8 bn cu metres of pipeline gas, while Libya and the UAE each provided 1.5 bn cu metres of liquefied natural gas (BP, 1996: 21). Since then, a new gas pipeline has been opened from Algeria across Morocco to Spain and Portugal which is currently carrying 8 bn cu metres annually and will expand towards 10 bn cu metres a year, thus helping Algeria move towards its objective of 62 bn cu metres of gas exports to Europe annually by the early years of the twenty-first century. A new gas pipeline is planned from Libya to Sicily – the $5.5 billion West Libya Gas Project, which will also deliver up to 8 bn cu metres of gas each year into the European gas grid via Italy. Plans also exist – once the Middle East

Table 11.3   Trade patterns in the Maghrib, 1991–1997

	1991	*1992*	*1993*	*1994*	*1995*	*1996*	*1997*
(a) Imports ($m)							
Algeria							
EU	5,021	5,783	5,397	5,731	6,699	5,589	5,401
USA	764	954	1,311	1,372	853	695	764
Total	7,638	8,648	8,761	9,510	10,123	8,329	8,889
Libya							
EU	3,355	3,228	3,662	2,790	3,289	3,497	3,432
USA	70	–	–	–	–	–	–
Total	5,339	5,164	5,371	4,169	4,879	5,187	5,477
Morocco							
EU	4,023	4,177	3,906	4,049	4,321	4,469	6,420
USA	400	435	692	618	505	612	482
Total	7,520	8,020	6,858	7,168	7,705	8,257	10,021
Tunisia							
EU	3,987	4,712	4,603	4,728	5,643	5,600	5,732
USA	247	320	358	433	391	348	302
Total	5,530	6,426	6,218	6,571	8,032	7,749	7,918
(b) Exports ($m)							
Algeria							
EU	8,733	8,386	7,118	6,105	7,039	7,841	8,616
USA	2,038	1,553	1,607	1,414	1,643	2,064	2,405
Total	11,750	11,137	11,098	8,591	10,422	12,599	13,923
Libya							
EU	9,668	8,251	6,639	6,592	6,859	8,053	7,967
USA	–	–	–	–	–	–	–
Total	11,212	9,942	7,535	7,849	8,483	10,099	9,816
Morocco							
EU	2,709	2,582	2,410	2,556	2,565	2,915	4,894
USA	108	149	130	140	136	164	298
Total	4,728	4,405	3,803	3,971	4,072	4,745	7,060
Tunisia							
EU	2,966	3,140	3,022	3,724	4,539	4,418	4,203
USA	24	34	27	49	69	75	45
Total	4,087	4,048	3,811	4,643	5,785	5,519	5,363

Source: IMF, *Direction of Trade Statistics Yearbook 1998.*

Table 11.4   World oil trade, 1990–1997 (000 b/d)

	1990	*1991*	*1992*	*1993*	*1994*	*1995*	*1996*	*1997*
Imports								
USA	8,026	7,791	7,888	8,620	8,929	8,831	9,400	9,907
Western Europe	9,801	10,171	10,319	10,399	9,840	9,567	9,539	9,413
Total world	31,441	32,338	33,397	35,100	36,052	36,776	38,618	40,098
Exports								
Middle East	14,212	13,829	15,453	16,456	16,513	16,651	17,170	18,184
North Africa	2,604	2,781	2,849	2,685	2,652	2,696	2,756	2,743
Total world	31,441	32,338	33,397	35,100	36,052	36,776	38,618	40,098

Table 11.5   Oil imports from the MENA region (000b/d)

	Middle East				*North Africa*			
	1991	*1993*	*1995*	*1997*	*1991*	*1993*	*1995*	*1997*
North America	2,052	1,965	1,677	1,880	284	336	305	387
USA	1,958	1,852	1,607	1,750	277	293	263	324
Western Europe	3,878	4,462	3,582	3,778	2,083	1,998	2,017	1,979
Central Europe	–	–	348	390	–	–	100	80

peace process is complete – to link North African gas producers to Turkey via Egypt, Israel and Syria, with a spur line delivering gas from Gulf producers, particularly Qatar where the North Gas Field is now on-stream. By the end of the first decade of the twenty-first century, Europe will, in effect, be inextricably linked into an energy supply system based on fixed pipeline installations across the Mediterranean into the Maghrib, the Mashriq and Turkey and extending into the Gulf, the Caucasus-Transcaucasus and Central Asia.

The current European dependence on the Mediterranean region for natural gas (45.8 bn cu metres from the Maghrib alone in 1997) and on the high capital-cost pipelines to deliver it will thus be intensified when Caucasian and Central Asian oil and gas begin to flow in significant quantities, via Iran and/or Turkey. At present, in economic terms the Maghrib, in particular, is of crucial economic importance to Europe, for it is the source of much of Europe's energy supply, generating a quarter of its natural gas and 29 per cent of its oil in 1997. Although the region is of minor importance in terms of total trade with Europe – only 10 per cent of extra-European trade is with the MENA region overall – Europe is vital for Maghribi commercial interests as both a consumer and a provider.

Table 11.6   Gas imports to Europe

	Middle East				North Africa			
	1991	*1993*	*1995*	*1997*	*1991*	*1993*	*1995*	*1997*
(a) by pipeline (bn cu metres)								
Western Europe	–	–	–	–	14.1	13.6	17.4	22.9
Central Europe	2.5	0.5	–	–	–	0.3	0.4	0.4
(b) as LNG (bn cu metres)								
USA	0.0	0.0	0.0	0.1	1.9	2.3	0.6	1.6
Western Europe	0	0.0	1.5	14	18.6	19.5	14.0	20.9
Central Europe	–	–	0.0	0.0	–	–	1.2	2.9

Source: BP *Statistical Review of World Energy*, various years.

2.3 The security issue

These economic considerations alone make it clear that a close, symbiotic relationship is bound to exist between Europe and the south Mediterranean rim – and indeed, this relationship extends far further afield, for Europe's energy supply also depends on the Gulf, and in the future will depend also on hydrocarbon energy from the Caucasus-Transcaucasus complex and Central Asia, supplied through Turkey and Iran. Conversely, the Mediterranean states depend on Europe as a source of essential imports – both because of a colonial past and because of the dominant position of Europe in the global economy. This economic interdependence, however, takes on a specific security dimension, primarily for Europe, because of geographical propinquity; and this factor alone provides a rationale for the development of the kind of open regionalism symbolized by the Barcelona process. The security issue, of course, would continue to exist even if Europe's sources of energy were more distant. The particular form it takes and the measures adopted to respond to it are, however, acutely conditioned by the geographical relationship between Europe and its energy suppliers.

Indeed, the contemporary pattern of regional integration in the Mediterranean stems from such considerations, although it was not initially prompted by concerns about energy security. Historically, European concern over the south Mediterranean rim developed from the French colonial experience and France's desire to maintain economic interests in North Africa. The economies of France's colonies there had been developed as specific outliers of the French metropolitan economy and, in the postcolonial world, France was anxious to provide continuing support to them. The 1957 Treaty of Rome, the founding document of what was to become the European Union, therefore made specific reference to the need to provide such economies with support. From 1969 onwards, the new European Community developed a policy of bilateral economic support with the Maghrib states which was later extended around the Mediterranean basin (Marks, 1996).

Behind these purely economic considerations, however, lay other concerns. One of these certainly reflected growing anxieties over energy supply, particularly after the oil-producing states of the Middle East began to redefine the relationship between the major oil producer companies and themselves in the early 1970s (Ghanem, 1986). The loss of control over oil prices, coupled with the subsequent loss of concession acreage as oil producers began to nationalize their oil sectors, made European consumers increasingly aware of their own vulnerability, particularly after the oil price shocks of 1973 and 1979–80. Even though it soon became apparent that, in real terms, energy prices had not been significantly affected and that oil producers, in the final analysis, had little option but to sell oil, the marginal effects of price instability and interruptions to supply were extremely disturbing. It was only at the end of the 1980s, however, that Western states came to realize that they could respond to such developments through hard security measures – first in the American intervention on behalf of Kuwait and against Iran in 1987 during the Iran–Iraq War and subsequently, of course, in the multinational coalition against Iraq after its invasion of Kuwait in August 1990.

Europe, however, did not possess either the means or the will – as an integrated political unit – to engage in hard security initiatives. Instead, it either relinquished such initiatives to the United States, in both the energy and the geopolitical spheres – over the Arab–Israeli conflict and the consequences of the Iranian revolution in 1979, for example – or resorted to soft security responses through economic support and confidence-building measures, such as the Euro-Arab Dialogue. One consequence of such an approach was, inevitably, that the European security vision tended to be holistic, rather than particularistic and addressed to specific problems. In essence, however, Europe continued to rely, as it did over hard security issues along its eastern borders, on American military support, albeit not articulated through a formal alliance, such as NATO – despite the role of the American Sixth Fleet in the Mediterranean and, later, the Fifth Fleet in the Gulf.

Europe's security concerns about the Mediterranean region also reflected the fact that it formed part of the European periphery or hinterland. It was both Europe's 'forgotten frontier' and a geographical arena for vital European security interests, however articulated. Neither European states nor the political European entity created by the Union could remain indifferent to developments there. Such concerns have been quite explicit for north Mediterranean states, from Greece to Portugal; but developments over the past forty years have forced north European states to address these issues as well. In their case, the problem has not merely been one of energy dependency; it has also been enshrined inside their separate domestic policies. This has been particularly true in respect of the migration issue.

Migrant labour from the Mediterranean has a long history in Europe. North Africans were first introduced into the French labour market during the First World War as replacement labour for French nationals recruited for military service. During the interwar period, the Algerian migrant community in France became an important focus for the development of Maghribi nationalism as part of the anti-colonial struggle (Julien, 1954: 93–123). After the Second World War, European reconstruction created a massive demand for labour, with the result that Mediterranean migrant communities spread throughout Europe: North Africans into France, the Benelux countries, northern Germany and, later, in Italy and Spain; Turks into Germany and northern Europe. Only Britain remained isolated from this migrant flow, relying instead on its former colonies in the Indian subcontinent and the Caribbean. By the 1970s, however, as the populations of migrant communities were transformed from temporary migrant workers to settled permanent migrants with families, problems of integration, together with growing problems of indigenous unemployment as the postwar boom came to an end, led most governments to introduce restrictive immigration policies in the hope that net migration flows would be reduced to zero or even reversed.

During the 1980s and 1990s, however, European governments and, latterly, the European Commission, came to realize that this would not occur. First, established migrant communities cannot be easily dissolved; and second, the driving factors encouraging migration have constantly increased (Collinson, 1996). These include tangible concerns, such as lack of employment opportunities in countries of origin, as well as more intangible factors, such as lifestyle opportunities, political threat and educational opportunity. In the face of the continuing inward flow, the greatest concern in Europe has been the economic pressure over employment in south Mediterranean countries, particularly in view of the recrudescence of xenophobia throughout the continent during the past twenty years. Associated with this issue are specific security concerns linked to drug smuggling, organized international crime and political terrorism. The issue of terrorism, in particular, has affected European popular and political perceptions in recent years, largely because of the crisis in Algeria.

It is generally accepted throughout Europe that restrictive immigration policies alone cannot deal with the issue. It is estimated that, of the 10 million foreign workers in Europe at present, 2.4 million come from the Maghrib; and at least a further 1.58 million Turks are located in Germany.[4] Mediterranean countries provide a significant source of potential migration into the European continent, not least because, as the European Commission (1994) itself pointed out, south Mediterranean economies had failed to grow sufficiently fast to create the employment opportunities needed to cancel out the economic impulse involved in migration, and the discrepancy between growth rates and labour demand had accelerated. Migration pressures on Europe – with all the attendant security risks and dangers, whether real or imagined – were likely, therefore, to increase.

3. The Euro-Mediterranean Partnership Initiative

The collective European response to these Mediterranean problems has been moulded primarily by concerns over their likely effects on Europe itself, rather than as part of a regional solution. In this respect, of course, European leaders are merely reflecting the objective political reality in which Europe, as the dominant partner in Mediterranean affairs, is in a position to impose solutions on its peripheral hinterland. It is, therefore, open to question as to whether the outcome of this process – the Euro-Mediterranean Partnership Initiative – is really an exercise in 'open regionalism', in that the two sides of the Partnership are linked in a profoundly asymmetrical relationship which is reflected in the nature of the Partnership itself.

In effect, although the major European concerns are essentially security issues – energy security and security problems linked to migration, not to speak of possible spillover effects from conflict in the south Mediterranean region (the Arab–Israeli conflict or the crisis in Algeria, for instance) or further afield (in the Persian Gulf, for example) – the collective response that Europe has encouraged is primarily economic in nature. In part, this reflects the weakness of European institutions, for when the Partnership was introduced the second pillar of the Maastricht Treaty had not really been put in place. The common foreign and security policy only acquired substance after the Amsterdam intergovernmental conference, with the appointment of Xavier Solana as its first secretary-general in 1999 and with European determination to create a credible collective defence capacity in the same year.[5] It also reflected a deeply held European belief that the long-term solution of the problems of the MENA region depended upon effective economic development,[6] together with the construction of viable political institutions – a soft security response that was also holistic in nature (Rhein, 1998: 3–15), since the prescription could be applied to all regional states except for Israel. The Arab–Israeli dispute was seen as primarily an American responsibility, particularly after the debacle of the 1980 Venice Declaration by the European Union,[7] while Israel was accepted as the sole example of a democratic political system in the region.

There was also an evolutionary factor at work – a typical feature of collective European policy. After 1990, it was quite clear that the old pattern of bilateral association and cooperation agreements that had been drawn up with south Mediterranean states and which provided tariff-free and quota access to the European marketplace for south Mediterranean industrial goods and agricultural produce respectively, together with development aid in a series of five-year financial protocols, was inadequate as a means of encouraging successful economic development, even in the modified form proposed by the Union in its 'renovated south Mediterranean policy' of 1992. There were other factors, too – embarrassment at the denial of financial aid to Morocco and Syria in 1992 by the European Parliament, and anxiety among south European states over the diversion of European aid and private investment flows from the Mediterranean towards the former Soviet bloc (Marks, 1998: 48) – but they were ancillary to the basic concern that European intervention to resolve the problems of relations across the Mediterranean required effective economic reform. That reform process was conceived in Brussels and in most European capitals as the one defined by IMF and World Bank experience during the 1980s as the 'Washington Consensus' (Hunt, 1998: 18–32; Hoekman, 1998: 89–104).

The result of these considerations emerged at the Barcelona Conference in November 1995, which was attended by fifteen European Union members and twelve South Mediterranean states – all the littoral states except for Libya, together with Jordan – but not the United States (which, apparently at French insistence, was excluded from the conference, even as an observer). The declaration published at the end of the conference emphasized the common desire of participants to create a zone of shared peace, stability and prosperity, but its indications of how this was to be achieved bore a very obvious European imprint. The Partnership, as described in the declaration, was based on three baskets of measures in what appears to have been a conscious reflection of its inspiration in the Conference on Security and Cooperation in Europe (CSCE) declaration, made in Helsinki in 1975, as a confidence and security-building measure that initiated detente in the Cold War.[8]

One basket related to political and security issues of common concern. It proposed common measures to achieve political reform in south Mediterranean states, designed to make their political systems legitimate and participatory in nature – an important consideration, given the neo-patrimonial and authoritarian nature of virtually all participating south Mediterranean states. It also sought means to ensure respect for human rights among participating states. These requirements were not as radical as they appeared, as similar provisions had already been standard in the cooperation agreements and were to reappear in the new association agreements signed as part of the Barcelona process. Not surprisingly, southern governments have resisted attempts by the Union to interfere in processes which they consider their own sovereign concern and, apart from formal comment, little has been achieved in this direction. The one occasion when European governments were goaded into action – the massacres in Algeria in January 1998 – resulted in an effective whitewash by the British-led European 'Troika' and, subsequently, by a European Parliament delegation (Spencer, 1998a).

The security dimension of this basket has also experienced considerable delay, largely because of continuing tensions in the Middle East peace process involving not only regional states but also the European Union and the United States. There was also a profound south Mediterranean suspicion of all security initiatives emanating from Europe, as was made manifest in North African reactions to the EUROFOR and EUROMARFOR initiatives in 1997 (Spencer 1998b: 209). The result was that, despite French and Maltese proposals for a Mediterranean security pact and charter respectively in 1996, and notwithstanding common anxieties over international terrorism and organized crime, little progress was made in constructing such detailed arrangements for regional security until the end of the decade.

By then, further disagreements had developed over whether such a security charter should also act as a revision of the Barcelona Declaration itself – a powerful, albeit implicit, recognition that the Barcelona process is essentially a response to security concerns. This potential revision of the declaration, which reflected profound southern unhappiness about the economic implications of the process, was resisted by the European Union. Instead, in the wake of NATO's Kosovo intervention, the German presidency of the Union laid down guidelines after the Union's Stuttgart Summit in June 1999 for the detailed negotiations which were to produce a security charter in time for the new millennium. Given the continuing evolution of European security policies, this is likely to be a difficult task to complete – although a framework document was due in mid-2000. Surprisingly, no explicit attention is paid in these guidelines to issues of energy security, nor are the implications of the Persian Gulf included, even though the European Union has been negotiating a separate free trade relationship with the Gulf Cooperation Council – which would mirror the Barcelona process – for the past fifteen years!

The second Barcelona basket involved social and cultural issues. By its very nature it lacked specificity, providing instead guidelines for creating cross-cultural familiarity and supporting the development of civil society inside south Mediterranean states. In fact, it seems likely that this particular basket may turn out to be the most important element in the process, for it deals with issues that genuinely create cross-Mediterranean links as well as having the potential for generating profound cultural division. Its importance lies in the fact that it deals with issues of shared cultural experience that transcend national boundaries, particularly through modern media via satellite and cable television, and through the growth of the knowledge economy as the Internet spreads into the MENA region. The development of civil society is equally important, for it will generate the political diversity inside south Mediterranean states that will both limit the authoritarian and corporate nature of government there and create the variety of political experience that will force governments to legitimize themselves and accept participatory political models. The significance of this basket of the process is, however, long-term, and it will require slow nurturing outside the formal political institutions of the Barcelona process if it is to be successful.

The third basket contained by far the most elaborate and developed aspects of the Initiative, for it dealt with economic relations, building on the experience of the previous thirty years. It was based on very simple principles derived from the Washington Consensus and the economic mechanisms guiding development within the neo-liberal canon. In essence, it sought to encourage further liberalization of the economies of the states in the south Mediterranean region and to reduce the role of the state within those economies. The primary mechanism it exploited for this purpose was the development of free trade linkages between the Union and the individual states of the MENA region. Because of European problems related to the Common Agricultural Policy, agricultural exports to Europe remained under existing quota arrangements but industrial goods and services were placed under the free trade rubric.

The importance of this proposal lay in the fact that, although south Mediterranean industrial goods had long been allowed free access to the European market, European goods entering the south Mediterranean countries had been placed under national tariff arrangements. Now these tariff and non-tariff barriers were to be lifted, so that industries in southern economies were to be exposed to the full force of European competition (Rhein, 1998: 3–16). Lengthy transition periods were provided for the removal of barriers to trade, with 2010 being set as the ultimate end date. Thereafter, the basket provided for the integration of south Mediterranean economies into a single regional market, as part of the process of creating economies of scale and complementarity to improve indigenous competitiveness, working alongside the existing challenge of European industrial competition.

The sudden stimulus – both negative and positive – implied by this process was recognized by the Union, which provided for special financial aid in the '*Mesures d'Ajustement*' (MEDA) funding programme which was to provide 4,865 million ECU/euro over a five-year period, together with access to soft loans from the European Investment Bank for the same amount. Aid, however, was to be directed primarily towards the private sector rather than, as in the past, being made available to governments. The same principles have been followed in the MEDA II programme which will run for seven years up to 2010, with funding raised by 25 per cent.

Tunisia and Morocco, the first two countries to sign the new bilateral free trade association agreements in 1995, certainly anticipated serious industrial adjustment problems. Each country estimated considerable costs in their proposed *mise-à-niveau* (industrial adjustment) programmes – $2 billion in the case of Tunisia and $5.4 billion for Morocco – and European funding fell far short of these requirements. Without these expenditures it was estimated that 60 per cent of the Moroccan industrial sector would collapse and one-third of the Tunisian industrial sector would disappear, with a further third under severe threat. Many other dangers have been identified (Tovias, 1998: 75–88; Marks 1998: 54–8).

In the light of the imposed nature of the Barcelona programme, particularly in the economic basket, and the severe strains that it will almost certainly impose on economies that are already fragile, it is legitimate to ask why the south Mediterranean states should have accepted such an apparently one-sided bargain (for the Tunisian case, see Chourou, 1998: 38–54). And yet they have been anxious to do so. The Palestinian Authority and Jordan signed up to the economic basket of the process in 1996, Israel and Turkey already had their own specific free trade and customs union agreements, and Egypt, Algeria, Syria and Lebanon are in negotiation. Even Libya, now that the Lockerbie crisis is being resolved, has become an observer in the process and is expected, eventually, to join it.[9] The fact is, quite simply, that south Mediterranean states both perceive a utility in closer links with

Europe, given their economic dependence upon it and their geographic contiguity with it, and realize that they have very little choice in the matter. The overwhelming size of the European Union in almost every respect, compared with any other potential partner, obliges them to accept the European vision of a shared future, even if they may fear the consequences. The fact that Israel, despite its long-standing and close relationship with the United States, also recognizes the economic power of Europe only underlines the point (Tovias, 1998).

4. The implications – regionalization or peripheral dependence?

The fact of implicit coercion in the creation of the Euro-Mediterranean common space raises questions about the nature of regionalization. It must be a commonplace that the processes of globalization, internationalization and regionalization are coercive in nature. There can be little doubt that the intrinsic nature of economic integration over-rides the autonomous and sovereign power of national government and thus imposes its own logic on national policy. However, this is very different from the process in which a state or an entity similar to a state can impose its preferred solution on relations with neighbours simply because of its size and power. That, after all, is a very ancient international process reflecting a neo-realist vision rather than the idealism inherent in the European model – even when, as Mill suggested, there could be moral justification (see Joffé, 1997b). It is also very different from the free association of states into a wider political framework in which aspects of national sovereignty are voluntarily abrogated for the sake of wider objectives. This, after all, was the basis on which the European Union was formed and which has begun to transform the actual significance of the state there.[10]

This is not to say that there is necessarily reluctance among south Mediterranean states to accept the European vision. Both Turkey and Morocco have expressed a desire actually to join the Union (though, while Turkey's request has now been granted substance with its inclusion on the list of aspirant members at the Helsinki Summit, Morocco's 1987 application still languishes). For other states, however, which may have different visions of regional integration or association – the Arab world or the Maghrib, for instance – the Union's 1995 proposal for open regionalism within the context of the Barcelona Declaration was an invitation that, however reluctant they may have been, they could not ignore. Thus it was Europe that defined both the terms of reference for the process and its objectives – all of which primarily benefited European interests. Even the promise of economic development in the south, which for most southern states was the only justification for accepting what they felt in political and sociocultural terms to be a poisoned chalice, may well prove to be illusory (Marks, 1998; Chourou, 1998; Mahjoub, 1998).

In many respects, the EU's Mediterranean policy, which reflected European imperatives in resolving its hinterland problems by securing its southern periphery, was similar to the United States' decision to engage in the North America Free

Trade Area (NAFTA), at least as far as Mexico was concerned. Mexico may have been more anxious to engage in such a policy because of the perceived benefits of technology transfer and access to the American market, while American employers and employees may have been far less ready to accept the arrangement for the same reasons. For the United States, however, the NAFTA policy was to be a means of resolving a migrant labour problem through domestic economic development – although the *maquilladora* system seems to embody precisely the hub–spoke arrangement which has caused such anxiety in the south Mediterranean (Tovias, 1998).

In other respects, the Union's policy towards the south Mediterranean is less than holistic in dealing with its peripheral problems, despite its claims, and thus may not meet the typical criteria laid down for the so-called 'open regionalism' (Thompson, 1998: 63) – nor, indeed, for the development of a region (Calleya, 1997: 35–6). This is particularly the case with respect to security issues, with energy security concerns at the forefront, and the role in the region of the United States. Indeed, this concern calls into question one of the fundamental assumptions of the Barcelona process, namely that the Mediterranean can be considered, for security purposes, as a single regional unit.[11] Furthermore, it is difficult to argue that there is a social or cultural homogeneity, given the massive and growing tensions between the two sides of the Mediterranean, despite the unifying factors of communication and political concerns at the popular level on issues such as human rights.

In these circumstances, it might be more accurate to define the Euro-Mediterranean Partnership Initiative as an experiment in 'peripheral regionalism' in which a major power bloc, whatever its internal structures, imposes solutions along its periphery in which mutual benefit is an incidental consequence of unilateral security concerns. It is defective in that, because of the role and interests of the United States, it cannot be holistic in nature and because it ignores both the issue of energy security and the implications of Europe's relations with the Persian Gulf. It may, nevertheless, have profound consequences in that it could force two ancillary developments. First, south Mediterranean states may well be forced into south–south economic integration and thus achieve the necessary conditions for endogamous or indigenous, self-generated economic growth alongside the pressure exerted by exposure to the European economic model. And second, the very fact of European interest and ability in influencing domestic political development – both for altruistic social and ethical reasons, as much as to satisfy demands for economic transparency and accountability – may promote genuine political change in south Mediterranean states towards an internationally acceptable participatory model of political legitimization.

It is at this level, far more than at any other, that the Euro-Mediterranean Partnership is significant; for, if it achieves these objectives, it will have demonstrated the potential of regional systems for achieving genuine and beneficial political change. It may also be that, in doing so, it will have to review its own nature. Even though the creation of a common economic space is also a mechanism for ensuring cultural separation – economic development should, after all, remove a major driving force for migration, as should political evolution – the fact seems to be that south Mediterranean states will not tolerate indefinitely being excluded from the decision-making processes of the Union itself. The current mechanisms for consultation built into the Barcelona process will not, in the last analysis, be sufficient, as the advent of Turkey as a candidate member demonstrates. In such a case, new European structures for inclusion will have to be devised, to encompass the European hinterland as well as its core, and the Barcelona process will prove to have been merely a transitional system on the way to a wider concept of regionalization.

Notes

1   Quite apart from the issue of the future of the Westphalian state and its development between the sixteenth and seventeenth centuries from the Augsburg Compromise to the Treaty of Westphalia, there is also the crucial issue of the development of the concept of sovereignty and its severance from the ruling institution to become a key property of a uniquely self-defined society, the nation. This concept becomes an explicit source of state legitimization through the French Revolution. The issue is crucial in the context of the Mediterranean because the states along its southern shore have no innate concept of 'the nation' in this sense derived from an indigenous political culture. The Mediterranean 'imagined community' (Anderson, 1987) is holistic, not particularistic; regional, not national; and cultural, not political. The need to nation-build has therefore been a dominant concern of states there and does much to explain their inherent repressiveness, alongside their defective, neo-patrimonial nature (Murphy, 1999).
2   'Open regionalism' implies linkages between states that do not impinge directly upon their sovereign activities and rights. They therefore tend to be primarily economic in nature, even if, as is the case with the Barcelona Process the explicit objectives may involve common security or diplomatic factors (see Thomas, 1998: 63).
3   The future interrelationship between NATO and the Western European Union, together with the Franco-British proposal for a 60,000 member European projection force adopted by the Helsinki Summit, have particular relevance for the Mediterranean in view of the Kosovo intervention in April-May 1999 and the Stuttgart Mediterranean security charter proposals of June 1999.
4   Unofficial estimates of the Turkish immigrant population in Germany range as high as 5 million; there are also significant Turkish communities in Austria, the Benelux countries, France and Britain.
5   This capacity is still embryonic, but the decision to incorporate the Western European Union into the proposed European Security and Defence Identity, together with Anglo-French proposals for a 60,000-strong projection force and discussions over an intensified European role inside NATO, indicate the way in which this is likely to proceed.
6   The best analysis of the economic situation of the Mediterranean region is provided by Bensidoun and Chevallier (1996).

7   The Venice Declaration asserted the European view that Palestinian aspirations must be recognized and satisfied as part of any settlement of the Arab-Israeli dispute. The Union thereafter quietly promoted policies designed to encourage Palestinian autonomy, particularly in the economic field. Israel, however, interpreted this as unwarranted interference that ran counter to American attempts to resolve the Middle East crisis and set its face against any European involvement in a future Middle East peace process. The supine nature of European policy on the issue thereafter makes it difficult to avoid the conclusions that (a) several European states implicitly accepted the Israeli criticism and were determined to follow the American lead in future and (b) the European Union itself thankfully abandoned any activism over the issue in future unless in support of American policy initiatives.

8   The CSCE declaration involved a series of agreements over security, political and social contacts between East and West that were designed to build confidence between the two sides as a means of defusing military tensions. Coincidentally, they also provided mechanisms by which political and humanitarian conditions in the Eastern bloc could be influenced. The CSCE model was applied to the design of a comprehensive settlement process for the Mediterranean, designed to provide holistic solutions to the political, economic and social problems and disparities in a region covering the Gulf as well, which was proposed by the Italian foreign minister, Giovanni de Michaelis, with Spanish support, in 1990. The Italo-Spanish proposal was considered too complicated and was, in any case, overtaken by the Iraqi invasion of Kuwait. It was replaced by a more modest suggestion made by President Mitterrand – the "Four plus Five" negotiations, bringing together France, Italy, Spain and Portugal with the five UMA (Union Maghreb Arabe) states of Mauritania, Morocco, Algeria, Tunisia and Libya to discuss common problems as an addendum to European Union bilateral economic cooperation. This forum was later expanded to the "Five plus Five" talks by the inclusion, at its own request, of Malta and, in 1994, was assimilated into the "Mediterranean Forum process" under Egyptian patronage. The Mediterranean Forum continues to operate within the Barcelona process as a parallel but more restricted arena of debate in which western Mediterranean concerns can be expressed.

The importance of these antecedents to the Barcelona process – the Euro-Mediterranean Partnership Initiative – is that, in parallel to the long-established pattern of EU bilateral economic cooperation with south Mediterranean states, the practice of confidence-building measures was also developed. Although it might cynically be concluded that little else would have been possible, outside the arena of economic cooperation, given the disarray in Europe's capacity for constructing effective common diplomatic positions, this would be to underestimate the importance that should be accorded to what was, in effect, a new technique in diplomatic contact. Without this prior diplomatic experience, it would have been quite impossible for the Barcelona process to have been launched. It should also be borne in mind that this confidence-building measure also depended crucially on another, parallel process: the Middle East peace process. Without the initial success of that American-guided process, it would have been quite impossible to launch a holistic long-term approach to common regional problems – ostensibly the real purpose of the Initiative. However, it should also be borne in mind that the Initiative is a European-inspired process applied to a reluctant south Mediterranean rim which knows it has little choice in the matter (Joffé, 1997a).

9   Because of UN sanctions against Libya as a result of accusations of its involvement in the destruction of PanAm Flight 102 over the Scottish town of Lockerbie in December 1988 and of a UTA aircraft over Niger in September 1989, it was excluded from the Barcelona Conference. Libyan willingness to hand over the two persons accused of the Lockerbie incident for trial in the Netherlands under Scottish law, and British willing-ness to accept such a unique extraterritorial arrangement in 1999, made it possible for Libya – as south Mediterranean states had long demanded – to be brought into the process. Its full participation, however, will only occur once the UN has definitively removed the sanctions regime. At present that regime is only suspended, subject to six-monthly review, and the United States is hostile to its removal. Libyan involvement in the UTA affair was resolved by a trial *in absentia* in Paris in early 1999.

10 Robert Cooper has argued that the structure of the EU itself is not enough to ensure the restructuring of the state in the modern world. He points out that it is the combination of the effects of the Union structure and the *acquis communautaire,* together with the security implications of the Agreement on Conventional Forces in Europe, that truly defines the contemporary postmodernist state (Cooper, 1997). This view should be contrasted with that of Adam Roberts in which the future political arena will be "a civil society of civil societies".

11 An alternative view might be that there are four hard security arenas: Greece and Turkey; the eastern Mediterranean, involving the Arab Middle East and Israel; the Balkans, particularly in the wake of the Bosnia and Kosovo crises; and the western Mediterranean, where security issues are largely soft security concerns (although between the states hard security issues persist; see Mezran, 1998). To these four a fifth might be added: because of its influence on Mediterranean strategic conceptions the Persian Gulf. American strategists would also impose upon this fragmented security arena an additional unitary vision of the Mediterranean and the Gulf, linked through the Red Sea, as a "strategic line of communication", primarily for the transit of energy products. They would also argue that American interests in the region, being targeted primarily at the Levant and Turkey (although Algeria and Egypt are also key geo-economic interests as pivotal state and emerging market respectively) require any regional system for the region to take American interests into account – something which the Barcelona process manifestly does not do, although European states and the Union do recognize the paramount American political role in the Middle East peace process. Even inside Europe, a recognition is emerging that eastern and western Mediterranean security concerns are not identical, and this may well influence the final form of the promised Mediterranean security charter, even though there will be considerable misgivings among south Mediterranean states.

12. Europe – Super Power or a Scandinavia of the World?

Göran Therborn

On the world maps of the Peters Projection, Europe appears as a small, far north-ern periphery of peninsulae and islands, out on the western fringe of the huge Asian land mass, separated by the narrow Mediterranean waterway from the big central continent of Africa, and by the wide Atlantic Ocean from the impressive semi-continent of North America. In other words, Europe here looks very much like the Nordic countries on a standard European map, with the qualification that Scandinavia normally looks larger on these. A Scandinavian scenario, I am going to argue, is in the long run one of the most attractive futures left to an irreversibly ex-imperial continent.

The future standing of Europe in the world will depend on three complex variables: the relative weight, the relative specificity, and the relative unity of Europe.

1. Still heavyweight, but...

Western Europe has long since abdicated from claims to rule the world, although the Dutch, the French and the Portuguese had to be ousted from their colonies by force. The bungled Anglo-French–Israeli attack on Egypt in 1956 was the last attempt to play world power. The recent War of the Yugoslav Succession demon-strated Europe's weakness even as a regional power. The road from Berlin 1878 to Dayton 1995 has been a long one. In so far as the Soviet Union was a European power, its collapse entails a further weakening of Europe in the global theatre of power.

Commemorations are correspondingly scaled down as aspirations are lowered. The start of western Europe's outward expansion was remembered in the last World Exhibitions of the twentieth century, in Seville in 1992 and in Lisbon in 1998, in ecologically conscious theme parks for tourists, without any of the imperial glory and nation-state *braggadoccio* of the pre-Second World War exhibitions, or even the futurism of the Brussels 1958 Exhibition. The arrival of European modernity in

1789 was two centuries later turned into a pure media spectacle, while the politically correct opinion was that the French Revolution was both vicious and unnecessary.

1.1 Production and prosperity

Economically, of course, Europeans are still among the primary league players. In 1995, four of the six large economies of the world (those with a GDP of more than $1 million) are European: Germany, France, the UK and Italy. (The others are the United States and Japan.) After its latest expansion the economy of the EU as a whole is of the same size as that of the United States, each accounting for one-fifth of the world economy.

By the IMF's reckoning (IMF, 1997: 121), there are twenty-eight 'advanced economies' in the world in the mid-1990s. Eighteen of these are European, and five are European settlements: Australia, Canada, Israel, New Zealand and the United States. The remaining five are East Asian: Hong Kong, Japan, Korea, Singapore and Taiwan. The World Bank (1997: 215) list of 'high income economies' is fairly similar. With Iceland and Luxembourg added – excluded from the main table because of their small populations – and correcting for purchasing power differences among currencies, this list comprises twenty-nine countries, of which eighteen are European ones. Taiwan is missing for diplomatic reasons, and the oil sheikhdoms of Kuwait and the UAE have been added. With the recent ascent to prosperity of Portugal and Greece, no Western European country is in division two.

How significant average GDP per capita and its growth are among rich countries, unless median incomes, the overall distribution, and quality of life are taken into account, is far from obvious. Nevertheless, it offers a useful measure of the change in the relative wealth of Western Europe and the United States and Japan. If we put GDP per capita of the EU 15 in 1996 at 100, the US figure would be 144 and the Japanese 121. In 1970 the spread was wider: the US figure was 163 and the Japanese 95 (OECD, 1998a: 162–3). Moreover, this relative increase in wealth is even more marked in respect of the world outside North America and East Asia. In the mid-1990s the per capita GDP of the EU was about six and a half times that of the Third World. For the gap to narrow, then, the latter needed to grow at an annual rate more than six and half times that of Europe. But in fact, for 1990–6 the so-called 'developing countries' grew by only 3.9 per cent a year, as against the EU's 1.4 per cent (IMF, 1997: 136). In summary, Western Europe is a rich corner of the world, and it is growing relatively more prosperous.

Western Europe has also maintained itself well on the world trade markets (see Table 12.1). For western Europe, as for the United States, the OPEC price hike of the 1970s had a much more significant impact on its trade shares than the recent wave of globalization. The trade expansion of East and Southeast Asia has had no net effect on the OECD countries; the Third World has had to bear the full brunt of this. In other words, Europe is holding up well in terms of trade competitiveness.

Table 12.1   Shares of world exports (of goods and services) 1950–1996 (%)

	1950	*1970*	*1976*	*1996*
Western Europe	33	46	42	42
North America	21	20	17	16
Japan	1	6	7	7
Total OECD	61	75	68	68
Non-OECD Asia	–	6	7	18

Sources: UNCTAD, 1995, tables 1.9, 1.10; UN, 1995a: special table A; IMF, 1996: table 1; IMF, 1997: 120.

In fact, in the first half of the 1990s, the EU was (by a small margin) a net exporter of manufactures to the so-called emergent economies. This may of course change, but so far Europe is less exposed to low-wage industrial competition than North America and Japan (OECD, 1997: 104–5).

Europe is hardly the hub of the world economy, although London is still the world's major financial centre. But Europe is still fully reproducing itself as a small semi-Arctic outpost of prosperity, out of reach, and increasingly so, to the bulk of the earth's population. Statistically average prosperity is, to some extent, being undermined, though, by a tendential rise of unemployment. However, in many countries – France, Germany, Italy, and Scandinavia excepting Denmark (Vogel, 1997) – the European welfare state has been strong and generous enough to prevent any rise in poverty during the 1990s.

1.2 Population

In sheer numbers, Europe is becoming steadily lighter in the world (see Table 12.2). The population projection reflects the fact that Europe, together with Japan, is close to a static natural population equilibrium. Birth and death rates are almost cancelling each other out (see Table 12.3).

The outcome of this demographic trend is already visible in the age structure. In 1990, 14.5 per cent of the population of western Europe was over 65 years old; the corresponding figure was 12.3 per cent for the United States and 11.9 per cent for Japan, but just 4.8 per cent for the other Central, East, and South Asian states, 3.6 per cent for West and North Africa, and 4.6 per cent for Latin America. Extrapolations into the future suggest that in the 2020s, about a third of the Western European population will be more than sixty years old. (World Bank, 1994: tables A1, A2.) Death rates are now exceeding birth rates in Germany, Italy and Switzerland.(Eurostat, 1996: table 1). Since the end of the Soviet Union, deaths have exceeded births to a dramatic extent in Russia, Ukraine, Belarus and the Baltic Republics (UNICEF, 1995: tables A1–2). Part of Europe is dying out.

Table 12.2   Europe's proportion of the world's population, 1950–2025 (%)

1950	*1993*	*2025 (est.)*
22	13	9

Note: Europe includes Russia and the non-Caucasian and non-Central Asian republics of the former USSR.
Sources: UN, 1995b:12; World Bank, 1995a: 210–11, 228.

Whereas biologically Europe's population is tending towards decline, migratory flows keep up a certain momentum, although not (yet) enough to stop estimates of a slight population decline in the next decades. Europe turned from almost half a millennium of net outward migration to a net recipient of immigrants in the first half of the 1960s. But it is only since the mid-1980s that the pace of migration into (western) Europe has quickened. Between 1985–7 and 1992 the number of immigrants into western Europe almost trebled. (Therborn, 1995a: 41ff, 50). In the 1990s, migration has constituted the bulk of the population growth in the EU 15. Net migration into Germany in the 1990s has been more than twice that into the United States (6.7 and 3.3 per thousand population per annum, respectively; see Eurostat, 1996: fig. 1, table 2).

Putting together the diminished military strength of Europe, its persisting political division, its fairly stable but clearly not predominant economic capacity, the high and visibly unthreatened prosperity of its citizens – though partly eroded by unemployment – and its ageing and gradually shrinking native population, it seems clear that the continent has little, if anything, to gain from entering a race for world championship. Further, the world view of the global business consultants, with their vision of an inexorable struggle for world competitive rank, seems no more securely founded in what matters to most people than was the 1930s ideology of the inescapable struggle for *Lebensraum*. On the other hand, there is no evidence of European marginalization, either current or imminent.

In sum, western Europe is still heavyweight, but its right hook is not as hard as it used to be, by a long way. Part of the weight is fat rather than muscle, and it is getting slower. But it also looks unscathed, exuding good training and experience.

2. Specificity under pressure – and imitation

The specificities of European societies derive from the historical trajectory of Europe, ancient and modern. This writer would tend to give more weight to the European route to modernity than to its ancient traditions in accounting for contemporary European sociology (Therborn, 1995b), but the point will not be argued here. What seems to be called for, however, is some assessment of the future life expectancy of the peculiarities of the Europeans.

Table 12.3   Crude birth and death rates in the world, 1993 (per 000)

	Birth rate	*Death rate*
Europe	12	11
Japan	10	7
United States	15	9
Latin America	25	7
Africa	41	14
China	18	7
India	27	9
Southeast Asia	26	8
World	24	9

Sources: UN, 1999, table 1.4.

Significant European specificities may be summarized as of two kinds. One refers to the *aggregate* of European societies and their common characteristics in comparison with the rest of the world. The other refers to 'Europe', as a supranational, suprastate collective or social *mega-network*. Both kinds are subject to three sorts of challenges. First, there is the possibility of the characteristics being eroded, by internal processes and/or under external pressure. Second, the specific traits of Europe may recede into the background, having become marginal or irrelevant in relation to broader and stronger global processes. Third, Europe's special features may become increasingly difficult to discern, because they are taken up elsewhere, by imitation or by parallel developments.

2.1 European modernity: class and welfare state

Among the many particularities of European social relations as aggregates, this chapter will touch upon just two: the special significance in Europe of industrial class relations and of a socially interventionist 'welfare' state. The two are, of course, historically related, the latter pretty much an outcome of the former.

Modernity in Europe was a completely endogenous development, on the continent taken as a whole. This meant that the bitter and violent conflicts for and against modernity all took the character of civil war. This endogeneity had at least three important implications.

First, the European route to modernity pitted socioeconomic classes against each other more clearly than elsewhere. That was inherent in endogeneity, as classes are internal social divisions; but it was strongly reinforced by the unique importance of industrialization to European societies. Only in Europe did industrial employment become at least relatively dominant in a trisectoral employment structure (Therborn, 1995a: 68ff). The polarized industrial division of labour gave further impetus to class consciousness, class mobilization and class organization in

Europe. To this day, the west European political party system derives from clear-cut class cleavages, with one major party descending from specific working-class representation and the other from a core of bourgeois and middle-class representation, representing non-working-class politics, either by claiming transcendence of class through nation or religion (Christian Democracy), or by representing agrarian or middle-class interests.

Second, the internal conflict path meant that established religion was always clearly on the side of anti-modernity. When modernity finally won, this meant a serious defeat of established Christianity. Today, Europe is by far the most secularized part of the world once governed by what Max Weber called the world religions (Therborn, 1995a: 275). (The Confucian area is not quite comparable to the rest of the religious world.)

Third, the protracted internal struggles for and against modernity gave rise to a large set of elaborate doctrines and principled ideological systems. Europe was the womb of almost all the major 'isms' of the nineteenth and the twentieth centuries, from Legitimism, Monarchism and Republicanism to Liberalism, Conservatism, Traditionalism, Radicalism, Socialism, Marxism, Fascism and Anti-Fascism. Only Fundamentalism is of non-European origin, coined in the United States in the 1920s to designate anti-modern Christian Protestantism.

A party system historically based on class cleavages, with a relatively high element of class voting, still characterizes western Europe. Trade unions carry more weight in Europe than elsewhere, especially in Germanic Europe. Even their weakening in the 1980s and 1990s has not made the situation of west European unions significantly more similar to that of American or Japanese ones (Therborn, 1995: 309–10).

In terms of ideological doctrines, Europe is still the world's major producer of ideology, although the successful export drive has passed from the Soviet Union and the Socialist International to neo-Tory Britain. Recently, British Blairism is contending for a position as ideological 'beacon' to the world. The major item of ideological export is no longer 'socialism' but 'privatization' and (marketeering) 'economic reform'. The relatively meagre ideological output – outside Christian Fundamentalism – of the US right, via the Reagan presidency and the Gingrich Congress, is noteworthy.

On the other hand, de-industrialization and its concomitant sociopolitical realignments have hit Europe. The industrial class basis of European politics is being undercut, although it retains a relative advantage over the United States and Japan. The unique European preponderance of industrial over agricultural and services employment, or at least over all non-agrarian employment – characteristic of Britain since about 1820 and of western Europe since the early twentieth century – has been lost. Since 1980 Europe has even become less industrial than Japan, although it has by and large retained its position in relation to the United States.

Now, sociological experience teaches us that institutions usually do not go away as a result of being undermined. The institutions of industrial class society are still in place in Europe, and they are not likely to evaporate in the foreseeable future. But their significance, as rallying-points of collective identity and behaviour, has diminished as solid class voting has ebbed away to May Day marching or meeting attendance. The efforts of political parties of the centre-left to distance themselves from the unions and their more direct class allegiance is palpable all across Europe in the 1990s, from Scandinavia to the Iberian peninsula via the British Isles.

There are, however, no signs of any accelerating descent of class relations and class politics in Europe. Even the basis for predicting a continuous linear erosion is flimsy. Electoral politics in western Europe is still moving, up and down, right or left, within the classical social parameters. And the pattern of tendencies in non-electoral social conflicts is complicated; there may be a resigned adjustment to permanent mass unemployment, but one should also note the occasional flare-up of still potent class-based social protest.

The welfare state has come under siege, from global financial markets – generally manned by highly paid young males, to whom social issues are as distant as the other side of the moon – and from the bulk of the economics profession, while internal support is increasingly withheld by an upper middle class growing both in assertiveness and in preoccupation with itself. More options for the prosperous and more concentration on the very minimum for the 'really needy' are slogans in ascendance, while social rights, solidarity and social integration are being correspondingly demoted. But how far has this new ideological discourse eaten into actually existing institutions of public social rights? Table 12.4 shows how social security transfers and total current public disbursements have evolved since 1960.

On the whole, the specificity of the European state has maintained itself well so far (see ILO, 1995: 120–1). The pressure on it is likely to be kept up, and may well even mount further. But attacks on the welfare state are intensifying even more in the United States, and there are so far no visible signs of any cutting down of a west European state to American or Japanese proportions.

The two major characteristics of modern European societies, their industrial class pattern of social relations and conflicts, and their sizeable social state, are not currently celebrated as foci of a collective European identity. Both are being under-

Table 12.4   Social security transfers and total current public disbursements, 1960–1996 (%GDP)

	1960		*1974*		*1985*		*1996*	
	Transfers	*Total*	*Transfers*	*Total*	*Transfers*	*Total*	*Transfers*	*Total*
Europe[a]	9.5	31.4	13.3	40.0	17.7	49.5	20.3(b)	49.4(b)
US	5.0	27.2	9.5	36.4	10.9	37.0	12.9	35.2
Japan	3.8	17.5	6.2	32.9	10.9	32.3	13.5	36.5

Note: [a] Europe = OECD Europe; [b] EU15.
Source: OECD, 1999: tables 6.3, 6.5.

cut by powerful forces, internal as well as international. However, like all traditions and institutions, they are very resilient, and in practice they continue to shape the continent in characteristic ways.

2.2 Beyond the nation-state: bloc or model?

An intricate interstate – or, to begin with, inter-prince – system has characterized western Europe since the middle ages. From the mid-nineteenth to the mid-twentieth century that state system gave rise to a series of increasingly devastating wars. Eventually, these experiences generated a specific set of suprastate institutions.

This is not the place to analyse the process of European unification, or even to summarize it. What needs to be underlined is the global specificity of it, and thereby its relevance to the standing of Europe in the world, both today and in the future.

The construction of 'Europe' since the Second World War is a process of system integration, of building a loosely coupled, open system. As such, 'Europe' is a set of supranational, suprastate institutions and a social mega-network. The European Union is the most concrete and tangible member of this set, with a highly visible political apparatus and a substantial budgetary underpinning. The EU does not operate only as a 'common market' – its impact on trade has been uneven and unsystematic – but, more characteristically, as a pooling of economic resources and initiatives, and as a *normative area*, governed by an extensive body of rules, vigilantly and strongly protected by a European judiciary, to which even nation-states are held liable.

The Council of Europe, with the European Convention on Human Rights, its Commission and Court of Human Rights, and its European Social Charter, have made Europe into an area of human rights more specific and more binding than any other area of the world. The rulings of the Strasbourg Court of Human Rights are accepted as binding by the states which have ratified the jurisdiction.

A third major institution of normative Europe is the Organization for Security and Cooperation in Europe (OSCE), officially constituted in 1992 and 1994 (when the name changed from 'Conference' to 'Organization'), but going back to the institutionalized thaw of the Cold War, the Helsinki Agreement of 1975. The seventh section of the latter listed a set of fundamental freedoms and rights to act, and provided for a review process. The now permanent OSCE has a special monitoring and dialogue-initiating office on democratic institutions and human rights, located in Warsaw.

The global specificity of the current sociology of Europe resides most visibly in suprastate 'Europe'. This is not to say that the continental drawing together of the western part of Europe is unique, nor even pioneering. Pan-American efforts in this direction clearly antedate European ones, starting with more or less regular Pan-American state congresses in 1889, leading to a loose pre-war Pan-American Union and a set of hemispheric professional recurrent conferences and institutions, like the Inter-American Child Institute in Montevideo, and in 1948 to the Organization of American States. Ex-colonial Africa has created its Organization of African Unity, and, particularly in West Africa, a number of regional organizations, one of which was rather more successful in its intervention in the civil wars in Liberia than the EU was in the former Yugoslavia.

However, in contrast to the OAS and the OAU, the EU, and, for those countries that have ratified its human rights jurisdiction, the Council of Europe, are suprastate not just interstate organizations. Upon ratification, the treaties and their judicial interpretation are legally binding to member states. This framework is functioning in practice, as the rulings of the European Courts of Justice and of Human Rights, and their de facto acceptance by member states, show. The European Commission represents a Union, not just a set of sovereign member states. A rare combination of a relatively balanced internal composition of power, intensive socioeconomic internal exchange, and considerable economic strength on a global scale has meant that 'Europe' (i.e. the EU) is widely perceived in the world as one 'bloc'.

It was as such a bloc that Europe met the East Asian countries at the Bangkok summit in March 1996; and, as such, 'Europe' has inspired looser economic groupings in the Americas in the 1990s – NAFTA, Mercosur and, most recently, the agreement on an Andean Community. The European Commission and Court of Human Rights have provided models for the recently established American equivalents.[1] 'Europe' as a bloc of prosperity is what attracts a growing queue of applicants, from the long and probably hopelessly waiting Morocco and Turkey to the formerly communist East–Central strip of Europe from Estonia to Bulgaria.

Europe's future standing in the world will largely depend on the future of its suprastate organizations and institutions. Their problem is not one of erosion and descent, but rather of over-extension and emulation. What will happen to Europe as a normative area if the Council of Europe accommodates continuous violent suppression of minorities, in Turkey, Croatia, Macedonia or Russia? Will a European Union of twenty-five or thirty members become more like the proposed All-American Free Trade Area than a European Community? Will the OSCE achieve anything or fail entirely in its virtually impossible missions to postwar Bosnia, Chechnya and the Caucasus? In the best of worlds the Council of Europe would decrease in significance and specificity, yielding place to a strong UN system of human rights flanked by many regional institutions. Implosion by internal disunity is another risk, which will be dealt with in a section below.

As a unit, Europe may appear in the world, and to the world, as a power bloc, as a normative or institutional model, or as a nullity without significance. The last possibility is not in sight for the foreseeable future, although logically it cannot be ruled out for ever.

2.3 The limits of globalization

Tendencies towards globalization have acquired a large amount of attention in the recent decade or two. The transnational corporations flattening the earth into one chessboard of competitive locations; the financial markets interconnected across all the time zones of the globe and with a gambling turnover exceeding the annual GDP of any state on the planet; a worldwide mass culture encasing the earth in satellite radiation, audible in the remotest corners, visible in the same trainers and jeans, and digestible as global fast foods: they are all real and well known. On a more modest scale, some steps have been taken towards a normative globalization, with the big UN conferences on human rights, on population, on the environment, and on poverty, with ensuing declarations and conventions, and sometimes monitoring reporting systems and evaluating committees. Increasingly powerful and ambitious international economic organizations like the IMF and the World Bank are pushing liberal economic and social policies, largely derived from US education, on to all poor and/or indebted states of the world.[2]

All these developments constrain Europe, both as an economic power and as an institutional model. But there is little reason to assume that globalization trends are reducing Europe to the status of just another interchangeable chunk of the earth – or that they will do so in the foreseeable future. A global economic system is not yesterday's invention. Many would say it goes back to the colonial expansion of Europe in the sixteenth century. In a narrower sense, it is at least 150 years old: for it was the mid-nineteenth century when the British Navy opened up China to the international drugs trade (the 'Opium Wars'). Far from being extinguished, different 'corporate cultures' have been discovered recently by students and consultants of big corporate management. (See e.g. Hampden-Turner and Trompenaars, 1993; and, as a testimony from within the corporate world, Albert, 1991.)

Global mass culture is a more recent phenomenon and is mainly American or American–British. The United States and the United Kingdom, in that order, dominate both the music and the audiovisual markets. Among the OECD countries, only the United States ($2 billion dollars in 1992) and the UK ($25 million) run a surplus on film and television rights (OECD, 1995: table A.21.) But culture is effective largely within institutional structures, and the latter are still strongly shaped by states and by situated ethnicities. Therefore the global cultural radiation is largely received in forms of hybridization or creolization.

The 1990s have also seen one important turn towards de-globalization. The collapse of the USSR and the end of the Cold War meant the end of four decades of global cleavage and alignments. The Gulf War and the protection of the Kuwaiti oilfields proved a brief episode and not the beginning of a global Pax Americana. In international power politics, regional powers and regional cleavages are currently mounting in significance, at the expense of globalism.

The main forces of globalization no longer derive from Europe, and have not done so since Europeans launched the Second World War. True, the global Cold War took its script from the rival ideologies of European modernity and its centre stage was the heart of Europe; but, of the two main actors, one was a European expatriate and the other a cousin from the eastern countryside. So far, there are no signs of the globe driving continental (or smaller) regions out of business. And in the global economic games being played, European players are well represented, although perhaps in the risk of running offside. Globalization is cutting into European specificity culturally, including European political and corporate culture, and in the longer run this encroachment will inevitably leave new institutional imprints. But we are not witnessing a disappearance of historical geography. Europe will continue to have a standing in the world, whatever that standing may be.

3. Clouds over unity

If the earth as a whole has difficulties with unification, so too has Europe. However, from a worldwide future perspective the problems of the latter look somewhat different from those that dominated public debate in Europe prior to the 1996 EU Intergovernmental Conference. Since Europe is unlikely to become a first-rank global political and military power in the twenty-first century, the concerns about a unified foreign and security policy have little more than parochial interest. Nor is a European monetary union likely to have any crucial impact upon Europe's relative economic power in the world. The idea of EMU is mainly a peculiar conception of a political union. Economically, its overriding concern is neither competitiveness nor growth, but stability.

Only to the extent that future world markets will be carved up between protectionist blocs will European unity be very important to the economic power position of European corporations, trading sites and states. That direction is not where regionalization in the world is currently heading. On the contrary, the major thrust is towards the opening of markets, albeit regional more than (and before) borderless ones. European economic power will not depend directly on the unity of 'Europe' as one organization or collectivity, but on the dynamism and luck of the major European players. Nevertheless, social disintegration in Europe might very well have a negative effect on the dynamism of European actors.

3.1 Unemployment and ethnic multiculturalism

Europe is facing two major social unity problems. One is the mounting socioeconomic segmentation and polarization within the nations of western Europe, a product of rapid ethnic diversification in the big cities and sluggish labour markets, with unemployment steadily rising from one business cycle to the next over twenty years. The other is the discrepancy between, on one hand, an institutional/cultural adaptation of eastern Europe to western models and, on the other, a drastic widening of an already large divide in resources and life-chances for the bulk of the population, as the cost of breaking up the previous institutional structures.

Neither problem is very likely to lead to acute social disintegration in the foreseeable future, except perhaps in Russia, Ukraine and some of the Balkan states. Both look for the time being containable within existing institutions, both of

Table 12.5   Standardized open unemployment rates in the EC/EU, 1964–1999 (%)

1964–73	1974–9	1980–9	1991–7	1999
2.7	4.7	9.3	10.2	9.2

Sources: OECD, 1996: table 2.20; OECD, 1998b: table A; OECD, 2000: annex table 2.2.

the western cities and national states, and of the extensive forms of East–West cooperation. But if they are not tackled seriously and in a concerted and sustained way – and there is little indication of this at the time of writing – the divisions within the western half of the continent and the East–West divide are more likely to deepen than to close. If they do get worse, they will then bear heavily and negatively upon the quality of life of the whole European population. Virtually everybody is likely to have to pay a price for social exclusion, marginalization, poverty and despair: a price of fear, crime and occasional but recurrent violence.

The 'employment problem' is not represented only by the unemployment rate. Drop-outs, from the labour force as well as from school, early retirement, and unemployability disguised as disability are other aspects that require attention. The self-imposed fiscal constraints of Maastricht are increasing attempts to shuffle the problem around, by, for example, raising the statutorily 'normal' retirement age and tightening the disability criteria. How is the labour market going to bear that? Certainly not by any particularly expansionary economic policies such as those characteristic of Keynesianism, now held to be obsolete by economically correct opinion. The only recipe around is the creation of a dualistic labour market. Alongside the normal European labour market, there is to be one with much lower wages, few if any social rights, and no security. To what extent this deliberate division of labour into two lanes will be carried out remains to be seen.

The traditionally rather monoethnic cities of western Europe have in recent decades acquired a considerable amount of multicoloured diversity – approaching, indeed, the rich multiculturality characteristic of east European cities, from Constantinople/Istanbul to Helsingfors/Helsinki, before the waves of national assimilation and ethnic cleansings began. The change has been particularly marked because of its concentration in certain cities, mainly capital or otherwise central conurbations. In Amsterdam about half of school children are of immigrant background, and in Paris in 1990 a third of all youths below age seventeen lived in a family of immigrants. In the early 1990s 'non-whites' made up a fifth of the Greater London population. In Frankfurt and Brussels over a quarter of the resident population are 'foreigners' (Therborn, 1995: 49–50).

Even if one considers multiculturality as an asset, as this writer does, sociology and history teach us that it is not unproblematic. What 'Europe' will mean to the West Indians or Bangladeshis in Inner London, to the Mahgrebins in the suburbs around Paris, to the Turks and the Kurds in Berlin and Frankfurt, is far from self-evident. And if there is to be little or no proper space for them on the labour market, and for their cultures among the cultures of Europe, the ensuing society will not be the normative area of the Council of Europe, with its recognition of the rights of diversity.

The prospects for a rich, peaceful and stimulating multiculturality as against those of ghettoization, crime, and ethnic strife and violence are difficult to assess. The evidence available so far belies any straightforward extrapolation in either direction. Unemployment hits proportionately more immigrants and immigrants' children than natives. The immigrant population tends to have a higher crime rate than the native. Xenophobic and ethnic violence has become part of social life all over Europe. Nativist parties and politicians have gained widespread support in several countries, notably Austria, Belgium, France and Switzerland. Protest riots against racism and discrimination have occurred in Britain, France and Germany.

On the other hand, there are also a large number of positive inter-ethnic contacts, including marriages. Public policy and public opinion are strongly in favour of multicultural integration. The immigrants, for their part, are not reducible to passive objects of discrimination. As migrants they tend to represent the more vigorous and active part of their original population. Therefore it is not surprising that many of them, or their children, do very well at school. The raw school records do not take class into account, which gives a distorted picture of school performance and migration. In all countries there is a considerable new ethnic entrepreneurship, and also, in the areas of concentration, a new ethnic politics.

Even if disaster scenarios are unlikely, west European societies of the future are likely to be less cohesive than in the past, harbouring more mechanisms of exclusion than in the 1960s and 1970s. Certainly, there will be less unity or social integration rooted in ancient European culture and identity. Even the memory of the fatal national wars as a centripetal force is disappearing with the generation of Helmut Kohl leaving the political front stage. However, there are as yet no visible tendencies of socioeconomic and/or cultural polarization or segmentation of a kind likely to break up the institutional inertia, either of 'Europe' or of the west European nation-states.

3.2 The East–West divide

The adoption of capitalist democracy in eastern Europe has not produced a quick fix of northwest European prosperity. How high the costs of systemic change have been, and for how long they will have to paid, are controversial and uncertain, respectively. An analysis of these questions is completely outside the scope of this chapter. However, in order at least to hint at the magnitude of the project to construct a single Europe, we should look at a couple of indicators.

UNICEF data on life expectancy show a clear difference between, on the one hand, the countries of the former Soviet Union and the Balkans, and on the other, Poland, the Czech Republic, Slovakia, Slovenia and, with qualification, Hungary.

The latter group maintained their late-communist mortality rates during the first years of the 1990s and have already started to improve, although not yet at the rate of improvement seen during the 1980s . The successor states of the USSR (including the Baltics) and the Balkans, on the other hand, have experienced a dramatic decline of life expectancy, which was already considerably lower than in western Europe before 1989–91 (UNICEF, 1995: 24ff, 143). As increased life expectancy is one of the very few development indices in which even sub-Saharan Africa has been able to participate, the 1990s decline in post-communist eastern Europe is a serious sign.

By the turn of 1997–8 only Poland had regained its GDP level of 1989 (in the Polish case the figure was somewhat above both the pre-crisis peak of 1978 and 1989). At that point eastern Europe (except the ex-USSR) as a whole was about 8 per cent below its level of 1989. Before the crisis of 1998, the GDP of Russia was less than 60 per cent of its 1989 level. Consumption/expenditure figures give a somewhat brighter picture. According to them, the 1989 level was reached by 1995/6 in Croatia, the Czech Republic, Poland, Romania and Slovenia. In the other countries, however, real consumption expenditure has not yet reached its level under communism (UN, 1998: 146–7).

The costs of systemic change have caused the economic gap between eastern and western Europe, defined in terms of the standard of living of the median inhabitant, to widen since 1989. If the GDP gap between the EU and eastern Europe (excepting the ex-Soviet Union) in 1989 was 100, it was 126 by the end of 1997 (UN, 1998: 146; OECD, 1998c: 225). Of course, not everybody has lost out in the turn to capitalism; Rudolf Andorka (1995: 8; personal communication, 23 May 1996) calculated that about 10 per cent of the Hungarian population gained economically between 1989 and 1995.

The East–West divide and the internal polarization in the East will interact with the economic and ethnic segmentations and tensions in the West, and with political efforts at wider continental integration. This will probably involve a continental *rapprochement* among the upper middle class – indeed, this is already palpable; a tendency to aggravate the frustrations of the working and unemployed classes in both East and West, without bringing them closer to each other; and the development of complex webs of continental networks of crime and of illicit business.

4. Conclusion: a second West Germany – or Scandinavia enlarged?

The future of Europe in the world is a function of its weight, its specificity and its unity. Western Europe is still a global heavyweight, but it has lost some force and speed. The institutional specificity of European societies as an aggregate remains, but is subject to erosion from within and without. Globalization is not trumping European-type regionalization; but the most dynamic specificity of Europe, the effort at building a suprastate 'Europe' alongside the continental system of nation-

Table 12.6   Kinds of standing in the world

	Relative performance	*Model*	*Power*
Political	+/–	+/–	+/–
Economic	+/–	+/–	+/–

states, is facing difficulties, within the increasingly segmented west European societies as well as in bridging the recently much widened gap between the life-chances of the bulk of the population in eastern and western Europe.

We may summarize a set of important possible future positions in the world as shown in Table 12.6. A plus sign on either political or economic relative performance, in comparison with the average of the world according to prevailing criteria – which may be political efficiency and stability or armed might, and economic growth or level of wealth – is a prerequisite for influence or power. A minus sign on both means underdevelopment or marginalization. In order to distinguish sharply between power and influence, I have here called the holder of the latter a 'model'. A model is taken as influential only to the extent that other people choose to regard it as such. Lack of plus signs on both influence (model capacity) and power means insignificance, irrelevance, whatever the objective level of performance. Plus signs in all cells indicate the possession of both economic and political model influence as well as power.

Europe is not going to be underdeveloped or marginalized in the foreseeable future, either politically or economically. Europe in the next century will not become the, say, East Africa or Luxembourg of the twentieth century. But will it remain a significant, major player in the world? And if so, will this be as an institutional or policy model or as a power bloc?

'Europe' as a global role model might take two forms, not necessarily mutually incompatible. It might appear as an economic model, of market unification and suprastate economic organization, possibly but much less likely of economic institutions in general. 'Europe' might also be taken as a normative model, of human rights, citizenship, gender and generation relations, of supranational norms and institutions.

As a power bloc 'Europe' is most unlikely to manifest itself in any other form than an economic one, as a continental 'trading state' of the sort that the West Germans and the Japanese created so successfully after their military defeat in the Second World War. Even a successful EU agreement on a common foreign and security policy is unlikely to yield any globally impressive military power. And without the backing of force and willingness to use it, 'Europe' is unlikely to become a normative power, telling other parts of the world what political, economic, and social institutions they should have.

Table 12.7   Europe's futures

	Model	*Power*
Political	'Scandinavia'	—
Economic	—	'Trading state'/'Germany'

Europe is likely to keep a significant position in the world of the next century. But not all places in the sun look available. A position as a major politico-military power of global reach seems to be ruled out for Europe, as far into the future as any eye can see (except, perhaps, Jacques Chirac's). Acceptance as a significant economic institutional model appears very unlikely, for the time being. Lacking the American back-up of military muscle, mass culture and elite economics education, European economic role modelling would have to rely – at least to begin with – almost exclusively on clearly superior economic performance, once the inspiration to other regional market arrangements has been spent. There have been hardly any signs of that in the past twenty years, and it is unlikely that ageing Europe will provide the world with any new economic achievements impressive enough to compare with either side of the Pacific.

This leaves us with two possible options, which do not necessarily exclude each other, but could very well mix in various combinations. One is the position of a major purely economic power; the other that of a socio-political institutional model of significant influence, generally accepted as such. In the former case Europe would become a sort of postwar West Germany or Japan of the next century, i.e., an economically prominent 'trading state'; in the latter, a Scandinavia writ large.

Both variants are variants of Europe, and have therefore a common background and certain common preconditions of relative success. Both represented a break with an (in the end, disastrous) past based on military power – although the major Scandinavian defeats occurred in the century 1709–1809. Both chose instead to concentrate on internal socioeconomic construction, in neither case economically inward-looking and protectionist, but open to and reaching out for the markets of the world. Both the Federal Republic and the Scandinavian countries became eminently prosperous in that way.

They differ in two basic respects: most obviously, of course, in their size and significance in the world; but also in their interest in social experimentation and in universalistic social norms. 'No experiments' was once a winning electoral slogan in postwar West Germany, whereas 'social reform' has been a persistent aim of successful Scandinavian politics. Scandinavians have also been outstandingly active in pushing universalistic and suprastate norms, in the Council of Europe, in the United Nations and the UN conferences and conventions, in the Palme and Brundtland Commissions, and in the most recent Commission on Global Governance. German foreign policy has had a strong suprastate component in the commitment to European unification, but has not shown any strong universalistic interests.

Both variants are built on strong, if differently organized, forms of social integration, and both require a well-managed and prosperous economy. But there is one major difference in the economic prerequisites. The German-type economic power play requires the constant reproduction of a sharp competitive edge on a long economic blade. A Scandinavian-type role model needs only some sharply competitive niche capacity and the maintenance of a certain amount of relative prosperity.

For the future, both a German- and a Scandinavian-type Europe will require some positive solutions to the two major problems of European unity: the economic–cultural divisions within western Europe and the gaps between eastern and western Europe. A 'Scandinavian' Europe will demand a maintenance of characteristically European institutions as well as new endeavours with regard to human and citizenship rights in the world. A 'German' Europe' will have to produce new generations of large-scale competitiveness.

The choice between these two ideal types is a matter of preference. But my guess is that, at least by the second half of the twenty-first century, the best Europeans can hope for is to constitute a nice, decent periphery of the world, with little power but with some good ideas.

Notes

1   The issue of human rights is, of course, much more serious and difficult in the Americas than in western Europe, but according to Chilean human rights activists interviewed in Santiago in January 1996, the new American institutions are doing a good job.

2   A good example is the World Bank's country report on Hungary: 'International comparison shows that Hungary spends a far larger share [about the same as that of Austria or Italy] of its resources on welfare than other market economies at similar stages of development ... if Hungary is to join the ranks of high-income countries, reforming its welfare system is a *sine qua non*' (World Bank, 1995b: 25; italics in original.) The report then goes on to spell out that if you don't severely cut pension rights and abolish general family allowances, you will never join the rich.

Part IV
Reconsiderations

13. Reconsiderations: Three Scenarios

Mario Telò

1. Regional groupings as international actors in the making? The European case

The revival of the discussion, ongoing since the early seventies, concerning the external relations of the European Community and its international identity, is a crucial part of the broader debate on new regionalism. Many questions still remain open regarding both its institutional capabilities and its ability to cope with the uncertainties of the globalized world after the Cold War.[1] Before drawing a final conclusion regarding the future of European regionalism and of new regionalism in general, let us focus on the empirical and theoretical dimensions of the evolving role of the EU as an international entity.

The self-consciousness of the EC/EU as a proactive region of the world and its inter-regional cooperation are essential elements in understanding it as a new international actor. To deepen the theoretical implications of this crucial topic, we firstly need to introduce the empirical side of the evolving interaction between the economic and political dimensions of EC/EU external relations.

a) The *EC/EU as a global economic actor*. Even in the difficult times of the bipolar world, the European Community was considered as a highly significant example of the inadequacy of a state-centric paradigm, the declining role of force and the growing importance of transnational interdependence.[2] The famous definition of a "security community"[3] or area of peace is a concrete consequence of intense regional integration at economic and social levels, a successful internal foreign policy. The very first definition of Europe as a "civilian power" has such a theoretical background. Tocqueville already categorized trade policy as foreign policy. The Common Commercial Policy is the core of external economic relations.[4] In a few decades, the European Community became an economic and trade power with growing influence. It controlled 40% of world-exports (20% + 20% infra trade) since 1996, was net exporter of products to the so-called emerging economies and was the first foreign investor and aid provider. European states are no longer the predominant economic powers they used to be pre-WWII, however

247

four members of the G8 are European and, similar to the US, European Union constitutes one-fifth of the world's economy.[5]

It would be wrong to speak of the strength of individual Western European countries: such an enhanced global economic weight is largely the consequence of a successful regional integration process. Since the Single European Act and the Maastricht Treaty, the EC/EU is becoming even more proactive as a multilateral international entity. In fifteen years, the Community and Union have created, both on bilateral and increasingly on region-to-region bases, an important network of institutionalized international agreements. Europe acts either as a supranational unit (as it does within the WTO and international and interregional trade arrangements) or by cooperation and coordination among Member States (as it does in the political field, for example in the UN).[6]

Summing up, several crucial "post-Westphalian" features have to be stressed as far as the external relations of EC/EU are concerned: association pacts and bi-regional agreements often explicitly support regional cooperation among partners. For example, the ACP Convention and the regional arrangements in Africa, the bi-regional agreements with MERCOSUR and other Latin American groupings, the ASEM process, the association agreements with central and eastern European countries and the Mediterranean process, illustrate (with various degrees of success) an EC/EU strategic preference for *region-to-region cooperation*. Secondly, many international and domestic factors result in the border between economic and political dimensions of regional cooperation, no longer constituting a "Chinese wall". For example, the external representation and implications of the single currency are highly sensitive political issues, despite depending on the first pillar. The political impact of trade disputes and negotiations, particularly, the various difficult challenges related to the Uruguay Round and the Millennium Round of the WTO were also a feature of this change. The political dimension of economic and trade external relations is becoming clear, and the realistic classic criticism of the European economic and trade power, as a mere part of the bipolar balance of power, was largely questioned after the Cold War. To what extent is the scepticism expressed, by R. Gilpin among others, regarding, on the one hand, the huge dependency of EC regional integration on the "pax Americana" (i.e. on US hegemony), and on the other hand, the primacy of states?[7]

b) Regarding *the common foreign and security policy*, we are witnessing a spectacular evolution, spanning from the low profile of the very first decades after WWII, to the years after the end of the bipolar world. The growing expectations by third parties and the very ambitious self-defining aspirations asserted by the Treaty of European Union (TEU, Maastricht, 1992) are particularly significant in the current evolution. Recalling briefly the history of political cooperation may be helpful in better understanding its significance and limits.

After the failure of the European Defence Community in 1954, and the rejection of the 1961 Fouchet Plans, the political dimension became a taboo. A step in a new direction was the Summit of The Hague in 1969, the first summit of the "post de

Gaulle era" and of the new "Brandt era". The six Heads of State and government called at that time for "a united Europe capable of assuming its responsibilities in the world of tomorrow". The first declaration for political cooperation came in the next Luxembourg Summit and, already by 1973, the Nine established the EPC (European Political Cooperation) and a principle of consultation among Member States before taking political foreign policy decisions. Even if ineffective, the 1978 Venice Declaration on the Israeli–Arab conflict was the most famous example of this new activism and of the emergence of a partial disengagement from American policy.[8] The 1981 London Report, which associated the European Commission with the EPC process at all levels, replacing cooperation with joint action as an EPC main goal, and also the Single European Act of 1986, which institutionalized the ECP in the framework of the Treaty and associated the European Parliament to the process, were the next significant steps taken by the EPC. The EC identified nine areas in which European political cooperation could be developed: CSCE, Council of Europe, East–West, Cyprus, Middle East, Africa (South Africa and the Great Lakes), Latin America and the USA.

In the new international context, characterized by the declining power and cohesion of Russia and by the dramatic increase in the weight of the unified Germany, the 1989 Franco-German initiative was historically important, even if not as yet sufficient to achieve a political power in Europe. The preference by new Germany for deepening European cooperation, instead of asserting its new national identity, has been the crucial background for any further development and, in general, the tendencies towards a "renationalization of foreign policy" have been contained.[9] However, Maastricht's dual decision to create a monetary and political Union (including a common security policy) was unable to correct the internal asymmetry of the integration process, namely the gap between the huge international weight of the EC, as an economic and commercial world player, and its political role.

Indeed the objectives set by the Treaty of Maastricht, establishing the so-called "second pillar" (Common Foreign and Security Policy), independent from the European Community procedures but belonging to the same house,[10] the new European Union, emerged difficult to implement. The Lisbon European Council (1992) was a move in this evolution towards a settlement of concrete common priorities.[11] The European Councils of Essen (1994), Cologne and Helsinki (1999) also influenced this development. The balance of the achievements of the first years of CFSP is widely considered modest by international literature. The pan-European architecture and the "Ost-Politik" are more successful, as far as the pre-membership association agreements are concerned, than regarding partnership with neighbouring countries. The Mediterranean dialogue is very problematic. European policies regarding civilian wars and tragedies in the former Yugoslavia are considered a "Debutante Performance".

As regards the global action, the ASEM process, the framework cooperation agreement with MERCOSUR, the 1999 Rio bi-regional Summit and the new ACP

Convention have a double meaning. They give an initial answer to external expectations for an expanding and global role for the EU and they push the EU beyond the traditional trade dimension or cooperation policy. Political dialogue with the near abroad, Asia, Latin America and Africa increase European responsibilities in stabilizing world politics after the end of the Cold War. Nevertheless, there is no evidence that the previous large gap between stated aims and economic power on the one hand and, on the other, political actions, operational abilities and diplomatic representation has truly been overcome.[12] As far as common foreign and security policy is concerned, even if the Amsterdam Treaty increased visibility and allowed a more flexible decision-making process, the procedure still included a veto right.[13] As a consequence, very contradictory facts characterize the years 1998–2000. On one side there exists the confirmed political and technological dependency of Europe on American leadership regarding the revival of "power politics" (Kosovo war) and the reluctance of European states and peoples to provide for their military security. On the other side, the practice of collaboration, the institutional spillover and the new willingness of Member States to react collectively to external challenges, in particular Blair's government's desire "to bring Britain to the core of Europe", (namely the new European defence policy) and the Franco-German initiatives had innovative consequences at the Helsinki European Council (1999) and at the IGC 2000.

When analysing the described mix of discontinuity and continuity in a global assessment of the external relations and actions, one should mention two main points. The first is the increasingly *extended presence* of both the Union and Member States worldwide after the end of the Cold War,[14] and second, the more "active identity" of the EU.[15] The EU is the second global player and is considered thus by third parties. Since the end of the Cold War and the collapse of the USSR, European regionalism is less dependent than previously on American security framework and threat perceptions. Most of the chapters printed here underline such a discontinuity and, in particular, the importance of the inter-regional dialogue in the new institutional framework and international environment. Prior to the Treaty of Maastricht, the EC was an economic entity with initial political impact, playing a minor international role. The European states were under the umbrella of American multilateral hegemony. In the new international environment of the nineties, however, the will of Member States to cope more efficiently with external opportunities and responsibilities and also with the internal spillovers of the EC/EU process allow one to speak of a *new European regionalism*. That does not only refer to deepening integration policies but also to giving an active contribution – as a single entity and not only as a sum of Member States – to filtering and shaping more autonomous international economic and political relations.

2. Beyond the old concept of "civilian power Europe"

The concept of "civilian power Europe" is reoccurring, though with multiple meanings. One is a euphemism, a synonym of semi-sovereign power. Indeed, every observer notices that, if confronted with a revival of power politics (e.g. Iraqi war, Kosovo war), the EU remains under the American shadow. Despite the end of the Cold War and the EC/EU success story (Single Market and Monetary Union), the so-called "French way"[16] prescribed by H. Bull among others twenty years ago, still seems beyond European capabilities. Bull described it as a notion of European political power "comparable with the dignity of nations with the wealth, skills and historical position of those of Western Europe". What is behind the reluctance of many European states and citizens to devote a part of their wealth in order to provide for their security? Firstly, different national visions, as far as the future of Europe in the world and as far as the relationships with the US are concerned,[17] play a role. Secondly, controversies surrounding the institutional form of Europe as a political power can also explain this reluctance: for many, enhanced supranational unity would be a weakness and not strength in defence policy. Moreover, the current system of a rotating Council Presidency is structurally weak because it is temporary, part-time, and is not as yet based on any diplomatic apparatus. Finally, as far as the internal feed-back is concerned, the further external relations are extended, the more it is causing a huge coordination difficulty among the various dimensions of external relations (trade, economy, cooperation policy, foreign policy and humanitarian aid).[18]

However, the original concept of "civilian power Europe", born during the Cold War decades, even if largely obsolete and in need of being updated, is richer in nuances than the concept of semi-sovereign power. There are two good reasons for dwelling on the analysis provided by F. Duchêne and R.O. Keohane and J. S. Nye. The European Community had already been defined as more than a mere economic power but not as "a superpower in the making", by J. Galtung, in 1973. François Duchêne focused his pioneering notion of "civilian power Europe" both on its internal and external roles of civilizing and domesticating relations between Member States and also on spreading civilian and democratic standards. He wrote, "this means trying to bring to international problems the sense of common responsibility and structures of contractual politics, which have been in the past associated exclusively with 'home' and not foreign, that is alien, affairs".[19] In spite of the limits set by the bipolar world, the EC started to become an international entity, without any military dimension. However, it was also able to exercise its influence on states, international and regional organizations, multinational corporations and other transnational bodies through a wide variety of diplomatic, economic and legal instruments. Furthermore, the afore mentioned international relations scholars have studied the EC, emphasizing the theoretical implications of its successful integration process. It has particularly been stressed that the concepts of power and of foreign policy are no longer as clearly defined as in the past and also that the traditional distinction between political and economic dimensions and between high and low politics are becoming quite obsolete, even within international relations theories.[20]

The famous 1989 letter by Kohl and Mitterrand proposing to the twelve to strengthen the European political dimension, in order to be able to cope with the new post-Cold War challenges and the Maastricht decision to create both a Monetary and Political Union, are symbolic of the EC/EU opportunity to tremendously increase its presence and to strengthen its international identity.[21] The external acknowledgements and expectations are helpful in so far as the EU institutions are seeking international and inter-regional agreements, with the aim of enhancing both the EU's visibility and internal legitimacy.

What about the *terminus ad quem* of such an evolution? According to a large part of the literature, the EU is becoming a global actor, the second in importance after the US.[22] "Actorship" raises the question of the criteria of the actor's capability, in comparison with the model of the Nation State and, more particularly, with the US: a community of interests, a decision-making system, a system for crisis management, a system of independent management, a system of implementation, external communication channels and representation, community resources and a mobilization system and so on. To what extent has the EC/EU achieved a satisfactory degree of actorship in the main areas of external relations? The previous type of civilian power was able to cope as a second range power with the bipolar world, however there is no evidence that an enlarged EU, acting within the globalized and uncertain world of the 21st century, can maintain the achievements even of the «small» EC.

Thirdly there is a crucial theoretical problem: how and to what extent can a regional "civilian power" evolve towards a more open political dimension without following the classical French pattern of «Europe puissance», which was over-illustrated by H. Bull. It is not sufficiently clear what a non-state-like political Union can be, in terms of power definition. Secondly, what kind of political and military capacity is necessary to overcome the current, already mentioned, picture of a "Candide" Europe and to act effectively as a more independent, regional and global actor within the trade, economic and political system?

The new starting point is the evolving revision of the Treaties. The delicate topic of security policy, the "Petersberg tasks", included within the Amsterdam Treaty (1997), the programme to build a military capacity approved in 1999 and the defence cooperation strengthened in 2000 represent modest but concrete innovations. This applies even if their relationship with the US and their implementation in the case of regional crises are far from evident and even if, ultimately, such an evolving European defence identity is not as yet at the level of world political power.[23]

The institutional dimension of external relations is meriting an increasing place within international scientific literature. The present book emphasizes two points: first of all, the EU's legal status is still unclear because the Member States have not yet provided the status of an independent subject of international law, while in contrast legal status is granted to the EC.[24] This book secondly and most importantly emphasizes the gap between the existing EU and a full classical political and military actor. Decision-making and implementation of foreign policy and external relations are particularly affected by the lack of centralization, which causes incoherence and inconsistency. Decentralization makes the decision-making a two level game (national and supranational). Furthermore, a large part of the literature agrees on the fact that it is a matter of complex multilevel governance, one that differs from the American model. Europe lacks hierarchical, centripetal, legitimized decision-making, including – even if unlike the so-called "Imperial Presidency" of the USA – a stable, full-time, legitimized central Council presidency.[25] This would constitute centralization in difficult political matters, balancing the internal polyarchy and the fragmentation of private and public interests taking part in the decision and implementation processes. As T. J. Lowy pointed out, in the USA crucial foreign political issues, fragmented governance and polyarchy are centralized, better and clearly substituted by decisions of the unified élites.[26] On minor issues, decisions and implementation are taken according to the fragmented or polyarchic pattern and put to tender among public bodies and private interests.

Decentralized European multilevel governance originally combines both centripetal and fragmented tendencies. The European institutions, particularly the European Commission and the European Council, can in some cases support centralized decisions and actions, with the help of 'Mr CFSP' and the Commissioner in charge for external relations. Furthermore, national Ministries' so-called Europeanization process, namely the routine of working jointly with fourteen partners and of regularly taking their points of view and interests into account when formulating national preferences, substantially changed thousands of high-ranking civil servants' vision and practice, especially those who attended the various specialized Councils of Ministers. It provoked to a certain extent a dynamic of "fusion".[27] Finally, some observers stress the fact that, even if beside any teleological illusion, a so-called institutional spillover exists, which explains 50 years of progress and also some very ambitious statements, the sometimes positive sum play in the Council and some steps recently accomplished even by Eurosceptic Member States.[28] However, the growing international role of the EU and its relations with other regions of the world demand further pooling of national sovereignties and the further centralization of the decision-making process which seems very difficult to achieve.

Where are the structural causes of the still highly decentralized polity to be found? Firstly they are to be found in the heterogeneous national interests and different visions of the Union's future, as shown by the endless bargaining between the supporters of an increased internal consistency and the defenders of the symbols and practices of national sovereignties.[29] Secondly, they are to be found in the overlapping and conflicting competencies, the internal pluralism and lobbying, the lack of hierarchies, the continuous bargaining among different levels and various bodies, the multidimensional structure as far as European Commission external relations are concerned (divided among many DGs), which inevitably hinder the EU's ability to decide and to act in a consistent manner.

The current institutional evolution needs multiple approaches in order to be correctly interpreted. Inter-governmentalist approaches underestimate both the centripetal spillover provoked by common interests and common policies, as far as the first pillar and EMU are concerned. They also underestimate the simple fact that civil servants and national Ministries have been accustomed, through routine cooperation of many decades, to paying fundamental and continuous attention to the EU by stating national positions and agendas. But, contrary to the federalist hopes, the second global player is not a state, neither is it a republic of republics, nor a unique and coherent actor. It is instead a *sui generis* institutional construction. The very simple fact that the EU is not a super-state means that it has no President, no single and hierarchical diplomatic body and no single Minister of Foreign Affairs. Despite the fact that participating in the European common policy strengthens the international weight of the Member States, the simple coordination of national policies within international organizations and conferences sometimes far from happens. That is the problematic framework of current institutional reforms concerning external relations and foreign policy.[30]

Our conclusion is that *institutions fundamentally matter when dealing with regional civilian powers*. Changes in rules and legal settlements induce changes in the policies and behaviour of Member States. They largely explain, more so than aims and external expectations, the strength and the weakness of fifty years' achievements, the *sui generis* nature of the EU, as a special kind of international actor, a "strange power". Of course, the EU still contrasts with the actorship of a classical state and particularly with a superpower which gathers both influence and power, namely the means to implement its aims in different fields: ideology, politics, economics, finance, military field, nuclear technology. But regional integration is already so deeply advanced that the rescued European Nation State does not have very much in common with the sovereign state of the first half of the century.

3. New regionalism and multilateralism: three scenarios

The following three scenarios are based on different interconnections between new regionalism and globalization. To conclude the present introduction by drawing scenarios seems to be a realistic way of expressing the uncertainty of the current developments both of the European Union and of the international system. This avoids challenging in a trivial way Europe as it is, as opposed to Europe as it should be, or presenting black/white pictures of the present debate between alternative options. The evolving international identity of the EC/EU is not analysed only by an inward-looking approach, but is rather interpreted as a salient aspect of global trends.

3.1 Europe as a continental "trading state" within a globalized economy.

This book does not support the over-simplified image (paradoxically proposed both by "apocalyptic" and "integrated" visions of Europe as "a mere free trade area"). The first scenario shows an apparent continuity with the existing "civilian power", however under the condition of a stop in the deepening process of regional integration. In parallel, the already-decided Eastern and Mediterranean enlargement of the EC/EU would create a new geopolitical reality. There are two versions of this scenario. In the best hypothesis, the EU is conceived as diffusing the historical benefits of the European construction (peace, stability, democracy, and prosperity) on a continental scale and in the near abroad. In the worst hypothesis, given the widened economic gap between the two parts of Europe, the huge financial, social, political and cultural challenge linked to this enlargement and the ongoing uncertainties regarding the Eastern border, the traditional positive trade-off between widening and deepening of the EC/EU would be interrupted. The institutional inertia would provoke a major economic and political decline of political actorship and an increasingly overlapping and fragmented European polity.

Examining this scenario in more detail, regarding the other features of the EC/EU and their external role: EMU could either fail because of a lack of political authority, or it could survive. However, it would be very doubtful that the Economic Monetary Union would do more than stabilize the economies of Member States and prevent internal disintegration. The Single European Market would be largely diluted as a part of the continental and Mediterranean free trade area and within worldwide liberalization. The *acquis communautaire* would not disappear but would certainly be faced with gradual erosion. The model of deep regionalism would be transformed profoundly, by withdrawing to a special kind of regional grouping within American economic and political globalism.

What do we mean by a new, overlapping and fragmented European polity? According to the "new-Medievalist" school of thought the European Union would only become a diplomatic coordination of apparently "sovereign" Nation-States, occupying territorial spaces but no longer controlling what goes on in those spaces.[31] The political authority lost by Nation-States would not be centralized at supranational level but would mainly shift elsewhere, towards public and private bodies. Within European studies, an important school of thought emerges, analysing the consequences of the blockade of the dynamics of political integration. For the new European polity, as a non-hierarchical, centrifugal, variegating, overlapping set of policies, the concept of "condominio" – a complex mix of functional and territorial constituencies and forms of governance has been proposed.[32]

According to other observers a maintained intergovernmental cooperation including common rules and procedures, mutual expectations among partners could continue with a two-level game.[33] But while the national level would rather be a formal framework than a shell protecting what happens inside, the intergovernmental game would be more like an "international regime", or a set of regimes, than like a political and economic community.[34]

However, regarding the socio-economic contents of such a new European polity, two versions have been outlined. For this European-rich corner of the world, the present book presents on the one hand, a relatively optimistic view: should a certain degree of territorial stabilization of such a new multilevel polity be possible, it would partly be comparable with the semi-sovereign Bonn Federal Germany of 1949–1990. Europe could keep its international image of being a relatively ecologically and socially conscious continent, but politically divided and militarily weak. Such a heavyweight entity within the international economy, rich in specificity, would be challenged because of international competitiveness and of demographic changes (immigration flows and free movement of people, as a consequence of eastern enlargement). However it is true that these latter threats are frequently overestimated by protectionists. According to Therborn, 'there is no evidence of European marginalization either pending or current', in spite of the broadly diffused visions of an "inexorable struggle" for world competitiveness and market. Under this condition, in spite of eastern and southern enlargement and globalization, Europe will continue to play an influence-role in the world.

On the other hand, less optimistic comments emphasize that the "Bonn-GFR-type" Europe, in order to maintain social integration and a prosperous economy, would require a sharp competitive edge to survive within the global economy. Many observers agree that this scenario would necessarily diminish, on a global level, the political dimension of the EC/EU as an economic and trade giant and its ambitions not only as a European power but also as a European political influence. Somehow a "continental trading-state Europe" would go back to the kind of regionalism, typical of the first decades of European integration. To mention the Federal Republic of Germany, which existed in the decades before German unity, reminds one of the famous picture of an economic giant and half-sovereign political dwarf. According to R.N. Rosencrance, the "trading state" is a political system where economic growth has no implications at all, as far as political and military power are concerned, because the latter remains firmly monopolized in the hands of the leading power of the alliance.[35]

The current main supporters of this evolution are economic networks, transnational coalitions of social interests, particularly in the US, in every European country, and more precisely in the United Kingdom. However, even if the idea of a strengthened transatlantic bi-regional entity, including the EC/EU and the sole remaining superpower, is widely shared among the Member States, the trade disputes, political obstacles and the recent failure of the American transatlantic project for a Multilateral Agreement on Investment (1998), show the huge problems existing between and within European States on this issue.

What about its implication for new regionalism worldwide? Such a continental trading state would be part of a common trend: within the globalist strategy of *"emerging markets"*, creating free trade mega-arrangements between US and Latin America, FTAA; between US and Asia-Pacific, APEC with EU, a stronger NTA. Such an evolution of the EC/EU would probably have important implications for other regions of the world, putting a stop to European support of the developments for deeper regionalism in Asia, Africa and Latin America. Every country and region would only have the choice between adjustment of national economies to the imperatives of global markets and catastrophic isolation. Nationalistic or funda-mentalist movements, as a reaction to globalization imperatives, are likely to arise somewhere in the world, since these movements would no longer have a regional alternative, as a framework for setting a more gradual and compromising process. Less would be done against the current marginalization of the poorest countries, which would lose bargaining edges, allied within international organizations.

In conclusion, something would be amiss, if we maintain "New Medievalist" theories or new inter-governmental regime theories. As a consequence of such evolution of European governance, the globalized international system would be increasingly characterized by what J. Rosenau calls "a bifurcation".[36] This would involve, on the one hand, fragmented multilevel governance but, on the other, a concentration of high-level political decision i.e. a practical shift towards a perpet-ual dependency on US-centred globalism, both in economic and political terms. New regionalism would fail as a dynamic third way of multilateral world gover-nance, between unipolarism and fragmentation.

3.2 The second scenario: from "Fortress Europe" to a new-mercantilist power

In the uncertain framework of the globalized post-Cold War world, the EC/EU could strengthen current tendencies to set inward-looking priorities, reducing dependency from partners and allies, as a reaction to both external pressures and internal demands. Economic failures and international threats could exacerbate this. The combination of hard trade disputes and the social demands of economic security could force the EC/EU to set defensive economic and protectionist policies, and, according to international literature,[37] also ease a spillover towards enhanced political and military security. The politicization of domestic pressures could be particularly evident in the case of growing instability in the eastern and/or southern borders of the Union, as the crisis in former Yugoslavia clearly demon-strated.[38] The two demands are not necessarily linked, but the first one creates a background that is favourable to the second one and vice versa. Thirdly, the demands of internal security also play a role in strengthening such a double trend. The perceptions of threats linked to migration flows have already inspired defen-sive border-control policies at national and European level (as shown by some of the Schengen Treaty provisions regarding immigration and asylum policies).

A kind of "institutional big bang" caused by new conflicts and threats in the surrounding world or by a degradation of the international economic and trade system is not excluded, even if it would not necessarily occur in line with a federal pattern. In front of the undesirable consequences of the federal and functional patterns,[39] a new confederate polity would be the more realistic institutional conse-quence of that scenario.[40] The new polity would be based on the revival of the territorial sovereign logic as a major institutional principle.

Broadly diffused fears and a negative perception of external threats could act in support of the current utopian idea of *Europe puissance*, the plea to revive the classical concept of international power of many politicians. Paradoxically, such an evolution happens to be more likely in the case of the failure of the model of Europe as a civilian power that quietly contributes to peaceful external relations and world governance, as a regional stabilizer, and as a resource of economic dynamics for partners and neighbours. Indeed, even if the starting point were economic demands, the trend would be towards political and military power as the only one able to settle disputes and conflicts when the economic, juridical, and ideological powers fail.[41] Against the simple notion of influence, a European classical power would be "telling other parts of the world what political, economic and social institutions they should have".

To what extent is that scenario realistic in the early 21st century? Firstly, several socio-political streams in many Member States and interest networks openly support the idea of Europe as a classical economic political and military power. Relevant industrial and socio-economic sectors (interested in arms cooperation etc) need protection, as well as agricultural interests. Secondly, according to many observers, dramatic instability at the European borders can provoke such a reaction. Most importantly, the difficulties that emerged during the last decade for the EU in coping both with the difficult enlargement process and particularly with the challenges of a globalized economy make such a scenario less abstract than during the seventies and the eighties.

The latter challenge is on the very first point of the agenda. EU countries are lagging behind Japan and the US in the areas of information and communication technologies (ICT), employment and growth, and economic competitiveness in strategic sectors. New demands for protecting the domestic market and subsidizing exports (including NTBs) are about to surface because of urgent domestic problems. A vicious circle is possible since only a dynamic European economy can finance the costs of social cohesion and of enlargement, the stability plans in the Balkan subregion, the Mediterranean policies, and compensate the problems created by liberalization in sensitive economic sectors and local districts.

What would be the implications for new regionalism and world governance? A shift to multiple conflicts among competing regional and non-regional blocs could result. As far as Europe is concerned, much more than it already does, it could oppose US globalism with a general counter strategy of "Europe–centred" inter-regional agreements and a myriad of "EC centred free trade areas",[42] including Eastern Europe and Russia, Africa and Latin America. The FTAA and the APEC would evolve as a counter-reaction to PTA by the US. Most Favoured Nation clause could become a weapon in provoking trade wars. Setting global agreements would be increasingly difficult because of growing tensions as far as the global commercial, financial and monetary systems were concerned.[43] Furthermore, the costs of more blocs competition might be sidelined particularly in the developing countries and in the periphery, becoming the victim of struggles between spheres of influence, obliged to opt for one or another contender in the framework of inter-centres competition. Not only NATO but also UN system could suffer because of increasing transatlantic conflicts. In conclusion, the fundamental opposition theory of regionalism versus globalism would be largely confirmed.

However there are some important *caveats* about such an evolution towards scenarios of a kind of new-mercantilist "European fortress":

- It cannot but cause serious divisions among and within European States, according to various interests in expanding the open economy, to variations in the consequences of trade wars in defence of selected geo-economic interests and, lastly, to the various historical pressures of liberalism and protectionism.
- As for the political side of the demand for a stronger and centralized European super power, there are huge discrepancies according to national traditions. These include differences between the two nuclear powers themselves and the others, between the neutrals and the nuclear states, between the five countries with greater experience of power politics, and between the staunch defenders of symbols of national sovereignty and hard-line federalists. Lastly, an important cleavage is the acceptance of the cost of defense policy in terms of standard of living and of possible input into the democratic scrutiny of European and national decision making. The simultaneous explosion of some of these internal cleavages could possibly disintegrate the EU.

However, imagine the scenario of a hegemonic regional power managing the internal economic and political conflicts. What would be the international implications of a new-mercantilist European power for world governance? As previously mentioned, global economic and trade organizations would be jeopardized. There would be no automatic spillover; however, the strengthening of defensive regionalism or economic nationalism elsewhere in America and Asia would support various demands for tighter economic and military security. Most probably, the EU and every regional organization mentioned in this book would be profoundly transformed in the case of trade and political disputes between trade blocs: either they would disintegrate or they would become hierarchical spheres of influence by a regionally dominating State. Secondly, even if not highly militarized, the EU would be a factor in the tendency towards a multipolar world. Of course, theoretically, there are many possible forms of a multipolar world. The military concept of multipolarism, replicating the negative experience of the thirties, is no longer relevant. The transformation of multilateralism into hard bargaining between trade blocs, or the emphasis on the classical dimension of power politics in an ambiguous way (whatever the main actors would be – mega-States or regional blocs), is not far from the vision of international relations recently expressed by leaders in Asia and Europe. It could provide the background for a controlled nuclear proliferation. Traditional international theories consider the balance between various spheres of influence as a realistic basis for a better world government. However, is a step back to the international system of "balance of power" in the early 21st century conceivable? Such a vision of multipolarism lacks realism because there is no evidence that the legacy of fifty years of world history could be easily deleted. Consider the unipolar primacy of US, the role of international and multilateral organizations, the tremendous development of transnational relations, the development of peaceful and cooperative new regionalism. Certainly, given the uncertainties of the new global framework, the shift from benevolent to malevolent behaviour of regional entities should not be excluded. However, even the tendencies towards a new multipolar balance of power should cope with the historical transformations of the last decades at global, domestic and transnational levels.

3.3 The third scenario: a new kind of "civilian power Europe" as a pillar of a new multilateral world order

A 'new kind of civilian power' is both a realistic and idealistic scenario: it means the EC/EU evolving towards an international actor able to maintain its fundamental socio-economic and institutional achievements, better able to cope with the evolving internal context and the changing international environment, but unable and/or unwilling to build a European Superpower.

Many writers in this volume suggest new concepts for defining the European Union's international identity beyond the two previously mentioned scenarios. The contributions by Gamble and Padoan describe Europe as a "strategic" economic actor. Two further contributions are particularly explicit in setting new guidelines. While Göran Therborn elaborates the concept of "Europe as a Scandinavia of the World" in his chapter, emphasizing the socio-economic contents and the potential international influence, R. Seidelmann includes the two notions of *"political responsibility"* and *"historical learning"* in the concept of "soft power Europe". These visions are important pillars of a new concept of civilian power bringing together real trends and a normative dimension. However, the present reconsideration cannot but try to answer the following questions.

To apply the value "responsibility" to an international relations issue is to emphasize the need of radical innovation of the realist and neo-realist tradition. Already calling for democracy and accountability in foreign policies puts in question the "Chinese wall" between domestic democratic politics and international power politics, a perennial stake for democratic theory, since Rousseau, Kant, and Tocqueville. Furthermore, to explain EU foreign policies through the value "responsibility" goes even beyond F. Duchêne's definition quoted above. In examining what "international responsibility" exactly means, we focus on the weight of domestic democratic public opinion, and particularly on *memory of the past*: on the one hand, keeping alive the best legacy of 2500 years of Greek *polis*, Roman right, Renaissance and Enlightenment culture, Christian influences etc. and, on the other hand, emphasizing the democratic learning process, making of past tragedies and aggressive policies (fascism, colonialism, intolerance, infra-European civilian war, etc.) a resource for peoples understanding and good governance . For example, it is useful to compare the salient differences between the German/Italian/Portuguese/Spanish post-fascist learning processes and the Japanese post-war experience. That helps by explaining why Europe is more globally responsible for the public good of world governance than, for example, the US, Japan or China and makes the consistency of European foreign policies with the UN's and cosmopolitan values easier, by defending the common interests of humans (disarmament, peace, environment, economic growth, social justice, the fight against crime and drugs and so on).

We need to combine idealistic and realistic approaches to understand such an original combination of interests and ideas and the practical influence of normative values within the European construction. Furthermore, current constructivist approaches focus on the weight of historical learning and memory, by building people's consciousness and by influencing national and supranational preferences in many policy fields particularly linked to international identity and actorship. That is matter of fact in many European countries, either as a heritage of the post-fascist democratic reconstruction or as a traditional national commitment to democratic values, republican aims, or neutral proactive traditions.

The realistic background as far as interests and historical forces are concerned has been strengthened after the end of the Cold War: diminishing the weight of nuclear threats and hard security issues, enhanced role of "idealistic democracies", particularly Germany, Italy, Iberian countries, Benelux, Scandinavia within the European construction.

The "new civilian power" scenario has a second feature. To focus more on long-term benefits than on purely short-term utilitarian criteria, as far as foreign relations are concerned, raises the question of the time frame of foreign policy. The theoretical opposition between the "structural foreign policy of the EU" and the "conjunctural" foreign policy of traditional powers needs to be theoretically deepened. The crucial question is: in which meaning does the political dwarf of the western world conceive and implement a *"structural"* foreign policy? The Therborn socio-economic perspective provides insights for a first step regarding the present and future European regionalism. His concept of Europe as a "Scandinavia of the world" means much more than a mere economic entity and deepens explicitly an alternative to both the above-mentioned scenarios. A "Scandinavian Europe" is not essentially a prescriptive rather an analytical concept, consistent with realized economic and social features and with the awareness of the impossibility of simply importing the American model. Europe has maintained its peculiarities so far in spite of domestic and international attacks. The diffusion of social justice as a value influencing the social actors and the various national party systems, and, the relatively well developed Welfare States demonstrate resilience and continue to shape the continent in characteristic ways. Moreover, the European Union is a specific set of supranational institutions, a process of system integration, a "social mega-network", a normative area, and at least partly governed by European law and common rules. It includes relatively binding human rights protection, and inspiring concentric organizations like the

EU, the Council of Europe and the OSCE. A consistent set of common values regarding science and society (including control of genetic manipulation, the defence of human beings against the death sentence, etc.) is surviving globalization more than elsewhere. Lastly, as a result of the *acquis communautaire* and the dynamics of European integration the "EU is perceived in the world as one bloc and attracting many neighbour countries to apply for membership and to accept long and hard training to achieve it".[44]

However, such a socio-economic model is seriously challenged: it is currently facing a double erosion, both from inside (unemployment and huge demographic change) and from outside (competitiveness, immigration flows and so on). The future European "capitalist diversity" in the 21st century cannot be the same as in the second half of the 20th century, when Western European States were able to adjust to economic internationalization by high-performing national Welfare States, Keynesianism, "Rhenan capitalism"[45] and functional regional integration. Even in defending the past achievements, Europe has to be more proactive within the international arena. The huge pressure towards economic convergence and the technological, financial and trade trends towards an enhanced globalization are challenging European regionalism to combine competitiveness, technological innovation, economic reforms and social cohesion in new terms. By new terms, we mean more research, more investment in human resources, growth policy, and also new methodologies of vertical and horizontal coordination among Member States, going beyond the old federalism–confederalism debate. A concrete example of new regionalism with a strategic vision and innovation policy, including concrete benchmarking and monitoring, has been offered by the Lisbon Special European Council of March 2000 and by the ten years programme, which was approved there.[46] High unemployment and the awareness of lagging behind in the area of international competitiveness might break up the institutional inertia of Europe and of the Member States pushing them to start a new era, with a new strategic concept giving a soul to new European Regionalism.

Further coordination and deeper integration does not necessarily mean building a federal European State, and setting up a protectionist trade policy either. For instance, the new European socio-economic strategy started at the Essen E. Council (1984) and resulted in the Amsterdam Treaty, the "Luxembourg process" (employment policy), the "Cardiff process" (economic reforms), and the "Cologne process" (macroeconomic guidelines) strengthened, by the Lisbon European Council, by a long-term all-encompassing project rejects both new-mercantilism and mere adjustment to world globalization. Rather, it expresses the willingness of the Member States to reform their socio-economic model in order to build a more competitive and growing Europe, even if compatible with an internationally open economy.

Indeed, the troubles and tensions of world regulation show that "strategic regionalism", if conceived as a mere defence of regional competitiveness, would not be a responsible provider of the rare "public good" of world governance. By its very existence, the EU up to now moderates both wild liberal and protectionist Member

State's policies, but its ability to cope with growing protectionist demands is an open question.[47] Our conclusion is that the future of "Europe as a Scandinavia of the World", strictly depends on the necessary pre-condition that new regionalism could provide the background for a new multilateralism at global level.

According to Göran Therborn, among other scholars, neither the marginalization of Europe nor the building of a superpower Europe, are very realistic, while its capacity and influence as a policy model are much more likely to be diffused worldwide: "a model is taken as influential only to the extent that other people choose to regard it as such". Rather than a civilian power, one should speak about a civilian "influence", namely of a particular interest in social experimentation and in universalistic social norms as Scandinavian countries have already demonstrated through their action in the framework of the UN ("Bruntland Commission", "Palme Commission", "Global Governance Commission").

Let us moderate our agreement with some scepticism. The influence of Northern European social and political culture outside Europe is an essential part of the European international identity. Germany, France, Italy, Britain, Spain and smaller Member States also form an important part of such an international social identity, including values and practices. However, the common institutions are more salient in reviving and spreading out such a legacy than in the past. Secondly, the EC/EU can not be compared with a spiritual power, something like the Catholic Church: without strengthening its decision-making process and institutional capabilities and further developing towards a new path as a civilian power, "Scandinavian Europe" would risk falling into a Volterian "Candide"-Europe scenario.

What do we mean by a proactive and regulatory civilian power Europe? We have already stressed the importance of the notion of a peaceful, democratic, and just civilian power, inspired by common values, to be strengthened within the European Treaties. This further entails a realistic degree of democratic warning and also of constraining criteria for current and future Member States. The common foreign policy is already based on common principles and values in chapter VII of the Maastricht Treaty, which emphasizes the consistency with the universal goals of the UN and OSCE. However, within the post-Cold War world, much more is needed. If Europe as an international entity has not the means fit to shape the surrounding economic and political environment, malevolent actors, middle or great powers, will marginalize or even break up the EU values.

Many observers underestimate both the external vulnerability of the European experiment and the need to urgently provide more common and comprehensive security within the new international asymmetric environment. At the end of the bipolar world neither founding Member States of the EC nor Scandinavian and neutral States, can be satisfied any longer living (explicitly or not) in the shadow of the balance of power offered by the current transatlantic relationship within NATO. Europe needs to further strengthen its common institutions and be more proactive by pushing peace-keeping and peace-enforcing missions in the near abroad and beyond, even in view of preventing trade wars, settling North–South relations, and defending common strategic interests. Pursuing such objectives without strategic allies and interregional partnerships would be futile.

What concept can we use to describe such a new civilian, soft, responsible, democratic, long-term oriented, economic and political power? Both the Member States' foreign policies and the EC/EU's already made some important steps forwards in terms of conceiving and implementing a European external actorship. That was not only the second-best option, given the impossibility of becoming a traditional actor of power politics, but also because of the urgent need for a greater consistency with existing external relations and identity. According to the international scientific literature, the concept of "structural foreign policy"[48] is able to describe such a strategic and practical evolution. A "structural foreign policy" affects particularly the economic and social structures of partners (states, regions, economic actors, international organizations etc.), it is implemented through pacific and original means (diplomatic relations, agreements, sanctions and so on),[49] and its scope is not conjunctural but rather in the middle and long range. However, the concept of "structural foreign policy" should be deepened beyond its empirical side.

When speaking of structural power and structural policy within international relations theory, the main references are of the "structural" new realism developed by Kenneth Waltz[50] and the concept developed within the international political economy. Contrary to Marxist thought, the word structural is not synonymous with economics opposed to the superstructural dimension namely politics and culture. By "structure" Waltz means the political perennial structure of the international system. This structure is anarchical, centrifugal, and non-hierarchical. The definition of structural foreign policy should focus on the ability of an international unit to support, even gradually and partially, the changes brought about in such a structural feature of the international system. The very existence of the EU, making war between former enemies impossible, is already the best example of "internal" structural foreign policy. The relationship between Brazil and Argentina, between South Africa and neighbouring countries, and between Indonesia and some ASEAN Member States, as well, are salient in this respect. This is particularly noteworthy if compared with the India–Pakistan conflict, which has put a stop to regionalism in Southern Asia because of the resilience of great States and of nationalism elsewhere in Asia.

The comparative analysis of the regional variations brings us to the conclusion that "a structural policy" by the EU can be successful only when and if deep structural domestic trends exist within the partner region limiting anarchy among States. Only when successful regional arrangements emerge limiting the anarchical structure of the global system can the foreign policy of the EC/EU help to further reduce fragmentation and conflicts and strengthen regional cooperation.

While a realistic view would deny the relevance of the question itself, other theories have been supporting, for some time, a greater effort to understand what the EC/EU actually does in world affairs and what it is becoming. Firstly, regional integration studies benefit from the extraordinary development of the transnational complex interdependence studies. The concepts of regional integration and of civilian power would be inconceivable without the theoretical background of the critical analysis of neo-realism developed within the American and international political science field in the seventies and eighties.[51] Secondly, as an example of "international regimes", regional arrangements establish various sets of common rules and procedures, providing mutual information and expectations among Member States. This makes transnational interest coalitions easier, limiting uncertainty and security dilemmas. Even candidates for membership are influenced by the club's internal rules as far as their preferences are concerned. Thirdly, the growing multiple, informal and formalized, decentralized systems of governance do correct substantially the neorealistic vision of a structural anarchy. Even the current deficit of world government, typical of a post-hegemonic era, does not necessarily revive the tendency towards anarchy and fragmentation. Our conclusion is that both the multiple functional networks and also the new regional territorial entities are providing a third level of governance, between local and national fragmentation and unipolar concentration of political authority.

Indeed, the European structural foreign policy can be, at least to a certain extent, interpreted as an export of the internal communitarian method, setting peaceful political relations through economic interdependence. That is shown by means of external relations (economic agreements and sanctions, "Marshall plans" etc.) and particularly by the so-called international and interregional "pactomania", spreading out preferential trade agreements over the world. We already mentioned critical views of European "conditional" external relations, underlining their possible evolution towards a new hegemonic sphere of influence opposed to others and reviving the theories of growing dependency centre-periphery. Our comparative research on regional groupings in Africa, Asia and America proves that such an external support to regional arrangements can be successful if domestic pressures, coming from economic and political orientations of the partner Member States, are autonomously pushing towards regional cooperation. It fails because of asymmetrical balance between internal and external factors.[52] In conclusion, structural foreign policies are efficient only if they interact with deep structural trends. According to Machiavelli, "virtus" is efficient only if combined with "fortuna": proactive policies need a favourable objective context.

The international political economy provides a second concept of "structural power" opposed to the traditional realistic notion of "relational power". According to S. Strange, the structural powers are increasingly able to shape the structures of the globalized world. They are relevant in indirectly conditioning the actors' way of acting, by changing the conditions of their behaviour and without forcing them to do something. With the end of the bipolar world, the security structural power is declining while the economic, financial and knowledge-based structural powers are enhancing their role in changing the international economy and affecting world politics.[53] If accepted, this post-Westphalian approach recommends paying much more attention to the decline of EC/EU in terms of ICT and the knowledge society than to its gap in terms of military power. A regional organization, leader of the international trade and no longer disadvantaged as far as the technologies of knowledge are concerned, would balance its minor defence power. Our second conclusion is that, within the new framework of evolving structural power, the realistic argument (mentioned among others by H. Bull), opposing the "contradictory in terms" concept of civilian power to a European independent military power is no longer as conclusive as during the Cold War. However, Bull is perfectly right in emphasizing Europe's need to develop an international actorship "compatible with the dignity of nations with the wealth, skills and historical position of those of Western Europe". The huge transformations in the external nuclear confrontation and the international system, along with the consequence of the changing perception of threats (see Seidelmann), the multiple limitations of the anarchy of the international system, and the raising relevance of structural powers (Strange), drastically limit the pertinence of the realistic arguments for a European Union as a military power.

What are the current internal driving forces pushing the EC/EU beyond the previous minor stage of civilian power and structural foreign policy without moving to a new-mercantilist scenario? Let us list them in order to underline the realism of our third scenario: the EMU and its international implications; the mentioned Lisbon Council strategic long-term option for a "European way to a knowledge society"; a more strategic management of economic and trade power; the role of the EU as first investor and aid provider to the southern world; strengthening the network of interregional arrangements; speaking with a single voice within international organizations (IMF, World Bank, WTO, UN, ILO) and developing alliances to strengthen their rule setting capabilities, also on the basis of regional representation and a new concept of 'conditionality'.

However, in conclusion, two points are crucial: institutional settlement and security. As mentioned above, to become more efficient in the long and middle-term, to be more consistent and more adaptable regarding the external urgencies, a structural foreign policy needs to enhance clarity and coherence among the various dimensions of external relations. In itself, developing external relations can bring both more internal fragmentation and enhanced coherence of policies and political unification. Institutional reforms should, beyond the old federal State or confederational institutional models, allow the EU to orient the current decentralized multilevel governance towards selected common goals, which may be possible only through new methodologies of coordination and integration.[54] Secondly, without democratic scrutiny and increased legitimacy of foreign policy and external relations, no relevant international action can be implemented; even if was of a structural nature and with long-term scope. Thirdly, the new institutional architecture should conciliate deepening and widening. A broader Europe with an efficient and open "hard core" needs Treaty provisions supporting flexible integration and enhanced cooperation. Fourthly, whatever the final institutional path will be, the strategic political leadership of the EU has to be institutionally strengthened: jointly with the Council and the Commission, the European Council is the fundamental political body expressing the common willingness and international actorship of the heads of the European States.

Ultimately, European new regionalism faces the question of US–EU military cooperation. European perceptions are increasingly that traditional international and nuclear wars no longer pose a major threat and that security challenges are mainly regional.[55] However, how does the civilian power Europe react to wars in the near abroad? A realistic and innovative answer is represented by the gradual construction of an evolving European security identity, even if through a revived legitimization of the current American leadership of the Atlantic alliance. It is a very uncertain challenge, which will characterize the next decades. Of course, the historical roots of this alliance and of American primacy have the solid background of the victories against Fascism, Nazism, Stalinism, and European militarism. The present difficulties of a disengagement from the American understanding of the alliance carries a price in terms of the relationship with other regional organizations and world powers, as clearly shown by the reactions of Brazil, MERCOSUR, Japan, China, India, ASEAN etc. to the Kosovo war.

Indeed, an analysis of the credibility of this way cannot ignore the long-term dynamics of the two partners of the Atlantic alliance, firstly, because of what is happening within American society, which is making the global role of the country as a world leader more problematic and the concept of American hegemony as being obsolete while the defence of national interests is not.[56] Because of its political, economic and cultural interests, the US will not leave Europe as in 1919, but the balance between the European agenda and the transatlantic agenda will inevitably evolve. Secondly, differences between the EU and the US are increasing, as far as economic interests, perceptions of security threats, and the vision of the post-Cold War world are concerned. The international vision and action of Germany, the "junior European partner" of the US, is currently showing a more realistic balance between continuity and discontinuity. This makes Germany a potential – and partially already present – leader of European new regionalism, both as far as the security policy and the trade policy are concerned.

In conclusion, the concept of civilian power is not only a legacy of the past, declining within the new global post-Cold-War system. On the contrary, under certain conditions, it belongs to the *longue durée* evolution of the European ideal. However, many of the contradictory – even hypocritical – features of the concept, now belong to the past, since the very evolution of relations among States and of structural power is strengthening the chances of a new international actorship, of a new international entity within the economic and political international system. More so than in the past, the EC/EU can find allies and partners elsewhere to construct a less asymmetric world governance. New regionalism is not a panacea but it could eventually provide further means to brake the tendency towards an increased fragmentation without imposing controversial globalist rules. Europe is not only a laboratory to understand potentialities and limitations of regionalism, but also an actor in the making within the new globalized world. At best, the European experiment, again as in the past, could suggest new concepts to cope with a new reality: an international system in transition where new actors and new forms of governance emerge.

On the other hand, whereas multilateralism has no future chances without a fundamental reform, new democratic and civilian regionalism cannot express its potential without a new economic and political multilateralism.[57] New regionalism is not only an instrument for multilateralism; rather a driving force for a reformed world governance, beyond the mere *aggiornamento* of the old (1948), afore-mentioned, art. 24 of the WTO. Our third scenario shares with the first one the inevitability of growing economic convergence and globalization; however, it also shares with the second scenario the analysis of conflicts and obstacles the global-ized economy provokes, with possible salient political implications. Protectionism can only be fought by enhanced world regulation, provided by informal gover-nance but also by reformed multilateral central rules. New regionalism can be the best support of new multilateralism, limiting both arrogant unilateralism and nationalistic, ethnic or privatizing fragmentation of authorities and decision making. We do witness an array of evolving regional arrangements. A deep region-alism entails more than a set of policies: it is a pillar of world multilateral politics, adjusting the legacy of the former multilateral values within a less asymmetric framework. If so, new regionalism would combine what a large part of economic literature considers as non-compatible, that is, economic openness and representa-tion of territorial economic, cultural and political variations. A new principle of territoriality is emerging between obsolete sovereignty and functional globalism.

While in the thirties regionalism was against worldwide arrangements and in the sixties regionalism was part of international multilateralism dominated by the liberal American hegemony, today a better balance is on the agenda: new regional-ism and biregionalism can interact fruitfully with global multilateral regulation. We are witnessing a mix of continuity and discontinuity with the past decades, when the vocation of democratic capitalism was multilateral, but until the eighties it was accompanied by strategic hegemonic powers.

The conditioners and salient variables are certainly not only to be found within European States and common institutions; they largely depend on external factors and on the prevailing trends of the international economy and politics. However, new regionalism offers the EU the possibility of worldwide alliances and partner-ships with a view to implementing new multilateralism. The EU is particularly committed to strengthening this kind of alliance and cooperation between regional organizations. It can help to overcome the current gap between economic global-ization and the multilateral political and economical institutional framework.

We also mentioned the word "responsibility" as one of the components of the new concept of regional civilian power. Within international politics, we are currently witnessing an ambiguous flourishing of "word responsibility" – in fact power politics instrumentalizing global values, protection of human rights and the urgent need of better global governance.[58] How is new regionalism coping with a realistic notion of responsibility? New regionalism could also offer a normative opportunity for providing a third way between global regulation and fragmentation. In the framework of the current normative discussion about improving world governance and respect of human rights, we should mention the need to deepen new regionalism as an original way between juridical globalism and relativism, between cosmopolitan rhetoric and power politics.[59] Many authors of this book have been working on the question of to what extent Europe can be, thanks to its memory and values, the cradle of a universal idea of peace and cooperation, through its contribution to a pluralistic, multicultural and multilateral democratic government at national, regional and world levels. Of course, it can succeed only under the precondition of other regional and State actors with the same goals: a new multilateralism is more than mere international regime-building and more than a bigger role for international organizations. While military and economic unilateralism corrode universal values and do not stop fragmentation, some examples of new regionalism are providing first pieces of a better world governance, economic justice and respect of human rights through more structural symmetry among actors, economic and political dialogue, respect for diversities, and a cross-border pluralistic trans-national public sphere.[60] Reciprocally, an innovative concept of civilian power cannot seriously rise out of a new multilateral global framework based on structural change and on "post-Westphalian" power relations.

Notes

1   C. Rhodes, ed. (1998), and R. Ginsberg, Conceptualizing the EU as an International Actor: Narrowing the Theoretical Capability-Expectations Gap, in *Journal of Common Market Studies* vol. 37, No. 3 pp. 429–454.
2   R. Keohane and J. Nye, eds. (1970).
3   K. Deutsch et al. (1957) and E. Haas (1958).
4   As far as the economic dimension of external relations is concerned, the ECSC Treaty and the 1957 Treaties of Rome are the legal foundations of the EC's external competence: customs and trade policy, external implications of the common market and of all the common policies (agricultural, competition), cooperation with developing countries, and so on. According to the Treaties, the European Commission can, in part, act on behalf of Member States and the communitarian procedures can be applied (Majority Voting Procedure in the Council, competence of the European Court of Justice, role of the European Parliament), while in part intergovernmental cooperation is requested.
5   Furthermore, no Western European economy is in division II of prosperity according to World Bank and IMF lists, and they are behind the US and Japan as far as GDP per capita is concerned. They are however increasing their distance from developing countries
6   Article 133 (ex–113) of the Treaty of Rome (TEC) provides one of the most important legal foundations of common external action, allowing the Commission to make commercial agreements with "one or more States or international organizations".

Though submitted to the unanimous agreement of the Council of Ministers, the new Treaty of Amsterdam (1997) provides for the extension of the Commission mandate, to "international negotiations and agreements on services and intellectual property", for example the sensitive issues of the problematic "Millennium Round" of the WTO. The European Commission, on the basis of articles 300–301 (ex–228 and 228A) can negotiate international agreements with states and international organizations. Articles 302–304 (ex–229–231) provide a legal basis for the EU's participation in international organizations: WTO, GATT, European Bank for Reconstruction and Development (for Eastern European countries), the Council of Europe, the OSCE, the UN and some of the UN organizations and agencies.

Moreover, a particular Treaty provision is particularly meaningful from economic and political points of view: art. 310 (ex–238) of the TEC describes the "association making power", including "reciprocal rights and obligations, common actions and special procedures", applied to the concerned state (s) and organizations.

There are different types of association status: States belonging to the "Lomé Convention" (78 African, Caribbean and Pacific countries), Eastern European and Mediterranean states. Finally, applicant states for membership have special agreements, conceived as a kind of an antechamber. It is important to underline that from the very beginning of the integration process the successive enlargements (art. 49 of the TEU) were an essential part of European foreign policy as shown by the British and the Iberian enlargements and more particularly since 1989, by the Scandinavian and EFTA, the Central-Eastern European enlargements.

7   R. Gilpin, The Politics of Transnational Economic Relations, in R. Keohane and J. Nye (1970), pp.48–68.

8   By its emergence as an international political actor, the EC contributed already in the seventies to the decline of US international hegemony. The ECP is hard to explain only as the outcome of an internal dynamic. The first coordination process of national foreign policies was a response by the EC to its international environment.

9   S.Hoffmann, R. Keohane, J. S. Nye, eds. (1993). See also C. Hill (1996) and particularly the Introduction by C. Hill and W. Wallace.

10   The Preamble to the TEU stresses the aim to "reinforce the European identity and its independence in order to promote peace, security and progress in Europe and the world" (par. 9). Art. 11 (ex-title V, article J) of the TEU is the legal basis for the Common Foreign and Security Policy, which is part of the political Union and strengthens the former European political cooperation with the aim of "asserting its identity on the international scene", art. 2 (ex-art. B, par. 2). J.-M. Dumond and P. Setton (1999), *La Politique étrangère et de sécurité commune (PESC)*, La Documentation française, Paris.

11   European Council, Lisbon 26/27 June 1992, Conclusion by the Presidency, European Commission General Secretary, 1992. The European Council emphasized the importance of strengthening the economic and political external relations of the European Community. It stressed the common interests and areas open to joint actions as far as external relations are concerned (Eastern Europe and Russia, Mediterranean, Latin America, Middle East, developing countries). Inter-regional relations are also mentioned: "the easing of international tensions with the end of the Cold War provides new possibilities and resources for development but also favors the emergence of new forms of co-operation namely at inter-regional level" (p. 24).

12   See C. Piening (1997) pp. 193–97, Martin Holland, ed. (1997); K. A. Eliassen, ed. (1998).

13 See M. Telò and P. Magnette, eds. (1998), and particularly the articles by M. Telò and E. Remacle. The procedure of the Amsterdam Treaty is intergovernmental the very complex provisions of enhanced cooperation excludes security and defence issues (second pillar of the TEU) and art. 25 of TEU allows single Member States to stop common external actions – the 'Nice Treaty' makes "enhanced cooperation" easier in defence policy.

14 D. Allen and M. Smith (1990), Western Europe's Presence in the Contemporary International Arena, in: *Review of International Affairs*, n. 16, pp.19–37.

15 I. J. Manners and R. G. Whitman, International identity of the EU, in *Journal of European Integration*, n. 3, pp.231–49: the EU implements its "active identity", according to the authors, through a significant array of tools: informational (strategic, specific, informational instruments and reactive statements), procedural (regional, bilateral, and so on), transference (6% of the EU Budget for external actions in 1997) and overt (either on a transitory or on a permanent basis).

16 By 'French pattern' he means: "indigenous nuclear weapons, control of foreign bases, loyalty to NATO but insistence on a distinct personality within it" in H. Bull, (1982) p.160. Obviously, the international environment of the seventies and early eighties historically conditions the call by H. Bull for a distinctive European nuclear deterrent force, based on French-British collaboration.

17 C. Hill (1996).

18 The Treaty of Amsterdam expresses openly the wish to better coordinate these multiple dimensions, by strengthening art. 3 of the TEU (former art. C) requesting not only a coherence between the various dimensions of the external action but also a better coordination between the Council and the Commission. However, the current multiple responsibility system, including 'Mister CFSP' (General Secretary of the Council and of WEU, M. X. Solana since 1999), the Commissioner charged with external relations (Mr. Patten, in the Prodi Commission) and the rotating Presidency of the Council, does not yet show a clear division of competence in policy implementation.

19 F. Duchêne (1973), The European Community and the Uncertainties of Interdependence, in: M. Kohnstamm and W. Hager (1973), *A Nation Writ Large? Foreign Policy Problems before the EC*, Macmillan, London.

20 R. O. Keohane and J. S. Nye, (1970); and more recently, R. B. Walker (1993); W. Carlsnaes and S. Smith eds. (1994), *European Foreign Policy: the EC and Changing Perspectives*, Sage London.

21 R. G. Whitman, (1998), see note 18.

22 C. Piening (1997), pp.193–97.

23 See the Helsinki European Council decision to build up a new capability, namely a European "rapid reaction force" by 2003 (60,000 soldiers capable of being mobilized within a short period of time in the framework of the "Petersberg Tasks" (Amsterdam Treaty).

24 See articles 228 and 238 EC Treaty, granting a Treaty-making power, even if submitted to unanimous vote by the Council and "avis conforme" by the EP; revised in the Amsterdam Treaty articles 300 and 310.

25 A. Schlesinger (1979), *The Imperial Presidency*, New York.

26 T. Lowi (1967).

27 W. Wessels and D. Rometsch (1996).

28 See for instance the statement presented by the General Affairs Council to the Vienna European Council (Dec. 1998) in order to increase the weight and coherence of the Union, with the title "Common strategies", the proposals by Tony Blair concerning

defence cooperation (April 1999) and the progress made in 1998 and 2000 as far as defence cooperation is concerned (St Malo, 1998, Feira E.Council 2000 etc.).

29 Particularly useful is the analysis of the various national interests and aims provided by the book edited by C. Hill (1996). However, Hill underlined in his 1993 article, The Capability–Expectation Gap, or Conceptualizing Europe's International Role (in *Journal of Common Market Studies*, n. 3, Sept.) four common external interests of EU Member States: providing a second western voice in international diplomacy; stabilizing Eastern Europe; managing the globalized economy and the world trade; relations with the South.

30 As regards the Amsterdam Treaty: better visibility by "Mr. CFSP" even if he will not be much more than a spokesperson, dependent on the Council; improved decision-making process (even if the "enhanced cooperation" clause cannot yet be applied to the "second pillar"), strengthened Treaty-making power of the Commission (even if limited by the revised art. 300 and 310 and 133, submitting it to unanimous vote procedure of the Council).

31 S. Strange, Who are EU? Ambiguities in the Concept of Competitiveness, in *Journal of Common Market Studies*, vol. 36, No. 1, March 1998, pp. 101–113.

32 This elaborated version of "multilevel governance" takes into account the end not only of teleological visions of the EU, but also of the functional spill-over dominating the first three decades of European regional integration. The author considers non-realistic both the "Stato" and "Confederatio" scenarios, linked to the territorial logic; see P. C. Schmitter (1995), Examining the Present Euro polity with the Help of Past Theories and Imagining the Future of the Euro Polity with the Help of New Concepts, in G. Marks, F. W. Scharpf, P. C. Schmitter, and W. Streeck (1996).

33 The two-level game, analysed by among others A. Moravsik (1998), is only to some extent compatible with such a neoliberal scenario.

34 S. D. Krasner (1983).

35 R. N. Rosencrance (1986).

36 J. Rosenau has proposed for that scenario the concept of "fragmegration" (combining fragmentation and integration); however the authors of this book, in general, do not share his functional optimism, as far as decentralized governance is concerned and focus on the crucial question of the role of new regionalism by providing a synthesis between the two dialectical tendencies mentioned by J. Rosenau. See J. Rosenau and Czempiel, eds, (1992) and Rosenau (2000) A Transformed Observer in a Transforming World, in *Studia Diplomatica, Les théories des R. I. à l'épreuve de l'après-guerre-froide*, edited by C. Roosens, M. Telò and P. Vercauteren, vol. LII, n. 1, 2000, pp. 4–14.

37 R. Gilpin (1987) distinguishes between the "benevolent" and "malevolent" types of neomercantilism. See also Björn Hettne, The Double Movement: Global Market versus Regionalism, in R. Cox ed. (1997) pp.223–244 and Hettne (1999).

38 G. Bertrand, A. Michalski, L. R. Pench (European Commission, Forward Studies Unit), *Scenarios Europe 2010. Five Possible Futures for Europe*, working paper (1999).

39 A. S. Milward (1999), L'impossibile fuga dalla storia, in *Europa/Europe.Quale idea d'Europa? per il XXI secolo*, n. 5, edited by M. Telò, pp. 57–68.

40 A. Moravcsik (1999).

41 N. Bobbio (1981), and (1998), *Etat et démocratie internationale*, Complexe, Bruxelles, ed.by M. Telò.

42 Bhagwati (1993) and A. Sapir (1998), pp. 717–732.

43 Kébabdjian, G. (1999), pp.227–53.

44 On European exceptionalism, see W. Wallace (1994).

45 M. Albert has updated his famous concept of "Rhenan capitalism " in Albert (1999), Il capitalismo europeo nel quadro della mondializzazione: convergenze e differenze, in *Europa /Europe, Quale idea d'Europa per il XXI secolo?* ed. by M. Telò, n. 5.

46 Portuguese Presidency of the EU (January 2000), *Employment, economic reforms and social cohesion. For a Europe of innovation and knowledge*, Lisbon, and *Conclusion of the Presidency* (Lisbon, 23/24. 3. 2000). See also European Commission (February 2000), *The Lisbon European Council. An Agenda of Economic and Social Renewal for Europe*, Brussels, 28.

47 For two opposite viewpoints, see: D. Piazolo (1998) and S. Bilal (March 1998), Political Economy Considerations on the Supply of Trade Protection in Regional Integration Agreements, in *Journal of Common Market Studies*, vol. 36, No.1, pp. 1–31.

48 S. Keukeleire (1998) has explored the empirical side of this approach in, *Het buitenlands beleid van de Europese Unie*, Deeventer, Kluwer. We would like to further develop here its theoretical dimension.

49 T. de Wilde d'Estmael (1998).

50 K. Waltz (1979); and R. Keohane, ed. (1986).

51 R. O. Keohane and J. S. Nye (1989), examine the importance of transnational crossborder relations and the emergence of new private and public actors within the international system, and the decline of the traditional hierarchies of power and issues. It gives priority to security; it questions the traditional separation between inside and outside of the state; and it explores international cooperation as a possible positive sum game.

    However, liberal institutionalist models exaggerate the impact of trade interdependence on the building of institutions, (which is not true in the case of ASEAN). On the contrary, customs unions evolve easily to deeper institutional settlements: see S. Haggard, Regionalism in Asia and the Americas, in E. Mansfield and H. Milner (1997), pp. 47–48.

52 M. Telò and S. Santander (1999), *Can the EU contribute to a Less Asymmetric Multilateral World?* paper, IPSA Research Committee on European Unification, Brussels.

53 S. Strange (1988).

54 The internal cohesion and consistency can be enhanced only through institutional reforms: a) strengthening the political leadership of the European Council as the strategic options as far as the long-term decisions are concerned (see the example of the Lisbon European Council on technological modernization, economic reform, knowledge society and social model); b) reforming the General Affairs Council, to be divided in two, in order to correct its current fragmentation and depolitization. On the one hand, the Council responsible for foreign affairs and security issues, and on the other hand, a General Affairs Council composed of superministers (Deputy Prime Ministers) responsible for coordinating and leading the implementation of intergovermental cooperation, acting as an internal reference for the European policies; c) improving the executive role of the European Commission, its external role of representation and its political accountability d) organizing a European diplomatic body, even if coordinated with Member States.

55 Even part of French literature takes into account the need to overcome the past debate between the French and British security policies, both focusing on the nuclear threat. Cfr. N. Gnesotto (1998).

56 See P. Kennedy (1987) and R. Keohane (1984). D. A. Lake (1999), D. L. Boren and E. J. Perkins, eds. (1999).

57 See John Gerard Ruggie, (1993), *Winning the Peace*, Columbia, New York and R. Cox, ed. (1997), pp. 245–261.

58 B. Badie (1999), particularly the third part, Entre responsabilité et puissance, pp.223–285

59 M.Telò (1999), Lo Stato e la democrazia internazionale. Il contributo di N.Bobbio oltre globalismo giuridico e relativismo, in *Teoria politica*, XV, Turin edited by L.Bonanate, n.2–3, pp.533–562.

60 J.Habermas (1996), and Die europäische Nationalstaat unter dem Druck der Globalisierung, in *Blaetter fuer deutsche und internationale Politik* n.4 (1999). Regarding the international discussion on world governance, realism and cosmopolitism, F.D.Archibugi, D.Held and M.Koehler, eds. (1998), F.Cerutti, ed. (2000); H.Bull, (1986) H. Kelsen and International Law, in J. J. L. Tur, W. Twining, eds. *Essays on Kelsen*, Oxford, University Press, Oxford, and D. Zolo (1997 and 1998).

Appendix:
List of Regional and Interregional Arrangements

Sebastian Santander

1. Regional arrangements

The organizations listed below are grouped by geographical area (Africa, Americas, Arab World, Asia, Europe and Oceania) and listed within each area in alphabetical order.

1.1 Africa

CAO: Eastern African Community, 1967
Purposes
Customs union. Inactive.
Members
Kenya, Tanzania, Uganda.

CEEAC: Economic Community of Central African States, 1983
Purposes
Customs union. Common external tariff.
Members
Burundi, Cameroon, Central African Republic, Chad, Congo, Democratic Republic of Congo, Gabon, Equatorial Guinea, Rwanda.

CEPGL: Economic Community of the Great Lakes Countries, 1976
Purposes
Customs union and specialized agencies for common development: in the banking, energy, agronomy and animal technology sectors.
Members
Burundi, Democratic Republic of Congo, Rwanda.

COMESA: Common Market for Eastern and Southern Africa, 1994
Purposes
Successor to Preferential Trade Area of Southern African States which was established on 22 December 1981. The aims of COMESA are the following:
- attain sustainable growth and development of member states by promoting a more balanced and harmonious development of production and marketing structures; promote joint development in all fields of economic activity and the joint adoption of macro-economic policies and programmes in order to raise the standard of living of the peoples in, and to foster closer relations among, member states; cooperate in the creation of an enabling environment for foreign, cross-border and domestic investment, including joint promotion of research and adaptation of science and technology for development; cooperate in the promotion of peace, security and stability among member states in order to enhance the economic development of the region, cooperate in strengthening the relations between the Common Market and the rest of the world and adopt common positions in international forums, contribute towards the establishment, progress and the realization of the objectives of the African Economic Community.

Members
Angola, Burundi, Comoros, Democratic Republic of Congo, Ethiopia, Kenya, Madagascar, Malawi, Mauritius, Namibia, Rwanda, Sudan, Swaziland, Seychelles, Tanzania UR, Uganda, Zambia, Zimbabwe.
Botswana and South Africa are under conditions stipulated by the members.

CUSA: Customs Union of Southern Africa, 1969
Purposes
Customs union.
Members
Botswana, Lesotho, Namibia, South Africa, Swaziland.

ECOWAS: Economic Community of West African States (CEDEAO in French), 1975
Purposes
To become a common market.
To promote cooperation and development in economic activity, particularly in the fields of industry, transport, telecommunications, energy, natural resources, trade, monetary and financial questions and in social and cultural matters, for the purpose of raising the standard of living, of increasing and maintaining economic stability, of fostering closer relations among its members and of contributing to the progress and development of the African continent.
Members
Benin, Burkina Faso, Gambia, Ghana, Green Cape, Guinea, Guinea-Bissau, Ivory Coast, Mali, Mauritania, Niger, Nigeria, Senegal, Sierra Leone, Togo.

MRU: Mano River Union, 1973
Purposes
Customs union.
To expand trade, encourage productive capacity, and progressively develop a common policy and cooperation as regards harmonization of tariffs and regulations related to customs, qualifications and postal services; to promote joint development projects (hydroelectric construction, telecommunications, maritime activities); to secure a fair distribution of the benefits from economic cooperation. Under the Lomé Convention, to maintain links with the European Union.
Members
Guinea, Liberia, Sierra Leone.

SADC: Southern African Development Community, 1992
Purposes
Replaced the SADCC (Southern African Development Coordination Conference) which was established in 1980. The main purposes of this customs union are: deeper economic cooperation and integration, on the basis of balance, equity and mutual benefits, providing for cross-border investment and trade, and freer movement of factors of production, goods and services across national borders; common economic, political and social values and systems, enhancing enterprise and competitiveness, democracy and good governance, respect for the rule of law and the guarantee of human rights, popular participation and alleviation of poverty; strengthened regional solidarity, peace and security, in order for the people of the region to live and work together in peace and harmony. Particular concerns: human resources, science and technology, food security, natural resources and environment, infrastructure and services, finance, investment and trade, popular participation, solidarity, peace and security.
Members
Angola, Botswana, Democratic Republic of Congo, Lesotho, Malawi, Mauritius, Mozambique, Namibia, Seychelles, South Africa, Swaziland, Tanzania, Zambia, Zimbabwe.

UDEAC: Customs and Economic Union of Central Africa, 1964
Purposes
Customs union.
To establish an ever-closer union among member states so as to reinforce sub-regional solidarity, to promote the gradual and progressive establishment of a Central African common market, and subsequently, through establishment of this sub-regional grouping, to participate in the creation of a true African common market and the consolidation of African unity.
Members
Cameroon, Democratic Republic of Congo, Chad, Central African Republic, Equatorial Guinea, Gabon.

WAEMU: West-African Economic and Monetary Union (UEMOA in French), 1994
Purposes
To replace WAMU (West African Monetary Union), which was established in 1959. To make the economic and financial activities of Member States more competitive in the context of an open market based upon free competition, to set up a multilateral surveillance procedure to harmonize national legislations (particularly fiscal) and coordinate economic policies. To set up a common market and a Common External Tariff.
Members
Benin, Burkina Faso, Guinea-Bissau, Ivory Coast, Mali, Niger, Senegal, Togo.

1.2 Americas (The)

Acuerdos de Caracas: Caracas Agreement, 1993
Purposes
Free trade agreement set up by the Group of the Three (see below) and the Central American countries.
Members
Colombia, Costa Rica, El Salvador, Guatemala, Honduras, Mexico, Nicaragua, Panama, Venezuela.

ALADI: Latin American Association for Development and Integration, 1980
Purposes
Replaced the ALALC (Latin American Association of Free Trade). Preferential trade area. Its main purpose is to become a common market. The ALADI has contributed to transforming economic structures and creating the conditions for integration in countries where they were less favourable. It has contributed to establishing bilateral and multilateral relations among member states.
Members
Argentina, Bolivia, Brazil, Chile, Colombia, Ecuador, Mexico, Paraguay, Peru, Uruguay, Venezuela. *Observers:* China, Cuba, Dominican Republic, El Salvador, Guatemala, Honduras, Italy, Nicaragua, Panama, Portugal, Romania, Russia, Spain, Switzerland.

Andean Community, 1969 (previously Andean Pact)
Purposes
To establish the conditions for a common market within ALALC–ALADI (see below). Since 1995, the member states have been establishing a customs union.
Members
Bolivia, Colombia, Ecuador, Peru, Venezuela. Chile was a founder member but withdrew in 1973, the year Venezuela joined. Peru does not participate wholly in the integration process.

CACM: Central American Common Market, 1960
Purposes
To establish a customs union and political integration as a federation of Central American states.
Members
Costa Rica, El Salvador, Guatemala, Honduras, Nicaragua.

CARICOM: Caribbean Community, 1973
Purposes
Replaced CARIFA (Caribbean International Free Trade Association), which was established in 1965. Has established a common external tariff and economic integration. Incorporates the Organization of the States of Eastern Caribbean.
Members
Antigua-Barbuda, Bahamas (member of the Community but not of the common market), Barbados, Belize, Dominica, Grenada, Guyana, Jamaica, Montserrat, Surinam, Trinidad and Tobago. *Observer countries:* Anguilla, Aruba, Bermuda, British Virgin Islands, Cayman Islands, Colombia, Cuba, Dominican Republic, Dutch Antilles, Haiti, Mexico, Puerto Rico, Venezuela.

Grupo de los Tres: The Group of the Three, 1989
Purposes
Free trade agreement, customs union, agreement for abolition of tariffs (aimed to be achieved by 2004), to facilitate investment and public purchases.
Members
Colombia, Mexico, Venezuela.

MERCOSUR: Mercado Común del Sur (Common Market of the South, MERCO-SUL in Portuguese), 1991
Purposes
Before the establishment of MERCOSUR, the biggest member states, Argentina and Brazil, passed through two important stages. The PICE (Integration and Cooperation Program, 1986) established the first link between them in pursuit of further economic integration. In 1989 the two countries reached a new agreement: the PICAB (Integration, Cooperation and Development Treaty), which aimed to abolish tariffs barriers and coordinate policy in some specific areas (customs, science, technology) as well as macroeconomic policy. In 1990 new modifications were introduced with the Acta de Buenos Aires (Buenos Aires Act), which aimed to facilitate the setting up of the common market in 1994. One year later the Treaty of Asunción extended the Buenos Aires Act to Paraguay and Uruguay and established MERCOSUR, which came into force on 1 January 1995. Its aims are both political and economic: to stabilize democracy and to develop the economies in the region. An important aim of MERCOSUR is to be a mechanism for 'open integration'. It has bilateral trade links with Chile and Bolivia and multilateral trade links

with the EU; contacts in the field of trade have been made with India and APEC; member states are also planning a South American Free Trade Area (ALCSA or SAFTA) with the remaining Latin American countries, and intend to take part in the proposed Free Trade Area of the Americas.
Members
Argentina, Brazil, Paraguay, Uruguay. *Associated members:* Bolivia, Chile.

NAFTA: North American Free Trade Agreement, 1994
Purposes
Free trade; free movement of capital and services. It aims to abolish more than 20,000 barriers to trade by 2010; to promote conditions of fair competition and increase investment opportunities; to provide adequate provision for intellectual property rights and environmental protection; to establish effective procedures for implementing and applying the Agreement and for resolution of disputes; to encourage further trilateral, regional and multilateral cooperation.
Members
Canada, Mexico, United States.

SELA: Latin American Economic System, 1975
Purposes
Established by the governments of Latin America with the main purpose of reinforcing the region's capacity in international economic negotiations and contributing to the full development of the member states.
Members
Argentina, Barbados, Belize, Bolivia, Brazil, Chile, Colombia, Costa Rica, Cuba, Dominican Republic, Ecuador, El Salvador, Grenada, Guatemala, Guyana, Haiti, Honduras, Jamaica, Mexico, Nicaragua, Panama, Paraguay, Peru, Surinam, Trinidad and Tobago, Uruguay, Venezuela.

1.3 Arab World and Maghreb

Arab Common Market, 1964
Purposes
Formed by the Council of the Arab Economic Union, it encourages the development of the less developed members in order to prepare for further developments such as customs union, the creation of joint ventures, etc.
Members
Egypt, Iraq, Jordan, Libya, Mauritania, United Arab Emirates, Yemen.

ACC: Arab Cooperation Council, 1989
Purposes
To be a more efficient forum for economic cooperation and integration among Arab countries; to promote among member states the coordination and harmoniza-

tion of major economic policies in areas such as finance, customs and trade, industry and agriculture; to form an Arab common market. It is open to all Arab countries. The aim is eventually to bring together countries represented by organizations with more limited geographical coverage.
Members
Egypt, Iraq, Jordan, Yemen.

AMU/UMA: Arab Maghreb Union, 1989
Purposes
The goals of the AMU are to safeguard Maghrebian economic interests; to foster and promote economic and cultural cooperation among member states; to intensify mutual commercial exchanges as a necessary precursor to integration; and the creation of a Maghreb Economic Space (a free market in energy products; free movement of citizens within the region; joint transport undertakings, including a joint airline, road and railway improvements; formation of a Maghreb union of textile and leather industries; creation of a customs union).
Members
Algeria, Libya, Mauritania, Morocco, Tunisia.

CAEU: Council for Arab Economic Unity, 1964
Purposes
To provide a flexible framework for achieving economic integration in stages. To undertake research into the economic conditions and outlook of the member states, to collect and to distribute the information and to offer consulting services; to prepare the way for a customs union; to develop industry and agriculture.
Members
Egypt, Iraq, Jordan, Kuwait, Libya, Mauritania, Palestine Authority, Somalia, Sudan, Syria, United Arab Emirates, Yemen.

CCASG: Council of Cooperation between Arab States of the Gulf, 1947
Purposes
The organization's main purpose is to pursue coordination, integration and cooperation in the economic, social and cultural fields.
Members
Bahrain, Kuwait, Oman, Qatar, Saudi Arabia, United Arab Emirates.

LAS: League of Arab States, 1945
Purposes
The main purposes of this association are to reinforce the links between member states, to coordinate their policies and economics activities, and to work together towards a better common future.
Members
Algeria, Bahrain, Comoros (1993), Djibouti, Egypt, Iraq, Jordan, Kuwait, Lebanon,

Libya, Morocco, Mauritania, Oman, Palestine Authority, Qatar, Saudi Arabia, Somalia, Sudan, Syria, Tunisia, United Arab Emirates, Yemen.

1.4 Asia

ASEAN: Association of South-East Asian Nations, 1967
Purposes
According to its founding Bangkok Declaration, the objectives of the Association are: to accelerate economic growth, social progress and cultural development in the region through joint endeavours in the spirit of equality and partnership in order to strengthen the foundation for a prosperous and peaceful community of Southeast Asian Nations: to promote regional peace and stability through abiding respect for justice and the rule of law in relationship among countries of the region and adherence to the principles of the United Nations Charter; to promote active collaboration and mutual assistance on matters of common interest in the economic, social, cultural, technical, scientific and administrative fields; to provide assistance to each other in the form of training and research facilities in the educational, professional, technical and administrative spheres; to collaborate more effectively for the greater use of their agriculture and industries, the expansion of their trade, including the study of the problems of international commodity trade, the improvement of their transportation and communications facilities and the raising of the living standards of their peoples; to promote Southeast Asian studies; to maintain close and beneficial cooperation with existing international and regional organizations with similar aims and purposes, and explore all avenues for even closer cooperation among themselves.

The aims of ASEAN economic cooperation in the post-Cold War period include the following: to develop the region into a global base for the manufacture of value-added and technologically sophisticated products geared towards servicing regional and world markets; to enhance the industrial efficiency of the region through exploiting complementary location advantages based on the principles of market sharing and resource pooling; to enhance the attractiveness of the region for investment and as a tourist destination; to cooperate in enhancing greater infrastructural development which will contribute towards a more efficient business environment; to ensure that the rich resources (mineral, energy, forestry and others) of the region are exploited effectively and efficiently.
Members
Brunei, Cambodia, Indonesia, Laos, Malaysia, Myanmar, Philippines, Singapore, Thailand, Vietnam. *Observer governments:* Papua New Guinea.

CAEC: Central Asian Economic Community, 1994
Purposes
It aims at a deeper economic integration among participating states, with free movement of goods, services, capital and labour forces and agreed credit, account-

ing, budget, tax, pricing, customs and currency policy, leading to a free trade area and customs union for the single ecological system comprising the states of central Asia, which already benefit from a common geopolitical disposition, common boundaries, close economic relations, available transport and other communications and rich natural resources and raw materials. It also seeks to develop common approaches and directions of cooperation in economic, political, defence and humanitarian spheres.
Members
Kazakhstan, Kyrghizstan, Tajikistan and Uzbekistan. *As observer:* Russia

SAARC: South Asian Association for Regional Cooperation, 1985
Purposes
To promote the welfare of the peoples of South Asia and improve their quality of life; to accelerate economic growth, social progress and cultural development in the region and give all individuals the opportunity to live in dignity and realize their full potential; to promote and strengthen collective self-reliance among the countries of South Asia; to contribute to mutual trust, understanding and appreciation of one another's problems; to promote collaboration and mutual assistance in economic, social, cultural, technical and scientific fields; to strengthen cooperation with other developing countries; to strengthen cooperation among members in international forums or matters of common interest; to cooperate with international and regional organizations with similar aims and purposes.
Members
Bangladesh, Bhutan, India, Maldives, Nepal, Pakistan, Sri Lanka.

1.5 Europe

BENELUX, 1947
Purposes
Customs union. Regional trade agreements.
Members
Belgium, Luxembourg, The Netherlands.

BSECS: The Black Sea Economic Cooperation Scheme, 1992
Purposes
The Black Sea Economic Cooperation Scheme (BSEC) has been established by 11 countries of the region during the summit meeting held in Istanbul on 25 June 1992. It is based on two documents, the 'Summit Declaration on Black Sea Economic Cooperation' and the 'Bosphorus Statement'. The principles governing the BSEC are based on those of the Helsinki Final Act, the CSCE follow-up documents, the Paris Charter for a New Europe (1990).

   Its main purposes are: to achieve closer cooperation among the member states (and any other interested country) through the signing of bilateral and mutilateral agreements, in order to 'foster their economic, technological and social progress, and to encourage free enterprise'; to ensure that the Black Sea becomes a sea of peace, stability and prosperity, striving to promote friendly and good-neighbourly relations; to ensure economic cooperation to help implementing 'a Europe-wide economic area, as well as raching a higher degree of integration of the Participating States into the world economy'.

Members
Albania, Bulgaria, Greece, Romania, Turkey and the countries which emerged after the break-up of the Soviet Union: Armenia, Azerbaijan, Georgia, Moldova, Ukraine and the Russian Federation.

CIS: Commonwealth of Independent States, 1991
Purposes
Economic union.
Members
Armenia, Azerbaijan, Belarus, Georgia, Kazakhstan, Kyrghizstan, Moldavia, Russia, Tajikistan, Turkmenistan, Ukraine, Uzbekistan.

Common Market of the Baltic States, 1991
Purposes
Free trade area.
Members
Estonia, Latvia, Lithuania.

EC/EU: European Community/European Union, 1957
Purposes
The European integration process has passed through several stages. In 1985 the European Economic Community (EEC) set up in 1957 by the Treaty of Rome was modified by the Single European Act, which brought together the European Coal and Steel Community (ECSC), the EEC and the European Atomic Energy Community (Euratom). The EEC became the European Community and then, in 1992, with the signature of the Maastricht Treaty, the European Union. The EU today has a three-pillar structure: (1) the Community activities pillar, managed by mainly supranational procedures; (2) the Common Foreign and Security Policy pillar, managed by an intergovernmental Council; and (3) the justice and home affairs pillar also based on intergovernmental cooperation.

According to Article 2 of the Treaty of EU, the Union sets itself the following objectives: to promote economic and social progress which is balanced and sustainable, in particular through the creation of an area without internal frontiers, through the strengthening of economic and social cohesion, and through the establishment of economic and monetary union, ultimately including a single currency in accordance with the provisions of the treaty; to assert its identity on the international scene, in particular through the implementation of a CFSP including the framing of a defence policy cooperation; to strengthen the protection of the rights and interests of the nationals of its member states through the introduction of a citizenship of the Union; to develop close cooperation in the field of justice and home affairs; to maintain in full the *acquis communautaire* ensuring the effectiveness of the mechanisms and the institutions of the Community. The objectives of the Union should be achieved as provided in the treaty and in accordance with the condition of the schedule set out therein while respecting the principle of subsidiarity. Article C indicates that the Union shall in particular ensure the consistency of its external activities as a whole in the context of its external relations, security, economic and development policies.

The Treaty of Amsterdam (1997), which superseded the Maastricht Treaty, incorporated a number of changes: to sweep away the last remaining obstacles to freedom of movement and to strengthen internal security; to give Europe a stronger voice in world affairs. The Treaty of Nice (2000) had the main task to adopt the Union's institutional structure and to enable the Union to enlarge to new member states.

Members
Austria, Belgium, Denmark, France, Finland, Germany, Greece, Ireland, Italy, Luxembourg, Portugal, Spain, Sweden, The Netherlands, United Kingdom.
Any European state may apply to the Council to become a member of the Union, which acts unanimously after consulting the Commission and after receiving the assent of the European Parliament; ratification by each member state is requested. According to the Helsinki European Council conclusions, applicant countries are Bulgaria, Cyprus, Czech Republic, Estonia, Hungary, Latvia, Lithuania, Malta, Poland, Romania, Slovakia, Slovenia and Turkey.

EEA: European Economic Area, 1993
Purposes
Free trade area.
Members
EU and EFTA, minus Switzerland which rejected the EEA in a referendum.

EFTA: European Free Trade Association, 1960
Purposes
To promote in the area of the Association and in each member state a sustained expansion of economic activity, full employment, increased productivity and the rational use of resources, financial stability and continuous improvement in living standards; to secure conditions of fair competition in trade between member states; to avoid significant disparity between member states in the conditions of supply of raw materials produced within the area of the Association; to contribute to harmonious development and expansion of world trade and to progressive removal of barriers to this; to create a single market in western Europe.

Members
EFTA brought together the countries which did not want to join the Treaty of Rome in 1957: Austria, Denmark, Norway, Portugal, Sweden, Switzerland and United Kingdom. Today it consists of just four countries: Iceland, Liechtenstein, Norway and Switzerland.

Free Trade Agreement of Central Europe, 1992
Purposes
Free trade agreement.
Members
Czech Republic, Hungary, Poland, Slovakia Republic.

Visegrad, 1991
Purposes
Free trade agreement. It was replaced by the Free Trade Agreement of Central Europe in 1992.
Members
Czech Republic, Hungary, Poland, Slovakia.

1.6 Oceania

ANZCERTA (CER: Closer Economic Relationship, 1983)
Purposes
Established in 1983 as a successor to the New Zealand–Australia Free Trade Agreement (NAFTA) which had been set up in 1966. The Antipodean NAFTA applied only to certain products (excluding agriculture) and was therefore not a full free trade agreement. CER involved a stronger commitment to the establishment of free trade between the two countries, with trade in merchandise becoming fully free by 1990. There is also a commitment to economic integration in relation to services and the labour market. Integration has not been achieved in investment and currency matters; Australia unilaterally abrogated an agreement on a common aviation market in October 1994.
Members
Australia, New Zealand.

SPC: South Pacific Commission, 1947
Purposes
The Commission was established by the governments of Australia, France, the Netherlands, New Zealand, the United Kingdom and the United States. It became an NGO providing the member states with technical assistance, scientific knowledge and economic assistance for development. On 1 January 1996 the United Kingdom decided to leave the Commission.

Members
Australia, Cook Islands, Guam, Eastern Samoa, Fiji, France, French Polynesia, Futuna, Kiribati, Marianne Island (North), Marshall Island, Micronesia, Nauru, New Caledonia, New Guinea, New Zealand, New Island, Palau, Papuasia, Pitcairn Islands, Solomon Islands, Tokelau, Tonga, Tuvalu, United States, Vanuatu, Wallis, Western Samoa.

2. Interregional organizations

ACP: Countries of Africa, Caribbean and Pacific, 1975
Purposes
Established by the EU through the Lomé Convention (Togo), replacing the Yaoundé Convention and the Arusha agreements. Its purpose is to establish cooperation for development among its member countries, some of which are former European colonies.
Members
Angola, Antigua-Barbuda, Bahamas, Barbados, Belize, Benin, Botswana, Burkina Faso, Burundi, Cameroon, Central African Republic, Chad, Comoros, Congo, Democratic Republic of Congo, Djibouti, Dominica, Equatorial Guinea, Eritrea, Ethiopia, Fiji, Gabon, Gambia, Ghana, Green Cape, Grenada, Guinea, Guinea-Bissau, Guyana, Eastern Samoa, Haiti, Ivory Coast, Jamaica, Kenya, Kiribati, Lesotho, Liberia, Madagascar, Malawi, Mali, Mauritius, Mauritania, Mozambique, Namibia, Niger, Nigeria, Papua New Guinea, Rwanda, St Kitts and Nevis, St Lucia, St Vincent and Grenadines, Solomon Islands, Sao Tomé and Principe, Senegal, Seychelles, Sierra Leone, Somalia, Sudan, Surinam, Swaziland, Tanzania, Togo, Tonga, Trinidad and Tobago, Tuvalu, Uganda, Vanuatu, Zambia, Zimbabwe, South Africa (70+1).

APEC: Asia–Pacific Economic Cooperation, 1989
Purposes
To serve as a forum for regular discussion on regional trade questions and cooperation; to sustain the growth and development of the region for the common good of its peoples and contribute to the growth and development of the world economy; to enhance positive gains, both for the region and the world economy, resulting from increasing economic interdependence, to include encouraging the flow of goods, services, capital and technology, developing and strengthening the open multilateral trading system in the interest of Asia–Pacific and all other economies; to reduce barriers to trade in goods and services among participants in a manner consistent with WTO principles where applicable and without detriment to other economies. The main purpose is to set up a free trade area by 2020.

Members
Australia, Brunei, Canada, Chile, China, Hong Kong, Indonesia, Japan, Malaysia, Mexico, New Zealand, Papua New Guinea, Philippines, Russia, Singapore, South Korea, Taiwan, Thailand, United States, Vietnam.

ASEM: Asia–Europe Meeting, 1994

Purposes
In 1994 the European Commission proposed a "New Strategy for Asia" and the ASEAN member states approved the "Singapore Project". From both these initiatives emerged the principle of the Asia–Europe Meeting, with the main purpose of bringing the two continents closer. The first ASEM forum was held in Bangkok in March 1996, the second in London in April 1998. In January 1999 the European and Asian finance ministers met in Frankfurt. The three points on the agenda were the birth of the euro, the economic and financial situation in Asia, and restructuring the financial system and prudential surveillance system.

Members
The fifteen Member States of the European Union (through the European Commission); the seven member states of ASEAN; China, South Korea and Japan.

Barcelona Process, 1995

Purposes
After 20 years of increasingly intensive bilateral trade and development cooperation between the EU, its 15 Member States and its 12 Mediterranean partners, the Conference of EU and Southern Mediterranean Foreign Ministers in Barcelona (27–28 November 1995) marked the start of a new "partnership" phase including bilateral, multilateral and regional cooperation. The conference was a first step towards a "Euro-Mediterranean Partnership" (hence called "Barcelona Process"). The Barcelona Declaration adopted at the Conference expresses the 27 partners' intention to:

1. establish a common Euro-Mediterranean area for peace and stability based on fundamental principles including respect for human rights and democracy (political and security partnership);
2. create an area of shared prosperity through the progressive establishment of a free-trade area between the EU and its partners and among the Mediterranean partners themselves, accompanied by substantial EU financial support for economic transition and for the social and economic consequences of this reform process (economic and financial partnership);
3. develop human resources, promote understanding between cultures and bring peoples closer together in the Euro-Mediterranean region, as well as develop free and flourishing civil societies (social, cultural and human partnership).

Members
The 15 EU Member States, Algeria, Cyprus, Egypt, Israel, Jordan, Lebanon, Malta, Morocco, Palestinian Authority, Syria, Tunisia, Turkey. *Observer:* Libya.

FTAA: Free Trade Area of the Americas, 1994
Purposes
The project of the Initiatives of the Americas (1990) is at the root of the Free Trade
Area of the Americas, which was launched by US President Clinton in 1994 at the
Miami summit conference of thirty-four American countries. Implementation of
the Free Trade agreement is expected to be completed in 2005.
Members
All the countries of the Americas except Cuba.

NTA: The New Transatlantic Agenda, 1995
Purposes
On 3 December 1995 at the EU–US Summit in Madrid, European Commission
President Santer, Spanish Prime Minister Gonzalez, as President of the European
Council, and US President Clinton signed the New Transatlantic Agenda (NTA).
The agenda is essentially a political gesture. The US and EU have agreed a NTA
for making swifter and more effective progress towards the political, economic and
security goals they first set for themselves in the Transatlantic Declaration of 1990.
The Agenda drawn from a more detailed Action Plan identifies a joint work
programme in four areas: promoting peace, development and democracy around
the world; responding to global challenges such as international crime, the
environment and disease; contributing to the expansion of world trade and closer
economic relations; bulding bridges across the Atlantic.
Members
United States of America and the fifteen Member States of the European Union.

Rio de Janeiro Process, 1999
Purpose
The 'Rio de Janeiro Process' started in June 1999 in Brazil with the Euro-Latin
American summit. The main purpose of this initiative is to bring the two continents
closer, creating a strategic partnership.
The three points on the agenda were the political dialogue; economic and trade
relations; and education, culture and human dimensions.
Members
The fifteen member states of the European Union and all Latin American countries.

OSCE: Organization for Security and Cooperation in Europe, 1975
Purpose
The Organization for Security and Cooperation in Europe succeesed to the
Conference on Security and Co-operation in Europe started on 3 July 1975, and
originated the so-called "Helsinki Process". The basic act of the Conference on
Security and Co-operation in Europe was signed on 1 August 1975 in Helsinki, by
Heads of States or governments of 35 states.

Institutionalized as a permanent body on 21 November 1990 (Charter of Paris for a New Europe), the OSCE has been enlarged and further delineated by the Helsinki Document (July 1992). the current title has finally been adopted at the pan-European summit of Budapest, 5–6 December 1994, to be effective from 1 January 1995.

The OSCE is a security forum and its 55 participating States span the geographical area from Vancouver to Vladivostok. In this region, it is an important instrument for early warning, conflict prevention, crisis management and post-conflict rehabilitation. The OSCE includes three baskets:
a) a comprehensive and co-operative approach to pan-European security;
b) human rights and elections monitoring;
c) economic and environmental co-operation.

Members
Albania, Andorra, Armenia, Austria, Azerbaijan, Belarus, Belgium, Bosnia and Herzegovina, Bulgaria, Canada, Croatia, Cyprus, Czech Republic, Denmark, Estonia, Finand, France, Georgia, Germany, Greece, Holy See, Hungary, Iceland, Ireland, Italy, Kazakhstan, Kyrghizstan, Latvia, Liechtenstein, Lithuania, Luxembourg, Malta, Moldova, Monaco, Netherlands, Norway, Poland, Portugal, Romania, Russian Federation, San Marino, Slovak Republic, Slovenia, Spain, Sweden, Switzerland, Tajikistan, the former Yugoslav Republic of Macedonia, Turkey, Turkmenistan, Ukraine, United Kingdom, United States of America, Uzbekistan, Federal Republic of Yugoslavia.

TEP: The Transatlantic Economic Partnership, 1998
Purpose
Announced at the Birmingham summit of the TEP is economic pillar of the New Transatlantic Agenda, to be achieved by "progressively reducing or eliminating barriers that hinder the flow of goods, services and capital". A new private sector group, the Transatlantic Business Dialogue (TABD), was established to define and promote the specific trade and investment agenda needeed to bring the marketplace to fruition. Thanks in large part to the TABD, Washington and Brussels reached agreement in 1997 – after years of effort – on a package of mutual recognition agreements (MRAs) eliminating duplicative testing and certification in six sectors. The US government estimates that this package, which covers about $47 billion worth of trade, eliminates costs equivalent to two or three percentage points of tariffs. In the meantime, other problems arose that soured the prospects for broader transatlantic economic cooperation.
Members
United States of America and the fifteen Member States of the European Union.

3. Other institutions

ECFA: Economic Commission for Africa, 1958
Purposes
United Nations initiative. To facilitate economic development and relations between member states.
Members
Algeria, Angola, Benin, Botswana, Burkina Faso, Burundi, Cameroon, Central African Republic, Chad, Comoros, Congo, Democratic Republic of Congo, Djibouti, Egypt, Equatorial Guinea, Eritrea, Ethiopia, Gabon, Gambia, Ghana, Green Cape, Guinea, Guinea-Bissau, Ivory Coast, Kenya, Lesotho, Liberia, Libya, Madagascar, Malawi, Mali, Morocco, Mauritius, Mauritania, Mozambique, Namibia, Niger, Nigeria, Rwanda, Sao Tomé and Principe, Senegal, Seychelles, Sierra Leone, Somalia, South Africa, Sudan, Swaziland, Tanzania, Togo, Tunisia, Uganda, Zambia, Zimbabwe.

ECLA: Economic Commission for Latin America (CEPAL in Spanish), 1948
Purposes
United Nations initiative. It has been working in the field of industrial development.
Members
Antigua-Barbuda, Argentina, Bahamas, Barbados, Belize, Bolivia, Brazil, Canada, Chile, Colombia, Costa Rica, Cuba, Dominica, Dominican Republic, Ecuador, El Salvador, France, Grenada, Guatemala, Guyana, Haiti, Honduras, Italy, Jamaica, Mexico, Nicaragua, Panama, Paraguay, The Netherlands, Peru, Portugal, St Kitts and Nevis, St Lucia, St Vincent and Grenadines, Spain, Surinam, Trinidad and Tobago, United Kingdom, United States, Uruguay, Venezuela.

ESCAP: Economic and Social Commission for Asia and the Pacific, 1947
Purposes
United Nations initiative (today ECAFE). The main purpose of ESCAP is to encourage economic and social development in Asia and the Pacific. It acts as a regional centre of the United Nations and constitutes the only intergovernmental forum for all Asia and the Pacific. It implements a whole series of development programmes through technical assistance, services for governmental cooperation, research, training and information.
Members
Afghanistan, Australia, Azerbaijan, Bangladesh, Brunei, Cambodia, China, Eastern Samoa, Fiji, France, India, Indonesia, Iran, Japan, Kiribati, Kyrgizstan, Laos, Malaysia, Maldives, Marshall Island, Micronesia, Mongolia, Myanmar, Nauru, Nepal, New Zealand, North Korea, Pakistan, Papua New Guinea, The Netherlands, Philippines, Russia, Solomon Islands, Singapore, South Korea, Sri Lanka, Tajikistan, Tonga, Turkmenistan, Tuvalu, United Kingdom, United States, Vanuatu, Vietnam.

ESCWA: Economic and Social Commission for West Asia, 1974
Purposes
United Nations initiative. To undertake or to support studies on economic and social perspectives in the region, to collect and to diffuse the information, and to offer consulting services. The main work of the ESCWA is being led in collaboration with other members of the UN.
Members
Bahrain, Egypt, Iraq, Jordan, Kuwait, Lebanon, Oman, Palestine Authority, Qatar, Saudi Arabia, Syria, United Arab Emirates, Yemen.

Rio Group, 1986
Purposes
Forum dealing with political and development problems of external relations and issues of regional integration.
Members
Argentina, Bolivia, Brazil, Chile, Colombia, Ecuador, Mexico, Panama, Paraguay, Peru, Uruguay, Venezuela.

Planispheres

Pablo Medina Lockhart (ULB)

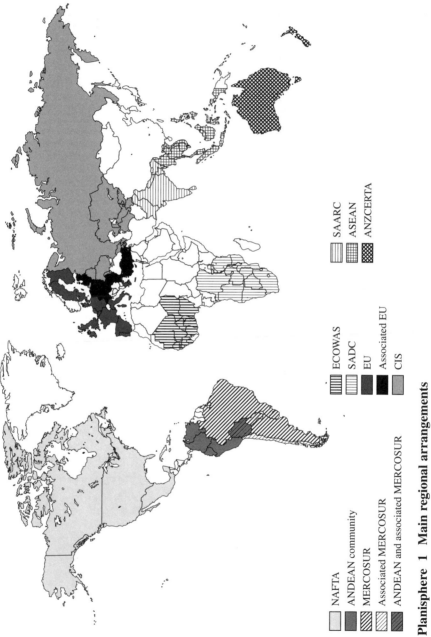

Planisphere 1 Main regional arrangements

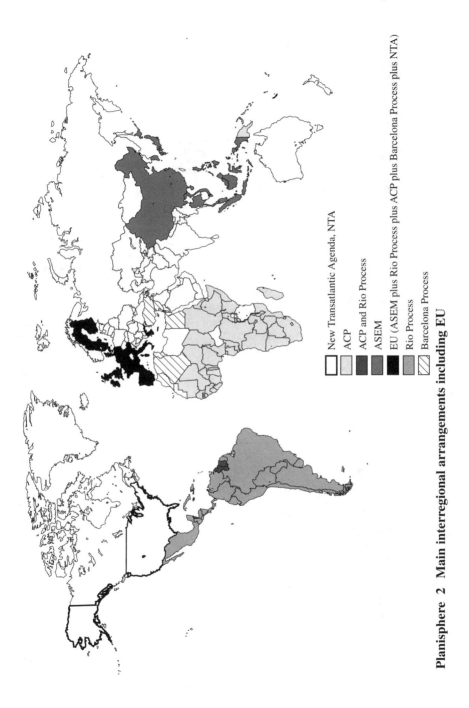

Planisphere 2 Main interregional arrangements including EU

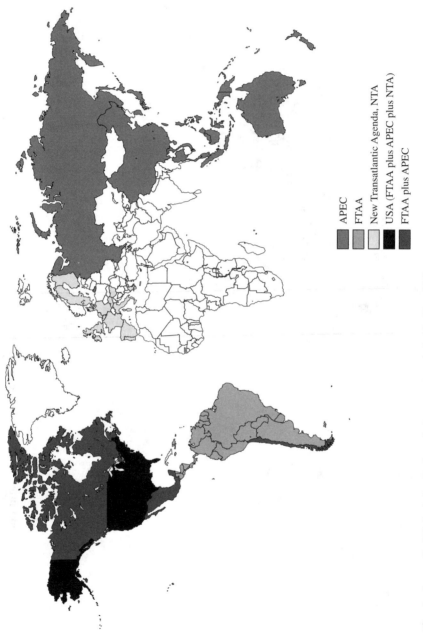

Planisphere 3 Main interregional arrangements including US

APEC

FTAA

New Transatlantic Agenda, NTA

USA (FTAA plus APEC plus NTA)

FTAA plus APEC

Bibliography

Acharya, Amitav (1997), Ideas, Identity and Institution-building: From the "ASEAN way" to the "Asia-Pacific way", in *Pacific Review*, vol. 10, no. 3, Department of Politics and International Studies, University of Warwick.

Aggarwal, Vinod (1994), Comparing Regional Cooperation Efforts in the Asia–Pacific and North America, in Andrew Mack and John Ravenhill, eds, *Pacific Cooperation: Building Economic and Security Regimes in the Asia–Pacific Region*, Allen and Unwin, St Leonards, New South Wales.

Albert, Michel (1991), *Capitalisme contre capitalisme,* Seuil, Paris.

Alesina, A. and Grilli, V. (1993), On the Feasibility of a One-Speed or Multi-Speed European Monetary Union, in *Economics and Politics*, vol. 5.

Algieri, Franco (1998), The EU's Asia Strategy – A Multiple Misnomer, in *EU CFSP Forum*, IEP, Bonn, 2.

Aliboni, R. (1990) *Southern European Security*, Pinder, London.

Allen, D. and Smith, M. (1990), Western Europe's Presence in the Contemporary International Arena, in *Review of International Affairs*, no. 16, 1990, pp.19–37.

Alter, Karen J. (1998), Who Are the "Masters of the Treaty"? European Governments and the European Court of Justice, in *International Organization*, vol. 52, no. 1, Winter, pp. 121–47.

Amato, Giuliano and Batt, Jud (1999), *Long-Term Implications of EU Enlargement: the Nature of the New Border,* Robert Schuman Centre, Florence.

Amin, Samir (1997), *Capitalism in the Age of Globalization*, Asterios, Trieste

Andersen, Svein S. and Eliassen, Kjell A., eds (1993), *Making Policy in Europe: The Europeification of National Policy-making*, Sage, London.

Anderson, Benedict (1987), *Imagined Communities*, Verso, London.

Anderson, James. and Goodman, J. (1995), Regions, States and the European Union: Modernist Reaction or Postmodernist Adaptation?, in *Review of International Political Economy,* vol. 2, no. 4, pp. 600–31.

Anderson, M. (1989), *Policing the World: Interpol and the Politics of International Police Cooperation*, Oxford University Press, New York.

Anderson, Perry. (1974), *Lineages of the Absolutist State*, Verso, London.

Andorka, R. (1995), The development of poverty during the transformation process, manuscript, University of Economic Sciences, Budapest.

Archibugi, Daniele, Held David and Koehler, M., eds. (1998), *Re-imagining Political Community. Studies in Cosmopolitan Democracy,* Polity, Cambridge.

Aron, Raymond (1998), L'Europe face à la crise des sociétés industrielles, in *L'Europe? L'Europe*, texts collected by Pascal Ory, Omnibus, Paris.

Axelrod, R. and Keohane, R. O. (1986), Achieving Cooperation under Anarchy: Strategies and Limitations, in K. A. Oye, ed., *Cooperation under Anarchy*, Princeton University Press.

Ayoob, Mohammed and Samudavanija Chai-Anan (1989), Leadership and Security in Southeast Asia: Exploring General Propositions, in M. Ayoob and Samudvanija Chai-Anan, *Leadership Perceptions and National Security: The SE Asian Experience,* Routledge, London.

Badie, Bertrand (1999), *Un monde sans souveraineté. Les Etats entre ruse et responsabilité,* Fayard, Paris.

Balassa, Bela (1961), *The Theory of Economic Integration,* Greenwood, London.

Baldwin, Richard (1993), *A Domino Theory of Regionalism,* CEPR Discussion Paper 732, Centre for Economic Policy Research, London.

Baldwin, R. (1994), *Toward an Integrated Europe,* CEPR, London.

Baldwin, Richard (1998), Le cause del regionalismo, in P. Padoan, ed., *Globalizzazione e regionalismo, Europa/Europe,* n. 6., pp.83–111, Rome.

Baldwin, Richard and Venables, Anthony (1994), Regional Economic Integration, in Gene Grossman and Kenneth Rogoff, eds, *Handbook of International Economics,* vol. 3, North Holland, Amsterdam.

Barahona de Brito, Alexandra (1997), Condicionalidade politica e cooperação para a promoção da democracia e dos direitos humanos, in *Além do Comercio,* IEEI, Lisbon.

Barber, Benjamin, R. (1995), *Jihad vs. McWorld,* Times Books, New York.

Barro, R. and Sala-i-Martin, X. (1991), Convergence Across States and Regions, in *Brookings Papers on Economic Activity,* 1, pp. 107–58.

Bauman, Zygmunt (1998), *Globalization. The Human Consequences,* Polity Press, Cambridge.

Baylis, J. and Smith, S. eds, (1997), *The Globalization of World Politics,* Oxford University Press, Oxford.

Bayoumi, Tamil (1994), *A Formal Model of Optimum Currency Areas,* CEPR Discussion Paper 968, Centre for Economic Policy Research, London.

Ben-David, D. (1995), *Trade and Convergence Among Countries,* CEPR Discussion Paper Series 1126, Centre for Economic Policy Research, London.

Bensidoun, I. and Chevallier, A. (1996), *Europe-Méditerranée: le pari de l'ouverture,* Economia-CEPII, Paris.

Berg, E. (1988), *Regionalism and Economic Development in Sub-Saharan Africa,* USAID,Washington DC.

Berger, Susan and Dore, R. (1996), *National Diversity and Global Capitalism,* Cornell University Press, Ithaca.

Bergsten, Fred (1996), Globalizing Free Trade, in *Foreign Affairs,* n. 3.

Bergsten, Fred (1997), *Open Regionalism,* Working Paper, Institute for International Economics, Washington DC.

Bernard, Mitchell and Ravenhill, John (1995), Beyond Product Cycles and Flying Geese: Regionalization, Hierarchy and the Industrialization of East Asia, in *World Politics,* vol. 47, no. 2, pp.171–209.

Bertrand, G., Michalski, A. and Pench, L. R. (European Commission, Forward Studies Unit) (1999), *Scenarios Europe 2010. Five Possible Futures for Europe*, Working Paper.

Bhagwati, Jagdish (1991), *The World Trading System at Risk,* Princeton University Press, Princeton.

Bhagwati, Jagdish (1993), Regionalism and Multilateralism: An Overview, in Ross Garnaut and Peter Drysdale, eds, *Asia Pacific Regionalism: Readings in International Economic Relations*, Harper Educational/ANU, Pymble.

Bhagwati, Jagdish and Arvind, P. (1996), Preferential Trading Areas and Multilateralism: Stranger, Friends or Foes? in J. Bhagwati and A. Panagariya, eds, *Free Trade Areas or Free Trade?*, AEI Press, Washington DC.

Bhagwati, Jagdish, Haass, R., Litan, R., Lincoln, E. M. and Bouton, M. (1998), Can Asia Recover?, articles published in *Foreign Affairs*, May/June 1998, vol. 77, n. 3.

Bhattacharaya, A., Montiel, P. and Sharma, S. (1996), Private Capital Flows to Sub-Saharan Africa: An Overview of Trends and Determinants, mimeo, International Monetary Fund, Washington DC.

Bobbio, Norberto (1981), Stato potere, governo, in *Enciclopedia Einaudi*, vol. XIII, Einaudi, Turin.

Bobbio, Norberto (1998), *Etat et démocratie internationale*, Complexe, Brussels, ed. by M. Telò (translated by Vogel, Magnette and Giovannini).

Bomber, E. (1994), Policy Network on the Periphery, in *Regional Politics and Policy*, vol. 4, pp.45–61.

Boren D. L., and Perkins, E. J. eds (1999), *Preparing America's Foreign Policy for the 21st Century*, University of Oklaoma Press, Oklahoma.

Bova, Russell (1994), Political Dynamics of the Post-Communist Transition: A Comparative Perspective, in: *World Politics*, 44, S. 113–138.

Boyd, Gavin (1997), Regional Economic Cooperation: EU, NAFTA, and APC, in Gavin Boyd and Alan Rugman, eds, *Euro-Pacific Investment and Trade: Strategies and Structural Interdependencies*, Edward Elgar, Cheltenham.

Boyer, Robert, et al. (1997), *Mondialisation. Au delà des mythes*, La Découverte, Paris.

Braudel, Fernand (1949/1972), *The Mediterranean and the Mediterranean World in the Reign of Philip II*, 2 vols, Fontana, London.

Bressand, A. and Nicolaidis, K. (1990), Regional Integration in a Networked World Economy, in William Wallace, ed., *The Dynamics of European Integration*, Pinter, London.

Brewer, A. (1990), *Marxist Theories of Imperialism*, Macmillan, London.

British Petroleum (various years: published annually), *BP Statistical Review of World Energy*, British Petroleum plc, London.

Buchanan, James (1965), The Economic Theory of Clubs, in *Economica*, vol. 37, pp.1–14.

Bull, Hedley (1977), *The Anarchical Society*, Macmillan, London.

Bull, Hedley (1982), Civilian Power Europe: A Contradiction in Terms? in *Journal of Common Market Studies*, n. 1/2, pp.149–164.

Bulmer, Simon (1994a), The Governance of the European Union: A New Institutionalist Approach, in *Journal of Public Policy*, vol. 13, no. 4, pp.351–80.

Bulmer, Simon (1994b), Institutions and Policy Change in the European Communities: The Case of Merger Control, in *Public Administration*, vol. 72, pp.423–44.

Buzan, Barry (1991), New Patterns of Global Security in the Twenty-First Century, in *Foreign Affairs*, vol. 67, no. 3, pp.431–51.

Cai, Penghong (1992), The Fourth ASEAN Summit Talk and its Influence over Regional Economic Cooperation, in *Asia–Pacific Economic Review*, no. 2, pp. 16–18.

Calleya, S. (1997), *Navigating Regional Dynamics in a Post-Cold War World*, Dartmouth, Aldershot.

Caporaso, James and Keeler J. (1993), The EC and Regional Integration Theory, paper presented at the Conference of the ECSA, May 1993, Washington DC.

Cardoso, Fernando Henrique (1998), speech delivered at the closing session of the Fifth Euro-Latin American Forum, IEEI, Lisbon.

Carr, Edward H. (1946), *The Twenty Years Crisis 1919–1939*, Macmillan, London.

Casella, Alessandra and Feinstein, James (1990), *Public Goods in Trade: On the Formation of Markets and Political Jurisdictions*, NBER Working Paper 3554.

Castells, Manuel (1996), *The rise of the network society*, Blackwell Publishers, Cambridge, MA.

Cavalcanti, Geraldo H. (1990), As opções da América Latina face às transformações de hoje, speech delivered at the First Euro-Latin American Forum, Federação das Indústrias do Estado de São Paulo (FIESP) and IEEI, São Paulo.

CEC (1996), *Creating a New Dynamic in EU–ASEAN Relations*, report from the Commission of the European Communities, COM (96) 314 final.

Cerny, Philip G. (1990), *The changing architecture of politics: Structure, agency, and the future of the state*, Sage, London.

Cerny, Philip G (2000), Restructuring the political arena: Globalization and the paradoxes of the competition state, in *Globalization and its critics: Perspectives from political economy*, Randall D. Germain, ed., Macmillan/St. Martin's Press, Basingstoke/New York.

Cerutti, Furio (1997), Identität und Politik, in *International Zeitschrift für Philosophie*, no. 2.

Cerutti, Furio, ed. (2000), *Gli occhi sul mondo*, Carocci, Florence.

Chalermpalanupap, Termsak (1997), *Enlargement of ASEAN: Prospects for Closer Regional Cooperation*, paper presented to the international conference "ASEAN at the Crossroads: Opportunities and Challenges", Malaysian Institute of Economic Research, November 1997, Kuala Lumpur.

Chirac, Jacques (1997), speech delivered to the Congress of the Federal Republic of Brazil, 12 March 1997, Brasilia.

Cho, Yong-sang and Chung, Chong-tae (1997), ASEM's Hopes and Apprehensions: An Interregional Organization in the 21st Century, paper presented to the International Political Science Association at the 17th World Congress, August 1997, Seoul.

Chourou, B. (1998), The Free-Trade Agreement between Tunisia and the European Union, in *Journal of North African Studies*, vol. 3, no. 1, Spring.

Clarck, Ian (1997), *Globalization and Fragmentation. International Relations in the Twentieth Century*, Oxford University Press, Oxford.

Cohen, Benjamin J. (1993), Beyond EMU: The Problem of Sustainability, in *Economics and Politics*, vol.5

Coleman, W. D. and Underhill, G. R. D. (1998), *Regionalism and Global Economic Cooperation*, Routledge, London.

Collier, Paul and Gunning, J. (1996), Trade Liberalization and the Composition of Investment: Theory and an African Application, WPS/96–4, Centre for the Study of African Economies, University of Oxford, Oxford.

Collier, Paul and Gunning, J. (1999), Explaining African Economic Performance, in *Journal of Economic Literature*, vol. 37, pp.64–111.

Collignon, S. (1997), *European Monetary Union, Convergence and Sustainability* (The Sustainability Report), AUME, Paris.

Collinson, S. (1996), *From Shore to Shore*, Royal Institute of International Affairs, London.

Commission Européenne (1997), *L'avenir des relations Nord-Sud*, Les cahiers de la cellule de Prospective, Bruxelles.

Commission on Global Governance (1995), *Our Global Neighbourhood*, Oxford University Press, New York.

Cooper, Richard (1994), World-wide Regional Integration: Is There an Optimal Size of the Integrated Area?, in Ross Garnaut and Peter Drysdale, eds, *Asia Pacific Regionalism: Readings in International Economic Relations*, Harper Educational/ANU, Pymble.

Cooper, Richard (1997), *The Postmodern State*, Demos, London.

Cornes, James and Sandler, Todd (1985), *The Theory of Externalities, Public Goods and Club Goods*, Cambridge University Press, Cambridge.

Cox, Robert W. (1996), *Approaches to World Order*, Cambridge University Press, Cambridge.

Cox, Robert W. ed. (1997), *The New Realism. Perspectives on Multilateralism and World Order*, United Nations University Press, Tokyo, New York, Paris.

CREFSA (1997), The South-East Asian Crisis and Implications for South Africa, in *Quarterly Review*, October, Centre for Research into Economics and Finance in Southern Africa, London School of Economics, London.

Crouch, Colin and Streeck, Wolfgang, eds. (1997), *Political Economy of Modern Capitalism. Mapping Convergence and Diversity*, Sage, London.

Cumings, Bruce (1984), The Origins and Development of the Northeast Asian Political Economy: Industrial Sectors, Product Cycles, and Political Consequences, in *International Organization*, no. 38, pp.1–40.

Decaluwé, B., Njinkeu, D. and Bela, L. (1995), UDEAC Case Study, paper presented at the AERC workshop on Regional Integration and Trade Liberalization, Harare.

de Grauwe, Paul (1992), *European Monetary Integration*, Oxford University Press, Oxford.

Delanty, Gerard (1995), *Inventing Europe: Idea, Identity, Reality*, Macmillan, Basingstoke.

de Melo, Jaime, Panagariya, A. and Rodrik, D. (1993), The New Regionalism: A Country Perspective, in J. de Melo and A. Panagariya, eds., *New Dimensions in Regional Integration*, Cambridge University Press, Cambridge.

de Senarclens, Pierre (1998), *Mondialisation, souveraineté et théorie des relations internationales*, Colin, Paris.

Deutsch, Karl, Burrell, S. and Kan, R. A. (1957), *Political Community in the North Atlantic Area*, Princeton University Press, Princeton.

de Wilde d'Estmael, T. (1998), *La dimension politique des relations économiques extérieures de la Communauté européenne, Sanctions et incitants économiques comme moyens de politique étrangère*, Bruylant, Bruxelles.

Dollar, D. (1992), Outward-oriented Developing Economies Really Do Grow More Rapidly: Evidence from 95 LDCs, 1976–1985, in *Economic Development and Cultural Change*, vol. 40, no. 2, pp.523–44.

Dowrick, S. and Nguyen, D. (1989), OECD Comparative Economic Growth 1950–1985: Catch-up and Convergence, in *American Economic Review*, vol. 79, no. 5, pp.1010–30.

Duchêne, François (1972), *Europe's Role in World Peace*, in: R. Mayne, ed., *Europe Tomorrow. Sixteen Europeans Look Ahead*, Fontana, London.

Duchêne, F. (1973), The European Community and the Uncertainties of Interdependence, in M. Kohnstamm and W. Hager (1973), *A Nation Writ Large? Foreign Policy Problems before the EC*, Macmillan, London.

Duff, A. (1994), The Main Reforms, in A. Duff, J. Pinder and R. Priye, eds, *Maastricht and Beyond*, Routledge, London.

Durand, Marie-Françoise and Vasconcelos, Alvaro (1998), *La Pesc. Ouvrir l'Europe au Monde*, Presses de Sciences Politiques, Paris.

ECSA World Conference (1998), *The European Union in a Changing World*, European Communities, Brussels.

Edwards, G. and Spence, D. (1995), *The European Commission*, Longman, London.

Edwards, G. and Regelsberger, E. (1990), *Europe Global Links: the EC and Inter-Regional Cooperation*, St Martin's Press, New York.

Edwards, S. (1993), Openness, Trade Liberalization and Growth in Developing Countries, in *Journal of Economic Literature*, vol. 31, no. 3, pp.1358–93.

Eichengreen, B. (1994), *International Monetary Arrangements for the 21st Century*, Brookings Institution, Washington DC.

EIU (1997) European Policy Analyst: Key Issues and Developments for Business, *Regional Monitor*, Economist Intelligence Unit, first quarter 1997.

Eizenstat, Stuart E. (1997), Our Future Trade Agenda, remarks before the House of Representatives, 24 September 1997.

Elbadawi, I. (1995), 'The Impact of Regional Trade/Monetary Integration Schemes on Intra-Sub-Saharan African Trade', paper presented at the AERC workshop on Regional Integration and Trade Liberalisation, Harare.

Eliassen, Kjell, A., ed. (1998), *Foreign and Security Policy in the EU*, Sage, London.

Ellwood, D. W. (1992) *Rebuilding Europe*, Longman, London.

Emerson, M. (1998) *Redrawing the Map of Europe*, Macmillan, London.

European Commission (1994), *The Economic Situation of the MENA Countries*, COM 94.

European Commission (1997) *Agenda 2000*, Brussels.

Eurostat (1996), *Statistics in Focus: Population and Social Conditions*, no. 6, Luxembourg.

Evans, Paul. M. (1994), The Dialogue Process on Asia Pacific Security Issues: Inventory and Analyses, in Paul M. Evans, ed., *Studying Asia Pacific Security*, University of Toronto–York University Joint Centre for Asia Pacific Studies and Centre for Strategic and International Studies, Toronto and Jakarta.

Fawcett, Louise and Hurrell, Andrew, eds (1995), *Regionalism in World Politics: Regional Organization and International Order*, Oxford University Press, Oxford.

Feldstein, Martin (1988), Distinguished Lecture on Economics in Government: Thinking about International Economic Coordination, *Journal of Economic Perspectives*, vol. 2, no. 2, pp.3–13.

Fine, J. and Yeo, S. (1994), *Regional Integration in Sub-Saharan Africa: Dead End or Fresh Start?*, mimeo, African Economic Research Consortium, Nairobi.

Fischer, Jens (1999), *Eurasismus*, Nomos-Verlag, Baden-Baden.

Fonseca, Gelson (1998), *A Legitimidade e outras questoes internacionais*, Paz e terra, Sao Paulo.

Foroutan, F. (1993), Regional Integration in Sub-Saharan Africa: Past Experiences and Future Prospects, in J. de Melo and A. Panagariya, eds, *New Dimensions in Regional Integration*, Cambridge University Press, Cambridge.

Fratianni, M. (1995), *Variable Interpretation in the EU*, mimeo, Indiana University, Indiana.

Fratianni, M. and Pattison, J. (1982), *The Economics of International Organisations*, Kyklos.

Frey, Bruno (1984), *International Political Economics*, Basil Blackwell, New York.

Froot, K. and Yoffie, D. (1991), Strategic Policies in a Tripolar World, in *The International Spectator*, n.3.

Fukuyama, Francis (1992), The End of History, *The National Interest*, Summer.

Fukuyama, Francis (1993), *The End of History and the Last Man*, Hamish Hamilton, London.

Furuki, Toshiaki (1998), *European Integration and the World-System*, ISS Chuo University papers, n. 3, Tokyo.

Gallant, Nicole and Stubbs, Richard (1996), Asia–Pacific Business Activity and Regional Institution-Building, in J. Greenwood and H. Jacek, eds, *Organized Business and the New Global Order*, Macmillan, London.

Galtung, Johan (1973), *The European Community: A Superpower in the Making*, Allen and Unwin, London.

Gamble, Andrew (1993), Shaping a New World Order, in *Government and Opposition*, vol. 28, no. 3, pp.325–38.

Gamble, Andrew (1997), Politics 2000, in P. Dunleavy, A. Gamble, I. Holliday and G. Peele, eds, *Developments in British Politics*, Macmillan, London.

Gamble, Andrew and Payne, A., eds. (1996), *Regionalism and World Order*, Macmillan, London.

GAO (1993), *North American Free Trade Agreement: Assessment of Major Issues*, vol. 2, Sept., US Government General Accounting Office, Washington DC.

GAO (1997), *North American Free Trade Agreement: Impacts and Implementation*, statement of Jay Etta Z. Hecker, Associate Director, International Relations and Trade Issues, National Security and International Affairs Division, testimony before the Subcommittee on Trade, Committee on Ways and Means, House of Representatives, 11 September, US Government General Accounting Office, Washington DC.

Garnaut, Ross and Drysdale, Peter, eds (1993), *Asia Pacific Regionalism: Readings in International Economic Relations*, Harper Educational/ANU, Pymble.

Garrett, Geoffrey, Kelemen, R. Daniel and Schulz, Heiner (1998), The European Court of Justice, National Governments, and Legal Integration in the European Union, in *International Organization*, vol. 52, no. 1, Winter, p.149.

Ghanem, S. (1986), *The Pricing of Libyan Crude Oil*, Adams, Malta.

Gilbreath, Jan and Tonra, John Benjamin (1994), The Environment: Unwelcome Guest at the Free Trade Party, in M. Delal Baer and Sidney Weintraub, eds, *The NAFTA Debate: Grappling with Unconventional Trade Issues*, Lynne Rienner, Boulder, CO, pp.53–96.

Gill, Ranjit (1998), *Asia under Siege: How the Asian Miracle Went Wrong*, Epic Management Services, Singapore.

Gills, B. K. (1997), East Asian Development in World Historical Perspective: Ascent, Descent, Ascent, paper presented to International Political Science Association at the XVIIth World Congress, August, Seoul.

Gilpin, R. (1970), in R. O. Keohane and J. Nye, *Transnational Relations and World Politics*, Harvard University Press, Cambridge.

Gilpin, R. (1981), *War and Change in World Politics*, Cambridge University Press, Cambridge.

Gilpin, R. (1987), *The Political Economy of International Relations*, Princeton University Press, Princeton.

Ginsberg, Roy (1999), Conceptualizing the European Union as an International Actor: Narrowing the Theoretical Capability–Expectations Gap, in *Journal of Common Market Studies*, vol. 37, n.3, pp.429–54.

Gnesotto, Nicole (1998), *La puissance et l'Europe*, Presses de Sciences Po, Paris.

Goldstein, Judith (1996), International Law and Domestic Institutions: Reconciling North American "Unfair" Trade Laws, in *International Organization*, vol. 50, no. 4, Autumn, pp.541–64.

Goldthorpe, J. H. ed. (1984), *Order and Conflict in Contemporary Capitalism*, Oxford University Press, Oxford.

Golebiowski, Janusz, ed. (1995), *Poland, Germany, Russia: Perspectives on Collaboration*, University of Warszawa, Warszawa.

Gompert, D.C and Larrabee, S., eds. (1997), *America and Europe: A Partnership for a new Era*: Cambridge University Press/RAND Corporation, Cambridge.

Gowa, Johanne and Mansfield, E. (1993), Power Politics and International Trade, in *American Political Science Review*, vol. 87.

Gowan, Peter and Anderson P., eds. (1997), *The Question of Europe*, Verso, London.

Gramsci, Antonio (1975), *Quaderni del carcere*, Einaudi, Torino.

Gray, John (1998), *False Dawn. The Delusions of Global Capitalism*, Granta Publications.

Grayson, George W. (1995), *The North American Free Trade Agreement: Regional Community and the New World Order*, University Press of America, New York.

Greenwood, J. (1997) *Representing Interests in the EU*, Macmillan, London.

Grieco, Joseph M. (1997), Systemic Sources of Variations in Regional Institutionalization in Western Europe, East Asia and the Americas, in E. D. Mansfield and H. Milner eds., *The Political Economy of Regionalism*, pp.164–187, Columbia University Press, New York.

Grossman, G. and Helpman, E. (1991), *Innovation and Growth in the World Economy*, MIT Press, Cambridge MA.

Grossman, G. and Helpman, E. (1994), Protection for Sale, in *American Economic Review*, vol. 84.

Grossman, G. and Helpman, E. (1996), Sunk Costs and Liberalization Policies, in *European Economic Review*, May.

Guéhenno, Jean-Marie (1998), The Impact of Globalisation on Strategy, paper delivered at the 40th Annual Conference of the International Institute for Strategic Studies, Oxford, 3–6 September 1998.

Guerrieri, Paolo. and Padoan, P. C., eds (1988), *The Political Economy of International Cooperation*, Croom Helm, London.

Guerrieri, Paolo and Padoan, P. C. eds. (1989), *The Political Economy of European Integration: Markets, States and Institutions*, Wheatsheaf, Brighton.

Guerrieri, Paolo and Scharree, Hans-Eckart, eds. (2000), *Global Governance, Regionalism and the International Economy*, Nonos-Verlag, Baden-Baden.

Haas, Ernst, B. (1958), *The Uniting of Europe. Political, Economic and Social Forces*, Stanford University Press, Stanford.

Haas, Ernst B. (1964), *Beyond the Nation-State:Functionalism and International Organization*, University Press, Stanford.

Haas, Ernst, B. (1975), *The Obsolescence of Regional Integration Theory*, Institute of International Studies, Berkeley, California.

Habermas, Juergen (1996), *Kant's Idee des ewigen Friedens aus dem historischen Abstand von 200 Jahren*, Suhrkamp Verlag, Frankfurt.

Habermas, Juergen (1999), Der Europäische Nationalstaat unter dem Druck der Globalisierung, in *Blaetter fuer Deutsche und internationale Politik*, n.4.

Haggard, Stephan (1997), Regionalism in Asia and the Americas in E.D. Mansfield and H. Miller, eds, *The Political Economy of Regionalism*, Columbia University Press, New York.

Hall, J. (1996), *International Orders*, Polity Press, Cambridge.

Hampden-Turner, C. and Trompenaars, A. (1993) *The Seven Cultures of Capitalism*, Doubleday, New York.

Hanks, P. (1986), *Collins English Dictionary*, Collins, Glasgow.

Harvey, D. (1989), *The Condition of Post Modernity*, Blackwell, Oxford.

Heclo, Hugh (1978), Issue Networks and the Executive Establishment, in A. King, ed., *The New American Political System*, American Enterprise Institute, Washington DC.

Held, David (1995), *Democracy and the Global Order*, Stanford University Press, Stanford.

Henderson, Callum (1998), *Asia Falling? Making Sense of the Asian Currency Crisis and its Aftermath*, McGraw-Hill, Singapore.

Henning, R. (1996), Europe's Monetary Union and the United States, in *Foreign Policy*, Spring.

Hernandez, Carolina G. (1996), Controlling Asia's Armed Forces, in L. Diamond and M. Plattner, eds, *Civil–Military Relations and Democracy*.

Hess, A. C. (1978), *The Forgotten Frontiers: A History of the Sixteenth-Century Ibero-African Frontier*, University of Chicago Press, Chicago.

Hess, R. (2000), Constraints on Foreign Direct Investment, in C. Jenkins, J. Leape and L. Thomas, eds, *Gaining from Trade in Southern Africa: Complementary Policies to Underpin the SADC Free Trade Area*, Macmillan, London.

Hettne, Björn (1999), The new regionalism: A prologue, in Björn Hettne, András Inotai and Osvaldo Sunkel, eds, *Globalism and the new regionalism*, Macmillan/ St. Martin's Press, Basingstoke/New York.

Higgott, Richard (1995), Economic Cooperation in the Asia Pacific: A Theoretical Comparison with the European Union, in *Journal of European Public Policy*, vol. 2, no. 3, pp. 361–83.

Higgott, Richard (1997), Globalization, Regionalization and Localization: Political Economy, the State and Levels of Governance, paper presented to the 25th Joint Sessions of Workshops of the European Consortium for Political Research, February–March, Bern.

Higgott, Richard and Reich, S. (1998), *Globalization and Sites of Conflict: Towards Definition and Taxonomy*, GSGR working paper 3.

Hill, Christopher (1993), The Capability–Expectations Gap, or Conceptualizing Europe's International Role, *Journal of Common Market Studies*, no. 3, Sept.

Hill, Christopher, ed, (1996), *The Actors in Europe's Foreign Policy*, Routledge, London and New York.

Hirst, Paul, and Thompson, Grahame (1996), *Globalization in Question: the International Economy and the Possibilities of Governance*, Polity Press, Cambridge, UK and Cambridge, MA.

Hirst, Monica (1995), A dimensão politica do Mercosul: especificadades nacionais, aspectos institucionais e actores sociais, in *Integração Aberta*, Euro-Latin American Forum/IEEI, Lisbon.

Hix, Simon (1994), The Study of European Community: The Challenges of Comparative Politics, in *West European Politics*, vol. 17, no. 1, pp.1–30.

Hobsbawm, Eric (1994), *Age of Extremes: The Short Twentieth Century 1914–1991*, Abacus, London.

Hoekman, B. (1998), Free Trade Agreements in the Mediterranean: A Regional Path towards Liberalization?, in G. Joffé, ed., *Perspectives on Development: the Euro-Mediterranean Partnership Initiative, Journal of North African Studies* special issue, vol. 3, no. 2, Summer, Cass, London.

Hoffmann, Stanley, Keohane, R. and Nye, J. S. eds (1993), *After the Cold War, International Institutions and State Strategies in Europe. 1989–1991*, Harvard University Press, Cambridge.

Hofstede, Geert (1980), *Culture's Consequences: International Differences in Work-Related Values*, Sage, Beverly Hills, CA.

Hofstede, G. (1994), *Cultures and Organizations: Intercultural Cooperation and its Importance for Survival*, Harper Collins, New York.

Holland, Martin, ed. (1997), *Common Foreign and Security Policiy. The Record and Reforms*, Pinter, London.

Holland, K. M. (1994), NAFTA and the Single European Act, in T. D. Mason and A. M. Turay, eds, *Japan, NAFTA and Europe: Trilateral Cooperation or Confrontation?*, St Martin's Press, New York.

Hunt, D. (1998), Development Economics: The Washington Consensus and the Euro-Mediterranean Partnership, in G. Joffé, ed., *Perspectives on Development: the Euro-Mediterranean Partnership Initiative, Journal of North African Studies* special issue, vol. 3, no. 2, Summer, Cass, London.

Huntington, Samuel P. (1993), The Third Wave: Democratization in the Late Twentieth Century, Norman, Oklahoma.

Huntington, Samuel P. (1993), The Clash of Civilisation?, in *Foreign Affairs*, vol. 72, no. 3, pp.22–49.

Huntington, Samuel P. (1996) *The Clash of Civilizations and the Remaking of World Order*, Simon and Schuster, New York.

Hurrell, Andrew (1995), Regionalism in Theoretical Perspective, in Louise Fawcett and Andrew Hurrell, eds, *Regionalism in World Politics: Regional Organization and International Order*, Oxford University Press, Oxford.

Hyde, G. V. and Price, Adrian G. V. (1994), Democratization in Eastern Europe: the External Dimension, in: Geoffrey Pridham and Tatu Vanhanen, eds, *Democratization in Eastern Europe*, London/New York.

IEEI (1998), Report of the Fifth Euro-Latin American Forum, *Setting Global Rules*, Lisbon.

ILO (1995), *World Labour Report 1995*, International Labour Organization, Geneva.

IMF (1988), *International Financial Statistics: Supplement on Trade Statistics*, International Monetary Fund, Washington DC.

IMF (1995), *International Financial Statistics Yearbook 1995*, International Monetary Fund, Washington DC.

IMF (1996), *Direction of Trade Statistics Quarterly*, September, International Monetary Fund, Washington DC.

IMF (1997), *Direction of Trade Statistics Yearbook*, Washington DC.

IMF (1997), *World Economic Outlook*, May, International Monetary Fund, Washington DC.

Inglehart, Ronald and Abramson, P. A. (1995), *Value Change in a Global Perspective*, University of Michigan Press, Michigan.

IRELA (1998), *European Direct Investment in Latin America*, Madrid.

IRELA (1998), *Latin America at the Brink? Effects on the Global Finance Crisis*, Madrid.

Jaguaribe, Helio (1996), Uma nova concepção de segurança para o Brasil, in *Estrategia: Revista de Estudos Internacionais*, nos. 8–9, Lisbon.

Jaguaribe, Helio (1998), *Mercosul e as alternativas para a ordem mundial*, Instituto de Estudos Politicos e Sociais, Rio de Janeiro.

Jameson, F. (1984), Postmodernism, or the Cultural Logic of Late Capitalism, in *New Left Review*, no. 146, pp.53–92.

Jameson, F. (1989), Marxism and Postmodernism, in *New Left Review*, no. 176, pp. 31–45.

Jenkins, Carolyn (1997), Regional Integration is Not Enough, in *Quarterly Review*, April, Centre for Research into Economics and Finance in Southern Africa, London School of Economics.

Jenkins, Carolyn and Thomas, Lynne (1998), Is Southern Africa Ready for Regional Monetary Integration? in L. Petersson, ed., *Post-Apartheid Southern Africa: Economic Policies and Challenges for the Future*, Routledge, London.

Jenkins, Carolyn and Thomas, Lynne (2000), The Macroeconomic Policy Framework, in C. Jenkins, J. Leape and Lynne Thomas, eds., *Gaining from Trade in Southern Africa: Complementary Policies to Underpin the SADC Free Trade Area*, Macmillan, London.

Jenkins, Carolyn, Leape, J. and Thomas, L. (2000), Gaining from Trade in Southern Africa, in Carolyn Jenkins, J. Leape and L. Thomas, eds, *Gaining from Trade in Southern Africa: Complementary Policies to Underpin the SADC Free Trade Area*, Macmillan, London.

Joffé, Emil George Howard (1997a), Southern Attitudes towards an Integrated Mediterranean Region, in R. Gillespie, ed., *The Euro-Mediterranean Partnership: Political and Economic Perspectives*, Cass, London.

Joffé, Emil George Howard (1997b), Sovereignty in the Developing World, in M. Heiberg, eds, *Subduing Sovereignty*, Pinter, London.

Julien, Ch-A. (1954), *L'Afrique du Nord en marche*, Presses Universitaires de France, Paris.

Kahler, Miles (1995), *Regional Futures and Transatlantic Economic Relations*, Council on Foreign Relations Press, New York.

Katzenstein, Peter (1996), *Regionalism in Comparative Perspective*, working paper no. 1/96, ARENA, Oslo.

Kébabdjian, G. (1999) *Les théories de l'économie politique internationale*, Seuil, Paris.

Kehoe, Timothy J. (1994), Assessing the Economic Impact of North American Free Trade, in M. Delal Baer and Sidney Weintraub, eds, *The NAFTA Debate: Grappling with Unconventional Trade Issues*, Lynne Rienner, Boulder, CO, pp.3–33.

Kennedy, Paul (1987), *The Rise and Fall of the Great Powers*, Random House, London.

Kenwood, G. and Lougheed, A. L. (1992), *The Growth of the International Economy 1820–1990*, 3rd ed., Routledge London.

Keohane, Robert O. (1980), *The Theory of Hegemonic Stability and Changes in International Economic Regimes, 1967–1977*, Westview Press, Boulder.

Keohane, Robert O. (1984), *After Hegemony. Cooperation and Discord in the World Political Economy*, Princeton University Press, Princeton.

Keohane, Robert O., ed. (1986), *Neorealism and its Critics*, Columbia University Press, New York.

Keohane, R. O. and Nye, J. S. (1970), *Transnational Relations and World Politics*, Harvard University Press, Cambridge.

Keohane, R. O. and Nye, J. S. (1989), *Power and Interdependence*, Harper Collins, New York.

Keukelaire, S. (1998), *Het buiterlands beleidvande EU*, Kluven, Deeventer.

Kindleberger, Charles P. (1973), Economic Integration, in *International Economics*, Richard D. Irwin Inc., Illinois.

Kindleberger, Charles. P. (1973), *The World in Depression 1929–1939*, University of California Press, Berkeley.

Kirchner, Emil and Wright, Kevin, eds (1997), Security and democracy in transition societies, Conference Proceedings, Essex 1998, and *Journal of European Integration, Special Issue Problems of Eastern Europe*, no. 2–3.

Kobrin, S. (1996), Back to the Future: Neomedievalism and the Postmodern World Economy, paper presented at the 1996 Annual Meeting of the International Studies Association, San Diego, California, 17 April.

Krasner, D. Stephen, ed. (1983), *International Regimes*, Cornell University Press, Ithaca.

Krishna, K., Ozyildirim, A. and Swanson, N. (1998), *Trade, Investment and Growth: Nexus, Analysis and Prognosis*, Working Paper 6861, National Bureau of Economic Research, Washington DC.

Krugman, Paul (1993a), Regionalism versus Multilateralism: Analytic Notes, in R. Garnaut and P. Drysdale, eds, *Asia Pacific Regionalism: Readings in International Economic Relations*, Harper Educational/ANU, Pymble.

Krugman, Paul (1993b), Regionalism: Some Analytical Notes, in de Melo J., Panagariya, A. and Rodrik, D., eds, *New Dimensions in Regional Integration*, Cambridge University Press, Cambridge.

Krugman, Paul (1994), *Peddling Prosperity*, Norton, New York.

Krugman, Paul (1998), *La mondialisation n'est pas coupable*, La Découverte, Paris.

Kuznets, S. (1966) *Modern Economic Growth*, Yale University Press, Cambridge, MA.

Lafer, Celso (1999), *Comércio Desarmamento Diretos Humanos*, Paz e terra, Sao Paulo.

Lafer, Celso and Fonseca, Gelson, (1995) A problemática da integração num mundo de polaridades indefinidas, in *Integração Aberta*, Euro-Latin American Forum/IEEI, Lisbon.

Lake, D. A. (1999), *Entangling Relations.American Foreign Policy in its Century*, Princeton University Press, Princeton.

Lake, D. A. and Morgan, P. M. (1997), *Regional Orders. Building Security in a New World*, State University Press, Pennsylvania.

Latouche, Serge (1998), *Il mondo ridotto a mercato*, Edizioni Lavoro, Rome.

Laursen, Finn (1991), The EC in the World Context: Civilian Power or Superpower, in *Futures*, pp.747–59.

Lavigne, Marie (1998), *L'intégration des pays d'Europe centrale dans l'économie mondiale: régionalisation ou mondialisation*, papier présenté au colloque OCDE, CEPII, Sept. 1998, Paris.

Lavigne, Marie (1999), *The Economics of Transition. From Socialist Economy to Market Economy*, Macmillan, London.

Lawrence, R. (1996), *Regionalism, Multilateralism and Deeper Integration*, Brookings Institute, Washington DC.

LeClair, Mark S. (1997) *Regional Integration and Global Free Trade: Addressing the Fundamental Conflicts*, Avebury, Aldershot.

Leslie, Peter M. (2000a), The European regional system: a case of unstable equilibrium?, in *Journal of European Integration.The Fuzzy Edges of Community*, edited by Peter Leslie and Charles Pentland, n.23

Leslie, Peter M. (2000b), Abuses of Asymmetry: Privilege and Exclusion, in Karlheinz Neunreither and Antje Wiener, eds, *Amsterdam and Beyond: The European Union on its Way into a Twenty-first Century*.

Lijphart (1994), *Democracies*, Yale University Press, London.

Lim, Robyn (1998), The ASEAN Regional Forum: Building on Sand, in *Contemporary Southeast Asia*, vol. 20, no. 2, pp.115–36.

Little, R. (1989), Deconstructing The Balance of Power: Two Traditions of Thought, in *Review of International Studies*, vol. 15, no. 2, April, pp.92–97.

Lorenz, Ditlev (1992) Economic Geography and the Political Economy of Regionalization: The Example of Western Europe, in *American Economic Review*, vol. 82, no. 2, pp.84–97.

Lowi, Theodore (1967), Making Democracy Save for the World, in J. Rosenau ed., *Domestic Sources of Foreign Policy*, The Free Press, New York, pp.295–331.

Lucas, Michael R. (1998), The CIS and Russia, in: Eric Remacle and Reimund Seidelmann, eds, *Pan-European Security Redefined*, Nomos-Verlag, Baden-Baden, pp.319–351.

Luttwack, George (1990), From Geopolitics to Geoeconomics. Logic of Conflict and Grammar of Commerce, in *National Interest*, Summer.

Maasdorp, G. (2000), Microeconomic policies, in C. Jenkins, J. Leape and L. Thomas, eds, *Gaining from Trade in Southern Africa: Complementary Policies to Underpin the SADC Free Trade Area*, Macmillan, London.

Mackinder, H. (1904), The Geographical Pivot of History, in *Geographical Journal*, vol.23

Mahjoub, A. (1998), Social Feasibility and the Costs of the Free Trade Zone, in G. Joffé, ed., *Perspectives on Development: the Euro-Mediterranean Partnership Initiative*, *Journal of North African Studies*, special issue, vol. 3, no. 2, Summer, Cass, London.

Maier, Charles (1987), *In Search of Stability: Explorations in Historical Political Economy*, Cambridge University Press, Cambridge.

Majone, Giandomenico (1996), *Regulating Europe*, Routledge, London.

Manners, I. J. and Whitman, R. G., International Identity of the EU, in *Journal of European Integration*, no. 3, pp.231–49.

Mansfield, Edward and Branson, Rachel (1994), Alliances, Preferential Trading Arrangements, and International Trade, paper presented at the annual meeting of the American Political Science Association, 1–4 September 1994, New York.

Mansfield, Edward D. and Milner, Helen. V., ed. (1997), *The Political Economy of Regionalism*, Columbia University Press, New York.

Mansfield, Edward D. and Milner, Helene, V. (1997), Introduction, in *The Political Economy of Regionalism*, Columbia University Press, New York.

Marks, J. (1996), High Hopes and Low Motives: The New Euro-Mediterranean Partnership Initiative, in *Mediterranean Politics*, vol. 1, no. 1, Summer, pp.1–24.

Marks, J. (1998), The European Challenge to North African Economies: The Downside to the Euro-Mediterranean Policy, in G. Joffé, ed., *Perspectives on Development: the Euro-Mediterranean Partnership Initiative*, *Journal of North African Studies*, special issue, vol. 3, no. 2, Summer, Cass, London.

Marty, Martin E. and Appleby, R. S. (1991), *Fundamentalisms Observed*, University of Chicago Press, Chicago.

Mattingley, G. (1964), *Renaissance Diplomacy*, Penguin, London.

Mattli, W. (1999), *The Logic of Regional Integration. Europe and Beyond*, Cambridge University Press, Cambridge.

Mattli, Walter and Slaughter, Anne-Marie (1998), Revisiting the European Court of Justice, in *International Organization*, vol. 52, no. 1, Winter.

Mayer, F. (1992), Managing Domestic Differences in International Negotiations: The Strategic Use of Internal Side-Payments, in *International Organization*, vol. 46.

Mayhew, Alan (1998), *Recreating Europe. The EU's Policy towards Central and Eastern Europe*, Cambridge University Press, Cambridge.

Mazey, S. and Richardson, J. eds (1993) *Lobbying in the EC*, Oxford University Press, Oxford.

McSweeney, Dean and Tempest, Clive (1993), The Political Science of Democratic Transition in Eastern Europe, in *Political Studies*, XLI.

Meyer, Thomas (1997), *Identitäts-Wahn: Die Politisierung des kulturellen Unterschieds*, Aufbau, Berlin.

Mezran, K. (1998) Maghrib Foreign Policies and the Internal Security Dimension, in *Journal of North African Studies*, vol. 3, no. 1, Spring, pp. 1–24.

Milner, Helen V. (1995), Regional Economic Cooperation, Global Markets and Domestic Politics: A Comparison of NAFTA and the Maastricht Treaty, in *Journal of European Public Policy*, vol. 2, no. 3, pp. 337–60.

Milner, Helen V. (1997), *Interests, Institutions, and Information*, Princeton University Press, Princeton.

Milward, Alan (1992), *The European Rescue of the Nation State*, Routledge, London.

Missiroli, Antonio (1999), European Security and Defense, the Case for Setting Convergence Criteria, in *European Foreign Affairs Review*, vol 4, pp.485–500.

Mittelman, J. and Falk, R. (1999), Regionalism and Globalization in the Post-Cold War World, in Stephen Calleya, ed., *Regionalism in the Post-Cold War World*, Ashgate, Aldershot.

Montes, Manual F. (1998), *The Currency Crisis in Southeast Asia*, Institute of Southeast Asian Studies, Singapore.

Moravcsik, Andrew, ed. (1998), *Centralization or Fragmentation? Europe Facing the Challenges of Deepening, Diversity and Democracy*, Council of Foreign Relations Press, New York.

Moravcsik, Andrew (1999), *The Choice for Europe: Social Purpose and State Power from Messina to Maastricht*, Cornell University Press, Ithaca.

Mullen, Paul (1998), Legitimate Options: National Courts and the Power of the European Court of Justice, in *ECSA Review*, European Community Studies Association, vol. 11, no. 1, Winter, pp. 2–7.

Murphy, E. (1999), *Economic and Political Development in Tunisia: From Bourguiba to Ben Ali*, British Academic Press, London.

Nairn, Tom (1981), *The Breakup of Britain*, Verso, London.

Nelsen, B. F. and Stubb, A. C-G., eds. (1994), The European Union: Readings on the Theory and Practice of European Integration, in *Cooperation and Conflict*, vol. 28, pp.373–402.

Nohlen, Dieter (1997), Demokratie, in: Dieter Nohlen, Peter Waldmann and Klaus Ziemer, eds, *Lexikon der Politik* Bd 4: *Die östlichen und südlichen Länder*, Beck Verlag, München, pp.118–127 and 122.

OECD (1995), *Services: Statistics on International Transactions*, Organization for Economic Cooperation and Development, Paris.

OECD (1996), *Historical Statistics 1960–1994*, Organization for Economic Cooperation and Development, Paris.

OECD (1997), *Employment Outlook*, June, Organization for Economic Cooperation and Development, Paris.

OECD (1998a), *National Accounts 1960–1996*, vol. 1, Organization for Economic Cooperation and Development, Paris.

OECD (1998b), *Employment Outlook*, June, Paris: Organization for Economic Cooperation and Development, Paris.

OECD (1998c), *Economic Outlook*, June, Organization for Economic Cooperation and Development, Paris.

OECD (1999), *Historical Statistics 1960–1997*, Paris.

OECD (2000), *Economic Outlook*, no. 67, Paris.

Ohmae, Kenichi (1993), The Rise of the Region State, in *Foreign Affairs*, 72, pp.78–87.

Ohmae, Kenichi (1995), *The End of the Nation-state. The Rise of Regional Economies*, HarperCollins, London.

Oliveira Martins, Guilherme (1993), *O enigma Europeu*, Quetzal Editores, Lisbon.

Oliveira Martins, Guilherme and Vasconcelos, Alvaro (1995) A lógica de integração aberta, base de un novo multiregionalismo, *Integração Aberta*, Euro-Latin American Forum, Institute for Strategic and International Studies, IEEI, Lisbon.

Olson, Mancur (1965), *The Logic of Collective Action*, Yale University Press, New Haven.

Oman, Charles (1994), *Globalization and Regionalisation: The Challenge for Developing Countries*, OECD Development Centre, Paris.

Oye, Kenneth., A., ed. (1985), *Cooperation under Anarchy*, Princeton University Press, Princeton.

Oye, Kenneth A. (1992), *Economic Discrimination and Political Exchange*, Princeton University Press, Princeton.

Padoan, Pier Carlo (1997), Regional Agreements as Clubs: The European Case, in Mansfield and Milner.

Padoan Pier Carlo, ed. (1998), Globalizzazione e regionalismo, special issue of *Europa/Europe*, Rome n. 6.

Palmer, Norman D. (1991), *The New Regionalism in Asia and the Pacific*, MA: Lexington Books, Lexington.

Pape, Wolfgang, ed. (1998), *East Asia by the Year 2000 and Beyond: Shaping Factors*, a study for the European Commission, Curzon Press, Surrey.

Peng, Dajin (1997), *An East Asian Model of Regional Economic Cooperation*, Centre for European and Asian Studies, Norwegian School of Management, Oslo.

Perraton, J., Goldblatt, D., Held, D. and McGrew, A. (1997) The Globalization of Economic Activity, in *New Political Economy*, vol. 2, no. 2, pp.257–78.

Perroni, C. and Whalley, J. (1994), *The New Regionalism: Trade Liberalization or Insurance?*, NBER Working Paper 4626.

Petersen, Thomas, (1998), *Realism and Regional Institutionalization. A Theory of Cooperative Hegemony*, paper presented at ISA meeting, Sept. 1998.

Peterson, J. (1992), The European Technology Community: Policy Networks in a Supranational Setting, in D. Marsh and R. Rhodes, eds (1992), *Policy Networks in British Government*, Oxford University Press, Oxford.

Peterson, J. (1995), Decision-making in the European Union: Towards a Framework for Analysis, in *Journal of European Public Policy*, vol. 2, no. 1, pp.69–93

Piazolo, D. (1998), European regionalism and Multilateral Trade Negotiations, in *Journal of European Integration*, vol 21 n. 3, pp.251–271.

Piening, Christopher (1997), *Global Europe. The EU in World Affairs*, Rienner, London.

Poh, Steven (1997), Just Don't Expect a Feast, in *Asia Week*, 25.4.

Polanyi, Karl. (1957) [1944], *The Great Transformation: The Political and Economic Origins of our Time*, Beacon Press: Boston.

Powell, R. (1994), Anarchy in International Relations Theory: The Neorealist-Neoliberal Debate, in *International Organizations*, no. 31, pp.313–44.

Prakash, Aseem and Hart, Jeffrey A. eds (1999) *Globalization and Governance*, Routledge, London and New York.

Putnam, R. (1988), Diplomacy and Domestic Politics: The Logic of Two-Level Games, in *International Organization*, vol. 42.

Regelsberger, Elfriede (1988), EPC in the 1980s: Reaching Another Plateau? in A. Pijpers, Elfriede Regelsberger, and Wolfgang Wessels, eds, *European Political Cooperation in the 1980s: A Common Foreign Policy for Western Europe?*, Martinus Nijhoff, Dordrecht.

Regelsberger, Elfriede (1990), The Dialogue of the EC/Twelve with other regional groups: a New European Identity in the International System? in G. Edwards and E. Regelsberger, eds (1990), *Europe's Global Links: The European Community and Inter-Regional Cooperation*, Pinter, London.

Reich, Robert (1991), *The Work of Nations*, Knopf, New York.

Remacle, Eric and Seidelmann, Reimund, eds (1998), *Pan-European Security Redefined*, Nomos-Verlag, Baden-Baden.

Rhein, E. (1998), Euro-Med Free Trade Area for 2010: Whom Will It Benefit?, in G. Joffé, ed., *Perspectives on Development: the Euro-Mediterranean Partnership Initiative*, *Journal of North African Studies* special issue, vol. 3, no. 2, Summer, Cass, London.

Rhodes, Carolyn, ed. (1998), *The European Union in the World Community*, Lynne Rienner, Boulder, CO.

Rhodes, Carolyn and Mazey, S. (1995), *The State of the European Union: Building a European Polity?* Lynne Rienner, Boulder, CO.

Richardson, Jeremy R. (1995), Actor Based Models of National and EU Policy-making: Policy Communities, Issue Networks and Epistemic Communities, in A. Menon and H. Kassim, eds, *The EU and National Industrial Policy*, Routledge, London.

Richardson, Jeremy R., ed. (1996), *European Union: Power and Policy-making*, Routledge, London.

Richardson, Jeremy R. and Jordan, Grant (1979), *Governing Under Pressure: The Policy Process in a Post-parliamentary Democracy*, Martin Robertson, Oxford.

Risse-Kappen, Thomas, ed. (1995), *Bringing Transnational Relations Back In*, Cambridge University Press, Cambridge.

Rodriguez, F. and Rodrik, D. (1999), *Trade Policy and Economic Growth: A Skeptic's Guide to Cross-national Evidence*, Working Paper 7081, National Bureau of Economic Research, Washington DC.

Rodrik, Dani (1997), *Has Globalization Gone Too Far?*, Institute for International Economics, Washington DC.

Roett, Riordan (1998), *The EU and Mercosur: US Perspectives*, text prepared for the Fifth Euro-Latin American Forum, Lisbon.

Roney, Alex (1995), *EC/EU Fact Book*, Chamber of Commerce and Industry, London.

Rosenau, J. (1995), Governance in the Twenty-First Century, in *Global Governance*, 1, pp.13–43.

Rosenau, J. (2000), A Transformed Observer in a Transforming World, in *Studia Diplomatica, Les théories de R. I. à l'épreuve de l'après-guerre-froide*, edited by C. Rosens, M. Telò and P. Vercauteren, vol. LII, no. 1, pp.4–14.

Rosenau, J. and Czempiel, E. O. eds (1992), *Governance without Government: Order and Change in World Politics*, Cambridge University Press, Cambridge.

Rosencrance, Richard N. (1986), *The Rise of the Trading State: Commerce and Conquest in the Modern World*, Basic Books, NewYork.

Ruggie, John G., ed. (1993), *Multilateralism Matters.The Theory and Praxis of an Institutional Form*, Columbia, New York.

Ruggie, John G. (1993), Territoriality and Beyond: Problematising Modernity in International Relations, in *International Organization*, vol. 47, no. 1, pp.139–74.

Ruggie, John. G. (1996), *Winning the Peace*, Columbia, NewYork.

Ruggie, John G. (1998), *Constructing the World Polity*, Routledge, New York.

Sachs, J. and Warner, A. (1995), Economic Reform and the Process of Global Integration, in W. Brainard and G. Perry, eds, *Brookings Papers on Economic Activity*, 1, pp.1–118.

Sachs, J. and Warner, A. (1997), Sources of Slow Growth in African Economies, in *Journal of African Economies*, vol.6, no.3, pp.335–79.

Sala-i-Martin, X. (1997), I Just Ran Two Million Regressions, in *American Economic Review Papers and Proceedings*, May 1997, vol. 87, no. 2, pp.178–83.

Sandler, Todd and Tschirhart, James (1980), The Economic Theory of Clubs: An Evaluative Survey, in *Journal of Economic Literature*, vol. 18.

Santos, Paulo (1993), The Spatial Implications of Economic and Monetary Union, in *European Economy*, no. 54.

Sapir, André (1998), The Political economy of EC Regionalism, in *European Economic Review*, n. 42, 1998, pp.717–32.

Sbragia, Alberta (1992), Thinking about the European Future: The Uses of Comparison, in Alberta Sbragia, ed., *Euro-politics: Institutions and Policy-making in the 'New' European Community*, Brookings Institution, Washington DC.

Sbragia, Alberta (1996), Environmental Policy, in Helen Wallace and William Wallace, eds, *Policy-making in the European Union*, Oxford University Press, Oxford, pp.235–56.

Sbragia, Alberta (1998), The Transatlantic Relationship: A Case of "Deepening" and "Broadening", in Carolyn Rhodes, ed., *The European Union in the World Community*, Lynne Rienner, Boulder, CO, pp.147–64.

Sbragia, Alberta and Pierre, Jon (2000), The European Union as Coxswain: Governance by Steering, in Jon Pierre, ed., *Debating Governance: Authority, Democracy, and Steering*, Oxford University Press, Oxford and New York.

Scharpf, Fritz W. (1998), *Governing in Europe*, Oxford University Press, Oxford.

Schiavone, Giuseppe, ed. (1989), *Western Europe and South-East Asia. Cooperation or Competition*, Macmillan, London.

Schmitter, Philippe C. (1993), The International Context of Contemporary Democratization, in *Stanford Journal of International Affairs*, n. 2, pp.1–34.

Schmitter, Philippe C. and Terry Karl, Lynn (1995), The Conceptual Travels of Transitologists and Consolidologists: How Far to the East Should They Attempt to Go?, in *Slavic Review*, pp.111–127.

Seidelmann, Reimund, (1992), The Old and New Soviet Threat: the Case for a Grand New Western Strategy towards the Soviet Republic in the 1990s, in Peter Ludlow, ed., *Europe and North America in the 1990s*, CEPS Paper No 52, Brussels, pp.69–88.

Seidelmann, Reimund, ed. (1996), *Crisis Policies in Eastern Europe*, Nomos-Verlag, Baden-Baden.

Seidelmann, Reimund, (1997), NATO's Enlargement as a Policy of Lost Opportunities, in *Journal of European Integration. Special Issue Problems of Eastern Europe*, n. 2–3, pp.233–245.

Seidelmann, Reimund (1998), Amsterdam e la sicurezza europea. Un' opportunità nuova o perduta, in *Europa/Europe*, Rome, n. 1, pp.66–86.

Simon, José Luis (1998), Lessons from Paraguay, in *Open Integration Newsletter*, IEEI, Lisbon.

Sjôstaedt, G. (1977), *The External Role of the EC*, Saxon House, Farnborough.

Smith, Alisdair and Tsoukalis, Loukas (1996), Report on Economic and Social Cohesion, mimeo, College of Europe, Bruges.

Snidal, Duncan (1991), Relative Gains and the Pattern of International Cooperation, in *American Political Science Review.*

Snitwongse, K. (1990), Meeting the Challenges of Changing Southeast Asia, in R. Scalapino, ed., *Regional Dynamics: Security, Political, Economic Issues in the Asia–Pacific Region*, Centre for Strategic and International Studies, Jakarta.

Spencer, C. (1998a), The End of International Enquiries? The UN Eminent Persons Mission to Algeria: July–August 1998, in *Mediterranean Politics*, vol. 3, no. 3, Winter 1998, pp.127–34.

Spencer, C. (1998b), Security Implications of the EMPI for Europe, in G. Joffé, ed., *Perspectives on Development: the Euro-Mediterranean Partnership Initiative, Journal of North African Studies*, special issue, vol. 3, no. 2, Summer 1998, Cass, London.

Stavridis, Stelios et al, eds. (1999),*The Foreign Policies of the EU's Mediterranean States and Applicant Countries in the 1990s*, Macmillan, London.

Steinberg, Richard H. (1997), Trade–Environment Negotiations in the EU, NAFTA, and WTO: Regional Trajectories of Rule Development, in *American Journal of International Law*, vol. 91, no. 2, April 1997, pp.231–67.

Stevens, C. (1997), The EU and South Africa: Slow Progress towards "Free" Trade, in *Quarterly Review*, April 1997, Centre for Research into Economics and Finance in Southern Africa, London School of Economics.

Strange, Susan (1988), *States and Markets. Introduction to International Political Economy*, Pinter, London.

Strange, Susan (1996), *The Retreat of the State. The Diffusion of Power in the World Economy*, Cambridge University Press, Cambridge.

Strekal, Oleg (1999), Nationale Sicherheit der unabhängigen Ukraine (1991–1995). Zur Analyse der Sicherheitslage und der Grundlagen der Sicherheitspolitik eines neu entstandenen Staates, Nomos-Verlag, Baden-Baden.

Suite101.com (1997), Cambodia and ASEAN: A Separation of Economics and Politics, 25 July: see http:www.suite101.com.

Summers, Lawrence H. (1991), Regionalism and the World Trading System, in R. Garnaut, and P. Drysdale, eds, *Asia Pacific Regionalism: Readings in International Economic Relations*, Harper Educational/ANU, Pymble.

Summers, Larry, ed. (1991), *Policy Implications of Trade and Currency Zones*, and particularly, Regionalism and the World Trading System, Federal Reserve Bank of Kansas City, Kansas City.

Summers, Robert. and Heston, Alan (1991), The Penn World Table (Mark 5): An Expanded Set of International Comparisons, 1950–1988, in *Quarterly Journal of Economics*, 327–68.

Sweet, Alec Stone and Brunell, Thomas L. (1998), Constructing a Supranational Constitution: Dispute Resolution and Governance in the European Community, in *American Political Science Review*, vol. 92, no. 1, March, pp.63–81.

Sweezy, Paul (1942), *The Theory of Capitalist Development*, Monthly Review Press, New York.

Syrquin, M. and Chenery, H. (1988), *Patterns of Development, 1950–1983*, World Bank Discussion Paper no. 41, World Bank, Washington DC.

Tanaka, A. (1996), *A New Medievalism: The World System in the Twenty-first Century*, Nihon Keizai Shimbun, Tokyo.

Taylor, Paul (1993), *International Organisation in the Modern World: the Regional and Global Process*, Pinter, London.

Telò, Mario, ed. (1993), *Towards a New European Union?* Editions de l'Université de Bruxelles, Brussels.

Telò, Mario, ed. (1994), *L'Union Europénne et les defis del'élargissement*, Editions de l'Université de Bruxelles, Brussels.

Telò, Mario, ed. (1995), *Démocratie et construction européenne*, Editions de l'Université de Bruxelles, Brussels.

Telò, Mario and Magnette, Paul, eds (1996), *Repenser l'Europe*, Editions de l'Université de Bruxelles, Brussels.

Telò, Mario and Magnette, Paul, eds (1998), *De Maastricht à Amsterdam. L'Europe et son nouveau traité*, Complexe, Brussels.

Telò, Mario and Santander, Sebastian (1999), *Can EU Contribute to a Less Asymmetric World?* December 1999, ECPR-IPSA, Brussels.

Telò, M., Vercauteren, P. and Rousens, C. (2000) eds, *Studia Diplomatica les théories des Relations Internacionales á l'épeure de l'aprés-guerre-procòle*, vol. L11, no. 1, Brussels.

Therborn, Göeran (1995), *European Modernity and Beyond. The Trajectory of European Societies 1945–2000*, Sage, London.

Thomas, G. (1998), Globalization versus Regionalization?, in G. Joffé, ed., *Perspectives on Development: the Euro-Mediterranean Partnership Initiative*, *Journal of North African Studies*, special issue, vol. 3, no. 2, Summer, Cass, London.

Thurow, Lester (1992), *Head to Head: the Coming Economic Battle between Japan Europe and America*, Nicholas Brealey, London.

Tibi, Bassam (1998), *The Challenge of Fundamentalism*, University of California Press, Berkeley, CA.

Tovias, A. (1998), Regionalization and the Mediterranean, in G. Joffé, ed., *Perspectives on Development: the Euro-Mediterranean Partnership Initiative*, in *Journal of North African Studies*, special issue, vol. 3, no. 2, Summer, Cass, London.

Tovias A. (1999), Israel's Free Trade Agreement with the European Union, EuroMeSCo Occasional Paper no. 5, IEEI, Lisbon.

Trautmann, Günther (1997), Russia and the Euro-Atlantic Community, in *Journal of European Integration* no 2–3, pp.201–32.

Tsakaloyannis, Panos (1996), *The European Union as a Security Community*, Nomos-Verlag, Baden-Baden.

UN (1995a), *International Trade Statistics Yearbook*, vol. 2, United Nations, New York and Geneva.

UN (1995b), *Statistical Yearbook*, 40th ser., United Nations, New York and Geneva.
UN (1998), *Economic Survey of Europe 1998*, no. 2, United Nations, New York and Geneva.
UN (1999), *Demographic Yearbook 1997*, New York.
UNCTAD (1995), *Handbook of International Trade and Development Statistics*, United Nations, New York and Geneva.
UNICEF (1995), *Poverty, Children and Policy: Responses for a Brighter Future*, Economies in Transition Series, Regional Monitoring Report no. 3, UNICEF, Florence.
Valladão, Alfredo (1993), *Le XXIe siècle sera américain*, La Découverte, Paris.
Vernon, Raymond (1991), The Community in the Global System: A Synthesis, in Armand Clesse and Raymond Vernon, eds, *The European Community after 1992: A New Role in World Politics*, Nomos-Verlag, Baden-Baden.
Vogel, J. (1997), *Living Conditions and Inequality in the European Union 1997*, Eurostat Working Papers E/1997: 3, Luxembourg.
Walker, Rob B. J. (1993), *Inside/Outside: International Relations as Political Theory*, Cambridge University Press, Cambridge USA.
Wallace, Helen (1989), The Best is the Enemy of the "Could": Bargaining in the European Community, in Secondo Tarditi, Kenneth J. Thomson, Pierpaolo Pierani, and Elisabetta Croci-Angelini, eds, *Agricultural Trade Liberalization and the European Community*, Clarendon Press, Oxford, pp.193–206.
Wallace, William (1994), *Regional Integration: The Western European Experience*, The Brookings Institution, Washington DC.
Wallace, William (1995), Regionalism in Europe: Model or Exception?, in Louise Fawcett and Andrew Hurrell, eds, *Regionalism in World Politics: Regional Organization and International Order*, Oxford University Press, Oxford.
Wallerstein,Immanuel (1974), *The Modern World System*, Academic Press, New York.
Wallerstein, Immanuel (1991), *Geopolitics and Geoculture*, Cambridge University Press and Maison des Sciences de l'Homme, Cambridge.
Waltz, Kenneth (1979), *Theory of International Politics*, Addison Wesley, Reading MA.
Weidenfeld, Werner and Janning, Joseph, eds (1993), *Europe in Global Change. Strategies and Options for Europe*, Bertelsmann Foundation Publishers, Gütersloh.
Weiler, Joseph J. H. (1999), *Fundamental Rights and Fundamental Boundaries: Common Standards and Conflicting values in the Protection of Human Rights in the European Legal Space*, paper, Law Schoool Harvard.
Weintraub, Sidney (1997), The North American Free Trade Agreement, in Ali M. El-Agraa, ed., *Economic Integration Worldwide*, St Martin's Press, New York, pp.203–26.
Welsch,Wolfgang (1994),Transkulturalität: die veränderte Verfassung heutiger Kulturen, in *Sichtweisen. Die Vielheit in der Einheit*, Stiftung Weimarer Klassik, Frankfurt am Main.

Wessels, Wolfgang and Rometsch, D. (1996), *European Union and Member States*, Manchester University Press, Manchester.

Westerlund, Percy (1997), *Kan ASEM stärka den svaga länken i triangeln EU-Ostasien-Nordamerika?*, Directorate General I, European Commission, Brussels.

Whitehead, L. (1996), *The International Dimension of Democratization: Europe and the Americas*, Oxford University Press, Oxford.

Whitman, R. G. (1998), *From Civilian Power to Superpower? The International Identity of the European Union*, Macmillan, London.

Widgren, Michel (1994), *The Relation between Voting Power and Policy Impact in the European Union*, CEPR Discussion Paper 1033, London.

Wijkman, Per Magnus and Sundkvist Lindström, Eva (1989) Pacific Basin Integration as a Step Towards Freer Trade, in John Nieuwenhuysen, ed., *Towards Freer Trade Between Nations*, Oxford University Press, Oxford, New York, pp.144–62

Winand, Pascaline (1993), *Eisenhower, Kennedy, and the United States of Europe*, St Martin's Press, New York.

Winters, Alan (1993), Expanding EC Membership and Association Accords: Recent Experience and Future Prospects, in K. Anderson and R. Blackhurst, eds, *Regional Integration and the Global Trading System*, Harvester Wheatsheaf, Brighton.

Winters, A. (1999) Regionalism vs. Multilateralism, in *Market Integration. Regionalism and the Global Economy*, R. Baldwin, D. Cohen, A. Sapir and A. Venables, eds, CEPR, Cambridge University Press, Cambridge.

World Bank (1994), *Averting the Old Age Crisis*, Oxford University Press, Oxford and New York.

World Bank (1995a), *World Development Report 1995*, Oxford University Press, Oxford and New York.

World Bank (1995b), *Hungary: Structural Reforms for Sustainable Growth*, World Bank,Washington DC.

World Bank (1996), *From Plan to Market: World Development Report 1996*, Oxford University Press, Oxford and New York.

World Bank (1997), *The State in a Changing World: World Development Report 1997*, Oxford University Press, Oxford and New York.

World Bank (1998), *Global Development Finance*, World Bank: Washington DC.

Wrobel, Paulo S. (1998), A Free Trade Area of the Americas in 2005?, in *International Affairs*, vol.74, no 3, July, pp.547–561.

Yearbook of International Organization (1998), V.I.A., München, New York, London and Paris.

Young, Soogil (1993), Globalism and Regionalism: Complements or Competitors?, in R. Garnaut and P. Drysdale, eds *Asia Pacific Regionalism: Readings in International Economic Relations*, Harper Educational/ANU, Pymble.

Zellner, Wolfgang and Dunay, Pal (1998), *Ungarns Außenpolitik 1990–1997*, Nomos-Verlag, Baden-Baden.

Zielonka, Jan and Prava, Alex, eds, (1997) Democratic Consolidation in Eastern Europe: International and Transnational Factors, in Press, Dieter Nohlen, Demokratie in Dieter Nohlen, Peter Waldmann and Klaus Ziemer (Hrsg.), *Lexikon der Politik*, vol. 4. Die Östlichen und Südlichen Länder, Beck Verlag, München, 1997, pp.118–27.

Zielonka, Jan (1998), *Explaining Euro-Paralysis*, Macmillan, London.

Zolo, Danilo (1997), *Cosmopolis, Prospects for World Government*, Polity Press, Cambridge, 1997.

Zolo, Danilo (1998), *I signori della pace. Una critica del globalismo giuridico*, Carocci, Roma.

Zviagelskaia, Irina (1998), Russia's Security Policy and Its Prospects, in: Eric Remacle and Reimund Seidelmann, eds, *Pan-European Security Redefined*, Nomos-Verlag, Baden-Baden, pp.305–318.

Zysman, J. (1996), The Myth of a Global Economy: Enduring National Foundations and Emerging Regional Realities, in *New Political Economy*, vol. 1, no. 2, pp.157–84

Index